I0715771

The Atlantic World and the Manila Galleons

The Atlantic World

EUROPE, AFRICA AND THE AMERICAS, 1500–1830

Series Editors

Wim Klooster (*Clark University*)
Benjamin Schmidt (*University of Washington*)

Editorial Board

Juliana Barr (*Duke University*)
Christopher Brown (*Columbia University*)
Trevor Burnard (*University of Melbourne*)
Cécile Fromont (*University of Chicago*)
Michiel van Groesen (*Leiden University*)
Jane Landers (*Vanderbilt University*)
Ricardo Padrón (*University of Virginia*)
Gabriel Paquette (*Johns Hopkins University*)

VOLUME 37

The titles published in this series are listed at *brill.com/aw*

The Atlantic World and the Manila Galleons

*Circulation, Market, and Consumption of Asian
Goods in the Spanish Empire, 1565–1650*

By

José L. Gasch-Tomás

BRILL

LEIDEN | BOSTON

Cover illustration: Detail of the folding screen "Palace of the viceroy of New Spain" (late 17th century). The detail depicts the main square of Mexico City, where a weekly market (*Parián*) took place. It also depicts a coat of arms, a horse-drawn carriage, and some members of the main social groups of the Mexican society – Spaniards, Creoles, mestizos and natives. Source: Ministerio de Educación, Cultura y Deporte (Spain). Museo de América, Madrid (Spain). For a full view of the folding screen see Illustration 1.

The Library of Congress Cataloging-in-Publication Data is available online at http://catalog.loc.gov
LC record available at http://lccn.loc.gov/2018960505

Typeface for the Latin, Greek, and Cyrillic scripts: "Brill". See and download: brill.com/brill-typeface.

ISSN 1570-0542
ISBN 978-90-04-36928-3 (hardback)
ISBN 978-90-04-38361-6 (e-book)

Para mis padres, José Luis y Dori, porque el esfuerzo también es vuestro
A Marta, por tantos años

∴

Contents

Acknowledgments

This book, which is the product of research spanning several years, is indebted to many people and institutions. Here I would like to thank those individuals whose help, concern, and support were essential in bringing this book to press.

First of these is Bartolomé Yun Casalilla, European University Institute of Florence and *Universidad Pablo de Olavide* of Seville, whose counsel, fruitful conversation, and expertise have been fundamental to the development and form of this book. It was a privilege to work with him at the European University Institute of Florence during my scholarship. At the European University Institute I was also inspired by Luca Molà, Sebastian Conrad, Antonella Romano, Jorge Flores, and Regina Grafe – all of whom helped me to approach the research from new perspectives.

I thank Harold James (Princeton University) and Jan de Vries (University of California at Berkeley) for their sage advice concerning aspects of global history and the history of consumption in preindustrial times.

Ana Crespo Solana, at the *Instituto de Historia* of the *Consejo Superior de Investigaciones Científicas*, was indispensable for her guidance regarding early modern trade networks. I am also grateful to the ForSeaDiscovery team and project (PITN-GA-2013-607545), directed by Ana and financed by the European Comission through "Marie-Curie Action: Initial Training Networks," where I have shared intellectually stimulating time, ideas, and debates with many colleagues.

Many thanks are due to Manuel Herrero Sánchez, Bethany Aram, Igor Pérez Tostado, and Fernando Ramos Palencia, at the *Universidad Pablo de Olavide*, to whom I am deeply indebted for their kind support and useful suggestions during my stays in Seville.

I am grateful to Carmen Yuste, Gustavo Curiel, Ivvone Mijares, and Flor Trejo, whose excellent suggestions and support during my stays in Mexico City helped to augment my research with insight on the histories of New Spain, and colonial art.

I am very grateful to Mariano Ardash Bonialian, who contacted me and shared his excellent work on the Pacific Ocean during the eighteenth century. Our e-mail exchanges deepened my understanding of the Manila Galleon trade's economic structures and dynamics in that period and confirmed that such structures and dynamics remained virtually intact until the early nineteenth century, which extends the conclusions of this book to later periods.

I also thank Ben Marsh, University of Stirling, to whom I am indebted for fruitful conversation and clues concerning *Archivo General de Indias*,

Richard L. Garner, who kindly resolved my doubts as regards silver currencies in New Spain, and Manuel González-Mariscal, who kindly provided prices for Seville's wheat which he collected at the Hospital of Santa Clara.

I was aided immensely by participation in seminars and workshops organised at the European University Institute from 2008 to 2012. This book has been enriched by discussions with professors and students whose names would require several paragraphs (if not pages) to list.

Funding for my research was provided by *Ministerio de Asuntos Exteriores y Cooperación* and by *Fundación Española para la Ciencia y la Tecnología* of Spain and also by the European University Institute of Florence. In addition, essential support was provided by *Junta de Andalucía*, which financed the research project "New Atlantic Products, Science, War, Economics and Consumption in Spain during the Old Regimen. The Case of Andalusia, 1492–1824" (P09- HUM-5330), and the and the *Ministerio de Economía, Industria y Competitividad* of Spain, which financed the research project "Iberian Globalisation: Networks between Asia and Europe, and Changes in the Patterns of Consumption in Latin America" (HAR2014-53797-P), in which I was privileged to take part.

I extend my gratitude to Evelien van der Veer, Gerda Danielsson Coe, Malathy Chandrasekaran and the editors of Brill's series in the Atlantic World.

I am especially grateful to the knowledge and cooperation of the archivists and administrative staff of several archives, without whose help this research would have been severely compromised: the *Archivo General de Indias* of Seville, the *Archivo Histórico Provincial* of Seville, the *Archivo General de la Nación* of Mexico, and the *Archivo General de las Notarías del Distrito Federal* of Mexico.

Early Modern Hispanic Measures and Currencies

Weight Units

In Castile
1 *fanega* = 54.7 litres
1 *arroba* = 25 *libras* (25 lb)
1 *libra* (1 pound) = 16 *onzas* (16 oz)
1 *libra* (1 pound) = 460.09 grammes

In New Spain
1 *fanega* = 55.5 litres
1 *arroba* = 25 *libras* (25 lb)
1 *libra* (1 pound) = 16 *onzas* (16 oz)
1 *libra* (1 pound) = 460.09 grammes

In the Philippines
1 *pico* = 10 *chinantas* = 137.5 *libras* (137.5 lb)
1 *arroba* = 25 *libras* (25 lb)
1 *chinanta* = 13.75 *libras* (13.75 lb)
1 *cate* = 1/10 *chinanta* = 1.375 *libras* (1.375 lb)
1 *libra* (1 pound) = 460.09 grammes

Length Units

1 *codo* = 0.5 *varas*
1 *pie* = 0.333 *varas*
1 *vara* = 0.836 metres

Currency Units

In Castile
1 *real* = 34 *maravedís*
1 *real de a 4* or *tostón* (1 real of 4 pieces) = 136 *maravedís*
1 *real de a 8* or *peso* (1 real of 8 pieces / "pieces of eight") = 272 *maravedís*
1 *ducado* = 375 *maravedís*

In New Spain and the Philippines

1 *peso de oro común* (1 peso of 8 pieces / "pieces of eight") = 8 *reales* or *tomines*
= 272 *maravedís*

1 *real* or *tomín* = 34 *maravedís*

1 *peso de oro de minas* = 450 *maravedís*

Abbreviations of Archives

ACS	*Archivo de la Catedral de Sevilla*, Seville
AGI	*Archivo General de Indias*, Seville
AGN	*Archivo General de la Nación*, Mexico City
AHAM	*Archivo Histórico del Ayuntamiento de México*, Mexico City
AHPS	*Archivo Histórico Provincial de Sevilla*, Seville
ANotDF	*Archivo General de las Notarías del DF*, Mexico City
BN	*Biblioteca Nacional*, Madrid

Figures, Illustrations, Maps, and Tables

Figures

Illustrations

Maps

Tables

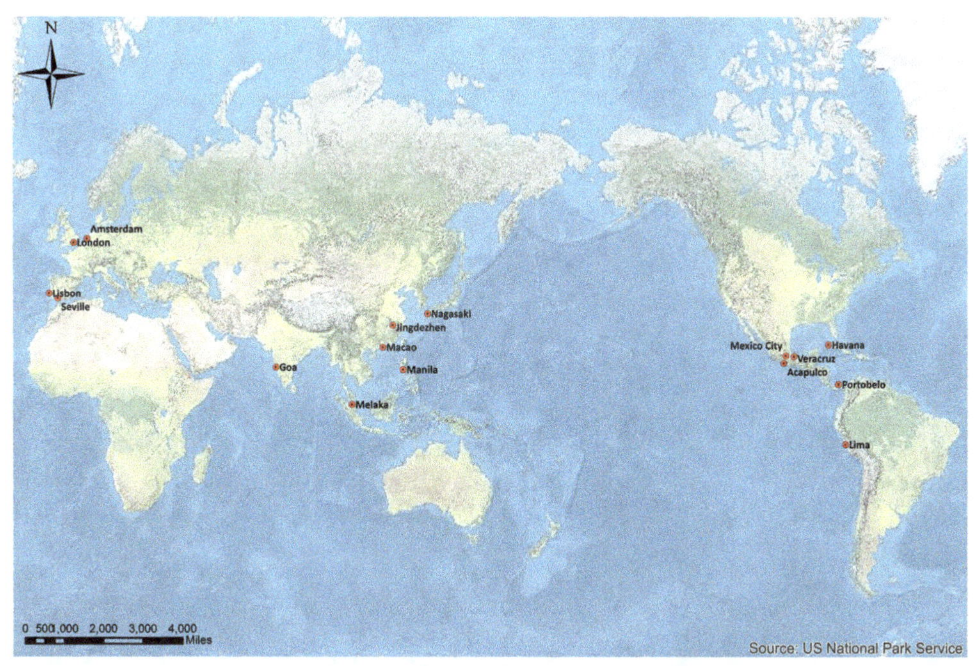

MAP 1 Some main *entrepôts* where Asian goods-for-silver exchanges were conducted, *c.* 1565–1650

Introduction

> I say that I am poor. Given that I have neither resources nor occupation, I would like to freely sell some merchandise from China and Castile, in order to support my mother and two sisters who live in poverty. I ask and beg Your Honour to give me a licence to sell my merchandise in a box in the main square and markets and streets of this city.
>
> BERNARDO DE MANSILLA, MEXICO CITY, 1602[1]

∴

Globalisation is a term that has been much used by the media, political leaders, and social scientists since the 1990s. Convergence of markets, the cultural hybridisation of clothing regimes, food, and forms of leisure across the world, and the development of supranational institutions, financial interdependence, and international social movements are among the most influential and defining elements of today's world. However, global interdependence is seen less as a Eurocentric and Western process now than in the 1990s, especially after the financial crisis of 2007–2008. The emergence of areas such as China, India, and Latin America is driving a widely shared vision of the world as a multi-centred environment with several different areas of economic achievement. The early modern world was also multi-centred. Most current historians view the early modern era as the time during which the rise of the West occurred. Moreover, they view the early modern era as a world in which non-European areas – such as China, Islamic regions, and colonial Latin America – were globalising forces where processes of economic and cultural interaction intensified and laid the groundwork for later, modern-day globalisation. Spanish America and the

---

1 *Bernardo de Mansilla, digo que soy persona pobre, y para poderme sustentar y faborecer a mi madre y dos hermanas que tengo con neçesidad, y sustentarlas ansimismo por no tener las dichas otro recurso ni trabajo, y asi para el dicho efeto queria vender algunas mercadurias de China y Castilla, y para que lo pueda hazer libremente a V. E. pido y suplico me mande dar lizenzia para que las pueda vender en la plaza publica desta ziudad y tianguis della y calles della en una caja.* México, 1602: AGN, *Indiferente Virreinal, Industria y Comercio.* Caja-exp.: 4371–022.

Pacific Ocean, whose waves wash against the shores of East and Southeast Asia as well as the Americas, was another of these areas.

This book aims to articulate a contribution to, and revises, the traditional understanding of the Atlantic World by emphasising the historical connections between the Atlantic and the Pacific Ocean, and the importance of Spanish America in those connections. The chapter-opening quote reveals that in 1602 a poor peddler of Mexico City, Bernardo de Mansilla, made a request to the commercial authorities of the city to be given permission to sell Chinese and also Castilian merchandise in the streets of the city. Asian goods were already being sold in the streets and public squares of Spanish American cities such as Mexico City. This contrasts with the limited penetration of Chinese goods into most parts of Europe at that time. Portugal had begun to import Chinese products via its *entrepôts* in Asia, especially Macao, but in most European countries (including England and the Netherlands) the import levels for these products were far from the peaks they would reach in subsequent decades.[2]

When researching the Atlantic–Asian encounter of the early modern era, many historians have focused on the European commercial companies and their commercial and cultural exchanges across the Cape route and the Indian Ocean. Yet historians typically fail to mention that, until the mid-seventeenth century, trade between Spanish America and Asia was flourishing – in some years surpassing even the trade between Europe and Asia across the Cape route.[3] So to a certain extent, the Americas and the colonial American elite are the forgotten part of the encounter between the Atlantic World and Asia during the sixteenth and seventeenth centuries. *The Atlantic World and the Manila Galleons* hopes to fill that gap in the literature. This book explores the degree to which the colonial Spanish American elite and cities were main components of the economic and cultural encounter between the Spanish Empire and Asia in the late sixteenth and seventeenth centuries, and the reason why the Manila Galleon route was superseded by the Cape route as the main venue

---

2 In 1602, the very same year in which Bernardo de Mansilla made his request to sell Asian merchandise in the streets of Mexico, the Dutch seized two Portuguese carracks laden with Chinese porcelain. The auction of that merchandise in the Netherlands had an enormous effect on the country's consumer and commercial circles both: Maxine Berg, "In Pursuit of Luxury: Global History and British Consumer Goods in the Eighteenth Century," *Past and Present* 182 (2004): 85. That year the *Verenigde Oostindische Compagnie* (VOC) was founded and the Dutch began their Asian enterprise.

3 Jan de Vries, "Connecting Europe and Asia: A Quantitative Analysis of the Cape-route Trade, 1497–1759," *Global Connections and Monetary History, 1470–1800*, ed. Dennis O. Flynn, Arturo Giráldez, and Richard von Glahn (Burlington, VT: Ashgate, 2003), 77–81.

of exchange between the Atlantic World and Asia around the mid-seventeenth century.

In 1565 the Spaniards established themselves in Cebú conquered the Sultanate of Maynila 5 years later. Although thy never entirely controlled Luzon, the biggest island of the archipelago, the Spaniards opened a new commercial route. The shipping of Chinese goods, such as silk and porcelain, in the galleon *San Pedro* from the Philippines to Spanish America across the Pacific Ocean marked the beginning of a direct trade between Asian traders (mostly Chinese) and the Creoles and Europeans who lived in Spanish America. In 1571 the Spaniards founded Manila and opened the commercial route of the Manila Galleon, also known as the China Ship (*nao de China*). This route linked Acapulco, on the northwestern coast of the Americas, with Manila and the commercial area of Southeast Asia. It was used for 250 years. For almost every year between 1565 and 1815, one to four galleons –laden with silver –crossed the Pacific from the American viceroyalty of New Spain to Manila. Silver was re-exported to other Asian countries, mainly China, after which the galleons returned to New Spain full of Asian goods consisting mostly of Chinese silk and porcelain. Asian goods were then distributed from New Spain to other regions of the Americas and also to Castile. Such a rich exchange of Asian goods for American silver across the Pacific entailed a series of economic and cultural transformations in the Spanish Empire, including its European territories, whose main protagonists resided in the Americas and the Philippines. The Manila Galleon trade contributed to strengthening the colonial economy of Spanish America. At the same time, Asian goods began circulating in the Atlantic territories of the empire to an unprecedented extent. Furthermore, the flow of Asian goods was to transform the cultural practices of some of the empire's elite. This trade also favoured technical and skill transfers of product manufacturing across the Pacific Ocean. Moreover, the export of American silver and import of Asian manufactured goods into New Spain via the Pacific triggered clashes of interest, between the Hispanic elite of both sides of the Atlantic, in which the Crown was seriously involved. *The Atlantic World and the Manila Galleons* provides a history of these phenomena, which took place between about 1565 and the mid-seventeenth century and gave substance to the encounter between Asia and the Spanish Empire via Manila and New Spain.

The rise of the Atlantic World and the Cape route as indisputable globalising force in the world, and of the latter as the main route of exchange between the Atlantic and Asia, began during the second third of the seventeenth century and continued unabated during the eighteenth century. During this time, the Manila Galleon and New Spanish traders were pushed into the background of the global arena. Yet earlier, during the early decades of the seventeenth century, Manila – along with its hinterland, the Pacific Ocean, and the traders and elite of colonial Spanish America – were better positioned than were the Cape route, the *Verenigde Oostindische Compagnie* (VOC), and the English East India Company (EIC) to become the main areas and agents of the exchanges between the Atlantic and Asia in the new global times of the early modern era. It is worth asking why the Manila Galleon route lost ground against other globalising spaces of the world. This book provides an explanation that goes beyond the common understanding that Iberian powers lost the "battle" in Asian seas against the Dutch and English commercial companies during the seventeenth century. That is a correct but insufficient explanation. We must also examine the internal dynamics of the Spanish Empire in its American territories, because the Spanish American elite and traders were key to the working of the Manila Galleon route. In doing so, this book provides a comprehensive understanding of the significance of Spanish America in the connections between the Atlantic World and East Asia.

1.1   Historical Issues and Debates: Globalisation, Trade, and Consumption History

The literature on the Manila galleons is extensive. However, most works on the commercial route that connected the Philippines and New Spain during the early modern era are extremely dated.[4] The most notable exceptions are works by Carmen Yuste López, Salvador Bernabéu, Carlos Martínez Shaw, and Mariano Ardash Bonialian. These works focus mostly on commercial exchanges across the Pacific Ocean in the eighteenth century. By studying the commercial mechanisms of Mexican traders in the Manila galleons, the development of trade in Manila and Acapulco, and the establishment of the merchant guild of

---

4   The work by Schurtz is classic: William L. Schurtz, *El Galeón de Manila* (Madrid: Ediciones de Cultura Hispánica, 1992). Summaries of the literature on Manila galleons can be found in: Pedro Pérez Herrero, "El Galeón de Manila. Relaciones Comerciales Entre Extremo Oriente y América (Estado de la Cuestión)," in *El Extremo Oriente Ibérico. Investigaciones Históricas: Metodología y Estado de la Cuestión*, ed. Francisco de Paula Solano Pérez-Liria (Madrid: CSIC, 1989), 445–57; Vera Valdés Lakowsky, "Problemas y Posibilidades en el Estudio de la Historia Económica y las Relaciones Internacionales en el Pacífico," in *El Extremo Oriente Ibérico. Investigaciones Históricas: Metodología y Estado de la Cuestión*, ed. Francisco de Paula Solano Pérez-Liria (Madrid: CSIC, 1989), 459–69; María F. García de los Arcos, "El Comercio Manila-Acapulco: Un Intento de Estado de la Cuestión," in *Comercio Marítimo Colonial. Nuevas Interpretaciones y Últimas Fuentes*, ed. Carmen Yuste López (México, DF.: Instituto Nacional de Antropología e Historia, 1997), 165–80.

Manila in 1769, Yuste López has shed light on how the trans-Pacific became an alternative to the intracolonial trade in New Spain during the eighteenth century.[5] The works edited by Bernabéu and Martínez Shaw address, with respect to the Manila Galleon trade, such diverse issues as Spanish debates over spice trade across the Pacific, the Manila galleons' effect on the municipal life of Manila, the management of "contracts of cards" (*asientos de naipes*) in the Philippines, and the links between the Manila galleons and California, among many others.[6] The book by Ardash Bonialian deserves special mention because, unlike most works on the Manila Galleon route, it locates the trans-Pacific route in the context of the whole Pacific Ocean and points out the importance of the Manila Galleon route for Atlantic trade in the eighteenth-century political economy of the Spanish Empire.[7] Despite the volume of books and articles, few have explicitly integrated Asian, American, and European historical processes with explanations regarding commercial exchanges between Chinese and Euro-American actors connected via the Manila galleons.[8]

This book explores how the Manila Galleon route emerged as one of the most important globalising forces of the early modern world from 1565 until the mid-seventeenth century. In this study, some of the most fruitful fields of historiography in recent years – such as the history of the Atlantic World, international trade, and the history of consumption and material culture in

---

5   Carmen Yuste López, *Emporios Transpacíficos. Comerciantes Mexicanos en Manila, 1710–1815* (México, D.F.: UNAM, 2007).

6   Salvador Bernabéu Albert and Carlos Martínez Shaw, eds., *Un Océano de Seda y Plata: El Universo Económico del Galeón de Manila* (Sevilla: CSIC, 2013); Salvador Bernabeu Albert, Carmen Mena García and Emilio J. Luque Azcona, eds., *Filipinas y el Pacífico: Nuevas miradas, nuevas reflexiones* (Sevilla: Universidad de Sevilla, 2017).

7   Since the 1960s, when Pierre Chaunu published his quantitative work about the evolution of trade in the Pacific Ocean during the early modern era, few had made an effort to relate the dynamics concerning the Manila Galleon to those of the Atlantic Ocean: Mariano Ardash Bonialian, *El Pacífico Hispanoamericano. Política y Comercio Asiático en el Imperio Español (1680–1784). La Centralidad de lo Marginal* (México, D.F.: El Colegio de México, 2012); Mariano Ardash Bonialian, *China en la América Colonial. Bienes, Mercados, Comercio y Cultura del Consumo desde México hasta Buenos Aires* (México, D.F.: Instituto Mora, 2014). As I have found and show in the following pages, some of the Manila Galleon trade's political dynamics addressed by Ardash Bonialian did not arise in the eighteenth century (the time period on which he focused) but they had previously emerged as early as the late sixteenth century.

8   The only notable exceptions are those of historians who have dealt with bullion and the worldwide circulation of silver: Dennis O. Flynn and Arturo Giráldez, "Arbitrage, China, and World Trade in the Early Modern Period," *Journal of Economic and Social History of the Orient* 38, no. 4 (1995): 429–48; and "Cycles of Silver: Global Economic Unity through the Mid-Eighteenth Century," *Journal of World History* 13, no. 2 (2002): 391–427; Ardash Bonialian, *El Pacífico hispanoamericano,* 29–52.

pre-industrial times – converge. I shall address the trade of Asian manufactured goods (e.g., Chinese silk, Chinese porcelain, Japanese furnishings) along the Pacific Rim, their re-exportation from the Americas to Castile, the non-commercial circulation of such goods, the production of Asian-like products in the Americas, and the consumption and use of Asian manufactured goods by the Hispanic elite from New Spain and Castile from about 1565 to the mid-seventeenth century.

Before the 1990s, the historiographical agenda of world historians had focused mostly on analysing the hierarchies and dependencies between countries and areas of the world as sources of their poverty or wealth. Many works in world history were published as part of the debate over "dependency theories." Thereafter, when the word "globalization" became fashionable in the media and social movements, economic historians and academics began to focus more on global *integration* than on the hierarchy and imbalance of power relations at a global level.[9] A renewed and fruitful interest in the old question of why and when Europe emerged as the dominant world power has been a favourable environment for the publication of ground-breaking and influential works.[10] In these discussions, the history of the early modern period is now being recognised by scholars as a crucial period. Historians including Antony G. Hopkins and Christopher A. Bayly have defined the early modern era as a period of "proto-globalisation" marked by an increase in the movement of people, animals, plant crops, goods, and technologies within and between different areas of the world. Furthermore, these two authors in particular have emphasised that global connections in the early modern period was a non-lineal, complex process characterized by interruptions as well as many globalising areas.[11] This book takes the approach to early modern globalisation developed by Hopkins and Bayly and integrates it into the history of the Atlantic World.

---

9   Joseph E. Inikori, "Africa and the Globalization Process: Western Africa, 1450–1850," *Journal of Global History*, 2 (2007): 63–86; Kevin O'Rourke and Jeffrey G. Williamson, *Globalization and History: The Evolution of a Nineteenth Century Atlantic Economy* (Cambridge, MA: MIT Press, 1999).

10   Roy B. Wong, *China Transformed. Historical Change and the Limits of the European Experience* (Ithaca, NY: Cornell University Press, 1997); Kenneth Pomeranz, *The Great Divergence: China, Europe and the Making of the Modern World Economy* (Princeton, NJ: Princeton University Press, 2002); Peer Vries, *Via Peking back to Manchester: Britain, the Industrial Revolution, and China* (Leiden: Leiden University, 2003).

11   Antony G. Hopkins, ed., *Globalization in World History* (London: Pimlico, 2002). See also Jürgen Osterhammel and Niels P. Petersson, *Globalization: A Short Story* (Princeton, NJ: Princeton University Press, 2003), 21–35.

The Manila Galleon route connected the European commercial houses with headquarters based in Seville to the Philippines, Southeast China and Japan. This link was formed through the New Spanish commercial houses and networks. *The Atlantic World and the Manila Galleons* studies the structure of such networks and also the New Spanish wholesalers' commercial decision making in the context of this new, vast trading space that spread from Asia to Castile via the Americas. The explanation of how Southeast Asia and the Spanish Empire interacted will lie within the agency of New Spanish traders and their commercial networks. That being said, this book seeks to contribute to the recent history of the Atlantic World in the early modern era by clarifying three points as follows.

The first concerns the main historical characters of this book. The work presented here focuses primarily on the elite of New Spain and the Spanish Empire as connectors of different spaces of the world, consumers of Asian goods such as Chinese silk and porcelain, and agents of the emergence of a market of Asian goods in the Spanish Empire. In the early modern era, empires were global, and their agents mainly operated within and across the boundaries of empires. This phenomenon has driven historians, including Jorge Cañizares-Esguerra and Eric R. Seeman, to highlight the need for geographically expanding the Atlantic paradigm beyond the boundaries of the Atlantic Ocean. The reason is that "Atlantic" processes cannot be properly understood without accounting for other global phenomena – especially when one considers that most Atlantic empires were actually global empires.[12] This book takes that fact explicitly into account. It is likewise assumed here that globalisation (and deglobalisation) processes in the early modern era were entangled not only with the clash between different empires but also with internal dynamics of each empire. Within this framework, *The Atlantic World and the Manila Galleons* puts the crisis of the trans-Pacific trade of the late 1630s, which has been studied by some historians of Spanish and Mexican academia,[13] in context with the increase in trade via the Cape route and also addresses that crisis from a global perspective. It included the wars of the Hispanic Crown against the English and Dutch empires in different regions of the world, especially Southeast Asia; it also includes the difficulty for the Crown to finance war as well as the lack of

---

12   Jorge Cañizares-Esguerra and Eric R. Seeman, eds., *The Atlantic in Global History, 1500–2000* (Upper Saddle River, NJ: Pearson, Prentice Hall, 2007).

13   Carmen Yuste López, ed., *Comercio Marítimo Colonial. Nuevas Interpretaciones y Últimas Fuentes* (México, D. F.: Instituto Nacional de Antropología e Historia, 1997); Ostwald Sales Colín, *El Movimiento Portuario de Acapulco. El Protagonismo de Nueva España en la Relación con Filipinas, 1587–1648* (México, D. F.: Plaza y Valdés, 2000).

trade efficiency faced by merchants during this adverse political and economic time. The book examines and connects topics that are usually addressed separately: the fall of the trans-Pacific trade, the rise of the trade across the Cape route, and the socio-economic and consumer dynamics of the Hispanic elite of Spanish America (more specifically, of New Spain) during the first half of the seventeenth century.

The second point concerns the forces of the Atlantic World during the sixteenth and seventeenth centures – more specifically, the principal drivers of the increase in the distribution of goods from the Pacific Ocean to Castile via Spanish America. Although most research on global and Atlantic history in the early modern era stresses the significance of market forces, and even though I shall emphasise the significance of New Spanish trading forces in the expansion of Asian goods in the Spanish Empire, these were not the only forces impelling globalisation. Other forms of goods circulation also played a role in the emergence of foreign goods markets and entanglement with distant regions. The power of market phenomena today has obscured other forms of circulation in our study of the past. Bureaucrats, nobles, and other elites who did not directly trade in the Manila galleons also shipped Chinese silk and porcelain (among other goods) with no commercial aims, for instance as presents to their relatives, whereas merchants who did trade with Asian goods also circulated silk and porcelain as gifts for relatives and members of their networks. This merits attention because it contributed to the emergence of new markets in the Atlantic World.

This leads to the third point. This book stresses a point that some of the most recent approaches to Atlantic history neglect: the contradictory and sometimes problematic processes that triggered global economic expansion for certain sectors of early modern empires. In other words, not all agents of the Spanish Empire benefited from the opening of the Manila Galleon route. On the contrary, some of them – especially those from Seville and other Iberian cities – saw how the growth of commercial operations of New Spanish wholesalers in the Pacific Ocean, and the re-exportation of products such as Chinese silk to Castile, damaged their own business with Spanish America and other Castilian markets. It is worthwhile to consider how the different players in this global game reacted to such contradictions and to observe just how they were resolved.

Many debates and new ways of writing Atlantic – and global history – are related to new studies on consumption history in pre-industrial times. Current historians studying consumption and changes in demand during the early modern era from economic, cultural, and sociological perspectives are not doing so at the national level. Indeed, the history of material culture and consumption is one of the richest historiographical fields in global history. The most recent publications on consumption history stress the significance of the multi-directional flow of some commodities and, thereby, the multi-directional character of their values and consumption.[14] Material culture, aesthetic practices, and consumption in both the modern and early modern eras are becoming more widely understood as the fruit of cultural interactions within and between continents, where local and global scales were continually interacting. One recent example of the new way of approaching material culture and changes in consumption habits and designs of objects and textiles during the early modern era is the study of the production in European countries of ivory caskets imitating those carved in Sri Lanka (Ceylon) and of rhinoceros goblets from Goa. Other examples include the importing of bezoar stones into Europe from Asia, the global connections of Jingdezhen porcelain, and the cross-cultural connections between Asia and the Italian Renaissance.[15] This book participates in these new historiographical trends, which transcend national perspectives, while dealing with an element that recent publications in the field have barely addressed: the role of Spanish America as a cultural and economic bridge between Asia and Europe.

The expansion of the trans-Pacific trade from the last third of the sixteenth century until the mid-seventeenth century resulted in a growing influx of Asian manufactured goods to American markets, mostly Chinese silk and porcelain and furnishings from Japan. The American markets extended a taste for Asian goods and aesthetics among some of the elite of the Spanish Empire. This work explores how Asian manufactured goods were integrated into the clothing fashions, forms of leisure, furnishing, and material culture of the elite residing in two outposts of the empire, the viceroyalty of New Spain and Castile. The book not only confirms that the New Spanish elite consumed more Asian goods than did their Castilian counterparts; it also gives the reasons for that difference. One might argue that the Mexican elite purchased more Asian goods than their Castilian peers because they had a closer doorway to Asia through Acapulco and the Manila Galleon route, but this is hardly a sufficient explanation. New Spaniards may well have rejected the new goods, given that

---

14 John Brewer and Frank Trentmann, eds., *Consuming Cultures, Global Perspectives: Historical Trajectories, Transnational Exchanges* (Oxford: Berg, 2006); Bethany Aram and Bartolomé Yun-Casalilla, ed., *Global Goods and the Spanish Empire, 1492–1824. Circulation, resistance and Diversity* (New York, NY: Palgrave, 2014).

15 Michael North, ed., *Artistic and Cultural Exchanges between Europe and Asia* (Farnham: Ashgate, 2010); Glenn Adamson, Giorgio Riello, and Sarah Teasley, eds., *Global History Design* (London: Routledge, 2011).

the consumption of luxuries and semi-luxuries (as these Asian manufactured goods were considered) was regulated as much by taste as by such strictly economic factors as supply.[16] Therefore, the motive for the greater consumption and use of Asian manufactured goods by the American elite must lie in several reasons, among them the tastes and identities of consumers.[17] Historians who have studied consumption and material culture in colonial Spanish America have introduced goods into the power schemes of that society; in other words, they have identified the "civilising" role that goods such as wine, bread, and fabrics (among others) played, alongside political domination, in the colonising process.[18] Although the consumption and use of Asian goods was mostly elitist and hence were largely inaccessible to the lower classes of New Spain and Castile by the early seventeenth century, that consumption was affected also by power schemes. In addressing the diffusion and consumption of Asian goods throughout the Spanish Empire from an Atlantic perspective, one that considers both American and European territories as well as agents of the empire, this book offers an account of the different cultural mechanisms and identities that contributed to determining the taste for Chinese silk and porcelain, Japanese furniture, and other Asian goods in the Spanish Empire – on both sides of Atlantic.

1.2   Approach, Sources, and Methodology

The approach taken in this book is Atlantic and trans-"national", and the methodological framework is situated at the intersection of cultural and economic history. By Atlantic and trans-"national" I mean an approach that transcends national perspectives; it is neither a theoretical paradigm nor a methodology, but a way of seeing the past. The approach employed in this work stresses the importance of movement, flow, circulation, linkages, and networks across

---

16   Arjun Appadurai, "Commodities and the Politics of Value," in *The Social Life of Things, Commodities in cultural perspective*, ed. Arjun Appadurai (Cambridge: Cambridge University Press, 1986), 3–63.

17   For a socio-cultural perspective on historical consumption, see Colin Campbell, "Capitalism, Consumption and the Problem of Motives," in *Consumption and Identity*, ed. Jonathan Friedman (Amsterdam: Harwood, 1990); Lorna Weatherill, *Consumer Behaviour and Material Culture, 1660–1760* (London: Routledge, 1988); Stephan S. Halikowski, " 'Profits Sprout Like Tropical Plants': A Fresh Look at What Went Wrong with the Eurasian Spice Trade, c. 1550–1800," *Journal of Global History* 3 (2008): 389–418.

18   Arnold J. Bauer, *Goods, Power, History: Latin America's Material Culture* (Cambridge: Cambridge University Press, 2001).

boundaries.[19] In doing so, it makes explicit the "tangled" nature of historical processes and thus follows the historiographical perspectives initiated by studies in Atlantic History and connected histories. On the one hand, Atlantic historians (most of whom work in the Anglophone world) explicitly view the Atlantic Ocean as a geographic basin for exchange at all human levels, which made the history of all Atlantic empires profoundly entangled.[20] On the other hand, "connected histories" (as developed mainly by Sanjay Subrahmanyam) emphasize that "porosity" characterized the Spanish and Portuguese empires worldwide throughout the sixteenth and seventeenth centuries.[21] This view can help us overcome Eurocentric views of history and, in this book, "Castile-centric" views of processes occurring within the Spanish Empire.[22] The approach of *The Atlantic World and the Manila Galleons* incorporates findings based on these research perspectives. Furthermore, this book's Atlantic History viewpoint follows the recent trend whereby such history covers more than the ocean itself and the shores on which its waves wash.[23] This book is also germane to the work of historians who transcend "national" perspective and have emphasised the relevance of local scale (amid the complexity of local, regional, and global facts) in the early modern era. The importance of local scale is particularly evident in the case of the European "composite" monarchies, such as the Spanish Empire, where local groups and institutions and web of

19   Understood in this way, global history bears some similarities to transnational history: Christopher A. Bayly, Sven Beckert, Matthew Connelly, Isabel Hofmeyr, Wendy Kozol, and Patricia Seed, "AHR Conversation: On Transnational History," *American Historical Review* 111, no. 5 (2006): 1441–65. However, I reject the use of a transnational approach in this work because it would not be appropriate to view and write early modern history in terms of nineteenth- and twentieth-century nation states. A more updated reflection on global history and the approaches and methods related to it is Sebastian Conrad, *What is Global History?* (Princeton and Oxford: Princeton University Press, 2016).

20   Philip D. Morgan and Jack P. Green, "Introduction: The Present State of Atlantic History," in *Atlantic History: A Critical Appraisal,* ed. Philip D. Morgan and Jack P. Green (Oxford: Oxford University Press, 2009); David Armitage, "Three Concepts of Atlantic History," in *The British Atlantic World,* ed. David Armitage and Michael J. Braddick (New York, NY: Palgrave, 2002), 11–17. For a history of the term and practice of Atlantic History, see Bernard Bailyn, *Atlantic History: Concept and Contours* (Cambridge, MA.: Harvard University Press, 2005).

21   Sanjay Subrahmanyam, "Holding the World in Balance: The Connected Histories of the Iberian Overseas Empires, 1500–1640," *American Historical Review* 112 (2007): 1359–85.

22   Serge Gruzinsky, "Les monde mêles de la Monarchie Catholique et autres 'connected histories'," *Annales HSS* 1 (2001) : 85–117 ; Serge Gruzinski, *Las Cuatro Partes del Mundo. Historia de Una Mundialización* (México, D.F.: Fondo de Cultura Económica, 2010).

23   Jorge Cañizares-Esguerra and Eric R. Seeman, eds., *The Atlantic in Global History, 1500–2000* (Upper Saddle River, NJ: Pearson/Prentice Hall, 2007).

merchants, in which both global movement and local components (e.g., senses of commonality and identity, make-up of the community) were present and played an indispensable function.[24] Within this framework, the importance of certain elites of the Spanish Empire – such as the wholesalers of Mexico City, Seville, and Manila – stressed in this book, will be more understandable.

If we define the approach of this book in this way – as an approach that transcends "national" perspectives while stressing the flows, circulations, linkages, and networks that drive historical processes –, then it need not be tied to any particular method. On the contrary, the book takes methodological tools from several fields, including the viewpoints of Atlantic History and "connected histories." Doing so helps to integrate cultural, political, and economic processes: for example, the Hispanic elites' taste for Asian goods, the political economy of the Spanish Empire, and the trade of Asian goods from Southeast Asia to Castile across the Americas. Thus the cultural–economic false dichotomy can be broken, which enables a better understanding of the historical processes described in this book.

This book makes use of a wide range of primary sources, such as the *almojarifazgo* and *avería* taxes that were charged on trade and were collected in the ports of Acapulco on the western coast of New Spain and in Veracruz on the eastern coast, and the *avería* tax collections and "arrival registers of ships from New Spain to Seville" (*registros de venida de Nueva España*), which are the registers of each ship and the merchandise they annually transported from Veracruz to Seville. The documents of the merchant guild of Mexico City have also been used. Other sources include minutes of the meetings of the city council (*cabildo*) of Mexico City, letters of the viceroys of New Spain, and minutes of the merchant guild of Seville. In Appendix A there is more detailed information regarding these sources and the use that I make of them. Two sets of sources deserve special mention: dozens of private and business letters belonging to Mexican merchants, and a sample of 286 probate inventories of the elite population.

Access to private letters of merchants has been central to this research because they contain not only the business correspondence from some of New Spain's main wholesalers but also reports of goods that Mexico's merchants received from their agents in Acapulco and the Philippine Islands. Many such letters belonged to the Mexican merchant Santi Federighi, who was the "prior" (head) of Mexico City's merchant guild in the 1630s. He died in 1643, but, for

---

24 Bartolomé Yun Casalilla, " 'Localism', Global History and Transnational History. A Reflection from the Historian of Early Modern Europe," *Historik Tidskrift* 127, no. 4 (2007): 668–72.

unknown reasons, many of his documents have survived in the archive. Santi Federighi was a member of a powerful merchant family of Florentine origin (his grandfather, Giovanni Federighi, was governor of the Florentine village of San Gimignano and emigrated to Seville in the second half of the seventeenth century). He took charge of the Federighi family branch of the business in New Spain in the 1610s and guided it to commercial success. This led to his appointment as prior of the merchant guild of Mexico, making Santi Federighi one of the most powerful merchants of New Spain in the first half of the seventeenth century.[25]

The second set of sources, a sample of almost 300 probates involving the elites of Mexico City and Seville, will be used as a base from which to compare the reception and use of Asian manufactured goods – mainly Chinese silk and porcelain as well as Japanese furniture and folding screens, among other products – by the elite in these two cities of the Spanish Empire.[26] That comparison will be used to gauge just how much the quantity and use of Asian goods diverged between American and European urban centres of the Spanish Empire. The choice of Mexico City rather than (for instance) Lima was dictated by the New Spain's viceroyalty being the only American region that had been licenced to trade directly with Asia since 1587.[27] That distinction rendered Mexico City (the capital of New Spain) an extraordinary centre of trade, especially in the export and diffusion of Asian goods to other parts of the Americas and to Castile.

------

25   Francisco Núñez Roldán, "Tres Familias Florentinas en Sevilla: Federighi, Fantoni y Bucarelli (1570–1625)," in *Presencia Italiana en Andalucía. Actas del III Coloquio Hispano-Italiano* (Sevilla: CSIC, 1989), 23–50. José L. Gasch-Tomás, "Agents of globalisation: An approximation to Santi Federighi's commercial network, c. 1620-1643," in *Merchants and Trade Networks in the Atlantic and the Mediterranean, 1550–1800: Connectors of Commercial Maritime Systems*, ed. Manuel Herrero Sánchez and Klemens Kaps (London: Routledge, 2016), 130–144.

26   For the principal methodological precautions when using probate inventories as a historical source to study consumption, see Bartolomé Bennasar, "Los Inventarios Post-mortem y la Historia de las Mentalidades," in *La Documentación Notarial y la Historia.*, vol. 2, VVAA (Santiago de Compostela: Universidad de Santiago de Compostela, 1984), 139–46; Bartolomé Yun Casalilla, "Inventarios Post-mortem, Consumo y Niveles de Vida del Campesinado del Antiguo Régimen. Problemas Metodológicos a la Luz de la Investigación Internacional," in *Consumo, Condiciones de Vida y Comercialización*, ed. Bartolomé Yun Casalilla and Jaume Torras Elias (Valladolid: Junta de Castilla y León, 1999, 27–40; and Weatherill, *Consumer Behaviour*, 201–7.

27   Carmen Yuste López, *El Comercio de la Nueva España con Filipinas, 1590–1785* (México, D.F.: Instituto Nacional de Antropología e Historia, 1984), 14–15.

1.3   Mexico City, Seville, and Manila in 1600: Population and Institutions

I have already mentioned the significance of local scale during the early modern period. Networks of the elite were global in character; nonetheless, wholesalers and consumers of imported goods of early modern empires as well as their horizons, sense of community, and institutions were strongly rooted in the local area. The elite's networks were based on a certain type of location: large, cosmopolitan cities. A brief overview of the societies, institutions, and political structures of the cities in which this book's protagonists – the elite of Mexico City, Seville, and Manila – experienced their day-to-day lives is necessary for the history described here to be properly contextualised.

Mexico City was erected by the Spanish conquerors on the ruins of Tenochtitlan; see illustration 1. From the very beginning of the conquest, Mexico City became the political, economic, and administrative capital of New Spain – one of the two viceroyalties (the other was Peru) founded in the Americas by the Spaniards. By the second half of the sixteenth century, the Castilian monarch had already established the political structure that organised the American territories until the Bourbon reforms of the eighteenth century. All colonial institutions along with their competences, their development, and their collaboration and clashes over time are exemplars of the jurisdictional fragmentation that characterised a composite monarchy such as the Spanish Empire.[28]

The head of the viceroyalty was the viceroy – etymologically, "in the King's place" – established by the King in 1535 in New Spain for America's northern territories and seven years later in Peru for its southern territories. The court of the New Spanish viceroy was in Mexico City, and the court of the archbishop of Mexico was also located here. The viceroy and archbishop were the two most powerful political figures in this "kingdom." A preexisting political institution of some importance was the *audiencia* (royal appellate tribunal), created in 1528 and consisting of six to eight members with judicial and government powers.[29] These three institutions (viceroy, archbishop, and the *audiencia* members) were directly appointed by the King with the advice of the Indies Council (*Consejo de Indias*). Despite having jurisdiction in all territories of the viceroyalty, the viceroy and *audiencia* both had their headquarters in Mexico City. From this concentration of the elite flowed extraordinary consequences for the city's political and social life, which was filled with lackeys and employees

---

28   John H. Elliot, "A Europe of Composite Monarchies," *Past and Present* 137 (1992): 48–71.

29   Ignacio Bernal, *Historia General de México* (México, D.F.: Colegio de México, 2000), 248–251.

in administrative positions such as scriveners, notaries, and civil servants of all types. In addition there were *corregidores*, who were also (in the Americas) called *alcaldes mayores*, a type of mayor at the head of an administrative territory known as a *corregimiento*. The *corregidores*, who had several local responsibilities that included collecting taxes, exercising judicial powers, and maintaining public order in the city, were present only in the largest American cities. In New Spain, there were *corregidores* in Mexico City, Veracruz, and Zacatecas.[30]

The city council was relatively independent of the city's "royal" power. The council was composed of two mayors (*alcaldes ordinarios* or *regidores mayores*) and ten aldermen (*regidores ordinarios*) along with other local and government employees such as the *alférez real*, the *alguacil mayor*, the *fiel ejecutor*, the *procurador*, and scriveners – all with different functions that regulated everyday life in the city. The city council's duties were of an administrative nature: distributing property among neighbours, managing the city food supply, controlling prices, and so forth.[31]

From a social point of view, the institutions of Mexico City reflected to some extent the difficulties and tensions that, owing to the particularities of colonial society, were not present in peninsular cities such as Seville. The struggles that brought the Iberians (*peninsulares*) face-to-face with the Creoles – the people of peninsular origin that had been born in the Americas – became manifest during the first decades of the seventeenth century. Those struggles increased in the second half of the seventeenth century and again in the eighteenth century. The *peninsulares* controlled the most important political organs of power in the viceroyalty: the viceroys, archbishops, and *corregidores*; but local institutions, such as the city council, were controlled by Creoles. The Mexican elite were largely Creole, but the Iberians were a powerful minority group.

A similar situation arose with respect to positions in the Church. Although the Creoles did not occupy the most distinguished clerical posts (e.g., those of the archbishops of Mexico, Puebla de los Ángeles, Michoacán, and Guadalajara), they acceded to important posts of secular and regular clergy. In general terms, the regular clergy were the richer of the two, especially from the end of the sixteenth century onward – that is, upon expiration of the initial impetus of conquest that necessitated large numbers of religious men to evangelise

---

30   Antonio Domínguez Ortiz, *La Sociedad Americana y la Corona Española en el Siglo XVII* (Madrid: Asociación Francisco López de Gomara, 1996), 169–70.

31   Jonathan I. Israel, *Razas, Clases Sociales y Vida Política en el México Colonial, 1610–1670* (México, D.F.: Fondo de Cultura Económica, 1980), 100–4.

ILLUSTRATION 1   View of Mexico City on a folding screen (*Palacio de los virreyes de México*).
Anonymous, *c.* 1676–1700.
SOURCE: MINISTERIO DE EDUCACIÓN, CULTURA Y DEPORTE (SPAIN).
MUSEO DE AMÉRICA, MADRID (SPAIN)

natives. In Mexico City there were more Franciscan, Agustin, and Jesuit monasteries and convents than in any other city of the viceroyalty.[32]

There is one social group that deserves special attention: the merchants.
They were a highly significant social group in Mexico City because of their
control over the silver mining, their trade with the Philippine Islands and Castile, and many other economic segments of the viceroyalty. In addition to these
important and powerful traders, many people had small businesses in the city
thanks to the substantial trade that flowed within it. Mexico was a city full of
merchants – from petty dealers, peddlers, and shopkeepers to wholesalers that
specialised in silver and other expensive products. There were also merchant
agents who brokered for companies with links to Seville, Manila, Lima, or Havana, among other places.[33] Moreover, the different types of merchants inject-
ed life into the city's principal area: the main square, known as *Zócalo*, where
stood cathedral buildings and palaces of the viceroy and the archbishop. Full
of arcades, the famous Arcade of the Merchants (*Portal de los Mercaderes*) of
the *Zócalo* was over-run by stalls belonging to peddlers, booksellers, and craftsmen who sold items as varied as silk, books, crystals, jewels, spices, and articles
imported from Castile, Asia, and other American regions.

----

32   Leonard A. Irving, *La Época Barroca en el México Colonial* (México D.F.: Fondo de Cultura
      Económica, 1974), 74–77.

33   For a complete study of these merchants, see Louisa S. Hoberman, *Mexico's Merchant
      Elite, 1590–1660. Silver, State, and Society* (Durham, NC: Duke University Press, 1991).

So far I have focused only on the white Mexican elite, who accounted for some ten per cent of Mexico City's population in *circa* 1600. This was the wealthiest group. The rest of the city's population consisted mostly of natives who lived in specific neighbourhoods with limited autonomy, *mestizos* (a cross of native American and European parents), mulattoes, blacks, and other categories that were relatively low on the social scale of that era.

Between 1580 and 1640, Mexico City had about 100,000 inhabitants. Indigenous Americans, despite being a decimated population group, made up the majority of the city's denizens. During the sixteenth century the native population of Mexico-Tenochtitlan was dramatically reduced, much as in the rest of the viceroyalty. That reduction was due first to effects of the Spanish conquest and subsequently to overwork, enslavement, and epidemics that spread because natives had no immunity against the European diseases imported by the conquerors.[34] From the end of the sixteenth to the middle of the seventeenth century, the native population of Mexico City was stable; about 80,000 native American lived there during that period.[35]

Unlike native Americans, the populations of black, mulatto, *mestizo*, and white inhabitants did not suffer long-term declines. Contemporary estimates put the white population (composed mainly of the Spanish and Creole elite) at between 10,000 and 40,000 during the period 1580–1650.[36]

Population figures for the city's black, mulatto, and *mestizo* inhabitants are less reliable than those for the white and Indigenous population. Contemporary sources gave estimates of 40,000 or 50,000 for black, mulatto, and *mestizo* groups in the mid-colonial period, but those numbers are apparently exaggerated and unreliable. The inflated figures are likely due to the difficulties experienced by contemporaries in counting these groups – perhaps because slaves

---

34 Woodrow W. Borah and Sherburne F. Cook, *The Population of Central Mexico in 1548. An Analysis of the Suma de Visitas de Pueblos* (Berkeley, CA: University of California Press, 1960); Woodrow W. Borah and Sherburne F. Cook, *Essays in Population History. Mexico and the Caribbean*, 3 vols. (London: University of California Press, 1971, 1974, and 1979).

35 Charles Gibson, *The Aztecs under the Spanish Rule. History of the Indians of the Valley of Mexico, 1519–1810* (Stanford, CA: Stanford University Press, 1964), 136–41, 378, 381; Nicolás Sánchez-Albornoz, *La Población de América Latina. Desde los Tiempos Pre-Colombinos al Año 2000* (Madrid: Alianza, 1973), 60–72, 89–91; Linda A. Newson, "The Demographic Impact of Colonization," in, *The Cambridge Economic History of Latin America*, vol. 1, ed. Victor Bulmer-Thomas, John H. Coatsworth, and Roberto Cortés Conde (New York: Cambridge University Press, 2006), 167.

36 The white population peaked in about 1625; at that time, it was estimated that from 30,000 to 40,000 whites lived in Mexico City. Yet after the floods of the late 1620s, many Spanish and Creole families died or emigrated from Mexico City. The white population declined by as much as 20,000 in 1629 and by some 8,000 in 1646: Gibson, *The Aztecs*, 381.

and mixed racial groups tended to concentrate in those sectors with the largest numbers of white population. Given the size of native and white populations, more trustworthy estimates appear to be 2,000 mulatto and 1,000 black people in the city during the second half of the sixteenth century.[37]

These estimates allow us to calculate Mexico City's population at about 100,000 at the turn of the century. Even if we suppose that the population was smaller by several thousand, Mexico City had approximately the same population as some of the biggest European cities of that time: Rome, Lisbon, Seville, and Milan.[38]

On the eastern side of the Atlantic, Seville was one of the most important cities of the Atlantic World. Seville was not the capital city of Castile but was, along with Lisbon, an extremely important *entrepôt* of the Iberian Peninsula. Seville was an early modern city that best exemplified a mix of the preceding (medieval) era and the new era – namely, the importance of blood and nobility in social organisation, on the former hand, and the growing economic importance of commerce on the latter. Examining Sevillian institutions reveals just how important the aristocracy was in that city. Even though Seville underwent profound social changes during the sixteenth century as the trans-Atlantic trade expanded, noblemen retained a remarkable degree of power. They controlled Seville's city council to such an extent that it was considered one of the most "aristocratised" councils of Castile. The main income of titled noblemen came from rural rents and taxes, though they also controlled municipal life through administrators under their rule.[39] That being said, the nobility was a heterogeneous group and not all of its members were rich and powerful. This became clear during the sixteenth and seventeenth centuries, when nobility suffered from a process of inflation and economic change.

Besides aristocrats, merchants were the other significant social group of Seville. Indeed, merchants were sometimes virtually indistinguishable from the aristocratic nobles. Nobles took part in commercial operations and, conversely, high-ranking merchants aimed to achieve nobility. Evidence for the latter is that the most important Sevillian merchants purchased rural properties, married in to noble families, bought high municipal positions, and obtained

---

37   Gibson, *The Aztecs*, 380, 576.

38   Jan de Vries, *European Urbanization, 1500–1800* (Cambridge, MA: Harvard University Press, 1984), 278–87.

39   Ruth Pike, *Aristócratas y Comerciantes. La Sociedad Sevillana en el Siglo XVI* (Barcelona: Ariel, 1978), 37–41.

aristocratic titles.[40] Thus evolved social flux and a merging of the high merchants and noblemen in Seville. These new social and economic features of the city facilitated the development of a powerful commercial class that controlled the merchant guild (*Consulado de Mercaderes*), which had been created in 1543.[41] The merchant guild was an institutional lobby used by merchants to defend their economic interests, and it also acquired some legal jurisdiction to regulate trade. Prior to the merchant guild's founding, trans-Atlantic trade had been exclusively regulated by the House of Trade (*Casa de la Contratación*).[42]

Seville's monopoly on trade with the Americas made possible the development of these new social, economic, and political characteristics of the city; see illustration 2. The tradition in commercial activities, which had begun in the thirteenth century with the Genoese commercial initiatives and the city's commercial relations with other Mediterranean ports, was the starting point that allowed Seville to monopolise American trade in the sixteenth century. Geographically, this trade was facilitated by the Guadalquivir River's flowing into the Gulf of Cádiz in the Atlantic Ocean. The consequences of such commercial activity included the spread of new institutions that regulated trade (e.g., the House of Trade) as well as the proliferation of greater social complexity and the attraction of people from such diverse areas as Guipuzcoa, Florence, Genoa, Portugal, Flanders, England, Ireland, France, and Germany.

Like Mexico City, Seville was full of squares where craftsmen, fruit sellers, barbers, peddlers, and tradesmen of all sorts offered their services and sold their products. The main square of Seville was San Francisco, where the city council, the *audencia*, the cathedral, and the archbishop's palace were all located. The uses of the main square changed over time; in addition to being a scene of religious and noble fiestas, San Francisco square became a commercial area used to buy and sell bread, meat, fish, vegetables, and all the other commodities and objects imported from the Americas. It was also a centre of activities for silversmiths, moneychangers, and financiers.[43]

The monarchy's choosing it as the only Castilian port connected to the Americas made Seville, at the beginning of the sixteenth century, a huge cosmopolitan city – to the extent that its population grew to nearly 130,000 by the

---

40   Antonio Domínguez Ortiz, *Orto y Ocaso de Sevilla* (Sevilla: Universidad de Sevilla, 1981), 85–89; Enriqueta Vila Vilar, *Los Corzo y los Mañara. Tipos y Arquetipos del Mercader con Indias* (Sevilla: Escuela de Estudios Hispano-Americanos, 1991).

41   Today, the Indies General Archive is located in the building of the old merchant guild.

42   Antonio García-Baquero González, *La Carrera de Indias. Suma de Contratación y Océano de Negocios* (Sevilla: Algaida, 1992), 55–84.

43   Francisco Núñez Roldán, *La Vida Cotidiana en la Sevilla del Siglo de Oro* (Madrid: Sílex, 2004), 19–50.

ILLUSTRATION 2   View of Seville from the Triana neighbourhood. Attributed to Alonso
                 Sánchez Coello, *c. 1576–1700*.
                 SOURCE: MINISTERIO DE EDUCACIÓN, CULTURA Y DEPORTE (SPAIN).
                 MUSEO DE AMÉRICA, MADRID (SPAIN)

year 1600. This was larger even than Madrid, home to the King's Court, whose population was about 60,000. According to various sources, the population of Seville reached its highest point during the 1580s and then declined after the plague of 1599–1601. Thereafter, and until the eighteenth century, the number of Seville's inhabitants never surpassed 100,000.[44] Most people living in Seville were poor and, without the resources to save or invest, often subsisted on the bare essentials. Within this majority group were *pecheros* (non-nobles) as well as those people not integrated into Catholic society: the Moorish (*moriscos*), the Christians who were descendants of Jews (*conversos*), and slaves.[45]

Now we can direct our attention to the other side of the world – namely, to Southeast Asia. Manila was the capital city of the Philippine Islands, which had been under Spanish control since 1565. As part of Southeast Asia, the Philippines are an area clearly marked by natural boundaries; the area has similar flora and fauna throughout, with water and forests as the dominant elements. This particular environment supported a diet derived mainly from rice, fish, and various palms.[46] Notwithstanding this geographical unity, the Philippines

---

44   León C. Álvarez Santaló, "La Población de Sevilla en las Series Parroquiales, Siglos XVI–
      XIX," in *Actas II Coloquio Historia de Andalucía. Andalucía Moderna* (Córdoba: Monte de
      Piedad y Caja de Ahorros, 1983), 3–4; and Pike, *Aristócratas y Comerciantes*, 13–31.

45   Pike, *Aristócratas y Comerciantes*, 167–82.

46   Anthony Reid, *Southeast Asia in the Age of Commerce, 1450–1680. Volume One: The Lands
      below the Winds* (New Haven, CT: Yale University Press, 1988), 1–10.

featured some unique aspects prior to being conquered by the Spaniards. The Philippine archipelago was characterised by political fragmentation. The native population was divided into many small towns, each one home to between 20 and 100 families (*barangays*). These towns, governed by strong hierarchies, were units of production and consumption. During the fifteenth century Muslims established themselves in certain areas of the Philippines, where they organised different systems of population control and introduced their religion (which merged with the established polytheist and monotheist religions). The Muslim areas – especially Mindanao (which, after Luzon, was the second largest island of the archipelago) and the mountainous area of northwestern Luzon – were the ones that most strongly resisted the Spanish conquest through the seventeenth century.[47]

The Spaniards founded Manila in 1571, but its conquest of the Americas was not complete at the time Europeans first set foot on the Philippine archipelago. It was in 1521 that the Portuguese Fernâo de Magalhâes, who served the Crown of Castile, arrived on the Philippine Islands and claimed them as part of the Habsburg Empire. However, the Spaniards did not manage to settle there for another two generations. Several expeditions from the Americas to Southeast Asia were organised in the years following 1521. These included the 1525–1536 expedition mounted by Juan García Jofre de Loaysa and Álvaro de Saavedra, who failed to take the Spice Islands (Maluku Islands) from the Portuguese. Another expedition was that of Ruy López Villalobos, during 1542–1549, when the Islands were named the "Felipinas" in honour of Prince Philip (the future Philip II). The main problem with these Spanish expeditions was that they did not find a route back to the Americas across the Pacific Ocean. Such a route was later discovered during an expedition led by Miguel López de Legazpi and Andrés de Urdaneta in 1564. The settlement on the Philippine Islands was possible because the conquerors finally discovered the Kuro Siwo ocean currents, which could ride ships across the Pacific to the western coast of New Spain on a journey taking about six months.[48]

The Philippines were initially disappointing lands for the Spaniards. There was scant production of spices, such as cinnamon and pepper. More important was the production of cotton, of which some textiles (e.g., the *lampotes* and blankets from Ilocos) were exported to New Spain in the years immediately

---

47   John L. Phelan, *The Hispanization of the Philippines: Spanish Aims and Filipino Responses, 1565–1700* (Madison, WI: University of Wisconsin Press, 2010), 3–30, 153–64.

48   Antonio García Abásolo, "La Primera Exploración del Pacífico y el Asentamiento Español en Filipinas," in *Las Relaciones entre España y Filipinas. Siglos XVI–XX*, ed. María D. Elizalde Pérez-Grueso (Madrid: CSIC, 2002), 21–35.

after the conquest.[49] During the decade following 1565, the conquerors made an effort to evangelise natives and control Luzon, the archipelago's main island. However, the Spanish population in the Philippines never exceeded 5,000 during the early modern period. Hence Spanish control over the islands was limited; it was restricted to the area surrounding Manila, some coastal areas of Luzon, and the plains of some of the smaller islands. Withdrawing altogether from the Philippines was often advocated by those among the King's circle of counsellors during the 1570s and 1580s. The development of Manila as a worldwide centre of exchange of silk for silver occurred after the arrival there of American silver and Chinese merchants during the 1580s and 1590s. This transformation into an international *entrepôt* guaranteed a place for the Philippines within the Spanish Empire. That became especially important during the Union of Crowns (1580–1640), when the Portuguese from Macao intensified their trade.[50]

The economic and political centre of the Philippine Islands was Manila. Unlike New Spain and Peru, the Philippines never constituted a viceroyalty. The archipelago was instead a Captaincy General (*Capitanía General*) that was both integrated with and economically dependent upon the viceroyalty of New Spain, from which the Philippines received an annual *situado* (subsidy) designated for the maintenance of Spanish imperial structures on the Islands. The most important of the Spanish institutions were the Governor General (*Gobernador General*), the Bishop of Manila, the *audiencia*, and the city council. Most of the Spanish and American Creole population of the Philippines lived in Manila. The only exceptions were friars of the Augustinian and Franciscan orders, who lived in rural areas – where they tried to convert as many natives as possible. Over time, when trade had developed further, even the landowners (*encomenderos*) who controlled native populations through the pre-Hispanic *barangays* in Luzon and other islands preferred to live in Manila.

The small number of Spaniards was even more pronounced in Manila than in American cities. The population of the Philippines was subject to constant setbacks. Along with the Spanish war against the Dutch, which intensified in Asia after 1600, the population of Manila also suffered natural disasters: the fires of 1583 and 1603 and the earthquake of 1600. These catastrophes discouraged many Spanish American Creoles and Spaniards from settling in Manila.

49	Luis Alonso Álvarez, *El Costo del Imperio Asiático. La Formación Colonial de las Islas Filipinas bajo Dominio Español, 1585–1600* (México, D.F.: Instituto Mora, 2009), 29–34; Yuste López, *Emporios Transpacíficos*, 21–26.

50	Birgit Tremml-Werner, *Spain, China, and Japan in Manila, 1571-1644. Local comparisons and global connections* (Amsterdam: Amsterdam University Press, 2015), 267–290.

The American Creole and European population of Manila, mostly Spaniards and Portuguese, was about 1,500 in 1601; this had increased to 2,800 people by 1612. From that year onward, sources chart a continuous decline in the Spanish, Portuguese an American Creole population, which became more precipitous in the 1630s and the 1640s. Of the 1,500 to 3,000 Europeans and American Creoles who lived in Manila around the year 1600, there was an elite made up of Spanish civil, military, and religious sectors. It is worth noting the significant number of widows in Manila – a result of constant attacks on the city (by the Dutch and by Chinese pirates) and the ongoing recruitment of men to fight against the Crown's enemies in the area.[51]

The Spaniards were a privileged minority in Manila, which (like Mexico City) was populated by people from all over the world. Filipinos, Chinese, Japanese, Africans and natives from Spanish America all lived in Manila. Africans and natives from the Americas usually worked as servants in the homes of the wealthiest elite. The Japanese, unlike the Chinese, rarely established their homes in Manila; their stays in Manila were normally short and related to the Manila Galleon cycle, although over time they built a small neighbourhood within an area of the city. The majority of Manila's population was native to Luzon. The populations of Mindanao and Joló, which were normally moved to Manila as slaves of war, were much smaller. Historical sources do not contain details concerning even the approximate number of Filipinos living in Manila, but they almost certainly formed the great majority of the city. These natives devoted their time to agriculture and raising cattle. Over time, even the Filipinos became involved in commerce – especially selling cotton to the Chinese, with whom miscegenation was more common than with Spaniards.[52]

The Chinese formed the largest population of continental Asians living in Manila. The only Chinese merchants who were allowed to trade with the Philippines, most of whom lived in Manila, were the so-called *sangleyes*. Although there had been Chinese on the Philippine archipelago before the Spanish conquest, the number of Chinese merchants rose sharply with the increase of

---

51 Inmaculada Alva Rodríguez, *Vida Municipal en Manila* (*Siglos XVI–XVII*) (Córdoba: Universidad de Córdoba, 1997), 30–34; Antonio García-Abásolo, "El Poblamiento Español de Filipinas (1571–1599)," in *España y el Pacífico*, ed. Antonio García-Abásolo (Córdoba: Asociación Española de Estudios del Pacífico, 1997) 145–55; Juan Mesquida Oliver, "La Población de Manila y las Capellanías de Misas de los Españoles: Libro de Registros, 1642–1672," *Revista de Indias* 70, no. 249 (2010): 469–500; Ostwald Sales Colín, *El Movimiento Portuario de Acapulco. El Protagonismo de Nueva España en Relación con Filipinas, 1587–1648* (México, D.F.: Plaza y Valdés, 2000), 34–36.

52 Alva Rodríguez, *Vida Municipal en Manila*, 34–36; Phelan, *Hispanization of the Philippines*, 3–30.

trade in Manila. The governor Francisco Tello estimated that in 1601 there were roughly 6,000 Chinese living in Manila in addition to several thousand others who visited every year for trading purposes. The growing number of Chinese – who lived in the *Parian* (their own neighbourhood) and also on the city's outskirts – worried the Spanish authorities. Despite their mutual dependence stemming from the exchange of silver for Asian products, a growing number of Chinese in Manila considered trade with the Spaniards to be unequal because of the legal restrictions that they imposed. These impositions caused social problems, as when the attempts of Spanish authorities to expel Chinese merchants from Manila led to Chinese rebellions in 1603 and 1639.[53]

Life in Manila depended to a large extent upon trade. The arrival of between one and four galleons – although from 1593 onward only two were legally allowed to sail – of, according to law, 300 tonnes at the port of Cavite from Acapulco every spring, and their sailing on to Acapulco every summer, marked the economic cycles of the city and its hinterland.[54] Trade with the Americas was free at first; over time, however, regulations were enacted by Spanish authorities from Madrid. Trade was limited to Manila's port (Cavite) and Acapulco, on the western coast of New Spain. In order to limit trade between the Philippines and the Americas, the Crown introduced a legal condition that no more than 500,000 pesos of "pieces of eight" (*pesos de oro común*) and 250,000 pesos worth of merchandise could be shipped, respectively, from Acapulco to Manila and from Manila to Acapulco. The organisation of trade, the distribution of ship cargo space, and the issuance of licences to load goods onto the galleons were all controlled by the colonial institutions of Manila. These tasks took considerable time and also required a significant amount of clerical manpower. All resident Spaniards in the Philippines had the legal right to load merchandise onto the galleons, a procedure that was organised through committees established by a royal decree of 1603. The Committee of Distribution (*Junta de Repartimiento*)

---

53   Antonio García-Abásolo, "Relaciones Entre Españoles y Chinos en Filipinas. Siglos XVI y XVII," in *España y el Pacífico. Legazpi*, vol. 2, ed. Leoncio Cabrero (Madrid: Sociedad Estatal de Conmemoraciones Culturales, 2004), 231–48; Marta M. Manchado López, "Chinos y Españoles en Manila a Comienzos del Siglo XVII," in *Un Océano de Intercambios: Hispanoasia (1521–1898). Homenaje al Profesor Leoncio Cabrero Fernández*, vol. I, ed. Miguel Luque Talaván and Marta M. Machado López (Madrid: Ministerio de Asuntos Exteriores, 2008), 141–59.

54   Until 1720, the law established that two galleons of 300 tonnes each would sail every year from Acapulco to Manila (and vice versa). In practice, however, there were one to four galleons of more than 300 tonnes each. The 300-tonnes limit would nearly always be exceeded during the journey from Acapulco to Manila, when the galleons were loaded with silver.

and the Committee of Valuation (*Junta de Avalúo*) consisted of representatives from merchants and the main colonial institutions: governor, archbishop, *audiencia*, and city council. The Committee of Distribution registered the Spaniards who loaded merchandise onto the galleons every year, and it gave these Spaniards a receipt (*boleta*) that reported the value and space required for the cargo on board every galleon. All this information was registered in a Book of Distribution (*Libro de Repartimiento*). Some social sectors, such as widows and soldiers, had certain trading privileges – for instance, more space for loaded merchandise than was granted to other Spanish residents. The Committee of Evaluation was in charge of producing a report containing all the details of distribution. In 1769 the merchant guild of Manila was founded, and all these proceedings were put into its hands. Unfortunately, no documents produced by the Committee of Distribution during the seventeenth century have survived. Even though all Spaniards of Manila could, in principle, load merchandise onto the galleons bound for New Spain, that trade was eventually reduced to a few merchants who purchased receipts (made out to other people) and the concomitant right to ship goods on the galleons. These Manila merchants were usually commercial agents of Mexican merchants, who also controlled the business of the fair of Acapulco through agreements with the merchants in that city.[55]

∵

The book is organised along the lines of circulation of goods and commerce, political economy, production, and consumption, which are formulated into seven chapters, including this first introductory chapter and a final chapter of conclusions. Chapter 2 deals with the circulation of Asian goods across the Spanish Empire as gifts and products that were distributed over global networks, which could be commercial, noble, familial, and/or socio-professional networks. Chapter 3 connects the Manila Galleon trade to the wholesale trade of Asian products on the trans-Atlantic commercial axis. In particular, it discusses the main agents for the trade of Asian merchandise along the trans-Pacific and trans-Atlantic axes as well as the rise and fall of this trade from 1580 until the mid-seventeenth century. Furthermore, Chapter 3 addresses the international context of trade and the Spanish Empire, especially its war against other European powers.

In order to illustrate how the economic performance of the Manila Galleon route affected institutional changes in the Spanish Empire (and vice versa),

---

55   Schurtz, *El Galeón de Manila*; Yuste López, *El Comercio de la Nueva España*, 20–24; and
      Yuste López, *Emporios Transpacíficos*, 34–40.

Chapter 4 tackles several issues. These include effects of the growth (and later contraction) of trans-Pacific trade as well as the commercial strategies employed by Philippine and Mexican merchants who faced, over time, not only changing trends in that trade but also the opposing interests of the Spanish Empire elite as regards the Manila Galleon trade. These conflicting interests, the international context, and a decline in trade accounted for some of the regulations and institutional changes that affected commercial trading across the Pacific. Chapter 5 explores the effect of Chinese silk, Chinese porcelain, and Asian furniture on some productive sectors of New Spain and of Castile. That chapter also looks at the transmission – from Asia to Spanish America via the Manila Galleon route – of skills and techniques for producing certain goods. Chapter 6 addresses the elite consumption of Asian manufactured goods in New Spain and Castile by comparing Mexico City and Seville with respect to the meanings and uses of Asian textiles and objects imported by those cities. Chapter 7 offers conclusions based on the finding of previous chapters.

From Asian Goods to Asian Commodities in the Spanish Empire

Both the shipment of gifts and the commission of orders were common practice in the early modern era. In a society such as that of the Old Regime, where membership in guilds and social strata (and where the culture of honour and rank) were so important, it was common for gifts and specially requested products to be transferred to another member of the same family or socio-professional status. The medieval practice of gift transfer took off in the sixteenth century and responded to the new possibilities offered by development of a market economy. Social and political relations were facilitated by the giving of gifts, inheritances, and alms – whether monetised or in kind. Natalie Zemon Davis and Martha C. Howell have pointed out that, during the early modern era, gifts simultaneously forged relations among individuals, fed social and cultural interactions, and fuelled commercial exchanges. Although transmission of goods via gift might sometimes have competed with transmission via sales, they commonly overlapped. For instance, it was typical for some commercial payments to be accompanied by gifts.[1]

It is worth asking to what extent Asian products – including Chinese silk and porcelain as well as Japanese furniture, folding screens, and jewels – were involved in the transmission of products shipped under order and gift transfer in the Spanish Empire in the sixteenth and seventeenth centuries. A related concern is identifying which social groups took part in the transmission of Asian goods as gifts across the Empire from the Philippines to Spanish America and then to Castile. In the historical context studied here, answering these questions can yield considerable information about how Asian manufactured products fuelled relations between peers within the social groups prevalent in the Spanish Empire. This investigation is important because it informs us about the uses and meanings that Asian goods had at a time when the market for them was hardly developed in the Atlantic World and when goods in the form of gifts and merchandise were part of the same shipment; it also sheds light on how the demand for Asian goods increased during a time of limited

---

1 Martha C. Howell, *Commerce before Capitalism in Europe, 1300–1600* (Cambridge: Cambridge University Press, 2010), 145–207; Natalie Zemon Davis, *The Gift in Sixteenth-Century France* (Madison: University of Wisconsin Press, 2000), especially 73–109.

expansion in the commercialisation of Asian goods in some parts of the West. In discussing the agents and forms of that Asian goods transfer – and also the degree to which such goods were integrated into the systems of retail distribution of New Spanish cities such as Mexico – this chapter explores how gift transfer and the commission of Asian manufactured goods served to improve social and political relations across the Spanish Empire. The chapter also explains how this transfer of goods promoted the recognition of Asian manufactures, which did not become widely known, desired, or demanded by European consumers until later in the second half of the seventeenth century and the eighteenth century.

2.1   Agents and Forms of Transfer of Asian Goods

As early as the late sixteenth century, the Manila Galleon route and the elite of Spanish America became agents who supplied, alongside Portuguese living in Macao (China), Chinese and Japanese silks and porcelains to the elite of the Iberian Peninsula.[2] These goods were decorated with either Christian or Asian designs. Although Chinese raw silk, silk fabrics, and porcelain circulated via commercial avenues from the Philippines to the Americas and then to Castile, these and other goods from Asia were also being transferred across the Empire as gifts and requested items. Indeed, on occasions Asian gifts and merchandise were shipped in the same package. Many documents – including merchandise reports and business letters from merchants, notarial records, and letters from emigrants to the Americas – have left traces of such circulation of Asian items in the Spanish Empire during the late sixteenth century and the first half of the seventeenth century. The most important of these documents are the "inward registers from New Spain of ships that came into the port of Seville" (*registros de venida de la Nueva España*), which record the cargoes, including gifts, of all ships and vessels that sailed from Veracruz (New Spain) to Seville. They also record the fleet and *avería* tax charged on each consignment: all transcontinental consignments, including gifts, were taxed by the Crown. The transfer of gifts and the shipment of Asian goods as personally commissioned orders determined the extent to which Asian goods were spread throughout the Spanish Empire around 1600. This circulation required the performance of different

---

2   Teresa Canepa, "The Portuguese and Spanish Trade in *Kraak* Porcelain in the Late 16th and Early 17th Centuries," in *Proceedings of the International Symposium: Chinese Export Ceramics in the 16th and 17th Centuries and the Spread of Material Civilization* (Hong Kong: City University of Hong Kong, 2012), 257–85.

types of agents who gave gifts and shipped them with diverse aims and in accordance with various codes. The registers of ships that sailed from New Spain to Castile are more complete than other sources; this makes them a good starting point from which to explore the main agents of such transference.

The members of the Philippine, New Spanish, and Castilian aristocracy – together with the highest positions of the Spanish Empire's religious, colonial, royal, and municipal administration – were the most relevant groups in the transmission of Asian gifts and orders. These rich elites, who in many cases were titled nobles, sent from East to West not only Chinese silk and porcelain but also more expensive (and rarer) products such as escritoires and other lacquered pieces of furniture from Japan, gold jewellery, and calico textiles from India. The elite of the Philippines sent Asian objects to New Spain and other places in the Americas; they also sent such objects to Castile via the Americas. There are some outstanding examples, among which the governors and archbishops of Manila (who occupied the highest positions on the Philippine Islands) are especially relevant. Don Alonso Fajardo, Governor of the Philippines between 1618 and 1624, dispatched several escritoires, writing desks, and beds of Japanese manufacture to Seville in 1618.[3] Likewise, Don Diego Vázquez de Mercado, Archbishop of Manila, made two consignments of Asian goods to Castile, one each in 1615 and 1616. In 1615 he sent two pieces of raw silk and 16 velvet *reposteros* (decorative cloths embellished with his coat of arms) from China, as well as four bedspreads adorned with his coat of arms from India, to Don Pedro de Mercado Vázquez, his nephew and an alderman of Madrid. This shipment of Chinese silk, with its inherently European decoration (coats of arms), confirms that the earliest commissions of made-to-order Asian items with Christian and Western motifs made by Castilian elites via the Philippines and New Spain were made during approximately the same period as those commissioned by Portuguese elites via Macao.[4] The archbishop's other consignment, of 1616, consisted of all the vestments a priest needed to conduct a mass: a chasuble, stole, and the robes called *almáticas*, all made of silk. The shipments of the Archbishop of Manila were not gifts but rather specific orders of items requested by his nephew. These were shipments that travelled across merchant networks, as the man responsible for receiving the objects in Seville was the captain and merchant Antonio Lorenzo de Andrada. However, other professional networks overlapped with these well-established commercial networks: the secretary de la Torre, from Mexico City, and the alderman

---

3 AGI, *Contratación*, 1849, 204–8.
4 Canepa, "The Portuguese and Spanish Trade," 271–73.

Benito González, from Veracruz, also took care of goods and sent them to Seville from their respective cities.[5]

The few aristocrats who lived in New Spain also made shipments of this sort to Castile. The case of the Count of Santiago is paradigmatic. In 1618 he sent his wife, who lived somewhere in Castile (probably Madrid), several pieces of satin from China, some thrown silk (*seda torçida*) from China, two folding screens, two writing desks from Japan, and a chest from Japan.[6] In 1621, he sent another crate of presents to his wife from New Spain containing several similar objects from Asia, mostly from China, along with some small boxes of chocolate.[7] It was common for Asian gifts and orders to be sent along with American products, such as chocolate, in the same package. There are many other cases of New Spanish nobles, or Castilian nobles who lived in New Spain, who sent Asian goods in the form of gifts or special orders to relatives and trusted people who lived in Castile. Examples include the Marquis and Marchioness of Villamanrique in 1604, the Count of Olivares in 1611, the Marquis of Salinas in 1614 and 1615, the Marquis of La Floresta in 1617, the Count and the Countess of Lemos in 1618, the Count of Peñaranda in 1618, the Countess of Santiago in 1618 and 1621, the Bishop of Palencia and Count of Pernia in 1619, and the Count of Benavente in 1621.[8]

When looking at the aristocratic elite on both sides of the Atlantic, the significance of the King's Court in Madrid as the centre of reception of Asian goods in Castile is evident. Many authors have stated that Madrid, where the Court was located, was also the location of the royal collections and the most powerful aristocrats' "chambers of wonders" (*cámaras de las maravillas*), among which Chinese porcelains and Japanese *namban* pieces of furniture were some of the most outstanding items.[9] The high number of consignments of Asian

---

5 AGI, *Contratación*, 1830, 850–52; AGI, *Contratación*, 1834, 1052–55. The Archbishop of Manila was not the only person who sent European objects manufactured in Asia. In 1615, the captain Francisco de Medina sent some items from Manila to Alonso Maldonado de Torres, priest of the King in Madrid. He sent 12 velvet *reposteros* from China, 24 velvet cushions from China, and one golden rosary: AGI, *Contratación*, 1830, 277–79.

6 AGI, *Contratación*, 1852A, 505–8.

7 AGI, *Contratación*, 1866, 651–54.

8 AGI, *Contratación*, 1805, 65–67; AGI, *Contratación*, 1809, 258–63; AGI, *Contratación*, 1823, 598–601; AGI, *Contratación*, 1832, 89–90; AGI, *Contratación*, 1841, 2183–86; AGI, *Contratación*, 1847, 236–40; AGI, *Contratación*, 1850, 78–79; AGI, *Contratación*, 1851, 63–67; AGI, *Contratación*, 1852A, 505–8; AGI, *Contratación*, 1866, 651–54; AGI, *Contratación*, 1856, 524–27; AGI, *Contratación*, 1866, 466–68.

9 José M. Morán and Fernando Checa, *El Coleccionismo en España. De la Cámara de las Maravillas a la Galería de Pinturas* (Madrid: Cátedra, 2005), 63–85; Pilar Cabañas Moreno, "Una Visión de las Colecciones de Arte Japonés en España," *Artigrama* (18, 2003): 107–24; Yayoi

gifts and personal orders destined for Madrid corroborate the role of the Royal Court as an area that attracted both Asian and American textiles, curiosities, and other items. Many members of the Court, including those close to the King himself, received Asian goods from New Spain. Moreover, some members of the Court appeared to be mediators in the distribution of these Asian goods to other Court members or to elites who lived in Madrid. Among those receiving Asian items in Madrid were King's servants, public prosecutors of the Royal Council (*Consejo Real*) and the King's Court, members of the King's Councils, and secretaries to the king, to name just a few. They received many types of items: Chinese and Japanese escritoires, various types of Chinese silks, Indian cottons, Japanese *katanas* and folding screens, ivory sculptures, and so forth. Sometimes the registers of ships sailing from New Spain to Castile did not specify the objects in a given package; they were simply labelled as "presents from China" or "presents from Japan." These Asian gifts and orders were often mixed with American products such as chocolate, *jícaras* (calabash bowls used to drink chocolate), escritoires from Michoacán, rosaries made of *coyoles* (fruits of the American tree *coyolli*), and tortoiseshell chests. The senders tended to have high-ranking positions in the administration of the viceroyalty of New Spain and in the Viceroy's Court of Mexico City. They included judges of the Royal Court of Mexico, royal accountants of the Royal Treasury of Mexico, secretaries of the Viceroy Guadalcázar, and even the viceroy's wife herself, the Marchioness of Guadalcázar, who sent several Asian and American objects in the form of gifts from Mexico City to her relatives in Castile.[10]

The Viceroy's Court of Mexico City was no less important as a point of diffusion of Asian goods to Castile. A person as close to power as Francisco de Párraga y Rojas, who was secretary of chamber of the Viceroy Guadalcázar, made shipments of Asian and American goods to different locations in Castile on several occasions. He sent consignments to Tello de Vilaragut from Madrid in 1614 and again in 1618, and to his sister Doña Maria de Párraga y Rojas from Madrid

---

Kawamura, "Coleccionismo y Colecciones de la Laca Extremo Oriental en España desde la Época del Arte Namban hasta el Siglo XX," *Artigrama* (18, 2003): 211–30.

10   AGI, *Contratación*, 1805, 49–52; AGI, *Contratación*, 1795, 319–22; AGI, *Contratación*, 1823, 479–82; AGI, *Contratación*, 1830, 593–94; AGI, *Contratación*, 1834, 264–66; AGI, *Contratación*, 1842, 1462–67; AGI, *Contratación*, 1849, 371–75; AGI, *Contratación*, 1881, 539–42; AGI, *Contratación*, 1882, 687–90; AGI, *Contratación*, 1887, 2858–61; AGI, *Contratación*, 1809, 313–17; AGI, *Contratación*, 1809, 268–70; AGI, *Contratación*, 1823, 598–601; AGI, *Contratación*, 1841, 2183–86; AGI, *Contratación*, 1848, 268–79; AGI, *Contratación*, 1854, 659–64; AGI, *Contratación*, 1865, 1448–51; AGI, *Contratación*, 1866, 466–68; AGI, *Contratación*, 1872, 71–73; AGI, *Contratación*, 1876, 2396–2404; AGI, *Contratación*, 1882, 660–63; AGI, *Contratación*, 1890, 2051–53.

ILLUSTRATION 3   Blue-and-white Chinese porcelain, late sixteenth century.
SOURCE: MINISTERIO DE EDUCACIÓN CULTURA Y DEPORTE AND
MINISTERIO DE DEFENSA (SPAIN). MUSEO NAVAL, MADRID (SPAIN)

in 1618. The shipments to Tello de Vilaragut were orders, but the consignments to Francisco de Párraga's sisters were designated as "presents" (*regalos*) on the crate.[11] To give an example of some of the consignments that Francisco de Párraga made, in 1618 the shipment was made up of two white satin skirts from China, a bedspread from China, twenty pieces of satins from China, an escritoire and a small writing desk from Japan, six dozen rosaries made of *coyoles*, miscellaneous small fruits, twelve woollen cloths for chocolate, two *tecomates* (bowls in the form of a pumpkin; of pre-Hispanic origins), and two tortoiseshell chests.[12] Another example is the survival of a shipment made by the viceroy's wife, the Marchioness of Guadalcázar, who in 1618 sent Asian and American

---

11   AGI, *Contratación*, 1824, 515–16; AGI, *Contratación*, 1847, 82–86; AGI, *Contratación*, 1866, 187–90.
12   AGI, *Contratación*, 1847, 82–86.

goods to her sister Doña Antonia Maria de Córdoba, who was Don Iñigo de Córdoba's wife and lived in Madrid.[13] Finally, the clearest case of the viceregal court in the conveyance of Asian items to Castile is a report of clothes, silver, and jewels that the Viceroy of New Spain, the Marquis of Cerralbo, brought back to Castile in 1636. This report is full of notes detailing the contents of the crates, which contained lavish clothes and jewels as well as dozens of Chinese silks, furnishings, and porcelains like the one in illustration 3.[14]

The importance of nobility notwithstanding, the overseas diffusion of Asian goods as gifts and specially ordered items was not limited to aristocrats and court members. Socio-professional relations were also sustained by (among other factors) sending gifts and ordering special goods. The consignments of presents between merchants seemed to be an important element in maintaining trust between them; their business letters contain references to Asian goods, because of their sumptuousness, taking the form of presents. For instance, in 1627 Lucián Espinel, *encomendero* (permanently employed as a commercial agent) of the Mexican merchant Santi Federighi in the port of Veracruz, asked him "to send some silken stockings from China for Jorgito and some small trinkets as presents for the cousins and children."[15] In 1636 Ascanio Guazzoni, commercial agent of Santi Federighi in Manila, sent Federighi an ivory sculpture of Christ as a gift.[16] Merchants were not the only corporate group to use gifts – and especially Asian goods – to strengthen social, political, and economic relations within their social spheres. There are cases of aldermen (*regidores*) and secretaries of Mexico City sending Chinese porcelains and silk canopies to other servants and secretaries of the King in Madrid, as mentioned previously.

Family relationships were also crucial to the circulation of gifts and placing of personal orders. The letters written by emigrants in the Philippines and the Americas to their relatives reveal how family members who lived on different continents sent each other Asian goods, among other products, in the form of gifts. The following fragment of a letter sent in 1593 by Juana de Quesada, who lived in Cebu (one of the largest islands of the Philippines), to her uncle Tomás del Rio, resident of Mexico City, shows the extent to which family relations were responsible for the networks through which objects – including Asian goods – circulated across the empire:

---

13   AGI, *Contratación*, 1847, 112–17.

14   "Memoria de Ropa, Plata Labrada y Joyas del Marqués de Cerralbo, Virrey de Nueva España," AGI, *Contratación*, 1918, 2196–2229.

15   "Se Trayga Algunos Pares de Medias de Seda de China para Jorgito y Algunas Cosillas Curiosas para Regalos de las Primas y Niños," Letter from Lucian de Espinel to Santi Federighi on 9 March 1627, AGN, *Indiferente Virreinal*, caja-exp.: 5651-017; AGN, *Consulado*, 159–60.

16   Letter of 14 July 1636, AGN, *Indiferente Virreinal*, caja-exp.: 5056-050, *Consulado*.

Dear Uncle,

I received a letter from you in the galleon *San Felipe*. It made us very happy to know that you, my aunt and the rest of my ladies are in good health. May God give you good health always to serve Him. Hernando de Carvajal does not write to you as he is gone with the expedition of Malua, and he had no time to manage his unfinished business here. Pray you for him to have a safe journey. By the time he is back, he will send you gifts of things that are here.[17]

Letters written by Castilian emigrants who lived in Mexico City contain similar information regarding the consignment of presents to their relatives on the other side of the Atlantic Ocean, in Castile.[18] The ship registers of New Spanish fleets are better indicators of the diffusion of Asian gifts and orders between members of the same family. In 1591, Juan de la Fuente Belluga, from Mexico City, sent "a box with things from China" to his sister Doña Teresa de la Fuente, from Granada.[19] In 1603, Lucio Gutiérrez, a Castilian emigrant who lived in Jalapa, sent his sisters, who still lived in Castile, several Chinese satins and damasks.[20]

There are also cases of this type of transfer from Manila to New Spain. For instance, Alonso Rodríguez de León, a commercial agent in the Philippines for his uncle, Alonso Rodríguez de Luado, sent his aunt, Doña Ana de Zaldívar, a box labelled "For my lady and the house." It contained three fine satins from Canton, three tablecloths with lace trimmings and lace corners, two white-and-orange satin petticoats, two tablecloths from Ilocos (Philippines), a piece of downy satin from Canton, ten coloured bowls from Japan, and a block of wax weighing 16 *arrobas*.[21] Most of these references to gifts and order transfers of Asian goods had something in common: women receiving items that were

---

17 "Carta 95. Juana de Quesada, desde Cebú (Manila), a su Tío Tomás del Río (Receptor de la Audiencia), en Méjico, 1593," in *El Hilo que Une. Las Relaciones Epistolares en el Viejo y el Nuevo Mundo (Siglos XVI–XVIII)*, ed. Rocío Sánchez Rubio and Isabel Testón Núñez (Mérida: Universidad de Extremadura, 1999), 217.

18 "Carta 73. Marta Díaz a su Hija Inés, en Sevilla. México, 31.III.1577," in *Cartas Privadas de Emigrantes a Indias, 1540–1616*, ed. Enrique Otte (México, D.F.: Fondo de Cultura Económica, 1996), 97–98. For other examples, see: "Carta 178. Hernán García a su Mujer Catalina Núñez, en Sevilla. Puebla, 4, XI, 1586," *Cartas Privadas*, 165–66; "Carta 204. Gaspar de la Torre a su Sobrino Juan Ruiz, en Palencia. Antequera, 14, IV, 1572," *Cartas Privadas*, 184–5.

19 AGI, *Contratación*, 1794, 163–5.

20 AGI, *Contratación*, 1804, 33–5. See other examples in AGI, *Contratación*, 1831, 131–2.

21 AGN, *Indiferente Virreinal*, caja-exp.: 0535-014; *Filipinas*, 53–5.

sent by men. This pattern should not be surprising given that most emigrants to the Americas and the Philippines were men.

Inheritance was another non-commercial means through which Asian goods were transferred and in which family relations were crucial. The increasing monetisation of life in comparison with medieval times meant that most inheritances, like other types of gifts, were increasingly received in cash in the early modern era.[22] In the Hispanic monarchy, when a relative died and bequeathed goods to his or her heirs, it was normal to sell the goods and properties at a public auction and then distribute the money among the heirs. That being said, it was also common for some treasured items of clothing to be passed from parents to children, like in such other parts of the Western world as England and America.[23] This was the easiest way for some people to acquire Chinese and other Asian textiles. Some testaments of Mexicans reveal this. In her last will dated 1614, Isabel Mexía (from Mexico City) bequeathed an old white blanket from China to her daughter.[24] Sebastiana Leal Palomino, also from Mexico City, in her last will dated 1 November 1617 ordered that her most expensive dresses and trousseaus be distributed among her daughters.[25] Since the probate inventory of Sebastiana was full of Chinese manufactured dresses, some of them must have been inherited by her daughters.[26] Cristóbal de Espinosa, a Mexico City scrivener born in the village of Santa María in Castile, was more explicit about the objects he left to his heirs. In his last will written on 6 February 1643, besides declaring to whom he owed money, he stated to which of his heirs he would like to bequeath his clothes; among those, to Esteban Franco de Balderas he left a pair of black stockings from China.[27] Sometimes, when the items making up these inheritances were owned by emigrants to the Americas, they were sent by ship to the heirs in Castile. This was the case for some goods owned by Cristóbal de Oviedo Montealegre, a merchant from Toledo who lived in Mexico City, where he died in 1592; his assets were transferred after being converted to cash at auction in Toledo. However, two golden necklaces from China were sent to his wife in Castile, Elena de Aguirre, along with the cash value of the remaining goods.[28]

---

22   Howell, *Commerce before Capitalism*, 159–71.

23   Carole Shammas, *The Pre-industrial Consumer in England and America* (Oxford: Oxford University Press, 1990), 203–10.

24   ANotDF, *Notario*: José Rodriguez (555), vol. 3839, no page.

25   ANotDF, *Protocolos*, 4147, Libro 11, 770–78.

26   ANotDF, *Protocolos*, 4158, Libro 11, 796–807.

27   ANotDF, *Protocolos*, 4338, Libro 2, 23–24.

28   AGI, *Contratación*, 244, N. 22.

The role of the Catholic Church and its members was essential in the non-commercial diffusion of Asian goods through different areas and continents. Three reasons can be cited for its involvement. First, the Catholic Church had some of the most global networks of the early modern era, which favoured the circulation of Asian goods across the empire.[29] Important church dignitaries living in Castile received Asian goods from Manila and Mexico City.[30] In 1624 the prioress of the convent of La Candelaria, in Cádiz, received a silk ornament for an altar made in China from the Mexican Inquisitor Don Juan Gutiérrez Flores.[31] In 1627 Doctor Gil de la Barrera, from Mexico City, sent some items to Don Diego Guerra, *procurador general* (representative) of the Mexican Church, who lived in Madrid. The items were sent as gifts; they consisted of three damasks, two satins, and five *gorgoranes*, all from China.[32] Many other examples could be cited.[33] Often the church institutions themselves placed orders for Chinese silks and other Asian goods for their properties. This is especially clear in the case of New Spain's ecclesiastical institutions. For instance, in 1601 the Hospital of Our Lady of Los Remedios, in Mexico City, placed an order for Chinese silks worth 346 pesos with the Philippine merchant Alonso Rodríguez de León. This order was made up of canopies, tablecloths, curtains, fabrics for the Virgin Mary's veils, chasubles, bedspreads, and ornaments for altars.[34] Church networks were so global that, according to the inward ship registers of Seville, they also transmitted Asian goods from the Philippines and New Spain to other European places beyond Castile. There are cases of New Spanish Augustinians and Jesuits that sent Asian goods such as silks, porcelain, and furnishings to rulers and members of their orders as far away as Antwerp and Rome.[35]

Second, as an institution the Church played a powerful role in the reception of such goods because many gifts took the form of alms that people sent to diverse churches and priests to whom they felt especially close – for example, the

---

29	Manel Ollé, *La Empresa de China. De la Armada Invencible al Galeón de Manila* (Barcelona: Acantilado, 2002); Juan Gil, *Hidalgos y Samurais. España y Japón en los Siglos XVI y XVII* (Madrid: Alianza, 1991).

30	Antonio J. Díaz Rodríguez, "Sotanas a la Morisca y Casullas a la Chinesca: El Gusto por lo Exótico Entre los Eclesiásticos Cordobeses, 1556–1621," *Investigaciones Histórica* 30 (2010): 31–48.

31	AGI, *Contratación*, 1876, 1616–20.

32	AGI, *Contratación*, 1892, 619–21.

33	AGI, *Contratación*, 1894, 1848–52; AGI, *Contratación*, 1899, 3473–76; AGI, *Contratación*, 1899, 4077–79; AGI, *Contratación*, 1917, 123–26.

34	AGN, *Indiferente Virreinal*, caja-exp.: 0535-014; *Filipinas*, 32–39.

35	AGI, *Contratación*, 1810, 255–57; AGI, *Contratación*, 1853, 181–85.

parish churches where they had been born, married, or lived near. Among the alms received by the churches of Castile from the Philippines and New Spain were silver objects (chalices, patens, candlesticks, relic boxes, lamps, crowns) and Chinese silks. The latter were usually in the form of priests' clothes and items such as chasubles, stoles, and *manípulos* (short stoles) as well as ornaments for altars and woven pieces to dress the Virgin Mary. Documents are full of references to Chinese damask fabrics, satins, and taffetas sent "to Our Lady of" (*para Nuestra Señora de*) and many churches and parishes in Castile.[36] In other cases the shipments were made to the priests responsible for the church or parish. For instance, Don Juan Bravo de Acuña, canon of the church of Toledo, received some Japanese objects in the form of gifts from Alonso Díaz de la Barrera, postmaster (*correo mayor*) of New Spain in 1604.[37] The Cathedral of Seville was among the most important of Castile; two of its canons received Asian products as alms in the early seventeenth century: Juan Checa, who in 1618 received some Chinese satins, taffetas, and damasks, along with rosaries;[38] and Juan Manuel Juárez, who in 1619 received a Japanese folding screen and a barrel of the American plant *cañafistula*.[39] Mexicans and Castilian emigrants to New Spain did not always personally handle shipments of Chinese textiles and American items as alms to the chapels and churches of their villages and cities yet sometimes ordered this in their last wills. For instance, Gonzalo de Francia, who was born in Seville but resided in Mexico City, ordered the following in his 1642 testament:

> He orders nine pieces of Chinese blue and yellow damasks to be taken from his goods and to be sent to Bartolomé Sánchez Utrera, his brother, who lives in the *Carretería* of Seville or, in his absence, to Miguel de Nebe. These must be sent to the church of Our Lady of La Consolación, in Utrera, in order to make a wall-hanging for the aforementioned church and chapel, within which is the aforementioned image.[40]

---

36   AGI, *Contratación*, 1798, 6–7; AGI, *Contratación*, 1805, 52–53; AGI, *Contratación*, 1805, 58–62; AGI, *Contratación*, 1808, 77–79; AGI, *Contratación*, 1809, 144–45; AGI, *Contratación*, 1809, 232–33; AGI, *Contratación*, 1831, 196–99; AGI, *Contratación*, 1871, 567–73.

37   AGI, *Contratación*, 1805, 496-48.

38   AGI, *Contratación*, 1851, 257–61.

39   AGI, *Contratación*, 1853, 181–85.

40   ANotDF, *Notario*, Juan Pérez de Rivera Cáceres, Reg. 4218, Libro 1, 78–84. This case is similar to that of Melchor García, who died in Mexico but had been born in Ajofrín (Toledo). He founded a chaplaincy of four pesos in this village and also bequeathed the following as alms to the Cathedral of Toledo: a bedspread from India, two ornaments for an altar decorated in China, and one altar stone from Tecal: AGI, *Contratación*, 527, N. 1, R. 9.

Monasteries and convents also received such objects. Probably one of the most important cases is that of the convent of Our Lady of Atocha, in Madrid, which along with some Chinese silk ornaments received products such as boxes of chocolate and alabaster stones (*piedras de tecali*) from one of its monks, Brother Juan Escajero, who was in New Spain in 1611.[41]

There is a third reason why the Castilian Church and its dignitaries were such important recipients of Asian goods in the form of gifts and alms. Unlike all other institutions and Castilians, they were the only ones who had the privilege of shipping and receiving gifts that were exempt from the *avería* tax. In a time like that of the early modern era, when transport costs were extremely high, this exemption made the shipment of alms and other consignments of "pious character" – such as Chinese silks for church buildings – cheaper.[42]

Of the social groups who participated in the diffusion and reception of Asian textiles and other items as gifts or personal orders across the Spanish Empire, one deserves particular attention: the merchants. The merchants, as elites of the New Spanish and Castilian societies and a well-defined social stratum, sent gifts and personal orders to one another as well as to their relatives and other members of society. There is another reason why merchants were central to such diffusion of Asian products. In addition to being agents of the Asian merchandise trade in the Spanish Empire, their privileged location in principal *entrepôts* of the empire (Manila, Acapulco, Mexico, Veracruz, Seville, etc.) put them in charge of the transmission of Asian goods that circulated as gifts and personal orders. We can see this in the following example. In the 1630s, the Mexican merchant Santi Federighi received a cargo from Manila consisting of personal orders placed by himself, members of his family, and significant people in Mexican society – to whom he would later distribute the items. For himself, he received a Japanese escritoire, several handkerchiefs, and a silver box with a rosary. For his wife, Doña Teresa Setin, he received a box containing a pair of silk gloves, a dozen handkerchiefs, and a dozen fans. For his young son, Gasparito, he received eight shirts, a dozen handkerchiefs, and five pairs of stockings. He even received items for the slaves and servants of his house: "For the little mulattoes," according to the document, there were seven shirts among the cargo items. Individuals who had placed personal orders of Asian textiles and furnishings through Santi Federighi included Doña Juana Farfán, the wife

---

41   AGI, *Contratación*, 1811, 516–19. Another case is that of the convent of Carmelites of Guadalcazar (Cordoba), which received five silver lamps and two boxes of Chinese porcelain in 1618 from the *corregidor* of Veracruz, Don Jerónimo de Benavides: AGI, *Contratación*, 1849, 212–18.

42   *Recopilación de Leyes de los Reynos de Indias – Tomo III* (3rd edition, 1791), 113.

of a Mexican mayor (*corregidor*), who received a piece of tawny-black damask and another of *chaúl* (blue silk from China); the mayor's *comadre* Doña María de Córdoba, who had placed an order for, among other things, 290 *varas* (242 metres) and four pieces of cloth, several *cates* of various types of silk, a piece of satin, two *tabíes*, and a small silver and gold box. For Luis Carrillo's wife there was a little box filled with toys (*niñerías*) from Japan; for Don Gonzalo de Legazpi's wife, a tortoiseshell box adorned with silver as well as a gold and agate rosary.[43] Most of the Asian gifts and orders shipped from New Spanish residents, bureaucrats, clerics, and emigrants to Castile were likewise distributed by merchant networks that extended through the Atlantic Ocean. Connections with a merchant and mercantile network was not only cheaper but in some cases indispensable for receiving objects from overseas, even when these objects were gifts or alms. Few migrant overseas networks existed for transmitting objects that were independent from the mercantile networks. Hence merchants were likely the most interested groups in the progressive commoditisation and consequent commercialisation of products that, like those of Asian origin, circulated as gifts. Those trends benefited their businesses enormously.

2.2   The Role of Women in the Transmission of Asian Goods

The role of women was paramount in the transmission of Asian goods, especially Chinese silks. As mentioned above, many women, especially widows, lived in Manila. We know from the huge quantity of surviving documents that concern the businesses and commercial network of the Mexican merchant Santi Federighi (as well as other sources) that women were active in the reception and shipment of silks and special items from Asia.

Doña Teresa Setin, who was Santi Federighi's wife, was involved in her husband's network that spanned the Pacific Ocean. She developed a taste for Asian goods and placed many orders of goods for herself by exchanging letters with her husband's commercial agent in Manila, Ascanio Guazzoni. Even more significant was that, although she wrote to Ascanio Guazzoni, it was not Guazzoni but rather his wife, Doña Ana María de Birués, who managed those orders in Manila. In a letter dated 17 July 1632, Ascanio Guazzoni reported to Teresa Setin that the 2,000 pesos she had sent to his wife could not be employed for the purchase of a Chinese slave and ribbons, which she had ordered that year. It explained that Doña Ana María de Birués had not found them to be of good

---

43   AGN, *Indiferente Virreinal*, caja-exp.: 5078-011, *Consulado*, 44–45.

quality, so she had bought only two pieces of *espolines* (silk patterned with flowers). Ascanio Guazzoni closed the letter thanking Doña Teresa for the gift she had sent him and his wife, which consisted of some chocolate and some boxes of quince cheese, and reported that he had sent some toys for her and Santi Federighi's daughters.[44] One year later, the 2,000 pesos that Doña Teresa Setin had sent were used to purchase clothes for herself and 60 bowls from Japan, which (according to Ascanio Guazzoni) "were very high in the estimation of the ladies of Manila."[45] In 1636, Ascanio Guazzoni shipped an order to Teresa Setin valued at 1,000 pesos. This order amounted to several jewels, four ivory sculptures of the baby Jesus, several rosaries and crosses, four skeins of fine yarn from China, a hundred buttons, and a female slave along with her clothing. In the report, there were also shipments for Santi and Teresa's daughters: an escritoire from Japan and several jewels for Doña Mayor, a gold brooch adorned with pearls and green stones for Doña Teresita, a gold necklace adorned with pearls and garnets for Doña Lucrecita, and a pair of gold and pearl earrings for Doña Gemita.[46] In a letter dated 6 August 1638, Guazzoni told Teresa Setin that he was sending her a shipment of a "good male slave, who is learning to be a good tailor and barber; he is a good cook, smart, and likes to serve."[47] The aforementioned shipment for Santi Federighi was managed not by Ascanio Guazzoni but by his wife. It also contained a Japanese escritoire, several handkerchiefs, and a silver box with a rosary for himself; a box containing a pair of silk gloves, a dozen handkerchiefs, and a dozen fans for his wife; and eight shirts, a dozen handkerchiefs, and five pairs of stockings for their son Gasparito.[48]

There are other cases like that of Teresa Setin. The Manila merchant Alonso Rodríguez de León sent his aunt, Doña Ana de Zaldívar, items personally ordered by her that consisted of silk stockings, tablecloths from India, tablecloths from Ilocos, velvets from Canton, silk cushions, taffetas, and blankets from *Lanquin* (maybe Nanking, in Jiangsu province, or a port in Fujian province),[49] among other textiles.[50]

---

44   AGN, *Indiferente Virreinal*, caja-exp.: 5078-011, *Consulado*, 8.

45   AGN, *Indiferente Virreinal*, caja-exp.: 5887-014, *Industria y Comercio*, 2–4.

46   AGN, *Indiferente Virreinal*, caja-exp.: 5056-050, *Consulado*.

47   AGN, *Indiferente Virreinal*, caja-exp.: 5078-011, *Consulado*, 48.

48   AGN, *Indiferente Virreinal*, caja-exp.: 5078-011; *Consulado*, 44–45.

49   According to Alfonso Mola and Martínez Shaw, Lanquin was the city of Nanking, in Jiangsu province. However, Sugaya has proposed that Lanquin was likely a port in Fujian province: Nariko Sugaya, "Spanish Colonial Manila in Transition: Trade and Society at the Turn of the Nineteenth Century," 愛媛大学法文学部論集. 人文学科編 36 (2014): 30.

50   AGN, *Indiferente Virreinal*, caja-exp.: 0535-014; *Filipinas*, 44–59; AGN, *Indiferente Virreinal*, caja-exp.: 5078-011, *Consulado*, 53–54; AGN, *Indiferente Virreinal*, caja-exp.: 4230-010, 7–10, *Filipinas*.

If women were in charge of ordering and choosing these textiles and other items both for themselves and for the home, it was because their taste was essential in sumptuously decorating houses and in selecting children's clothing. The Asian component was significant in the case of Mexico.

Besides their commissioning orders, the role of women as transmitters and recipients of gifts also seems to have been important in establishing relationships of trust between merchants. For instance, Juan de la Cruz Godines, commercial agent in Manila of the Mexican merchant Cristóbal de la Plaza, received several presents in the form of boxes of chocolate and cans of food in 1612, 1613, and 1624; these items were not from Cristóbal de la Plaza but instead from his wife, Doña Inés de Capellán.[51] Spousal behaviour of this sort is evident in both the trans-Pacific and trans-Atlantic trading routes of New Spain.[52] The "China Poblana" phenomenon of Mexico is indicative of the significance of wealthy women in the transmission of Asian goods, among them Chinese silk. According to the tradition, the "China Poblana" was an Asian woman who lived in Puebla (Mexico) and spread a new type of dress. In fact, the tradition reflects the use of a new dress style in New Spain which emulated the silk manufactures from China.[53]

The transmission of Asian goods as gifts between women is more visible in shipments from New Spain to Castile. So as not to repeat some of the previously mentioned examples, the following are three representative instances of women who sent each another Chinese silks and Asian goods as gifts in both directions across the Atlantic. In 1618 the Marchioness of Guadalcázar (wife of the Viceroy of New Spain) sent Doña Antonia Maria de Córdoba (her sister) a Japanese escritoire, a Japanese chest, several small boxes, some rosaries, an escritoire from New Spain, a piece of white satin, some *tecomates*, some lace from Campeche, and some "virtue stones" (*piedras de la virtud*).[54] In 1625, the Countess of Santiago of New Spain consigned the following items to the Marchioness of Belveder, who also lived in Madrid: three bedspreads from India, seven pieces of satin from China, and some American products that included

---

51   AGN, *Indiferente Virreinal*, caja-exp.: 1776-001, 55–57, 66–67, and 58–60.

52   AGN, *Indiferente Virreinal*, caja-exp.: 5651-017, *Consulado*, 135–36; AGN, *Indiferente Virreinal*, caja-exp.: 5651-017; *Consulado*, 191–92; AGN, *Indiferente Virreinal*, caja-exp.: 5651-017, *Consulado*, 201.

53   Gauvin A. Bailey, "A Mughal Princess in Baroque New Spain. Catarina de San Juan (1606–1688): the china poblana," *Anales del Instituto de Investigaciones Estéticas de la Universidad Nacional Autónoma de México* 71 (1997), 37–73.

54   AGI, *Contratación*, 1847, 112–27.

boxes of chocolate, cocoa, and rosaries.[55] Finally, in 1626 the Marchioness of Villamayor, also from Madrid, received several gifts from New Spain in the form of Chinese silks, grains of cocoa, and *tecomates*.[56]

In short, gender figured prominently in the development of a taste for and consumption of Chinese silks and certain other Asian goods. The role of women – more precisely, that of wealthy women who lived in Manila and Mexico City – in the purchase of Asian goods was instrumental in the emergence of a market for them.

2.3   The Retail Trade of Asian Goods in New Spain

Economic history has advanced greatly in analysing the evolution of the circuits of retail distribution along with the changes and spread of consumption and new tastes during the early modern period. The evolution of such retail distribution forms as shopping and peddling – and their relation to more traditional forms such as fairs, town markets, and direct sales by craft sectors – was linked to the development of more socially widespread consumption. Research in this field has paid special attention to the analysis of shops and shopping distribution.[57] Following the perspective of these studies, I have found a greater commoditisation of Asian goods in the viceroyalty of New Spain than in Castile. In the former, Asian goods were not only given as gifts and transferred as special orders (as described previously) but also increasingly consumed as merchandise bought from peddlers, second-hand markets, and shops. Specialisation in retail trade had not yet developed to the level of the eighteenth century, as shops and peddlers sold many different types of groceries and durables, yet New Spanish retailers supplied novelties that included Chinese raw silk and fabrics in addition to garments made of Chinese silk. To

---

55   AGI, *Contratación*, 1880, 221–31.

56   AGI, *Contratación*, 1885, 291–92.

57   John Styles, "Product Innovation in Early Modern London," *Past and Present* 168 (2000), 124–69; Bruno Blondé, Eugénie Briot, Natacha Coquery, and Laura van Aert, eds., *Retailers and Consumer Changes in Early Modern Europe. England, France, Italy and Low Countries* (Tours: Presses Universitaires François-Rabelais, 2005); Bruno Blondé, Peter Stabel, Jon Stobart and Ilja van Damme, eds., *Buyers and Sellers. Retail Circuits and Practices in Mediaeval and Early Modern Europe* (Turnhout: Brepols, 2006); Daniel Muñoz Navarro, "Espacios de Consumo en la Valencia Preindustrial. Notas para una Historia de la Comercialización en la España Moderna," in *Comprar, Vender y Consumir. Nuevas Aportaciones a la Historia del Consumo en la España Moderna*, ed. Daniel Muñoz Navarro (Valencia: Servei de Publicacions de la Universitat de València, 2011), 101–23

a lesser extent these retailers also sold, in the late sixteenth and early decades of the seventeenth century, more specialised items such as porcelains, beds, escritoires, and folding screens. This commerce was unimaginable in Castilian cities such as Seville, where Asian products were not sold in street markets and shops and where they could seemingly be purchased only through links with wholesale merchants, relatives, friends, or acquaintances in the Americas.

None of the probate inventories of Seville-based retailers studied for this book had Chinese silks among their supplies. Pedro de Bascuñán, a merchant from Seville who died in 1600, sold American sugar and ginger but did not have any Asian products for sale among his merchandise.[58] Hernando de Ovando, who died in 1602, had a shop in Seville where he sold dress trimmings such as laces, cords, and fringes as well as many types of silk – including silk from Murcia and Italy but none from China.[59] Martín González, who died in 1608, also had a shop in Seville where he sold sugar and many kinds of jams and fruits, such as quince cheese, pine nuts, morello cherries, pumpkins in syrup, pears in syrup, raisins from Almuñécar (Granada), and dried apricots (*orejones*) from Valencia. However, he did not sell any products from Asia, not even spices like cinnamon or pepper.[60] Andrea de la Cruz, who died in 1612 and whose husband was a tailor specialising in doublets (*maestro jubetero*), had many doublets, stockings, and sleeves in her husband's shop-*cum*-workshop, but none of them were made from Chinese silk.[61] Nicolás Fernández Pesquera, who died in 1620 and whose wife María Real owned a shop, possessed no merchandise from Asia.[62] When those in charge of Cathedral of Seville's factory sought small quantities of Chinese silk, they did not go to shops or other retail distribution networks but instead to wholesale traders. One such trader was Lope de Tapia, who imported Chinese silk from New Spain; the Cathedral of Seville bought 7 *varas* (5.9 metres) of purple silk from him in 1608.[63] Although the Cathedral of Seville, given its status as a great economic institution, bought most of its foodstuffs and non-perishable goods at wholesale markets, 7 *varas* of silk seems a small quantity to buy at such a market. In fact, several shops in

---

58   AHPS, *Protocolos*, Leg. 13734, 889–90.

59   AHPS, *Protocolos*, Leg. 12617, 621–66.

60   AHPS, *Protocolos*, Leg. 11689, no page.

61   AHPS, *Protocolos*, Leg. 3587, 1060–62.

62   AHPS, *Protocolos*, Leg. 9393, 659–76.

63   ACS, *Fábrica, Adventicios*, Libro 307 (sig. 9647A), 108. Lope de Tapia's commercial agent in Mexico City, who supplied him with Chinese silk, was Martín de Ynarra: AHPS, *Protocolos*, Leg. 14437, 895–1035. In 1603, Martín de Ynarra sent 12,000 pesos to the Philippines in exchange for Asian merchandise of that value: AGN, *Indiferente Virreinal*, caja-exp.: 5256-039, *Real Hacienda*.

Mexico City had many times that quantity of Chinese silk in stock. The evidence is scant, but it seems that Asian goods were not retailed in Seville in the first decades of the seventeenth century, or at least not in such great quantities as in New Spain.

In New Spain, Asian manufactured goods were regularly sold by retailers, peddlers, and shopkeepers. Requests to institutions of Mexico City, mainly the secretary's chamber (*secretaría de cámara*) of the viceroy and the city council (*cabildo*), for people to sell Asian goods in the streets of the city, or to transport them to other places of the viceroyalty, were common around 1600. As early as 1574, after the opening of the Manila Galleon route, the peddler Antonio Méndez made a request to the secretary's chamber of Mexico City to take ten pack mules loaded with Chinese and Castilian clothes from Mexico to Chiapas.[64] In 1598, Miguel Martínez applied to the city council for a licence to erect a shop to sell Chinese products – the request refers to "a Chinese shop," *una tienda china* – in the "street of the cloth sellers" of Mexico City.[65] There were many other similar cases.[66]

That Asian products were sold in the streets and shops of Mexico as early as the late sixteenth century can be gleaned also from documents as varied as probate inventories of peddlers and shopkeepers, notarial records that contain lists and valuations of shops, and the few account books of shops of this period that have survived in Mexican archives. Among goods belonging to the hawker (*mercachifle*) Juanes de Larralda, who died in 1619 and whose assets were then auctioned, there was a bundle of Chinese silk measuring 16 *varas*.[67] Of nine probate inventories of Mexican shopkeepers dated between 1580 and 1630, six of them had Asian merchandise designated to be sold in their shops. Francisco Ruiz Galán, who died in 1584 in Mexico City but had a shop in Michoacán, had merchandise consisting of musical instruments and large quantities of silk and other fabrics, most likely some from China, among the goods valued at the public auction that took place after his death.[68] Alexandre Mallón, a shopkeeper who died in 1592, had a shop in Mexico City in which he sold taffeta, *sinabafas*, floss silk, *gorgoranes*, and finished products such as wimples and stockings, all from China, along with other fabrics and wine.[69]

---

64 AGN, *Indiferente Virreinal*, caja-exp.: 5958-016, *Industria y Comercio*.

65 AHAM, *Actas del Cabildo* (6th July 1598), vol. 352A.

66 AGN, *Indiferente Virreinal*, caja-exp.: 4371-022, *Industria y Comercio*; AGN, *Indiferente Virreinal*, caja-exp.: 3681-045, *Industria y Comercio*.

67 AGI, *Contratación*, 470, N. 2.

68 AGI, *Contratación*, 312A, N. 8.

69 ANotDF, *Notario*: Juan Bautista Moreno (375), Reg. 2483, 199–205.

Antonio de la Fuente, a Mexican who died in 1602, owned a shop in which he had sold all sorts of products: needles, garnets and crystals, books, cords, ribbons, buttons, bells, scissors, paper, boxes, birdcages, tools, and so on. Among the textiles were raw and finished cloths from Castile and China. The most notable Chinese silks that Antonio de la Fuente sold were expensive fabrics including damasks, satins, and velvets and also smaller items such as hats and sleeves.[70] Alonso del Riego died in 1603. He was a craftsman – most likely a tailor, since he possessed tailoring tools and many fabrics in the form of merchandise; he had a shop in Mexico City that sold such fabrics as satins, taffeta, and raw silk from China. According to the proceedings of his probate inventory, he purchased the Chinese silks through the peddler Juan de Escudero from Acapulco, to whom del Riego owed 42 pesos.[71] Catalina de Villegas also died in Mexico City in the year 1603. She and her husband, Francisco Pérez, owned a shop in the neighbourhood of the *Amor de Dios* Hospital. In their shop they sold wine, vinegar, utensils, needles, funnels, scissors, buttons, razors, rosaries, wood, candles, salt, boxes, and books, among other merchandise. The couple also had some Chinese silk and porcelain, although it is not known whether the Asian merchandise was for their own use or for sale because it was not kept at the shop.[72] Juan Agustín, a Flemish resident of Mexico City who died in 1614, owned a shop along with his compatriot Juan del Monte in the village of Yuririapundaro (in the modern-day state of Guanajuato). He, too, sold Asian products in his shop, as evidenced by the 221 pesos and 5 tomines that he and his partner owed to the merchant Miguel Magdaleno for several Chinese raw and woven silks.[73]

The records written and signed by the public notaries of Mexico City also give information about the sale of Asian products in Mexican shops and streets. In 1600, the merchants Juan Ruiz (from Mexico City) and Hernando Covarrubias (from Zacatecas) agreed to establish a commercial company; the former contributed 10,000 pesos and the latter 1,000 pesos to buy wine and other merchandise from Castile, China, and New Spain. The products were sold in the shop that Hernando Covarrubias had in Zacatecas.[74] In 1612, Gaspar Gutiérrez de Salas and Martín de Pastrana signed a similar agreement to form a company for one year. The former contributed to the company with the shop that he had rented for 530 pesos a year, where the merchandise would be

---

70   ANotDf, *Notario*: Andrés Moreno (374), Reg. 2467, 465–78.

71   AGI, *Contratación*, 274A, N. 1, R. 11.

72   ANotDF, *Notario*: Juan de Porras Farfán (498), Reg. 3363, 672–78.

73   AGI, *Contratación*, 517, N. 2, R. 1.

74   ANotDF, *Notario*: Juan Pérez de Rivera (374), Reg. 1437, Libro 3, 158–61.

sold, and the latter with the merchandise, which was worth 9,653 pesos and 5 tomines. Among the merchandise were fabrics from Segovia, Avila, Florence, and Milan as well as taffeta and stockings from China.[75] In 1613, the indigenous American Pedro Martín (from Toluca) paid the merchant Diego López Román 150 pesos for *sinabafas* and other cloths from China that the former sold in the market squares (*tianguis*) of Mexico City.[76] Melchor García de los Reyes, shopkeeper of Mexico City, had a shop in the capital city of the viceroyalty whose merchandise was valued and auctioned after his death in 1625. He had fabrics in the shop from many places: Castile, Italy, Portugal, Flanders, and New Spain. Of the 21,045 pesos and 6 tomines that all the shop merchandise was worth, 4,388 pesos of this value was attributable to Chinese silks.[77] In 1643, Juan de Siguez filed a lawsuit claiming the goods of the deceased Gregorio Díaz Pico, who had died owing him 780 pesos and 6 tomines. Both had established a company to sell merchandise from China in Díaz Pico's shop, situated in Santo Domingo Street in Mexico City.[78]

Finally, four account books and sales memoranda of the period from 1580 to 1640 that are kept in the National Archive of Mexico contain records of purchases and sales of shops in Mexico City. There is one account book for 1583–1584 that lists all the transactions of an unknown shopkeeper during those two years; it registers sales of a wide range of products. From Asia there is a limited quantity of pepper and cloves but no silk or other manufactured products.[79] Another account book, which belonged to Gaspar de Castro's shop, lists his wholesale purchases between 1630 and 1639 – presumably goods that were to be sold in his shop. He bought items from Acapulco merchants and Mexican merchants who traded with Asia, among them Santi Federighi. Purchased items included not only silks but also folding screens, escritoires, beds, and perishable goods such as cinnamon and musk.[80] Another account book for the shop of an unknown Mexican records both sales and wholesale purchases, for the period 1631–1632, of oil, wine, vinegar, ham and bacon, olives, saffron, lavender, wax from Castile, reams of paper from Genoa and Granada, twine, buttons, wool, Portuguese yarn, yarn from Jerez, taffeta, flannelette, cloaks, and woollen stockings. Although the shopkeeper who created this account book

---

75   *Ibid.*, Reg. 3543, Libro 11, 141–46.

76   *Ibid.*, Reg. 3599, Libro 11, 295.

77   ANotDF, *Notario*: Andrés Moreno (374), Reg. 2476, 179–90; ANotDF, *Notario*: Andrés Moreno (374), Reg. 2476, 196–205.

78   ANotDF, *Notario*: Juan Pérez de Rivera (374), Reg. 4514, 2–9.

79   AGN, *Indiferente Virreinal*, caja-exp.: 1336-014, *Consulado*.

80   AGN, *Indiferente Virreinal*, caja-exp.: 0898-025, *Consulado*.

appeared to be more oriented toward selling Castilian and European products, the book also registers *capicholas* (a thin silk fabric in the form of lace) from China.[81] Finally, the accounts of another Mexican shop (owner also unspecified), contain a list of debts in favour of and against the shop as of 1641. Among the shop's sales in that year there are products including silk stockings from China and several *cates* of blue silk from China, along with other types of fabrics, cloaks from Campeche, sugar, and cocoa.[82]

2.4   Conclusions

Asian manufactured products played a privileged role in the exchanges between members of similar social and professional status who lived in different areas of the Spanish Empire. These products included Chinese silk and porcelain, Japanese furnishings and folding screens, Indian cottons, and American goods such as chocolate. Gifts, inheritances, alms, and commissions of special orders of Chinese silks and other Asian products confirmed and solidified the social relations – professional, commercial, and family ties – that had to be maintained across great distances. This form of Asian goods transfer was important for another reason: it overlapped with and contributed to supplying the Castilian elite with Asian manufactured goods from the Americas and the Philippines when, during the late sixteenth century and early seventeenth century, these goods were scarce and expensive in most of Europe. Both sociological and economic spheres overlapped in the diffusion of Asian goods as gifts and orders across the Spanish Empire.

Sources are scant and there are few historical studies of retail distribution in the Americas, but the evidence indicates that demand for Asian goods was better satisfied through retail forms of distribution in New Spain, particularly in Mexico City, than in Castilian cities like Seville. The greater provision of Asian goods in New Spain than in Castile meant that, along with gifts and specific orders for goods, the supply and demand of Asian goods was better matched in Mexico City than in Seville. The reason is that New Spain enjoyed direct commercial contact with Southeast Asia through the Pacific Ocean route. Asian goods, particularly Chinese silk, were included in the extensive retailing of Mexican peddling and shops, notwithstanding their lack of product specialisation in the sixteenth and seventeenth centuries. On the other side of the

---

81   AGN, *Indiferente Virreinal*, caja-exp.: 1818 -006, *Consulado*.
82   AGN, *Indiferente Virreinal*, caja-exp.: 5012-011, *Industria y Comercio*.

Atlantic, the demand for Asian manufactured goods was rising in cities such as Seville; however, its supply seems not to have been sufficiently great for distribution throughout the retail networks that existed in the first decades of the seventeenth century.

The consumption of Asian goods in New Spain, and above all in Castile, was partly due to the demand of noblemen, the church, members of some socio-professional strata, and familial networks in which wealthy women and their taste for Asian textiles and other goods were a significant presence. Women chose – and, on many occasions, ordered and distributed – the products in their social circle, thereby influencing the formation of a taste for Asian goods in the Empire. These familial and social networks were also, in many cases, merchant networks. In fact, merchants facilitated Asian gifts and special orders being diffused across their circuits, all the while establishing greater control over the commercial transmission of these products, as will be shown in the next chapter. These cultural, social, and economic spheres entangled from the Pacific to the Atlantic Ocean insofar as Mexican merchants transferred Asian goods from Manila to Seville, which shaped the interactions across such long distances and helped create the conditions that would commoditise, and form a proper market for, Asian goods in the Spanish Empire.

Commerce in the Pacific and the Atlantic and Interaction between the Two Oceans

As the circulation of Asian goods extended through the Spanish Empire, merchants of the New Spain viceroyalty were integrating the trade of Asian products into their businesses and thereby increasing the level of such trade. This growth in circulation of Asian goods stimulated the demand for them among the elite throughout the Empire. It is worth examining the extent of trade in Asian goods throughout the Empire in the late sixteenth and seventeenth centuries.

In 1565 the Spaniards conquered the Philippines, and in 1571 they founded Manila. This city was located at a privileged geographical point, for it was connected to the westward Chinese and Portuguese commercial networks and to the eastward American markets. Manila attracted both Chinese and Spanish American merchants, who exchanged Asian goods for silver. Thus began a flourishing trade between the Americas and Asia – China, Japan, Indonesia and India, among other places –, which extended alongside the growth of an initially weak but rising demand for Asian goods in the Spanish Empire. However, this trade of Asian goods between New Spain and the Philippines was not limited to trans-Pacific trading partners. The main New Spanish mercantile forces, the wholesalers of Mexico City and (to a lesser extent) those of Puebla de los Ángeles, sought to expand the supply of Asian merchandise eastward – to the Castilian markets.

The trade of Asian goods in the Spanish Empire followed two different trends between the last quarter of the sixteenth century and the mid-seventeenth century. The first was a period of ascent, from the 1580s to the 1630s, in which both the Manila Galleon trade and also trans-Atlantic trade of Asian goods escalated. The second trend was a period of decline from the 1630s onward. These trends cannot be explained simply by looking at the commercial changes that occurred in Southeast Asia, Manila, and along the Manila Galleon route. The trade of Asian manufactured goods across the Spanish Empire depended upon the connection of economic and geopolitical dynamics rooted in both the Atlantic World and East Asia. The rise of the trans-Pacific trade, the re-exportation of Asian goods to Iberia, and the later decline of the Manila Galleon trade all depended upon the convergence of a series of global factors. Once this chapter and the following (on the conflicting interests that surrounded the Manila Galleon trade) are read in the context of the Spanish Empire's political economy, we can assess the reasons offered for the decline – from the 1630s onward – of trans-Pacific trade in comparison with other commercial routes.

3.1   Transformations in the Philippine Economy

Manila was the *entrepôt* that made possible the delivery of American silver to China and that of Chinese products to New Spain. Before about 1590, the main economic sector of Manila and its hinterland was agriculture. What did occur between 1565, when Spaniards initiated their conquest of the Philippines, and the 1580s, when the southwestern area of Luzon definitively re-orientated their economy to global trade? The changes in the economy of Manila resulted from global and local tensions. Conflicts among the Spanish elite themselves – in addition to conflicts between the Spanish elite and the Tagalog populations, in which external military threats and changing Spanish fiscal policies in the archipelago played a critical part – are factors that must be taken into account.

Before the Spanish conquest of the Philippines in 1565, the Philippine economy was basically agricultural and production was based on rice, fish, and palms. The country's economy was organised as a system of consumption structured in autonomous units of settlement called *barangays*. Over time, the Islands came into contact with international trade, which flourished in Asia from the fifteenth century onward as Southeast Asia began to supply the Indian and Chinese demand for spices such as cloves and nutmeg.[1] In the sixteenth century the European newcomers, the Portuguese, joined the Chinese and Indians as the principal recipients of Southeast Asian spices. In the case of the Philippines, the main production that supplied international demand was cinnamon, although this was produced in only limited quantities in Mindanao. When the Spaniards founded Manila, the main economic base of its hinterland was still agriculture and cattle raising. The initial economic structures established by the Spaniards, which resembled those organised after Spain's conquest of the Americas, were oriented toward obtaining as much wealth as possible. Given the few spices that grew in Luzon, the main island of the archipelago, wealth was derived via exploitation of the land and the country's workforce.

---

1   Anthony Reid, *Southeast Asia in the Age of Commerce, 1450–1680. Volume One: The Lands below the Winds* (New Haven, CT: Yale University Press, 1988), 1–10.

The forced implementation of new economic protocols by the Spanish conquerors resulted in two structural contradictions that developed during the 1580s and 1590s and that favoured the internationalisation of Manila's economy. The first contradiction was economic. Following the Mexican model, the Spaniards restructured by force native settlements so as to gain total control over communities[2] – an approach that had catastrophic consequences for the economy. The conquerors divided the native *barangays* into new forms of settlements: first into *doctrinas* (as the initial aims of these new native settlements were missionary) and then into *reducciones* and *pueblos*. As Alonso Álvarez has pointed out, the changes led to reduced agricultural production and hence to a reduction in foodstuffs. These consequences were problematic, to say the least, because the demand for foodstuffs had actually increased owing to the arrival of Chinese and Spanish newcomers attracted by new commercial possibilities. The result was a severe crisis of underconsumption combined with an inflationary process that was aggravated by the importation of American silver, which commenced at about this time. The Spanish authorities sought to solve these problems by increasing production, even if doing so required fiscal coercion. The initial aim of Spanish conquerors had been to develop commercial agriculture: farming surpluses (such as rice) and local textiles (e.g., *lampotes* and *medriñaques*) were meant to be diverted to Mexican and American markets.[3] However, establishing commercial agriculture as the principal economic sector of the Philippines was from the start infeasible, mainly because of external factors.

Their lack of defence against external enemies – in particular, Muslims from the south, Chinese pirates, and European competitors – led the Spanish authorities of Manila to seek more financing for military objectives. The brunt of the fiscal pressure was borne by the native peasant population, who became subject to new taxes. This increase in fiscal pressure on natives was achieved

---

2　Patricio Hidalgo Nuchera, "Sistemas para la Explotación de las Islas: Encomiendas, Tributos y Comercio. La Recta Administración versus el Mal Comportamiento: La Situación de la Población Nativa en el Contexto del Marco Colonial Temprano," in *Las Relaciones entre España y Filipinas. Siglos XVI–XX*, ed. María D. Elizalde Pérez-Grueso (Madrid: CSIC, 2002), 75–86; John L. Phelan, *The Hispanization of the Philippines. Spanish Aims and Filipino Responses, 1565–1700* (Madison, WI: University of Wisconsin Press, 2010).

3　Luis Alonso Álvarez, "El Modelo Colonial en los Primeros Siglos. Producción Agraria e Intermediación Comercial: Azar y Necesidad en la Especialización de Manila como Entrepôt entre Asia y América, 1565–1593," in *Las Relaciones entre España y Filipinas. Siglos XVI–XX*, ed. María D. Elizalde Pérez-Grueso (Madrid: CSIC, 2002), 37–48. For inflation in the Philippines in the late sixteenth century, see Antonio de Morga, *Sucesos de las Islas Filipinas* (Madrid: Polifemo, 1997 [first published in 1609]), 202–3.

in the only way possible: by increasing cash collections. Paying taxes in cash, instead of in kind, actually meant less tributary charged to the peasants; they had to work less time in the fields because selling their products to the Chinese in the Philippine market was easier and more profitable than agricultural work.[4] In other words, the new fiscal organisation discouraged agricultural and livestock activities and encouraged commercial ones. This setup was solidified by the growing number of *sangleyes* (Chinese merchants) in the archipelago, who sold manufactured products, principally silk, at more competitive prices than the native goods. High profit margins when trading with the Chinese debilitated the collective mechanisms that had held the agricultural workforce together, especially in the area around Manila, and pushed the whole economy of that city toward international trade.[5]

The second set of contradictions stemming from the Spanish economic structures installed in the Philippines from about 1570 to 1590 had a social and institutional character, and was strongly related to the economic consequences just described. These social contradictions were a function of the different interests exhibited by members of the Spanish elite depending on their position within the controlled means of production. On the one hand, the landowners (*encomenderos*) obtained their incomes mainly from agriculture and from their exploitation of Filipino peasants,[6] so that landowners were forced to adapt their economic structures to a new situation arising from the re-orientation of Manila's economy from agriculture to trade. On the other hand, religious men (especially friars) had for some time been relatively more involved in commercial activities. Although it is difficult to ascertain how much the clergymen of the Philippines traded via the Manila galleons, there is little doubt that they did so extensively as soon as opportunities presented themselves. Moreover, many missionaries, for instance Jesuits, in Southeast Asia financed their missions in large part by trading silk, especially after the Union of Crowns between Spain and Portugal.[7] Letters of correspondence and other official documents

---

4   Luis Alonso Álvarez, "Don Quijote en el Pacífico: La Construcción del Proyecto Español en Asia, 1591–1606," *Revista de Historia Económica – Journal of Iberian and Latin America Economic History* 23 (2005): 251–62.

5   Luis Alonso Álvarez, *El Costo del Imperio Asiático. La Formación Colonial de las Islas Filipinas bajo Dominio Español, 1565–1800* (A Coruña: Universidade da Coruña, 2009), 54–62, 85–92.

6   The term *encomendero* has two meanings. It may refer to landowners and to the commercial agents who lived, sometimes for long periods or even their entire lives, in the assigned market.

7   Nicholas P. Cushner, "Merchants and Missionaries. A Theologian's View of Clerical Involvement in the Galleon Trade," *Hispanic American Historical Review* 47, no. 3 (1967): 360–69; Juan O. Mesquida, "The Early Years of the Misericordia of Manila (1594–1625)," *Review of Culture* 14 (2005): 59–81.

offer some clues as to how, in general terms, the secular elite and the religious elite represented opposing ways of generating wealth through different and conflicting economic structures during the 1580s and 1590s. The members of the *Audiencia Real* (royal tribunal) of Manila and also the Governor of the Philippines from 1589 to 1593, Gómez Pérez Dasmariñas, represented the interest of landowners, whereas Church officials were representatives of the elite most linked to commercial interests; examples of the latter group include Agustin and Franciscan friars as well as Domingo de Salazar, the Bishop of Manila from 1581 to 1594.[8] This conflict among the Spanish elite of the Philippines must be understood in the context of the Philippine economy's re-orientation from land to trade. A principal economic field in which the conflict became manifest was that of control over the system of commercial exchange between the Spaniards and the Chinese.

The so-called *pancada*, which was regulated by the Governor, was the official method used to establish the price of Chinese merchandise in areas of the archipelago controlled by the Spaniards. The *pancada* was initially devised as a system of collective bargaining. The Governor appointed two or three persons who in principle bargained with representatives of Chinese merchants over the prices of Chinese products; but instead of the Chinese and other foreign merchants freely agreeing on the prices with Spanish merchants, in practice those prices were imposed. It was the Governor and his closest circle of landowners and conquerors (and conquerors' descendants) who controlled the *pancada*.[9] This way of organising trade ran counter to the interests of the *sangleyes* and also to those of friars and other religious men who had profitable business relationships with the Chinese. There was so much hard-fought conflict over control of the *pancada* that the Bishop sent several complaints to the king, and the Governor of the Philippines sent several letters about this issue as well. According to the Governor's version of the problem, the Bishop and friars were fiercely opposed to the *pancada* system and considered its effects on commerce to be so serious that some clergymen ended up denying confession and absolution to those who negotiated within it. It is easy to understand the political scandal followed by these developments, since they shook the very principles of Catholic society:

---

8 Many letters and official documents record the clash between the different economic interests of the Spanish religious and secular elite sectors in the Philippines: "Carta de la Audiencia sobre situación y necesidades" (20 June 1585), AGI, *Filipinas*, 18A, R. 3, N. 13; "Carta del oidor Ribera Maldonado sobre situación" (24 June 1588), AGI, *Filipinas*, 18A, R. 6, N. 39; "Carta de la Audiencia sobre sublevaciones etc" (13 July 1589), AGI, *Filipinas*, 18A, R. 7, N. 47.
9 William L. Schurtz, *El Galeón de Manila* (Madrid: Ediciones de Cultura Hispánica, 1992).

In many other letters I have reported to Your Majesty about the introduction of the *Pancada*, which is to impose the price of Chinese merchandise, as Your Majesty commands in the Royal Order. And now I send
information about the difficulty that we have because the Bishop and
clerics do not want to absolve those who take part in this practice [*the
Pancada*].[10]

So stated Governor Dasmariñas in a letter sent to the King in 1592. The conflict
involved many witnesses who feared they would not be absolved of their sins
after negotiating on behalf of the Governor in the *pancada* system and thereby
imposing unfair prices on foreign merchants:

The aforementioned captain Luis de Vivanco died. He had wanted to con-
fess his sins, but his confessors had not wanted to absolve him because
he did not restore the damage that, according to them, he had caused
to the aforementioned Portuguese and Japanese [*merchants*], who could
not sell their merchandise freely and, they say, could have sold their merchandise with more profit than in the deal with the aforementioned Luis
de Vivanco.[11]

On the other side of the conflict, it is hard to find more impassioned discourse
in defence of the Chinese merchants – and of making trade as free as possible – than the rhetoric of Bishop Domingo de Salazar:

The commerce with the *sangleyes* is very important for the provision and
commerce of this city, and for those who come here to invest their money [...] In the beginning they [*the Chinese*] did not pay anything, later
they were charged the anchorage tax. The king charged the *sangleyes* the
anchorage tax in order to subject them to his authority, not for fiscal reasons. Last year and this year they were charged with a three per cent tax,
which has caused them much damage. The primary [*damage*] was that
this tax was collected when they were all enclosed in a house, to which
they were forced to enter, and there they had to pay higher prices than
outside [...] During the registration they [*the Spanish civil servants*] took
the best merchandise and at the prices that they chose [...] Those who
controlled this did not allow the *sangleyes* to sell merchandise to whom

---

10	"Carta G. P. Dasmariñas sobre oposición a la Pancada" (21 May 1592), AGI, *Filipinas*, 18B,
	R. 2, N. 4.
11	"Carta G. P. Dasmariñas sobre oposición a la Pancada," *ibid.*

they desired and at the prices they desired, and gave the rest to their servants and friends. Because of this, although 20 ships have arrived from China, and we have never seen so many in this port, not one thing from China have we seen this year. The merchandise is now so expensive that a piece of satin, which used to be worth 10 or 12 tostones here, is being sold at 40 and 45. The Church, which has so many needs, cannot find silk to make ornaments.[12]

This mistreatment of Chinese merchants and growing tensions between Chinese and Spanish authorities led to a Chinese revolt in 1603. The only reason for the revolt was not the commercial disagreements between the Chinese and a sector of the Spanish elite in Manila. There were other reasons, such as the growing insecurity in the city derived from pirate attacks. However, the rebellion and subsequent massacre could not be understood without taking into account the contradictory ways to address trade and the presence of Chinese merchants in Manila by the Spanish elites.[13]

Economic development centred on the exchange of American silver for Chinese silk and other Asian products. That exchange allowed the Philippine economy to fulfil a role in global trade that it need not have played given that, at the beginning of this period, much of the colonial elite were more interested in obtaining wealth from agricultural exploitation than from trade. Their preference in that regard was a result of internal contradictions – namely, requirements for military defence, fiscal changes, and social conflict between the elite for access to sources of wealth – for which external solutions were eventually found. Initial opposition by landowners was an economic hindrance to the economic re-orientation of the Philippines toward global trade. Resistance was finally overcome because of the new possibilities that trade offered and also because trade allowed landowners to obtain more resources for defending themselves against the possibility of military incursions from foreign powers. Key to this process was the integration of the American silver-for-Asian merchandise trade in Manila to the commercial dynamics of Southeast Asia, in which China played a dominant role. Cross-cultural trade between Chinese,

---

12   "Petición de Salazar sobre el estado de las islas" (6 June 1582), AGI, *Filipinas*, 6, R. 10, N. 180. Similar discourses can be found in "Carta de Domingo de Salazar sobre China" (4 August 1584), AGI, *Filipinas*, R. 74, N. 25.

13   José E. Borao, "The Massacre of 1603 Chinese Perception of the Spanish in the Philippines," *Itinerario* 22, no. 1 (1998): 22–40; Juan Gil, *Los chinos en Manila. Siglos XVI y XVII* (Lisboa: Centro Científico e Cultural de Macau, 2011).

Spaniards and Japanese in Manila was the driving force of that exchange.[14] The transformation of Manila into an international *entrepôt* indicates how much the local and global interests within the Spanish Empire were intertwined by means and networks shaping new processes that were not confined to local players and considerations.

3.2   The Trade of Asian Goods in the Spanish Empire at Its Apogee (1580–1630)

After Manila became an international *entrepôt*, the trans-Pacific trade continued to grow until the commercial decline of the 1630s. The *almojarifazgo* taxes imposed in Acapulco on silver exported from New Spain to Manila, along with the same type of taxes charged on all imports to and exports from Manila, provide strong evidence of the extent to which the trans-Pacific trade flourished in the period from the 1580s to the 1630s. Although the numbers are not entirely accurate because they do not account for contraband,[15] this trend is unequivocal. Data from the Royal Treasury of Acapulco on the *almojarifazgo* charged on silver exported to Manila reveals that the increase in trade lasted until about 1635, with continuous growth from 1585 to 1615 and a slight decrease between 1615 and 1620. Although trade grew slightly in the second half of the seventeenth century, trade across the Pacific Ocean hardly reached the levels of the early seventeenth century. The *almojarifazgo* tax in Manila – which was an ad valorem tax charged on all imported merchandise (from China, Japan, India, and New Spain) and on the merchandise exported to Acapulco – confirms this overall trend; see Figure 1.

The growth of trans-Pacific trade from the 1580s to the 1630s depended upon the general economic growth of the Americas. More specifically, it took place during an expansion of the New Spanish economy that was partly led by silver production.[16] However, the juncture of the New Spanish economy was not the only factor which determined the evolution of the trans-Pacific trade. Manila was located in a geographical space which might be understood under

---

14   Birgit Tremml-Werner, *Spain, China, and Japan in Manila, 1571–1644. Local comparisons and global connections* (Amsterdam: Amsterdam University Press, 2015), 125–238.

15   For levels of contraband in the trans-Pacific trade, see Louisa S. Hoberman, *Mexico's Merchant Elite, 1590–1660. Silver, State, and Society* (Durham, NC: Duke University Press, 1991), 218–20.

16   Ruggiero Romano, *Coyunturas Opuestas. La Crisis del Siglo XVII en Europa e Hispanoamérica* (México, D.F.: Fondo de Cultura Económica, 1993).

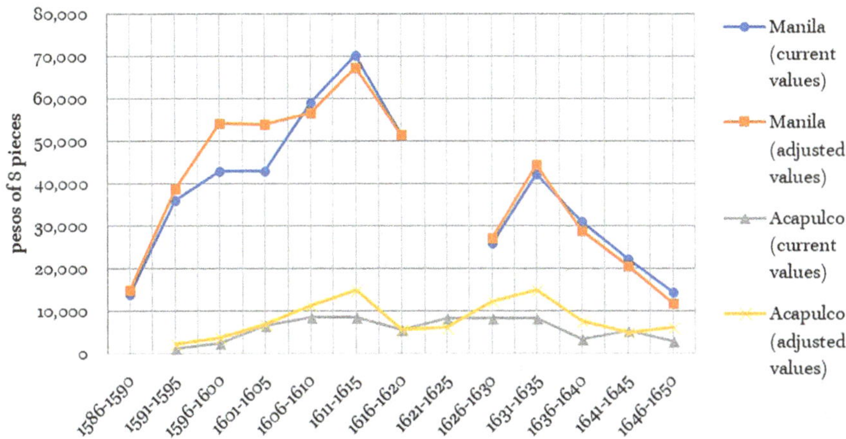

FIGURE 1 *Almojarifazgo* tax entries in the Royal Treasury of Manila and Acapulco (current and adjusted values, in pesos of "pieces of eight"), 1586–1650.
SOURCE: CHUANU, *LES PHILIPPINES*, 100,106, AND APPENDIX B.

a Braudelian perspective – Southeast Asia was a space where the South and the East China Sea framed and connected histories. It is worth remarking the significance of the connectivity between China, Manila and Japan, and that the international presence and expansion of Portuguese merchant networks in Southeast Asia at the end of the sixteenth century also drove commercial expansion of the Manila galleons.

Before the European arrival at East Asia, trade evolved in the South China Sea and in the East China Sea. China, Korea, Japan, Siam and Borneo, among other places, had exchanged such products as spices, porcelain, earthenware, silk, cotton and lacquerware furnishings, among other products, for centuries. That trade was articulated by a series of systems – tribute trade, mutual trade and visiting trade –, which sometimes coexisted, changed and conducted international trade, diplomacy and cultural interactions in Southeast and East Asia from the fourteenth century onward. When Europeans arrived at East and Southeast Asia in the sixteenth century, they participated in the Asian commercial networks which already existed. During the sixteenth and the seventeenth centuries, Europeans did not alter the trading patterns and networks. In fact, only exceptionally Chinese, Japanese and other Asian peoples allowed Europeans to found colonies and commercial cities in China and Japan. The Portuguese were the first Europeans who established themselves in Asia and participated in pre-existing commercial routes and networks.[17]

---

17   For the "tribute trade system," which was Chinese-centred and was based on the establishment of tributary missions as foundations of trade, see Takeshi Hamashita, *China,*

The Portuguese became essential agents in the trade between China, Japan and India, on the one hand, and the Philippines, on the other. The Portuguese and the Spaniards, who were subjects of the same king between 1580 and 1640, had a cold alliance in Southeast Asia that seems generally to have favoured their trade in the area – especially once the Dutch began to increase their presence in the commercial circuits of that area. In Iberia, the two kingdoms were kept separate during the Union of Crowns, and so were their institutional structures and armies. Philip II established the Council of Portugal (*Consejo de Portugal*), which was integrated into the system of councils of the monarchy, to deal with matters concerning Portugal.[18] Yet the Crown did not hesitate to take economic advantage of the new Portuguese subjects; many of these subjects were Jews and converts of Castilian origin (*conversos*), who played an important role in the export of wool from Castile to France and in financing the monarchy's treasury. This helped the King establish sources of credit beyond the Genoese bankers.[19]

In Asia, the Spaniards and Portuguese also kept their overseas territories politically separate. However, as Subrahmanyam has pointed out, divisions between the two empires were porous throughout the sixteenth and seventeenth centuries. Furthermore, connections between the two countries increased during the years of the Union of Crowns. The boundaries of the Asian and American territories in both empires were blurred in many areas. In Southeast Asia, the Castilian enclave of the Philippines and the Manila galleons were inserted into the Portuguese and Chinese trade networks. Manila was linked not only to China, as many Chinese merchants exported products and emigrated to the Philippines, but also to the triangular trade among Macao, Nagasaki,

---

East Asia and the Global Economy. Regional and historical perspectives (London: Routledge, 2008). More recently, scholarship has proposed the existence of several modes of trade in maritime and inner Asia, which coexisted during the Ming dynasty and the early times of the Qing dynasty. Alongside the "tribute trade system," which was predominant in East and Southeast Asia, there were the "mutual trade system" and the "visiting trade system," which were less hierarchical and predominated in the exchanges between China and inner Asia: Gakusho Nakajima, "The Structure and Transformation of the Ming Tribute Trade System," in *Global History and New Polycentric Approaches. Europe, Asia and the Americas in a World Network System*, ed. Manuel Pérez García and Lucio de Sousa (Singapore: Palgrave, 2018), 134–162.

18   John H. Elliot, "A Europe of Composite Monarchies," *Past and Present* 137 (1992): 48–71; John H. Elliott, "The Spanish Monarchy and the Kingdom of Portugal, 1580–1640," in *Conquest and Coalescence: The Shaping of the State in Early Modern Europe*, ed. Mark Greengrass (London: Edward Arnold, 1991), 48–67.

19   See for example James C. Boyajian, *Portuguese Bankers at the Court of Spain, 1626–1650* (New Brunswick, NJ: Rutgers University Press, 1983).

and Manila; in this, the Portuguese were (along with Chinese merchants) the leading actors. Manila was also connected to Goa and the Indian trade via Melaka, which was in Portuguese hands until 1641; see map 1. That connection fostered an increasing penetration of Portuguese traders, many of them New Christians, into the marketplaces of both New Spain and Peru.[20] Portuguese trade in Southeast Asia was also facilitated by the Chinese policy of opening up their maritime world. At the end of the fourteenth century, the emperor Hong Wu established the "sea ban policy" (*haijin*), which forbade the Chinese from leaving their country; however, the emperor Long Qing approved an "open sea policy" (*kaihai*) for the province of Fujian in 1567, which allowed the departure of Chinese ships to other ports in the surrounding area for trade purposes.[21]

The maritime commercial opening for Fujian coincided with the growth of Japanese demand for Southeast Asian lead and Chinese saltpeter. In this context, Japan fostered the *namban* trade – trade with foreigners – by allowing the Portuguese settling in the new city of Nagasaki in 1571. Portuguese merchants became the main intermediaries of Japanese *shuinsen* (foreign) trade in the late sixteenth century. They supplied the Japanese with military material and Chinese porcelain and silk, and exported Japanese goods, such as lacquered pieces of furniture, to Macao and Manila.[22]

In this context of trade expansion, the Portuguese gradually exported more Asian goods from Macao and other Asian ports to Spanish America via Manila. The Portuguese settlement had been conceded by Chinese authorities in 1556. The city soon became an *entrepôt* where merchandise and credit flowed, because of the attraction of Portuguese and Chinese businessmen and the role of such religious institutions as the Holy House of Mercy (*misericórdia*) of Macao in providing capital. Furthermore, the fact that Portuguese merchants in Macao came close to being treated as equal partners by Chinese merchants,

---

<ol start="20">
<li>Sanjay Subrahmanyam, "Holding the World in Balance: The Connected Histories of the Iberian Overseas Empires, 1500–1640," American Historical Review 112, no. 5 (2007): 1374–83; Charles R. Boxer, "A Note on the Triangular Trade between Macao, Manila, and Nagasaki, 1580–1640," Terrae Incognitae 17 (1985): 51–59.</li>
<li>Manel Ollé, La Empresa de China. De la Armada Invencible al Galeón de Manila (Barcelona: Acantilado, 2005), 9–25; Ivy Maria Lim, "From Haijin to Kaihai: The Jiajing Court's Search for a Modus Operandi along the South-eastern Coast (1522–1567)," Journal of the British Association for Chinese Studies 2 (2013): 1–26.</li>
<li>Mihoko Oka, "The Namban and Shuinsen trade in Sixteenth- and Seventeenth-Century Japan," in Global History and New Polycentric Approaches. Europe, Asia and the Americas in a World Network System, ed. Manuel Pérez García and Lucio de Sousa (Singapore: Palgrave, 2018), 163–181.</li>
</ol>

favoured trade in the area.[23] In the decades immediately following the opening of the Manila Galleon trade, the Portuguese of Macao concentrated their
commercial efforts in Manila. Starting in the late sixteenth century, the Portuguese – taking advantage of the development of Chinese and Japanese merchant activities and notwithstanding the English and Dutch expansion in the
area – diversified their contacts in mainland Southeast Asia and several ports
of the South China Sea. Thus did Manila remain one of the main Iberian ports
for trade during the years of the Union of Crowns. Even though trade between
Macao and Manila was illegal, it was explicitly encouraged by Spaniards and
Portuguese from the two cities between 1608 and 1636. Between 1580 and 1642,
a total of 77 ships made the journey from Macao to Manila; most of those voy-
ages occurred after the year 1600.[24]

For these reasons, the trade of Asian goods across the Pacific Ocean was very
much a matter of Portuguese and global networks. Indeed, many of those from
Mexico who financed the Asian trade via the Manila galleons were Portuguese.
Although most of the Portuguese merchants kept a low profile (some going so
far as to hide their Portuguese origins by "Castilicising" their family names and
thus conceal their Jewish origins), the main Portuguese commercial families
that traded between Asia, the Americas, and Iberia are well known. The more
prominent families included those of Gomes Solis, Fernandes Ximenes, Fernandes do Brasil e Tinoco, and Frias de Salazar; their members traded in places
as dispersed as Lisbon, Medina del Campo, Seville, Brazil, Goa, and East Asia.[25]
Among the most important Portuguese merchants whose private commercial activities between Macao and Manila proved to be very successful, it is
worth emphasising the names of Jorge (or Bastian) de Moxar and Bartolomeu

---

23   Jin Guo Ping and Wu Zhiliang, *Revisitar os primórdios de Macau: para uma nova abord-
      agem da história* (Macau: Instituto Português do Oriente, 2007); Isabel Leonor Seabra,
      *A misericórdia de Macau (séculos XVI a XIX): irmandade, poder e caridade na idade do
      comércio* (Macao and Lisbon: University of Macau and University of Porto, 2011); Roderich
      Ptack, "Sino-Portuguese Relations circa 1513/14-1550s," in *China, the Portuguese, and the
      Nanyang: oceans and routes, regions and trade (c. 100'-1600)*, ed. Roderich Ptack (Aldershot
      and Burlington, VT: Ashgate/Variorum, 2004), 19–46.

24   Rui D'Avila Lourido, "The Impact of the Macao-Manila Silk Trade from the Beginnings
      to 1640,"in *The Silk Roads. Highways of Culture and Commerce*, ed. Vadime Elisseeff (Par-
      is: UNESCO, 1998), 209–46; George B. Souza, *The Survival of Empire. Portuguese Trade and
      Society in China and the South China Sea, 1630–1754* (Cambridge: Cambridge University
      Press, 2004), 12–29, 46–86.

25   The activities of the Goan and Mexican Inquisitions have shown the extent to which New
      Christians took part in the Portuguese trade in Asia, including the trade among Macao,
      Nagasaki, Manila, and Mexico: James C. Boyajian, *Portuguese Trade in Asia under the
      Habsburgs, 1580–1640* (Baltimore, MD: Johns Hopkins University Press, 1993), 16–17, 53–85.

Landeiro. They signed an agreement with the governor of the Philippines, Don Diego Ronquillo (1583–1584), which allowed the former to annually sail a ship from Macao to Manila full of merchandise.[26]

Although sometimes the relations between Portuguese and Castilians were problematic in Asia, because the Portuguese merchants often saw the Castilian presence in Southeast Asia as a challenge to their monopoly on the spice trade,[27] they fought together when attacked by common enemies. One example is that of Ternate and Tidore (in the Maluku archipelago), which had been conquered by the Batavians and taken from the Portuguese in 1605. These islands were recovered for the Hispanic monarchy in 1606 after a Castilian attack by an army consisting of both Castilian and Portuguese soldiers. Several other proposals of Luso–Castilian collaboration were requested by the Portuguese and Castilian rulers of Goa, Macao, and Manila against the growing military power of the Dutch in Asia.[28]

Following the expansion of the Portuguese merchant networks in Southeast Asia and the trade of Manila and the Manila galleons, New Spain became an area from which Asian merchandise was re-exported to the metropole. The *avería* tax charged on exports from Veracruz, on the eastern coast of New Spain, to Seville (see Figure 2) indicates that the early seventeenth century was a golden period for direct trade between the Americas and Asia and also that some of

---

26   Lúcio de Sousa, *The Early European Presence in China, Japan, and the Philippines and Southeast Asia (1555–1590): The Life of Bartolomeu Landeiro* (Macao: Macao Foundation, 2010); Paulo Jorge de Sousa Pinto, "Manila, Macao and Chinese networks in South China Sea: adaptive strategies of cooperation and survival (sixteenth-to-seventeenth centuries)," *Anais de História de Além-Mar*, XV (2014): 79–100

27   Charles R. Boxer, "The Portuguese and Spanish Rivalry in the Far East during the Seventeenth Century," *Journal of the Royal Asiatic Society* 3 (1946): 150–64; Subrahmanyam, "Holding the World in Balance,": 1376–78; Ollé, *La Empresa de China*, 97–120. These growing interactions between the Portuguese and the Spaniards within imperial territories were more complex than can be detailed by a book of this scope. The interactions and tensions between the Spaniards and Portuguese of Asia were also reflected in the metropole, Iberia. For instance, there were Castilian projects planned to restructure the Hispanic empire between Castile and Portugal by exchanging the Philippines for Brazil, leaving Macao, and concentrating all the trade of Southeast Asia in Manila: Rafael Valladares, *Castilla y Portugal en Asia (1580–1680). Declive Imperial y Adaptación* (Leuven: Leuven University Press, 2001), 8–9, 13–36. The business transacted between the Spaniards and the Portuguese in Asia, and its impact on the institutions of the Monarchy based in Madrid, is a subject in need of further research: Domingo Centenero de Arce and Antonio Terrasa Lozano, "El Sudeste Asiáticos en las Políticas de la Monarquía Hispánica. Conflictos Luso-Castellanos entre 1580–1621," *Anais de História de Alem-Mar* 9 (2008): 289–332.

28   Boxer, "Portuguese and Spanish Rivalry," 150–64; Valladares, *Castilla y Portugal en Asia*, 13–64.

the supply of Asian goods was redistributed to Castile. Silk imports into Castile from New Spain rose in the first years of the seventeenth century. The second decade of that century saw an impressive rise in the silk trade between New Spain and Castile before its steady fall in the 1620s and later. A number of authors (often citing each other) have alluded to this re-exportation trade of Asian goods from the New World to the Old World.[29] This exportation of semi-elaborated products from a colonial space to the metropole is not unusual in early modern empires, as witnessed by the history of Indian calico in the British Empire.[30] However, New Spain and also the Portuguese *entrepôts* in Asia were pioneers in the re-exportation of Chinese silk fabrics.

It is certain that the development of this re-exportation coincided with the growth of trans-Pacific trade and also with the modest rise in Spanish Atlantic trade during the 1610s.[31] But these facts are not the principal reason for the re-exportation of Asian goods to Castile; rather, they define the economic context of that re-exportation, which was favourable to expansion – owing largely to the increase in American silver output, as will be described shortly. Some tentative reasons for this re-exportation can be found in the behaviour of the supply, demand, and prices of Asian products in the New Spanish market and in the commercial strategies developed by New Spanish merchants.

---

29   Pierre Chaunu, *Seville et l'Atlantique (1504–1650). Partie Statistique: Tome VI-2, Table Statistiques* (Paris: SEVPEN, 1956), 1020–21; Eufemio Lorenzo Sanz, *Comercio de España con América en la Época de Felipe II. Tomo I: Los Mercaderes y el Tráfico Indiano* (Valladolid: Diputación Provincial de Valladolid, 1986), 626; John E. Elliot, "España y América en los Siglos XVI y XVII," in *Historia de América Latina. 2. América Latina Colonial: Europa y América en los Siglos XVI, XVII, XVIII*, ed. Leslie Bethell (Barcelona: Crítica, 1990), 3–44; Hoberman, *Mexico's Merchant Elite*; Pedro Pérez Herrero, "Negocios y Redes Familiares en la Nueva España durante el Siglo XVIII," in *Capitalismo Mercantil en la España del Siglo XVIII*, ed. Rafael Torres Sánchez (Pamplona: EUNSA, 2000); Guillermina del Valle Pavón, "Expansión de la Economía Mercantil y Creación del Consulado de México," *Historia Mexicana* 51, no. 3 (2002), 529.

30   Giorgio Riello, *Cotton. The Fabric That Made the Modern World* (Cambridge: Cambridge University Press, 2013); Giorgio Riello and Tirthankar Roy, eds., *How India Clothed the World. The World of South Asian Textiles, 1500–1850* (Leiden: Brill, 2009); Beverly Lemire, *Fashion's Favourite: The Cotton Trade and the Consumer in Britain, 1660–1800* (Oxford: Oxford University Press, 1991).

31   Pierre and Huguette Chaunu, *Seville et l'Atlantique (1504–1650). Partie Interpretative. La Conjoncture, Tome VIII-2* (Paris: SEVPEN, 1960), 1276–96; Antonio García-Baquero, "Andalucía and the Crisis of the Indies Trade, 1610–1720," in *The Castilian Crisis of the Seventeenth Century. New Perspectives on the Economic and Social History of Seventeenth-Century Spain*, ed. Bartolomé Yun Casalilla and Ian A. A. Thomspon (Cambridge: Cambridge University Press, 1994), 115–17.

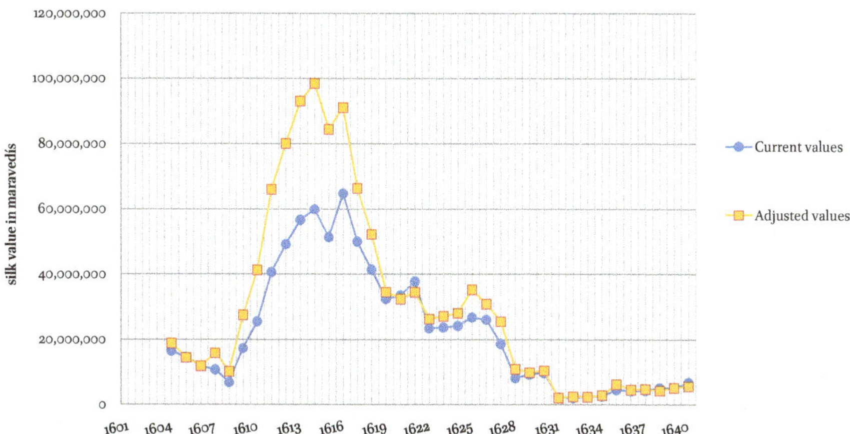

FIGURE 2   Chinese silk imports in Seville from New Spain (changing averages over six years,
current and adjusted values, in *maravedís*), 1600–1640.
SOURCE: AGI, CONTRATACIÓN, 4408–4477; CHAUNU, *SEVILLE*, 1020–1;
APPENDIX B.

The re-exportation of Chinese silk to Castile was an economic opportunity
for the merchants of New Spain when one considers the more than likely saturation of Asian goods in the New Spanish market. Given the small European
and Creole populations to which most imports, including Asian goods, were
directed, the size of the market for imported goods was small. At the end of the
sixteenth century, some 150,000 Creole and Spanish immigrants lived in the
Americas, of whom about 60,000 lived in New Spain. This number of Creole
and Spanish immigrants in the Americas was equivalent to approximately two
per cent of the population of Spain during the same period.[32] Such a market
could hardly absorb a supply of trade as buoyant as that delivered via the Manila Galleon route for so many decades – especially after the Portuguese introduced Asian merchandise (from the Cape route and Western Africa, through
Angola and then Rio de la Plata, or Brazilian ports) to Peruvian markets.[33] The
behaviour of Chinese silk prices in the early seventeenth century likely reflect
that the Americas provided only a small market for the high-volume Manila
Galleon trade. Although there is no way of distinguishing between flooding
of the market or decrease in the profit margin of merchants involved in the

---

32   Nicolás Sánchez-Albornoz, *La Población de América Latina. Desde los Tiempos Pre-
      Colombinos al Año 2000* (Madrid: Alianza, 1973), 60–72, 89–91; Bartolomé Yun Casalilla,
      "The American Empire and the Spanish Economy: An Institutional and Regional Perspec-
      tive," *Revista de Historia Económica – Journal of Iberian and Latin American Economic His-
      tory* 16, no. 1 (1998): 130–31.

33   Boyajian, *Portuguese Trade in Asia*, 141–45.

trans-Pacific trade, the fall of Chinese silk prices in New Spanish cities, such as Veracruz, in the second decade of the seventeenth century (see Figure 3) point to the hypothesis that the supply of Asian manufactured products imported from Southeast Asia overwhelmed the capacity of the New Spanish market to take in more Asian goods in the early decades of the seventeenth century. In fact, during the 1620s and the 1630s the merchant guild of Seville petitioned the delay or suspension of the fleet bound for New Spain because of the news that the New Spanish market was saturated of imports.[34] After several decades of increase in the trans-Pacific trade, the New Spanish demand for Chinese silk was likely manifesting the first signs of flooding. New Spanish merchants involved in the Manila Galleon trade could react to this commercial setback in a logical fashion: they looked for another market, beyond the Americas, that could absorb the surplus merchandise. The Castilian market was the best (if not the only) option because both the New Spanish and the Castilian markets had the same political structure and also because Castilian demand and taste for Asian goods had already begun to expand through the circulation of such goods in the form of gifts.

These changes in merchant strategies with regard to Asian goods in the New Spanish market led to new forms of interaction between the Pacific and Atlantic trades via colonial Spanish America. Networks of wholesale merchants based in New Spain joined and expanded from the Philippine Islands to Castile. The merchants who organised these commercial networks became the conduits through which Asian products circulated as gifts, special orders, and wholesale merchandise in both American and Castilian markets.

As can be seen from the maps of merchant networks involved in the Chinese silk trade in the Spanish Empire (Figures 4 and 5), the geographical scope of the trade of Asian goods from the Philippines to Europe across the Americas was extensive between the late sixteenth and early seventeenth century.[35]

---

34   Jeremy Baskes, *Staying Afloat: Risk and Uncertainty in Spanish Atlantic World Trade, 1760–1820* (Stanford, CA: Stanford University Press, 2013), 65. The fact that New Spanish merchants got well-stocked of imports, including Asian imports, happened other times later in the eighteenth century: Mariano Ardash Bonialian, *El Pacífico hispanoamericano. Política y comercio asiático en el imperio español (1680–11784). La centralidad de lo marginal* (México, D. F.: El Colegio de México, 2012), 153.

35   Two important points about these network maps are as follows. First, they illustrate the re-exportation of Asian goods (mainly Chinese silk) from New Spain to Castile; however, New Spain was also a redistribution point for Asian products being sent to other American areas. The documents used to construct the network maps of Figures 4 and 5 do *not* reflect commercial links between the New Spanish commercial elite and other areas of Central and South America. Second, the significance of Acapulco's merchants as commercial nodes between Mexican and Philippine merchants is misrepresented because

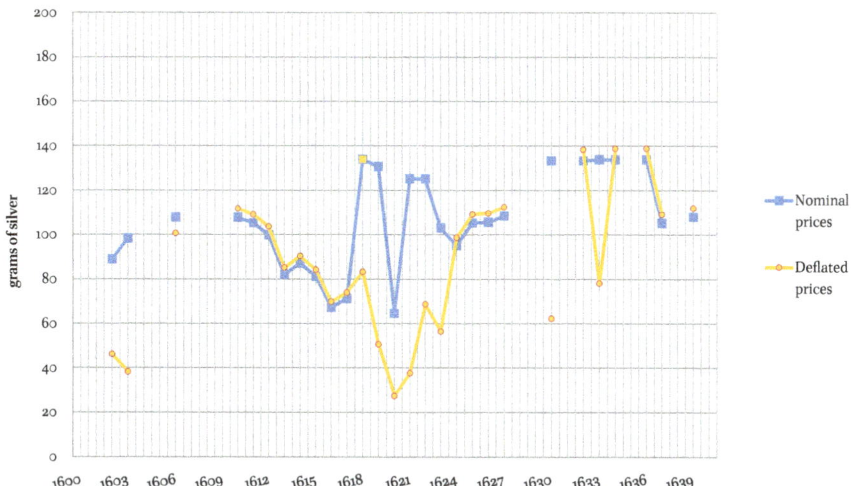

FIGURE 3   Nominal and deflated prices of Chinese raw silk in Veracruz (IN GRAMS OF
SILVER), 1600–1640.
SOURCE: APPENDIX A[1].

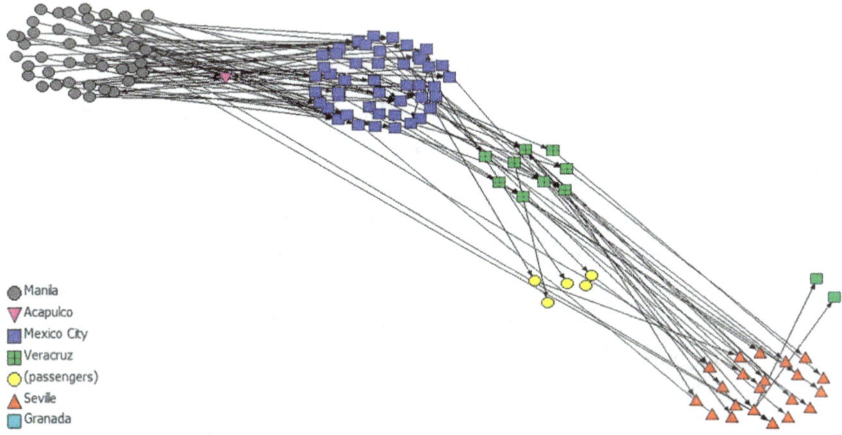

FIGURE 4   Networks of merchants involved in the Chinese silk trade, 1587–1600.
SOURCE: APPENDIX A[1 AND 11].

As the volume of the trans-Pacific trade grew and as New Spanish merchants
found that the Castilian market was receptive to products carried on the Manila galleons, merchants who invested in Asian goods multiplied across the

---

the documents used to construct the network in the Pacific Ocean make hardly any reference to such commercial intermediaries. Thus there were more Acapulco merchants than
indicated by these network maps. See Appendix A [11].

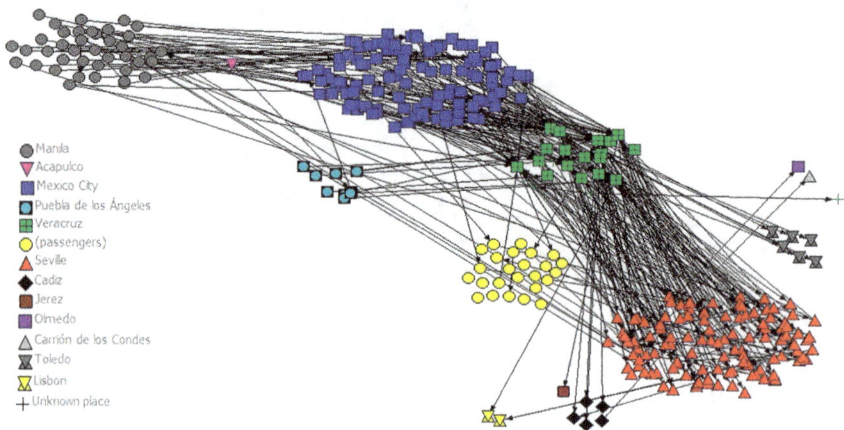

FIGURE 5   Networks of merchants involved in the Chinese silk trade, 1611–1615.
SOURCE: APPENDIX A[1 AND 11].

Empire. Increasing numbers of merchants and cities were involved in this trade. In the case of New Spain, it is noteworthy that merchants from Puebla de los Ángeles, which had been a main sericulture centre of New Spain during the second half of the sixteenth century,[36] became involved in this trade and even re-exported Asian manufactured goods from New Spain to Castile in the early decades of the seventeenth century. In Castile, besides the merchants of Seville and neighbouring cities (e.g., Cádiz and Jerez), traders from other cities also involved themselves in the importing of Chinese silk. Over time more Castilian cities received Chinese silks from the Americas. Of particular note is the case of Toledo and Granada, which became one of the main recipient cities of Chinese silks in Castile in the early seventeenth century. Even smaller cities in northern Castile, such as Olmedo and Carrión de los Condes, imported volumes of Chinese silk.

In Portugal, Lisbon also emerged as a centre for importing Chinese silk from Seville and likely re-exported silk to other locations in Europe. Thus the Portuguese imported Asian textiles not only from their colonies in Asia but also from the route that connected the Manila galleons with colonial Spanish America and Castile. This pattern contrasts with the circulation of Asian spices. In Europe, popular spices such as cinnamon were rarely introduced into the American markets from the Philippines and instead came from Europe – that is, from the Portuguese commercial networks that extended from Asia to Lisbon across the

---

36   Jan Bazant, "Evolución de la Industria Textil Poblana (1544–1845)," *Historia Mexicana* 13, no. 14 (1964): 473–516. More details are given in Chapter 6.

Cape route. The Manila galleons rarely carried spices from Southeast Asia to New Spain and from there to Iberia: the lists and reports of merchandise handled by Mexican merchants who traded in the Manila galleons are full of Chinese silks, porcelain, and (later on) Japanese furniture; however, spices such as pepper and cinnamon (and other perishable goods, such as benzoin) are very scant. For instance, the documents of the Mexican merchant Santi Federighi, who was active in both the trans-Pacific and trans-Atlantic trades, reveal that he received pepper from the Philippines only on exceptional occasions but received cinnamon on several occasions from Seville.[37] The implication is that early commercial specialisation existed at a global level between Portuguese trade networks that crossed the Cape route, which specialised both in spices and manufactures, and the New Spanish networks that traded with the Manila galleons, which specialised in Asian manufactured products that they re-exported to the Iberian Peninsula. The reasons for this specialisation during the Union of Crowns period can be found in the confluence of three factors. First, production of spices such as cinnamon was scarce on Luzon, the main island of the Philippines.[38] Second, Manila was growing ever more dependent – for their supply of goods – on China and on the Portuguese of Macao, who mostly traded in Chinese goods. Third, spices had been circulated mainly through Portuguese commercial circuits during the sixteenth century and so continued that pattern during the early decades of the seventeenth century.[39]

These merchant networks were global and geographically extended, but they followed the logic of early modern trade in also being extremely dense. A factor that clearly emerges from the merchant networks of the Chinese silk trade is the importance of Mexican and Veracruz merchants in the re-exportation of Asian goods from New Spain to Castile: the former as main investors in the Philippine market; the latter as *encomenderos* (commercial agents who lived permanently in the same town), who dispatched merchandise to Castile on behalf of the Mexican merchants. Because of the legal system that organised trade in the Spanish Empire until the eighteenth century, the trade of Asian goods had to pass through merchants hailing from a select few commercial cities. There were few cities that enjoyed the monopoly of trade with other commercial areas, which is especially evident in the coastal and maritime areas. Acapulco was the only city in colonial Spanish America that was allowed

---

37   AGN, *Indiferente Virreinal*, caja-exp.: 6015-023, *Consulado*; AGN, *Indiferente Virreinal*, caja-exp.: 5651-017, *Consulado*; AGN, *Indiferente Virreinal*, caja-exp.: 5651-017, *Consulado*; AGN, *Indiferente Virreinal*, caja-exp.: 0535-015, *Filipinas*.

38   De Morga, *Sucesos*, 314.

39   Boyajian, *Portuguese Trade in Asia*, 42–52.

to trade with Manila. Veracruz was the only commercial port in New Spain that traded with Seville; it shared this monopoly with Nombre de Dios-Portobelo (located in Panama) and such Caribbean cities as Havana. Seville was the only Castilian city that could legally trade with the Americas.

The monopoly trade system enjoyed by a select few cities in the Spanish Empire determined the importance of *encomenderos* in this trade. The *encomenderos* of the two main New Spanish port cities, Veracruz and Acapulco, were the main commercial intermediaries in the transmission of Asian goods from Southeast Asia to Castile across New Spain. Even though the capital investment for buying and re-exporting Asian goods was dominated by merchants of the two great commercial capitals of New Spain and Castile (Mexico City and Seville, respectively), the merchants of Veracruz and Acapulco were those who guaranteed the circulation of merchandise and information. The business letters of Mexican merchants reveal that their intermediaries in Acapulco and Veracruz were essential to the reception and delivery of Asian goods in (respectively) Mexico City and Seville.[40] The *encomenderos* of Acapulco took care of sending the silver to Manila on behalf of the wholesalers of Mexico City and Puebla every spring.[41] In winter, they received merchandise from the Philippines and guaranteed its subsequent transport via mule drivers and peddlers along the road linking Acapulco and Mexico City.[42] Furthermore, the role of Acapulco merchants in advising Mexico City wholesalers about market conditions was indispensable to the business of those wholesalers. Such information concerned various subjects, including the condition in which merchandise arrived from Manila, the climatic state of the seas, and the political situation in the Philippines. The *encomenderos* also updated wholesalers about any delays of fleets and galleons, which could prove catastrophic for business.[43]

In Veracruz, on the eastern coast of New Spain, the *encomenderos* played an essential commercial role in reporting to wholesalers in Mexico City and

---

40   AGN, *Indiferente Virreinal*, caja-exp.: 2427-032, *Consulado*, 1635, 29.

41   AGN, *Indiferente Virreinal*, caja-exp.: 2427-032, *Consulado*, 1635, 9.

42   AGN, *Indiferente Virreinal*, caja-exp.: 1776-001, *Consulado*, 1608–1616, 5–6, 40–48; AGN, *Indiferente Virreinal*, caja-exp.: 5887-014, *Industria y Comercio*, 1633, 9–11; AGN, *Indiferente Virreinal*, caja-exp.: 2427-931, *Consulado*, 1634, 4–7; AGN, *Indiferente Virreinal*, caja-exp.: 2427-029, *Consulado*, 1634; AGN, *Indiferente Virreinal*, caja-exp.: 2427-031, *Consulado*, 1634; AGN, *Indiferente Virreinal*, caja-exp.: 2427-032, *Consulado*, 1635, 15; AGN, *Indiferente Virreinal*, caja-exp.: 5845-077, *Consulado*, 1635, 8; AGN, *Indiferente Virreinal*, caja-exp.: 6564-039, *Industria y Comercio*, 1640–1641, 1–2.

43   AGN, *Indiferente Virreinal*, caja-exp.: 0778-006, *Consulado*, 1638–1639, 25–26. Other examples may be found in AGN, *Indiferente Virreinal*, caja-exp.: 0778-006, *Consulado*, 1638–1639, 41–42; AGN, *Indiferente Virreinal*, caja-exp.: 2427-031, *Consulado*, 1634. AGN, *Indiferente Virreinal*, caja-exp.: 5098-011, *Filipinas*, 1640–1660.

Puebla about the need to ship Asian merchandise to Castile. For instance, Lucián Espinel, *encomendero* of Veracruz, wrote the following to Santi Federighi in 1627:

> I see that you have shipped most of your merchandise and that you have little merchandise from China. I am happy that you never order me to take care of merchandise that can be easily damaged, such as fruit. We have much noise [*sic*] and anger and work with the rest of the merchandise, in order not to sell them at a loss. We do not know exactly what the situation is in Spain, but with war the price of merchandise always increases. We do not know what will happen with France either, nor whether the fleet is coming. In times of war there is much news.[44]

3.3 Silk for Silver in the Manila Galleon Trade

The production and transmission of silver from the Americas to the Philippines and then to China was one of the driving forces of the trans-Pacific trade. This statement does not mean that bullion was the only *raison d'être* of the Manila Galleon trade because many other variables, such as the escalation of Creole and Iberian population, agrarian production growth, (proto)industrial expansion and specialisation, and expansion of credit and improvement of credit techniques during the sixteenth and early seventeenth centuries, were also part of the conditions that favoured the expansion of New Spanish international trade, as will be shown in this and following chapters. However, the significance of silver, which provided the means of exchange for global trade, cannot be omitted.

The Manila Galleon trade was part of a commercial cycle in which merchants from all over the world participated and that involved the exchange of silver for Asian goods. This web of silver was a base and vehicle for connected histories and commercial transfers between remote places. Silver connected different parts of the world so fundamentally that its global variations in volume flow and value influenced many economic segments of – and international trade between – Europe, the Americas, and Asia. In fact, both the increase

---

44 AGN, *Indiferente Virreinal*, caja-exp.: 5651-017, *Consulado*, 1627, 125–26. Similar information can be found in AGN, *Indiferente Virreinal*, caja-exp.: 3815-002, *Consulado*, 1620; AGN, *Indiferente Virreinal*, caja-exp.: 5651-017, *Consulado*, 1627, 159–60; AGN, *Indiferente Virreinal*, caja-exp.: 5651-017, *Consulado*, 1627, 205; AGN, *Indiferente Virreinal*, caja-exp.: 5845-077, *Consulado*, 1640, 9.

in silver remittances through the Manila galleons from the 1580s to the 1630s and the fall of the trans-Pacific trade from the 1630s onward had serious consequences for the economic zones of China, Castile, and the Americas. New Spain and New Spanish merchants were at the centre of this web, wherein converged American silver production and the Chinese demand for it. The central location of New Spain in global silver markets led to changes in its colonial economy, the most important of which strengthened that economy.

There was element of truth to the European view of China as a bottomless well into which all traded silver sank. Events that resulted in the dominance of silver within the Chinese economy occurred during the Yuan Dynasty (1279–1368) and the first reigns of the Ming emperors. After some fruitless attempts to establish a nationwide currency system based on paper notes and copper coins and following the collapse of Southeast Asia's fiduciary system, the third Ming emperor Ch'eng-tsu (reigned 1403–1424) re-opened bullion mines, in several Chinese provinces, that had been closed for decades. The effect of these policies on government finances was immediate and substantial, and receipts from silver mining rose dramatically. Much additional bullion eventually filtered into circulation, and the entire fiscal system came to be organised under the parameters of silver. Local and regional taxes began to be paid in silver, and by the 1430s China was strongly committed to the silver standard – a commitment that lasted until the twentieth century.[45] The Chinese satisfied their demand for silver either by trading (legally and illegally) with Japan or by satisfying the growing demand for Chinese goods in Europe and, from the late sixteenth century, in the Americas as well. When Portuguese and Spaniards (and later the Dutch and English) sailed into Asian seas, the Chinese and other Asian countries were able to purchase silver more cheaply because they could sell their manufactured goods and spices to European and Euro-American merchants and companies without leaving the Chinese landmass.

The growth of the trans-Pacific trade from 1580 to the middle of the 1630s was related to two factors: this growing demand for silver in China; and a general expansion of the monetised sectors of economy in the viceroyalty of New Spain, whose driving force was the expansion of silver output. This period witnessed a boost in American silver output from New Spanish and also from

---

45   Richard von Glahn, *Fountain of Fortune. Money and Monetary Policy in China, 100–1700* (Berkeley, CA: University of California Press, 1996), 48–70; William S. Atwell, "International Bullion Flows and the Chinese Economy circa 1530–1650," *Past and Present* 95 (1982): 78–79; Dennis O. Flynn and Arturo Giráldez, "Arbitrage, China, and World Trade in the Early Modern Period," *Journal of Economic and Social History of the Orient* 38, no. 4 (1995): 429–48.

Peruvian mines. The mines of Potosí were consolidated as the leading silver producer of the Americas, and the Mexican mines – especially Zacatecas – dramatically increased production to unprecedented levels.[46] This increase of silver mining and production promoted international trade in all of the Americas, which by the end of the sixteenth century already had a solid commercial base thanks to the development of trade with Castile during previous decades.[47] Most silver and coin produced in New Spain escaped from the viceroyalty to other areas of the world.[48]

The levels of Atlantic trade between New Spain and Castile were always higher than the levels of trans-Pacific trade. This difference is indicated by the data on private remittances of silver; see Table 1, which charts commercial investments made by private merchants to the Philippines and Castile. Official records of the monarchy reveal that the remittance of silver and trade increased across both the Pacific and Atlantic Oceans during the last two decades of the sixteenth century and into the early seventeenth century. However, the export of bullion from New Spain to the Philippines (i.e., the Manila Galleon trade) grew at a faster rate than did exports from New Spain to Castile across the Atlantic. In the years 1571–1580, bullion privately imported into the Philippines from New Spain amounted to about 11 per cent of the total private remittances from New Spain to other continental areas; this figure rose to more than 30 per cent during 1621–1630 but declined thereafter.

Hence there was increased diversion of silver from the Atlantic to the Pacific as a consequence of the trans-Pacific trade boom in those years. The trade of New Spain and Manila, which was non-existent in the 1560s, was consolidated at the end of the sixteenth century and ended up rivalling the trans-Atlantic routes to Seville. However, the actual sum of silver shipped by the Manila galleons to Asia is the subject of much conjecture. Authors including Chuang, Flynn, Giráldez, and von Glahn have estimated about 51 tonnes of silver per annum for the first half of the seventeenth century; in contrast, Tepaske estimated an amount equal to only 17 tonnes.[49] De Vries assembled all estimates

---

46   John J. TePaske (edited by Kendall W. Brown), *A New World of Gold and Silver* (Leiden: Brill, 2010), 77–78, 112–13; Engel Sluiter, *The Gold and Silver of Spanish America, ca. 1572–1648* (Berkeley, CA: University of California Press, 1998), 7–35, 39–99.

47   Bartolomé Yun Casalilla, *Marte contra Minerva. El Precio del Imperio Español* (Barcelona: Crítica, 2004), 126–38.

48   Ruggiero Romano, *Moneda, Pseudomonedas y Circulación Monetaria en las Economías de México* (México, D.F: Fondo de Cultura Económica, 1998), 35–101.

49   John J. TePaske, "New World Silver, Castile, and the Philippines, 1580–1800," in *Precious Metals in the Late Medieval and Early Modern World*, ed. John F. Richards (Durham, NC: Duke University Press, 1983), 444–45. The estimates of Dennis O. Flynn and Arturo Giráldez are reported in their "Born with a 'Silver Spoon'. The Origin of World Trade in

TABLE 1   Private remittances of bullion from New Spain to Castile and the Philippines (in pesos of "pieces of eight" and percentages), 1571–1650

	Private remittances			
	To Castile	To the Philippines	To Castile	To the Philippines
Period	(in pesos of "pieces of eight")		(%)	(%)
1571–1580	7,763,754	928,288	89	11
1581–1590	21,698,886	4,646,164	82	18
1591–1600	23,602,458	5,184,812	82	18
1601–1610	25,952,906	9,411,695	73	27
1611–1620	28,423,325	5,682,490	83	17
1621–1630	22,161,725	11,166,567	66	34
1631–1640	12,673,065	3,542,454	78	22
1641–1650	8,865,489	1,900,023	82	18

Notes: Sluiter's data was collected (or estimated, in some cases) from the records of the Royal Treasuries of New Spain. The data include gold, which was about five per cent of the total American bullion exported from the Americas during the seventeenth century. Although Crown remittances of bullion followed a trend similar to that of private remittances, these have not been included because Crown remittances of silver across the Empire reflect not only the trade of state powers (i.e., the Crown) but also political decisions. For instance, financial subsidies to maintain colonial structures such as the *situado* were sent every year from New Spain to the Philippines, as were remittances of silver and gold to institutions such as religious orders: Sluiter, *Gold and Silver*, p. 146.

SOURCE: ENGEL SLUITER, *THE GOLD AND SILVER OF SPANISH AMERICA, CA. 1572–1648*, BERKELEY, CA: UNIVERSITY OF CALIFORNIA PRESS, 1983, P. 148.

of silver remittances worldwide during the early modern period. According to his data, between the years of 1600 and 1650 South and East Asia received about 56,000 kg of silver annually from the Baltic area, nearly 38,000 kg from

1571," *Journal of World History* 6 (1995): 204. See also Richard von Glahn, "Myth and Reality of China's Seventeenth-Century Monetary Crisis," *Journal of Economic History* 56, no. 2 (1996): 439; and von Glahn, *Fountain of Fortune*, 232. Recently, Bonialian has argued that Flynn and Giráldez's estimations of silver crossing the Pacific Ocean as an unjustified exaggeration: Bonialian, *El Pacífico hispanoamericano*, 44–9.

the Levant, and some 15,000 kg via the Cape route. In those same years, the Americas shipped between 17,000 and 51,200 kilograms of silver per annum to South and East Asia by way of the Manila galleons. This means that even the lowest estimates of silver crossing the Pacific Ocean are higher than those for the Cape route during the first half of the seventeenth century. The situation changed in the 1640s, when the shipment of silver across the Pacific Ocean declined even as shipments via the Cape route had been increasing over the previous years.[50] The relatively higher level of commercial exchanges cross the Manila Galleon route than across the Cape route during the early decades of the seventeenth century, which stemmed from increases in American silver output and absorption of the growing supply of Asian goods by the American and Castilian markets, favoured changes in New Spain that were linked to global economic re-adjustments.

The expansive cycle of silver output during the second half of the sixteenth century and first half of the seventeenth century, which expanded markets for Chinese silk and other manufactured goods (such as porcelain) in several areas of the world, culminated in the first global convergence of global silver values, which occurred around 1640, mainly because of the decline in Chinese silver values after decades of high import levels. The decline in Chinese silver values coincided with the transition from the Ming to the Qing dynasty, which was marked the military collapse of the Ming and, according to some scholars, the beginning of a new era of growing restrictions to international trade and industry in China.[51] Consequently, in the mid-seventeenth century China no longer offered the advantageous silver prices that had been available *circa* 1600.[52] The connection between the trans-Pacific and the Atlantic trade across

---

50   Jan de Vries, "Connecting Europe and Asia: A Quantitative Analysis of the Cape-route Trade, 1497–1759," in *Global Connections and Monetary History, 1470–1800*, ed. Dennis O. Flynn, Arturo Giráldez and Richard von Glahn (Burlington, VT: Ashgate, 2003), 77–81.

51   Kenneth M. Swope, *The Military Collapse of China's Ming Dynasty, 1618–44* (London: Routledge, 2014); Wang Yuan-kang, "Managing Regional Hegemony in Historical Asia: The Case of Early Ming China," *The Chinese Journal of International Politics* 5 (2012): 129–153. Some scholars have criticized the "Qing conquest theory," which stresses the bad economic performance of China during the seventeenth and eighteenth centuries, and they have emphasised the positive effects of the new Qing order on the Chinese economy: William T. Rowe, *China's Last Empire. The Great Qing* (Harvard University Press, 2010); Kenneth Pomeranz, *The Great Divergence. China, Europe, and the Making of the Modern World Economy* (Princeton and Oxford: Princeton University Press, 2000), 155–165.

52   Dennis O. Flynn and Arturo Giráldez, "Cycles of Silver: Global Economic Unity through the Mid-Eighteenth Century," *Journal of World History* 13, no. 2 (2002): 391–427; Kevin O'Rourke and Jeffrey G. Williamson, "After Columbus: Explaining Europe's Overseas Trade Boom, 1500–1800," *Journal of Economic History* 62, no. 2 (2002): 428–39.

the New Spanish economy figured prominently in the changes concerning international silver markets. Throughout the Spanish Empire, silver values finally fell to the cost level of American production around 1640, and the resulting sharp reductions in silver mining profits hastened the Empire's decline. Until then, American silver production (and the European and Chinese demand for it) had been one of the foundations of Spain's rise in the world.

In New Spain, the effects of increased silver production and increased Chinese demand for silver were profound in some economic segments of the viceroyalty, especially in the capital city and in the relatively more monetised sectors of the economy. The high levels of silver output, money movement, and credit extension that were associated with the arrival of the Manila galleons at Acapulco every year, when combined with the already well-established Atlantic trade with Seville, mobilised increasing amounts of economic resources in the viceroyalty. However, the New Spanish currency system was plagued by a persistent coin shortage and by the dominance of "strong" coins. Most coins minted in New Spain were silver pesos in "pieces of eight," which tended to move away from the viceroyalty and toward international commercial circuits. This trend was exacerbated by the rise of silver output and of trans-Pacific trade around 1600. The quantity of currency coined by Mexico City's mint (*Casa de la Moneda*) increased by a factor of nearly 4 between 1585 and 1610.[53] Furthermore, the last two decades of the sixteenth century saw an expansion of credit activity in Mexico City and more generally in the economy of New Spain.[54] One result was the rapid concentration of silver coin in the hands of the viceroyalty's wealthiest elite and in the few economic sectors most closely related to the colonial economy: mining, international trade, and the state's bureaucratic apparatus.[55] This concentration of currency is one reason why the elite of New Spain were better able – than the elite residing in central Castile – to face the economic problems that arose when the value of silver declined in China. As American silver production grew, international trade expanded and the connections between Atlantic and Pacific trade were reinforced. New Spain and its elites strengthened other sectors of the viceroyalty economy by

---

53   Hoberman, *Mexico's Merchant Elite*, 86–87.

54   María P. Martínez López-Cano, *La Génesis del Crédito Colonial en la Ciudad de México, Siglo XVI* (México, D.F.: UNAM, 2001), 190–201.

55   Ruggiero Romano, *Moneda, Pseudomonedas*; and Ruggiero Romano, *Mecanismo y Elementos del Sistema Económico Colonial Americano* (México, D.F.: Fondo de Cultura Económica, 2004).

investing capital in such economic activities as mining, private debt, urban estate, agriculture, and sinecures within the state administration.[56]

3.4   The Decline of Asian Trade in the Spanish Empire (1630–1650)

The fall in trans-Pacific trade over Atlantic commercial routes was a reflection of a shift in the economic cycle at a global level. This mid–seventeenth-century decline marked the emergence of the Cape route as the main avenue by which commercial exchanges between Asia and the Atlantic World transpired. By the eighteenth century, the Cape route had superseded the Manila Galleon route in terms of trade volume.[57]

Even recent estimates of eighteenth-century silver exports from New Spain to the Philippines, which indicate that American silver exports from the 1680s to the 1730s were higher than previously supposed, are far from Euro-Asian trade levels across the Cape route.[58] There was a progressive commercial diversion in Southeast Asia from east to west, from the Pacific to the Indian Ocean, from the 1630s onward which culminated in the eighteenth century. Recently, Birgit M. Tremml has addressed the "failure" of Manila to keep sustained economic development in the long run, thus its global significance after the mid-seventeenth century. She has brilliantly stressed the importance of political factors by shedding light on the political performance of the three main political powers which had commercial interests in Manila – Spain, China and Japan. Unlike the Americas, Spain could not successfully integrate Manila's economy into its territory-based empire, among other reasons because of its difficulties to deal with the rise of other European empires in Asia. China did not take advantage of the profitable businesses that great quantities of Chinese traders made in Manila, because of the limits of Chinese policies to maritime trade. Japan, even though proved to be a more successful state than the two former, withdrew from Manila after the *Sakoku* – external policy marked by growing isolation which was approved in the 1630s.[59] The commercial diversion in Southeast Asia from the Pacific to the Indian Ocean must be

---

56   For the diversification of economic investments of the New Spanish elite in the seventeenth century, see Hoberman, *Mexico's Merchant Elite.*

57   De Vries, "Connecting Europe," 77–81; Ward Barrett, "World Bullion Flows, 1450–1800," in *Rise of Merchant Empires. Long-distance Trade in the Early Modern World, 1350-1750,* ed. James D. Tracy (Cambridge: Cambridge University Press, 1993), 224–254.

58   Bonialian, *El Pacífico Hispanoamericano,* 222–6.

59   Birgit M. Tremml, "The Global and the Local: Problematic Dynamics of the Triangular Trade in Early Modern Manila," *Journal of World History* 23, no. 3 (2012): 555–86.

understood in connection not only with these political reasons, the transition from the Ming to the Qing dynasty in China and the aforementioned changes in global silver markets, but also with a number of economic and geopolitical changes that occurred both in the Atlantic World and Southeast Asia: the seventeenth-century crisis and its effects on the Spanish Empire, among them the consequent changes in the structure of Atlantic trade; the rise in military clashes and war between European powers in Southeast Asia; and the climatic, geographic and trading conditions of the Manila galleons. It must be also understood in the context of the political economy of the Spanish Empire, which is analysed in chapter 4.

Literature on the Castilian crisis of the seventeenth century has, over time, come to take a more balanced view – one that situates the crisis of Castile in its European context and that does not approach crisis as a homogeneous process which equally impacted all European spaces but as as process of economic and social divergence between regions in Europe and within Iberia.[60] During the first three quarters of the sixteenth century the population of Castile multiplied; urbanisation increased; the manufacture of silk and wool flourished in the textile centres of Toledo, Granada, Segovia, and Cordoba; wool exports were high until the 1560s; foreign trade expanded until the 1590s; and traffic with the Americas grew until the early seventeenth century. In the last quarter of the sixteenth century, all these trends first slowed and then reversed. This was the beginning of a general crisis that affected demography, agriculture, textile manufacturing, and trade in Castile. In contrast with northwestern European countries, which were barely affected by the crisis, Castile (along with Italy and the Ottoman Empire) suffered greatly during this period.[61] I write "Castile" because the crisis did not affect all territories of Iberia in the same way. Spain's seventeenth-century crisis, which had been overcome in some regions by the

---

60   Yun Casalilla and Thompson, *Castilian Crisis*; John H. Elliot, "The Decline of Spain," *Past and Present* 20 (1961): 52–75; Regina Grafe, *Entre el mundo ibérico y el atlántico. Comercio y especialización regional, 1550-1650* (Bilbao: Diputación Foral de Bizkaia, 2005), 19–25. Some classic works in the literature and debates addressing this topic are Eric J. Hobsbawm, "The Overall Crisis of the European Economy in the Seventeenth Century," *Past and Present* 5 (1954): 33–53; Hugh R. Trevor-Roper, "The General Crisis of the Seventeenth Century," *Past and Present* 16 (1959): 31–64; Jan de Vries, *The Economy of Europe in an Age of Crisis, 1600–1750* (Cambridge: Cambridge University Press, 1976); Trevor H. Aston and Charles H. Philpin, eds., *The Brenner Debate. Agrarian Class Structure and Economic Development in Pre-Industrial Europe* (Cambridge: Cambridge University Press, 1985).

61   Yun Casalilla and Thompson, *Castilian Crisis*, 1–3, 301–21. See also Antonio Domínguez Ortiz, ed., *Historia de España. La Crisis del Siglo XVII* (Barcelona: Planeta, 1988).

mid-seventeenth century, was accompanied by a shift of economic activity – including trade – from the center of Iberia to its coastal areas.[62]

Furthermore, changes arising from the seventeenth-century crisis did not have the same characteristics in Iberia as in its American colonies, in spite of their economic entanglement. In Spanish America, the conjuncture of these circumstances was not nearly as negative as in Castile.[63] Some scholars defined the seventeenth-century crisis in the Americas as neither a crisis nor a moment of stagnation but rather as a period of economic change.[64] Others contrasted the economic situation in America with that in Castile during the seventeenth century and denied the existence of an economic crisis in the Americas during this time.[65] Despite differences of opinion, most agreed that the seventeenth-century economic changes in Castile and New Spain were connected. However, this connection was not of the nature described by such twentieth-century scholars as John Lynch and John TePaske. Unlike traditional interpretations – which were based on viewing Spain as a predatory colonial state that intensified the exploitation of the Americas in order to finance its own military conflicts, address cash-flow problems, and preserve hegemony over Europe – more recent perspectives have shed light on the American fiscal system's redistributive character. In the Americas, the local elite either intervened heavily in taxation matters (case of the *cajas reales*) or managed them directly (case of the *alcabala* and *avería* tax). The revenue generated by these taxes was partly redistributed to other kingdoms and provinces of the Americas through a system based on constant net transfers between different fiscal districts (*situados*). Furthermore, the fiscal system was embedded in the credit system of the American kingdoms and merchants' businesses. Hence income for the Crown coming from the Royal Treasuries of the Americas was always irregular and unpredictable.[66]

---

62   Grafe, *Entre el Mundo Ibérico y el Atlántico*, 209–14.

63   Here I am following the relatively recent revisions of classic works – in particular those of Borah and Chaunu, who analysed the crisis in seventeenth-century America (especially in New Spain) in the 1950s: Woodrow W. Borah, *New Spain's Century of Depression* (Berkeley, CA: University of California Press, 1951); Chaunu, *Seville et l'Atlantique. VIII*.

64   John TePaske and Herbert S. Klein, "The Seventeenth-Century Crisis in New Spain: Myth or Reality?," *Past and Present* 90 (1981): 116–35.

65   Romano, *Coyunturas Opuestas*; John Lynch, *Spain under the Habsburgs* (Oxford: Oxford University Press, 1981), 212–27.

66   Bartolomé Yun-Casalilla, "The American Empire and the Spanish Economy: An Institutional and Regional Perspective," *Revista de Historia Económica – Journal of Iberian and Latin American Economic History* 16, no. 1 (1998): 123–56; Alejandra Irigoin and Regina Grafe, "The Spanish Empire and Its Legacy: Fiscal Redistribution and Political Conflict in Colonial and Post-Colonial Spanish America," *Journal of Global History* 1, no. 2

That system, alongside the extension of mining production and agrarian development in the sixteenth century, gave way to a growing regional specialisation and reinforcement of the New Spanish economy. The trans-Pacific trade played a key role in these trends. When combined with profits from the Atlantic trade and growing control of fiscal institutions by New Spanish local elite, the Pacific trade filtered into other segments of the colonial economy and favoured the consolidation of internal commercial circuits in New Spain. Creole merchants thus gained commercial independence from the metropole, which allowed them to enjoy a growing economic autonomy from the political decisions made in Spain.[67]

In the western Atlantic, Castile's seventeenth-century crisis coincided with changes in the structure of Atlantic trade, which were marked by displacement of the core of trade northward: from Seville and Lisbon to Amsterdam and London. In the last two decades, many scholarly assumptions regarding the supposed crisis of Atlantic trade during the seventeenth century have changed. In contrast to those who viewed the Atlantic trade as participating in the crisis of seventeenth-century Europe,[68] most scholars today view that seeming crisis of trade as rather a reflection of the growing participation in the Spanish American trade of traders from northwestern and other European countries. The arrival of American silver in Europe was not interrupted during the seventeenth century. Although tax collection records of seventeenth-century Spanish institutions indicate a decline in Atlantic trade, in reality this was a diversion of such trade toward northern Europe. The Dutch and the English expanded the commercial routes that Iberians had opened in the sixteenth century and,

---

(2006): 241–67; Alejandra Irigoin and Regina Grafe, "Bargaining for Absolutism: A Spanish Path to Nation-State and Empire Building," *Hispanic American Historical Review* 88, no. 2 (2008): 173–209; Alejandra Irigoin and Regina Grafe, "A Stakeholder Empire: The Political Economy of the Spanish Imperial Rule in America," *Economic History Review* 65, no. 2 (2011): 609–51; Regina Grafe, *Distant Tyranny: Markets, Power, and Backwardness in Spain, 1650–1800* (Princeton: Princeton University Press, 2012).

67   Yun Casalilla, *Marte contra Minerva*, 411–17; TePaske and Klein, "Seventeenth-Century Crisis,": 209–12. Romano, *Coyunturas Opuestas*, 151–58; Guillermina Del Valle Pavón, "Los Mercaderes de México y la Transgresión de los Límites al Comercio Pacífico en Nueva España," *Revista de Historia Económica – Journal of Iberian and Latin America Economic History* 23 (2005): 213–40.

68   Earl J. Hamilton, *El Tesoro Americano y la Revolución de los Precios en España, 1501–1650* (Barcelona: Crítica, 2000); Chaunu, *Seville et l'Atlantique*, 1136–1296; Antonio García-Baquero, "Andalusia and the Crisis of the Indies Trade, 1610–1720," in *The Castilian Crisis of the Seventeenth Century. New Perspectives on the Economic and Social History of Seventeenth-Century Spain*, ed. Bartolomé Yun Casalilla and Ian A. A. Thomspon (Cambridge: Cambridge University Press, 1994), 118–21.

in so doing, founded colonies in the Caribbean and on some South American coasts. Moreover, a growing number of merchant communities from northern Europe settled in such Iberian cities as Seville, Lisbon, and Cádiz and also in some Spanish American cities.[69] Indeed, English, Dutch, and (to a lesser extent) French trade in the Atlantic did not actually decline during the seventeenth century; the lone exception is the period 1645–1655, which saw a temporary reduction partly owing to the decline in American silver production in that decade.[70] The expansion of northern European commercial empires and merchants in the Atlantic made it impossible for the Spanish Empire to carry out its pretended monopoly of trade. The Spanish Atlantic trade, in theory a monopoly of the Castilian Crown and the traders of Seville's merchant guild, was in reality a business in which traders from most European countries were involved.[71] The Dutch entry into the American markets started in the 1590s, which was late when compared with the English. The main Dutch commercial objectives in Spanish America were the Caribbean Islands (Cuba, Puerto Rico, Hispaniola), Guiana, the estuary of the Amazon river and northern Brazil, Paraíba, and Ceará – all rich areas of sugar production. In these areas, the Dutch and English merchants imported great quantities of American silver and simultaneously introduced finished products.[72]

---

69 Michel Morineau, *Incroyables Gazettes et Fabuleux Métaux. Les Retours des Trésors Américains d'Aprés les Gazettes Hollandaises (XVIe–XVIIe Siècles)* (London: Cambridge University Press, 1985), 42–119; José M. Oliva Melgar, "La Metrópoli sin Territorio. ¿Crisis del Comercio de Indias en el Siglo XVII o Pérdida de Control del Monopolio?," in *El Sistema Atlántico Español Siglos XVII–XIV*, ed. Carlos Martínez Shaw and José M. Oliva Melgar (Madrid: Marcial Pons, 2005), 19–73.

70 John TePaske, Herbert S. Klein, et al., *Royal Treasuries of the Spanish Empire* (3 vols.) (Durham, NC: Duke University Press, 1982); Peter Bakewell, *Silver Mining and Society in Colonial Mexico. Zacatecas, 1546–1700* (Cambridge: Cambridge University Press, 1971); TePaske and Klein, "Seventeenth-Century Crisis,": 116–35; TePaske (ed. Brown), *A New World*, 77–78, 112–13.

71 Baskes, *Staying Afloat*, 6–7 and 45–58. For the large number of participants in the Spanish Atlantic trade, see Montserrat Cachero Vinuesa, "Should we trust? Explaining trade expansion in early modern Spain: Seville, 1500–1600" (PhD Thesis, European University Institute: Florence, 2010); Horst Pietschmann, ed., *Atlantic History. History of the Atlantic System, 1580–1830* (Göttingen: Vandenhoeck & Ruprecht, 2002); Nikolaus Böttcher, Bernd Hausberger and Antonio Ibarra, *Redes y Negocios Globales en el Mundo Ibérico* (Madrid: Publicaciones del Instituto Ibero-Americano, 2011).

72 Jonathan I. Israel, *The Dutch Republic and the Hispanic World, 1606–1661* (New York: Oxford University Press, 1982,), especially 1–28, 117–34; Jonathan I. Israel, *Dutch Primacy in World Trade, 1585–1740* (Oxford: Oxford University Press, 1989), 62–66, 171–87; Marius P. H. Roessingh, "Dutch Relations with the Philippines: A Survey of Sources in the General State Archives, The Hague, Netherlands," *Asian Studies* 5, no. 2 (1967): 377–407.

The entry of the Dutch West India Company (GWC) in Spanish Atlantic markets mainly reflected the different strategies of the northern and the Spanish Empires' traders for reducing transaction costs. On the one hand, the Dutch chartered company's new forms of capital investment and innovative forms of financing trade and war were efficient, especially in places where capital was scarce;[73] on the other, the Spanish Atlantic trade relied on the fleet system (*sistema de flotas y galeones*), which also proved effective at lowering the riskiness stemming from the unpredictability of supply, the danger of market saturation, and military threats. The monopoly of the port of Seville (despite failing to monopolise Seville's merchants), the periodicity of shipping departures and arrivals of two fleets (one to New Spain and another to Tierra Firme), and the influence of merchants over decisions about fleet departure timing were together able to control the volatility of market conditions and the negative effects derived from climatic disasters suffered by the fleets.[74] Yet this system – which enabled merchants to predict the setbacks and oversupply in markets and thereby reduce costs – hindered the possible diversifition of Spanish traders' businesses in the Atlantic World as compared with Dutch and English traders. Furthermore, from the rebellion of the United Provinces against the Habsburgs (in the second half of the sixteenth century) until the Peace of Westphalia, Europeans were in a nearly constant state of war on the Continent and at sea. War was the context in which Iberian empires lost ground against the commercial expansion of the Dutch and English empires in the Atlantic.[75] The difficulty of diversifying investments beyond Spanish America, increasing competition, and the results of land and sea warfare favoured the shift in hegemony from southern to northwestern Europe in the Atlantic World.

The decline of the Manila Galleon trade must be interpreted in these very same terms – that is, the terms used to interpret changes in the Atlantic World which take war and trading conditions into account.

---

73   Patrick O'Brien, "Contentions of the Purse between England and its European Rivals from Henry V to George IV: A Conversation with Michael Mann," *Journal of Historical Sociology* 19, no. 4 (2006): 341–63; Robert C. Allen, *The British Industrial Revolution in Global Perspective* (Cambridge: Cambridge University Press, 2009), 16–21; Jonathan Israel, *The Dutch Republic: Its Rise, Greatness, and Fall, 1477–1806* (Oxford: Clarendon Press, 1995).

74   Baskes, *Staying Afloat*, 43–68.

75   Geoffrey Parker, *The Army of Flanders and the Spanish Road, 1567–1659* (Cambridge: Cambridge University Press, 2004); Jan Glete, *War and the State in Early Modern Europe. Spain, the Dutch Republic and Sweden As Fiscal-Military States, 1500–1660* (London: Routledge, 2002); James D. Tracy, *The Founding of the Dutch Republic: War, Finance, and Politics in Holland, 1572–1588* (Oxford: Oxford University Press, 2008); John H. Elliot, *Empires of the Atlantic World: Britain and Spain in America, 1492–1830* (New Haven: Yale University Press, 2007).

When the Spaniards, Portuguese, Dutch, and many other Europeans moved into Asia, they brought their alliances and conflicts. In Southeast Asia, the Dutch increasingly wrested control from the Spanish and Portuguese over trade in the Manila–Macao–Nagasaki triangle. The founding of the Dutch East India Company (VOC) in 1602 and the Bank of Amsterdam in 1609, along with development of the Amsterdam Bourse during 1608–1611, were important steps in the Dutch expansion toward Asia. The VOC's activities continued unabated during the first decades of the seventeenth century. As early as the 1610s, the Dutch had taken as important *entrepôts* as Ambon and were already introducing Chinese silk and other Asian manufactured goods in the port of Manila, usually hidden in ships with flags of other countries. By the 1620s, the Dutch disrupted part of the trade between China and Manila.[76] Nonetheless, Dutch were not the only responsible for the decline of Portuguese trade in Asia. Internal politico-economic dynamics of Asia also played a role. The Portuguese lost Syriam against the Burmese king Anauk-hpet-lun in 1612 and Ormuz against Safavid Shah Abbas – with the support of an English navy – in 1622; in 1632 Qasim Hhan (Mughal governor of Bengal) expelled the Portuguese from Hughli.[77]

In Southeast Asia, the economic clash between Iberians (on the one hand) and the Dutch and English (on the other) was accompanied by such warlike methods as naval attacks against cargo ships and sieges of ports. Between 1609 and 1621, the Iberian empires were probably more threatened by the Dutch in the Pacific than in the Atlantic because the peace agreement between Spain and the Dutch Republic (the Twelve Years' Truce) was not respected in Asia. Attacks against the Manila galleons, which were sometimes taken or sunk, were especially shocking to those in Spanish and Portuguese political and merchant circles. Official reports from the time reveal that this was the case for the galleon *Santa Ana*'s capture off the Californian coast by the English corsair Cavendish in 1587 and for the naval attack against the galleon *San Nicolás* by the Dutch in 1620. These episodes, despite being short-term adversities, added uncertainty to the long-term perception of investors in Mexico City and Manila.[78] Indeed, in spite of the growing trend in trade, there were

---

76   Israel, *Dutch Primacy*, 73–79.

77   Sanjay Subrahmanyam, *The Portuguese Empire in Asia, 1500–1700. A political and Economic History* (London and New York: Longman, 1993).

78   "Carta de Vera sobre toma del galeón Santa Ana por ingleses" (23 June 1588), AGI, Filipinas, 18A, R. 6, N. 38; "Carta de Santiago de Vera sobre el corsario inglés Cavendish y otros asuntos" (25 June 1588), AGI, *Filipinas*, 34, N. 79; "Carta del oidor Ribera Maldonado sobre situación" (25 June 1588), AGI, *Filipinas*, 18A, R. 6, N. 39; "Carta de la Audiencia de Manila sobre situación en Filipinas" (26 June 1588), AGI, *Filipinas*, 18A, R. 6, N. 42.

more failed journeys across the Pacific Ocean than successful ones between 1580 and 1630.[79]

Whereas both the Spanish trade across the Pacific Ocean and the Portuguese trade in Asia declined in this context from the 1630s onward, Dutch trade in Asia continued to rise during the same period. Portuguese investments in Asian trade fell from the 1610s onward,[80] which coincided with the decline of the Manila galleons. In contrast, the amount of silver shipped from the Dutch *entrepôt* to Asia at the same time by the VOC rose steadily.[81] The ships returning to the Netherlands and Portugal from Asia followed exactly the opposite trends,[82] and the seizure of Melaka and concession of Dejima (Nagasaki) to the VOC in 1641 dealt a severe blow to the Iberian empires in Southeast Asia. Thereafter, the Dutch were able to engage Japanese sources of silver and so overcome their excessive dependence on American silver. Furthermore, the independence of Portugal from the Habsburgs and the collapse of the Ming dynasty in China in the 1640s hindered the trade between Macao and Manila. These events occurred at precisely the time when American silver output had begun to decline after being on the rise during previous decades.[83] After the mid-seventeenth century, Dutch superiority over the Iberians in Southeast Asia was indisputable.

The military scenario just described converged with the extreme dependence of the Manila Galleon trade on climatic circumstances, which heightened uncertainty about the trans-Pacific trade. Here uncertainty is understood as unmeasurable trading risks associated with poor information.[84] The Manila Galleon system, like the Atlantic fleet system, was based on concentrating trade on the outward and return journey of a limited number of strongly armed vessels. In the case of the Manila Galleon trade, two galleons sailed between only two ports (Acapulco and Manila), which helped Mexican and Manila merchants to predict market condition changes accurately and to repel enemy attacks. Yet sea climatic conditions were more dangerous in the Pacific Ocean than in the Atlantic. A comparison between the climatic and geographic conditions affecting the Manila Galleon trade

---

79 Carmen Yuste López, *Emporios Transpacíficos. Comerciantes Mexicanos en Manila, 1710–1815* (México, D.F.: UNAM, 2007), 31.

80 Boyajian, *Portuguese Trade in Asia*, 155, 226.

81 Israel, *Dutch Primacy*, 177.

82 De Vries, "Connecting Europe and Asia," 56.

83 Israel, *Dutch Primacy*, 171–73; De Vries, "Connecting Europe and Asia," 75–7.

84 Baskes, *Staying Afloat*, 1–4. More details about problems derived from uncertainty in the Manila galleons in Chapter 4.

with those affecting the trans-Atlantic trade can shed light on this point. Risks were more diversified in the Atlantic than in the Pacific because there were more routes and ships in the Atlantic trade and because there were not one but two annual departures of fleets from Seville to the Americas. Moreover, although both the trans-Atlantic and trans-Pacific trades were strongly affected by current and wind circuits, the limitations and dangers in the trans-Pacific route were greater and the travel times longer. The strong dependence of the trans-Pacific shipping route on the Kuro Siwo current was likely comparable to the dependence of the Spanish fleets on the Atlantic currents. However, the dangers that the Manila galleons suffered in their way out from the port of Manila (Cavite) to the Pacific, where they had to cross several perilous straits, were much greater than those of the Atlantic fleets in their way out from Seville to the Atlantic across the Guadalquivir River – the sandbar at the mouth of the Gualquivir became a problem later, in the late seventeenth century, when galleons became bigger and havier. The fall of several Manila galleons to an enemy contrast with fall of the 1628 Atlantic fleet in hands of the Dutch admiral Piet Heyn, which was the only time in the early modern era that an Atlantic Spanish fleet fell to the Spanish Empire's enemies.[85] Furthermore, in the Pacific and in the area around the Philippine archipelago there were monsoons and the strength of winds and oceanic currents was greater. The time required to cross the Atlantic from Seville to Veracruz was about two-and-a-half months; from Veracruz back to Castile, about four months. It took about three months to sail the Pacific from Acapulco to Manila, and the return journey lasted nearly six months.[86] These climatic circumstances meant that the Manila galleons had only a short time between their June arrival at Manila and their July departure back to Acapulco. It was necessary for the galleons bound for Acapulco to leave Manila in July (or August, at the very latest) if they wanted to arrive with their merchandise in New Spain and guarantee the passage of information across the ocean. A delay in the arrival of galleons at Manila would end up affecting the entire annual commercial cycle. Such delays, which became more and more common as war with other European powers developed in the South China Sea (see Table 2), led to doubts about the viability of some businesses on the

---

85   Carla Rahn Philips, *Six Galleons for the King of Spain. Imperial Defense in the Early Seventeenth Century* (Baltimore and London: The John Hopkins University Press, 1986), 3.

86   Schurtz, *El Galeón de Manila*, 209–26; Antonio García-Baquero, *La Carrera de Indias: Suma de la Contratación y Océano de Negocios* (Sevilla: Algaida, 1992), 180–81, 184–85.

TABLE 2   Main setbacks for Iberian trade in Southeast Asia and the trans-Pacific trade
             between 1570 and 1640

Year	Actions
1574	Naval attacks against Manila by the Chinese corsair Limahon
1586	English capture of the galleon *Santa Ana*
1587	English naval attack against Manila
1587	English naval attack against Acapulco
1596	Shipwreck of the gallon *San Felipe*
1600	Pursuit and capture of several merchant ships in the Philippines by the Dutch. Shipwreck of the galleon *San Diego* after a battle with Dutch vessels
1600	English attacks against Manila; sinking of the vessels *Santa Margarita* and *San Jerónimo* near the port of Manila
1600	Loss of the galleon *Santo Tomás* in the *Embocacadero*
1603	Naval attack against Goa by the Dutch
1603	Shipwreck of the galleon *San Antonio*
1605	Occupation of the Maluku Islands (Amboina, Ternate. and Tidore) by the Dutch (recovered in 1606 by the Spaniards and Portuguese)
1609	Naval attack against Iliolo (Panay Island, Philippines) by the Dutch
1610	Loss of the galleon *San Antonio* sailing to Acapulco
1610	Naval battle between the Dutch and the Spaniards in Mariveles (Bataan, Philippines)
1614	Blockade of Manila by the Dutch
1615–1618	Construction of the *San Diego* fortress in Acapulco to protect the harbour from Dutch and English attacks
1616	Bombardment against Iliolo (Panay Island, Philippines) and siege of Manila by the Dutch
1617	Naval battle between the Dutch and the Spaniards in Zambales (Central Luzon, Philippines)
1619	Pillage of Visayas (small archipelago of the Philippines) by the Dutch
1620	Naval attack against the galleon *San Nicolás* by the Dutch
1621–1622	Blockade of Manila and attacks on Chinese ships by the Dutch
1622	Naval attack against Macao by the Dutch
1624	Commercial blocking against Manila by the Dutch and naval battle
1624	Battle between Spaniards-Portuguese and the Dutch in Pescadores Islands (Penghu Islands, western coast of Taiwan)

TABLE 2 (*con't*)

1624	Occupation of southern Taiwan by the Dutch
1626	Occupation of northern Taiwan by the Spaniards
1628	Shipwreck of a Spanish galleon en route to Taiwan and Dutch attack against the shipyards of Taiwan
1639	Shipwreck of the two galleons sailing to Manila from New Spain

---

SOURCES: LUIS ALONSO ÁLVAREZ, "DON QUIJOTE EN EL PACÍFICO: LA CONSTRUCCIÓN DEL PROYECTO ESPAÑOL EN ASIA, 1591–1606," *REVISTA DE HISTORIA ECONÓMICA – JOURNAL OF IBERIAN AND LATIN AMERICA ECONOMIC HISTORY*, 23, 2005, P. 268; ANTONIO DE MORGA, *SUCESOS DE LAS ISLAS FILIPINAS* (FRANCISCA PERUJO, ED.), MÉXICO D.F.: FONDO DE CULTURA ECONÓMICA, 2007 (FIRST PUBLISHED IN 1609); JONATHAN I. ISRAEL, *THE DUTCH REPUBLIC AND THE HISPANIC WORLD, 1606–1661*, NEW YORK: OXFORD UNIVERSITY PRESS, 1982; JONATHAN I. ISRAEL, *DUTCH PRIMACY IN WORLD TRADE, 1585–1740*, OXFORD: OXFORD UNIVERSITY PRESS, 1989; CARLOS MARTÍNEZ SHAW, "MÁS ALLÁ DE MANILA," IN VVAA, *EL GALEÓN DE MANILA. CATÁLOGO DE EXPOSICIÓN*, MADRID: MINISTERIO DE FOMENTO, 2002, PP. 95–105; RAFAEL VALLADARES, *CASTILLA Y PORTUGAL EN ASIA (1580–1680). DECLIVE IMPERIAL Y ADAPTACIÓN*, LEUVEN: LEUVEN UNIVERSITY PRESS, 2001, PP. 13–36; "CARTA DE LA CIUDAD SOBRE SANDE, LIMAJON, ETC." (2 JUNE 1576), AGI, *FILIPINAS*, 27, N. 8; AHAM, ACTAS DEL CABILDO (14 AUGUST 1587), VOL. 348A; "CARTA DE VERA SOBRE TOMA DEL GALEÓN SANTA ANA POR INGLESES" (23 JUNE 1588), AGI, *FILIPINAS*, 18A, R. 6, N. 38; "CARTA DEL OIDOR RIBERA MALDONADO SOBRE SITUACIÓN" (24 JUNE 1588), AGI, *FILIPINAS*, 18A, R. 6, N. 39; "CARTA DE SANTIAGO DE VERA SOBRE EL CORSARIO INGLÉS CAVENDISH Y OTROS ASUNTOS" (25 JUNE 1588), AGI, *FILIPINAS*, 34, N. 79; "CARTA DE LA AUDIENCIA DE MANILA SOBRE SITUACIÓN EN FILIPINAS" (26 JUNE 1588), AGI, *FILIPINAS*, 18A, R. 6, N. 42; "CARTA DE ALONSO GÓMEZ A ÁLVARO DE ÁLVARO DE GRADO" (6 AUGUST 1601), AGN, *INDIFERENTE VIRREINAL*, CAJA-EXP.: 3008-020, *CONSULADO*; "RELACIÓN DE LOS SUCEDIDO EN MANILA DESDE EL AÑO 1627 HASTA EL PRESENTE 1628" (IN A LETTER FROM LUIS DE ARIETA TO SANTI FEDERIGHI), AGN, *INDIFERENTE VIRREINAL*, CAJA-EXP.: 5078-011, *CONSULADO*; "CARTA DE ASCANIO GUAZZONI A SANTI FEDERIGHI" (31 JULY 1628), AGN, *INDIFERENTE VIRREINAL*, CAJA-EXP.: 5078-011, *CONSULADO*, PP. 53F; "CARTA DE GASPAR DE TORRES A SANTI FEDERIGHI" (12 DECEMBER 1640), AGN, *INDIFERENTE VIRREINAL*, CAJA-EXP.: 5098-011, *FILIPINAS*.

part of Manila's commercial agents who traded on behalf of New Spanish wholesalers.[87] In this geographic context, the Manila Galleon's rigid system of an annual outward and return journey by two galleons was effective in predicting market conditions and reducing uncertainty, and in this it matched

---

87   The letters written by merchants are full of references to such delays in shipments and the consequent interruptions in the flow of information. Ascanio Guazzoni wrote to Don Fernando del Hoyo y Azoca in 1642: "I received two letters from you last year, after the

the performance of the Atlantic fleet system. Yet, unlike the Manila Galleon system, the Spanish Atlantic system had two trans-oceanic routes – to the northern and southern Americas. This diversification of uncertainty and investment was non-existent in the trans-Pacific trade. While the English and Dutch had *entrepôts* throughout all Asia (in the English case, India above all; in the Dutch case, Ambon, Ceylon, Taiwan, Melaka, and Dejima, among others), the Spaniards only had one *entrepôt* in Asia: Manila, whose only possible connection with the Americas – because of the riskiness and uncertainty associated to the trans-Pacific route – was through the Manila galleons, and whose relations with the Portuguese from Goa and Melaka were not always easy – despite all being subjects of the Portuguese Crown until 1640.

The geographic situation of Manila, which was in an area of monsoons and separated from the Pacific through many straits, combined with the expansion of Dutch and English powers in Southeast Asia and growing insecurity of trade in Southeast Asia, rendered the Manila Galleon trade extremely fragile. These circumstances fostered the conditions for a diversion of the main European centres of silver circulation, imports, and exports to the Dutch and English merchants and colonies – not only in the Atlantic but also in Southeast Asia. The entry of the Dutch and other Europeans (such as the English) in Southeast Asia and the American markets, in the latter case through the Caribbean Sea, weakened Spanish control over their commercial circuits on the two oceanic sides of the Americas. The Dutch merchants diverted increasing amounts of American silver from the Spanish Atlantic trade to their own trading routes in the Americas and Asia; at the same time,

---

galleons departed to New Spain. Because of this, I could not answer those letters and I am answering you now": AGN, *Indiferente Virreinal*, caja-exp.: 6015-023, *Consulado*. In the same year, Fray Domingo González wrote from Manila to Santi Federighi and expressed himself in the following terms: "I could not answer you last year because, although you sent me a letter with the receipt of the gold I shipped you, the letters were delayed because the galleons had already departed": AGN, *Indiferente Virreinal*, caja-exp.: 6015-023, *Consulado*. These problems – alongside others, such as the fires and earthquakes that repeatedly beset the Philippines and the Chinese uprisings against the Spanish authorities in Manila – were especially drastic in some years. In 1600, an earthquake destroyed many buildings in Manila, and in 1603 and 1639, the Chinese merchants of Manila rose up against the Spanish authorities. Merchant letters allude to these disasters as well. For instance, in a letter dated 31 July 1628, Santi Federighi refers to three fires that destroyed the *parian* neighbourhood of the Chinese merchants of Manila, the hospital and monastery of Saint Francis in Ternate, and Saint Augustine's monastery of Zebu: AGN, *Indiferente Virreinal*, caja-exp.: 5078-011, *Consulado*, 53f. In a 14 July 1636 letter to his wife (Teresa Setin), Santi Federighi entertains doubts regarding his stay in the Philippines and defines the land as "devious" (*trampossa*): AGN, *Indiferente Virreinal*, caja-exp.: 5056-050, *Consulado*.

they found new sources of silver in Japan. They also began surreptitiously to introduce foodstuffs produced in the American colonies (e.g., cocoa and coffee) into Castile and also, over time, such Asian manufactured products as Chinese porcelain,[88] which became a common practice in the eighteenth century.[89] Northern European empires entered Iberian markets both in the Atlantic and Southeast Asia to the extent that they could offer colonial imports at competitive prices in southern European markets themselves. Furthermore, the extraordinarily high protection costs of the Spanish Empire, which were paid by the Hispanic monarchy, benefitted not only the Empire's elite but also such foreign interests as those of the Dutch and English merchants and commercial companies in the Atlantic.[90] The commercial route between Manila and New Spain hardly could compete with the Cape route as the main commercial route between Asia and the Atlantic World in these conditions.

3.5 Conclusions

Data on silver imports into Asia reveal that the Pacific Ocean and the Americas were areas in which, according to the standards of the time, trade between Asia and the Atlantic World was strongly concentrated until the second half of the seventeenth century. By the eighteenth century, when the rise of Dutch and English in the Atlantic trade was definitive, the centre of trade between Asia and the Atlantic became concentrated on the Cape route and the Indian Ocean. The fall of the trans-Pacific trade in favour of the Cape route was a process driven not only by the alterations of the political-economic situation and relations between Spain, China and Japan in Southeast Asia, but also by the same global circumstances that drove changes in the Atlantic World. These circumstances were rooted in the hostilities between European powers that developed during the first half of the seventeenth century, when the Iberian hegemony began to manifest clear indications of decline and Dutch and English increased their commercial operations both in the Atlantic and Asia.

---

88 Manuel Herrero Sánchez, "La Política de Embargos y el Contrabando de Productos de Lujo en Madrid (1635–1673). Sociedad Cortesana y Dependencia de los Mercados Internacionales," *Hispania* 201 (1999): 177–91.
89 Bonialian: *El Pacífico hispanoamericano*, 202–7.
90 Yun Casalilla, *Marte contra Minerva*, 575.

For several decades, the Americas supplied the Spanish Atlantic trade with Asian merchandise, especially Chinese silk. When the trans-Pacific trade grew during three consecutive decades, from 1580 to 1610, Mexican merchants who controlled the Manila Galleon trade started re-exporting Asian merchandise not only to other American markets but also to Castilian markets. Such re-exporting was likely a solution that New Spanish wholesalers could find in answer to the increased saturation of Asian goods in the New Spanish market. Re-exporting transpired across reliable merchant networks that spanned the distance between the Philippines and Iberia and was centralised in the hands of Mexico City's merchants. When this trade expanded, investment in Asian trade was no longer limited to merchants in Mexico City and began to include merchants in other American cities (e.g., Puebla de los Ángeles), for whom the intermediary ports of Acapulco and Veracruz were crucial.

The rise in trans-Pacific trade during the late sixteenth and early seventeenth centuries was driven by many factors, among them silver. The silk-for-silver exchanges enabled by Manila galleons fed the expansion of global trade. Moreover, fluctuations in global silver markets connected and affected several regions of the world through means beyond a strictly cause-effect relationship between the expansion of silver output and trade growth. In New Spain and Mexico City, the increase in silver output and the growth of Atlantic and trans-Pacific trade favoured monetised economies as well as the growing economic autonomy of the viceroyalty and its Creole elites during the first half of the seventeenth century. However, these developments occurred just as Castile – especially central Castile – began to suffer a deep economic crisis and as the Iberian economies endured restructuring. This timing explains two facts. First, as is now known in historiogaphy, Iberia's seventeenth-century crisis was due in part to distribution problems and had a greater effect on the empire's core (Castile) than on its coastal areas. Second, seventeenth-century economic transformations resulted in a divergence of economic development both within Spain and across its empire. In the Americas, a leading factor in these transformations was trans-Pacific trade, which was necessarily related to the previously described fiscal, political, and economic structure of the Spanish Empire in the Americas.

The decline in trans-Pacific trade from the 1630s onward was not an isolated process influenced by the political instability in Ming China and the fall in silver value in China around 1640; it was also linked to developments in the Atlantic. The decline in importance of the Manila Galleon trade did not mark the beginning of a crisis in Southeast Asian trade. Rather, it was the beginning of a change – in an economic cycle – that was related to ongoing changes in the Atlantic area and that crystallised in the second half of the seventeenth century. After the settlement of the Portuguese in several East and Southeast Asian enclaves – Melaka, Macao, Nagasaki – in the sixteenth century, which did not alter the commercial patterns and networks existing in that area but contributed to growing trade, the history of the Atlantic World and East and Southeast Asia became more connected. These were changes that must be understood in terms of *longue durée*. The international commercial cycle of the sixteenth century, characterised by the dominance of the Spanish and Portuguese empires in the Atlantic and in certain areas of Asia, was being diverted toward the northwestern European empires. In the Atlantic, the Spanish monopoly on trade was losing ground to the Dutch and English empires; these empires were gaining more and more control over Spanish commercial routes, especially in the Caribbean Sea. In Southeast Asia, the Portuguese in particular suffered from the Dutch wresting of control over their commercial circuits. These changes notwithstanding, the Mexican merchants who controlled the trans-Pacific trade from the American side were able to adapt their businesses to the change of cycle. They could do so thanks to the strengthening of the colonial economy and their increasing control over it, in which their privileged location near the main silver mines of the world and direct participation in the fiscal system of the Empire played a key role.

It is worth asking the extent to which the rise–decline cycle of the Manila route was unavoidable once it was forced to compete with a regularised Cape route. Answering this question is essential to understanding the rise of the Dutch and English empires, and the relative fall of the Spanish Empire, during the seventeenth century. It is true that the decline of Chinese silk prices in New Spain in the 1620s (and earlier) was more pronounced that the fall of silver prices in China, which must have made trade more attractive to Mexican merchants. However, other factors played against the expansion of trans-Pacific trade. These pages have argued that – given the economic, geographic, and military conditions of the Spanish Empire in the seventeenth century – the decline of the Manila route and especially competition from the Cape route was practically ordained by four circumstances. First, the Dutch and English began penetrating Iberian commercial networks and markets both in the Atlantic World and in Southeast Asia, absorbing ever-larger quantities of American silver and (after 1641) Japanese silver; these developments, when combined with the Spanish Empire suffering a series of military defeats (especially from the 1630s onward), made it more difficult for the Mexican and Manila traders to maintain high levels of trade across the Pacific Ocean. Second, uncertainty about journeys of the Manila Galleons was greater even than that about Atlantic fleets and galleons owing to the Cavite's geographic location between the Pacific and several straits, which the Manila galleons had to cross every time they departed or arrived at Manila. Even though the Manila Galleon system significantly reduced uncertainty in trade by limiting journeys to only an outward and return journey each year in two strongly armed two galleons, it hardly could compete with the Cape trade, which was based on a greater diversification of trade sources across several *entrepôts* in Asia by the Dutch and English. Third, the New Spanish market could not easily absorb greater quantities of Asian goods owing to its fewer consumers (than in European markets), which also discouraged expansion of the Manila Galleon trade. Fourth, there were economic contradictions within the Spanish Empire that were inherent to its political-economic structure. The pressure from Seville's merchants to limit or even close the trans-Pacific trade route, along with tensions from the clashing interests (as in the 1630s) of Sevillian and Mexican merchants, weakened the commercial potential of the Manila galleons. This point is examined more closely in the following chapter.

Trans-Pacific Trade and the Political Economy of the Spanish Empire

Until this juncture in the narrative, it may seem that the Manila galleons and the re-exportation of Asian goods within the Spanish Empire amounted to a lucrative trade, one that benefited rich merchants from all areas of the Empire and that was disrupted only when agents external to the monarchy intervened in its Atlantic and Southeast Asian commercial routes. Yet that impression is far from reality. The approach employed so far, have been useful in addressing the circulation, trade, and incipient commoditisation of Asian goods in the Spanish Empire. However, there were not only cooperative elements in long-distance relations but also clashes of interest. We cannot examine the spread of goods and trade that expanded from Southeast Asia to Castile without also analysing in detail the institutional and economic relations between merchants from different areas of the Spanish Empire as well as those between merchants and the Crown. These relations were marked by rivalry between the Pacific and the Atlantic areas of trade. As the Manila Galleon trade grew, the trans-Pacific trade absorbed more and more bullion. This triggered an economic and political conflict between two of the most powerful elites of the Spanish Empire – the Mexican and the Sevillian wholesalers – which caused various institutional transformations within the Spanish Empire, especially in New Spain.

Scholars have recently discussed the institutional nature of the early modern Atlantic empires and how their institutions were either for or against the development of such important economic segments as capital markets and international trade.[1] Given the power and historical significance of the Spanish and Portuguese empires on one side, and the English and Dutch empires on

---

1   The New Institutional Economics (NIE) has supplied tools for empirical studies that have triggered new debates and approached old debates from new vantage points: Douglass C. North and Robert P. Thomas, *The Rise of the Western World: A New Economic History* (Cambridge: Cambridge University Press, 1973); Douglass C. North, *Structure and Change in Economic History* (New York: Norton, 1981); and Douglass C. North, *Institutions, Institutional Change and Economic Performance* (Cambridge: Cambridge University Press, 1990). The precedent for this "institutionalist" paradigm is Ronald H. Coase, "The Nature of the Firm," *Economica* 4, no. 16 (1937): 386–405. The course of some relevant debates within this paradigm can be followed in many books and articles. See for example Lee J. Alston, Thráinn Eggertson, and Douglass C. North, eds., *Empirical Studies in Institutional Change* (Cambridge: Cambridge

the other, the comparison between southern and northern Europe is recurrent – in particular, that between the English and Spanish cases. The Nobel Prize–winning Douglass C. North is an economic historian whose works have triggered debates over the institutional nature of early modern empires and its effects on economic growth. In his studies of early modern England, North linked the increasing economic efficiency of English economic growth to the institutional changes and limitations of royal power following the Glorious Revolution of 1688. After almost a century of bargaining between Parliament and the Crown for the control of financial resources – a process punctuated by such dramatic events as a civil war (1642–1651), the beheading of a king (1649), and restoration of the monarchy (1660) – the Glorious Revolution ended with a succession of institutional changes that affected the economy of England and its overseas empire. These changes included Parliament's gaining a central role in financial affairs, limitations on the Crown's independent sources of revenue, and the curtailment and subordination to Parliament of royal prerogatives in financial and judicial matters. Such institutional changes heralded a new period that guaranteed private property rights and reduced transactions costs, thus fostering economic growth.[2] Although North did not develop a systematic comparison with the cases of Spain and Portugal, his analysis abounded with references to the absence of similar processes of political bargaining in the Spanish and Portuguese empire (and also in France), whose economic failures are explained by their "centralised" and "absolutist" character. Following this interpretation, other studies have insisted on the same idea from new perspectives yet always based on a correlation between the relative lack of political constraints on the Crown's power by urban merchants on the one hand and, on the other hand, the (insufficiently supported) growth of Atlantic trade.[3]

University Press, 1996); and Elhanan Helpman, ed., *Institutions and Economic Performance* (Cambridge: Cambridge University Press, 2008).

2   Douglass C. North and Barry R. Weingast, "Constitutions and Commitment: The Evolution of Institutions Governing Public Choice in Seventeenth-Century England," *Journal of Economic History* 4 (1989): 803–32; this article was republished in Alston, Eggertson, and North, *Empirical Studies*, 134–65. See also Douglass C. North, "Institutions, Transaction Costs, and the Rise of Merchant Empires," in *The Polical Economy of Merchant Empires. State Power and World Trade, 1350–1750*, ed. James D. Tracy (Cambridge: Cambridge University Press, 1991), 22–41.

3   Daron Acemoglu, Simon Johnson and James A. Robinson, "Atlantic Trade, Institutional Change, and Economic Growth," *American Economic Review* 95, no. 3 (2005): 546–79; Mauricio Drelichman and Hans-Joachim Voth, "Institutions and Resource Curse in Early Modern Spain," in Helpman, *Institutions*, 210–47; Mauricio Drelichman, "The Curse of Moctezuma: American Silver and the Dutch Disease," *Explorations in Economic History* 42 (2005): 349–80.

However, other authors have offered alternative analyses of institutional change in the Atlantic empires. Firstly, Epstein proved that the supposed relation between financial security and republican regimes is not clear-cut when one adopts a historical perspective. For instance, he pointed out that the financial situation of the Dutch Republic worsened following independence from the Hispanic monarchy and that sixteenth-century Genoa enjoyed some of the lowest interest rates in Europe in spite of being a lender to that monarchy.[4]

Secondly, ground-breaking is the model developed for the Spanish and the Spanish American cases by Yun-Casalilla. The key to this scholar's view on the political economy and institutional change in the Spanish Empire is that he approaches the Spanish imperial institutional structure not as an "absolutist" or "centralised" regime but rather as a "composite monarchy."[5] Because it was far from a centralised structure, the Spanish Empire's administrative complexity triggered complicated institutional relationships between territories and the Crown; between territories and councils (*Consejos*); among the King, councils (*Consejos*), cities, and the Church and its diverse organisms; and between elites and the monarchy's institutions. The existence of continuous negotiations between the King and the different powers in the Empire, rather than the lack of negotiations, was precisely the problem that hindered the economic growth of Spain.[6]

Thirdly, along these lines, Grafe and Irigoin have posited why the Spanish imperial system survived through three centuries. The explanation is based on the strong ideology of contractual rule not only during the Habsburg period

---

4   Epstein concluded that English financial success subsequent to 1688 was related more to English convergence with continental European fiscal advances (exposure to which had been limited in England because of its military and political isolation) than to constitutional changes: Stephan R. Epstein, *Freedom and Growth. The Rise of States and Markets in Europe, 1300–1750* (London: Routledge, 2000), 12–37. More recent criticism of North and Weingast has highlighted the multiple mechanisms for creating commitment between monarchs and parliaments – as well as questioned the ability of their model to explain universally the structure of institutional change: D' Maris Coffman, Adrian Leonard and Larry Neal, eds., *Questioning Credible Commitment. Perspectives on the Rise of Financial Capitalism* (Cambridge: Cambridge University Press, 2013).

5   John H. Elliot, "A Europe of Composite Monarchies," *Past and Present* 137 (1992): 48–71.

6   Bartolomé Yun Casalilla and Fernando Ramos Palencia, "El Sur Frente al Norte. Instituciones, Economías Políticas y Lugares Comunes," in *Economía Política desde Estambul a Potosí. Ciudades Estado, Imperios y Mercados en el Mediterráneo y en el Atlántico Ibérico, c. 1200–1800*, ed. Bartolomé Yun Casalilla and Fernando Ramos Palencia (Valencia: Publicacions de la Universitat de València, 2012), 11–38; Bartolomé Yun Casalilla, *Marte contra Minerva. El Precio del Imperio Español* (Barcelona: Crítica, 2004), 121–73; Yun Casalilla, "Entre Mina y Mercado. ¿Fue América una oportunidad perdida para la economía española?," in *La historia sin complejos. La nueva visión del Imperio español*, ed. David García Hernán (Madrid: Actas, 2010), 204–9.

but also afterwards, during the Bourbon period, and on the strength of urban and local elites due to their control of consumption taxes. The Empire did not implode until its redistributive imperial fiscal organisation, and the King's consequent bargaining advantages, collapsed.[7]

This chapter addresses the political tensions that arose in the Spanish Empire as a result of trans-Pacific trade development and the attendant institutional changes. In so doing, it seeks to explicate how Spain's institutional structure affected that trade during trans-Pacific trade's periods of apogee (*ca.* 1580–1630) and decline (*ca.* 1630–1650). This connection will be studied in the context of commercial decision-making strategies employed by New Spanish merchants when responding to the trends in trade via the Manila galleons.

Section 4.1 seeks to explain how the expansion of New Spain's international trade and the opening up of trans-Pacific trade led to the founding of a merchant guild in Mexico City in the early 1590s, which in turn made it possible for New Spanish wholesalers to lower the transaction costs of international trade by the turn of the century. The focus here is on the establishment of a mercantile court of justice within that guild and the consequent reduction in trade costs for Mexican traders using either the trans-Pacific or trans-Atlantic route. Section 4.2 addresses the different commercial mechanisms that New Spanish elites utilised when trans-Pacific trade rose in the seventeenth century's early decades and when, thereafter, the Manila Galleon trade began to stagnate and decline. Section 4.3 explains how, in the 1630s, the Spanish Empire's institutional machinery served to constrain the performance of Pacific trade. By shedding light on the possibilities and limits of trade efficiency in the Spanish Empire, this chapter contributes to knowledge about the change of the economic cycle in trade via the Manila Galleon route, from a perspective which takes the dynamics of the political economy of the Empire into account.

4.1   Mexico's Guild of Merchants and the Trade of the Manila Galleons

The *Universidad de los Mercaderes* or *Consulado* of Mexico's merchants, founded in the late 1590s, was the first merchant guild in the Americas.[8] In the

---

7   Alejandra Irigoin and Regina Grafe, "Bargaining for Absolutism: A Spanish Path to Nation-State and Empire Building," *Hispanic American Historical Review* 88, no. 2 (2008), 173–75; Regina Grafe, *Distant Tyranny. Markets, Power, and Backwardness in Spain, 1650–1800* (Princeton: Princeton University Press, 2012).

8   Robert S. Smith and José Ramírez Flores, *Los Consulados de Comerciantes de Nueva España* (México, D.F.: Instituto Mexicano de Comercio Exterior, 1976); Guillermina del Valle Pavón, "El Consulado de Mercaderes de la Ciudad de México, 1594-1827. Historiografía y fuentes

medieval and early modern period, merchant guilds – known as *consulados* or *universidades* in the early modern Spanish-speaking world – were corporate associations of wholesale traders that guaranteed the privileges and interests of its members. The main privileges enjoyed by merchant guild members included the application of mercantile justice, delegations set up to deal with the King, and economic support for trade. In recent years, some economic historians have defined merchant guilds as institutions that contributed to reducing transaction costs and risk in long-distance trade.[9] In Castile, for example, merchant guilds such as those of Burgos (founded in 1494), Bilbao (1511), and Seville (1543) helped lower transaction costs by improving the fleet system and maritime insurance, actions taken in the context of the economic growth characteristic of sixteenth-century Castile.[10] Yet other economic historians have stressed the negative economic aspects of merchant guilds. For instance, some scholars have claimed that merchant guilds during the medieval and early modern periods thrived not because of their efficiency (i.e., their ability to promote economic growth) but rather because of their ability to transfer resources from the wider economy to the elites who supported the guilds, their members, and the country's rulers.[11]

The merchants of Mexico City achieved the privilege of establishing their guild after several decades of requests to the Crown. The expansion of the Manila Galleon trade in the late sixteenth century was a key driving force behind that establishment. As early as 1560, a group of merchants from Mexico City asked the viceroy and the *Real Audiencia* (royal appellate tribunal) of the city for permission to establish a guild of merchants there. This request was made when silver production in New Spain first peaked.[12] Among the main arguments in favour of establishing their own guild in Mexico City in 1560 was that

---

      sobre su historia," *América Latina en la Historia Económica* 9, no. 17 (2002): 11–21; Guillermina del Valle Pavón, "Expansión de la Economía Mercantil y Creación del Consulado de México," *Historia Mexicana* 51, no. 3 (2002): 522–26, and Antonio Ibarra and Bernd Hausberger, eds., *Comercio y Poder en la América Colonial. Los Consulados de Comerciantes, Siglos XVII–XIX* (México, D.F.: Colegio de México, 2003).

9   Regina Grafe and Oscar Gelderblom, "The Rise and Fall of the Merchant Guilds: ReThinking the Comparative Study of Commercial Institutions in Premodern Europe," *Journal of Interdisciplinary History* 40, no. 4 (2010): 480–81.

10   Yun Casalilla, *Marte contra Minerva*, 153–65.

11   Roberta Dessì and Sheilagh Ogilvie, "Social Capital and Collusion: The Case of Merchant Guilds," *Cambridge Working Papers in Economics* 417 (2004): 1–40; Sheilagh Ogilvie, *Institutions and European Trade. Merchant Guilds, 1000-1800* (Cambridge: Cambridge University Press, 2011); Grafe and Gelderblom, "Rise and Fall,": 482–89.

12   Peter J. Bakewell, *Silver Mining and Society in Colonial Mexico: Zacatecas, 1546–1700* (Cambridge: Cambridge University Press), 181–262; Del Valle Pavón, "Expansión": 522–26.

doing so would decrease merchant expenses resulting from lawsuits; thus the guild promised to resolve commercial litigation more easily and quickly than did the *Real Audiencia*, which was the royal body in charge of justice and the highest judicial organisation in the viceroyalty. Despite having the support of the city council (*cabildo*), the merchants of Mexico City were not allowed to form a guild at this time. In 1590, another group of Mexican merchants tried to found a merchant guild. The main arguments advanced were based on the increasing complexity of trade, on the judicial problems associated with it, and on the flourishing commerce of New Spain with the Philippines and Peru. On this occasion, the merchants achieved their objective. The report sent by this group of merchants to the King has never been located, but Philip II's answer has been published. The arguments used by these Mexican merchants, especially those concerning the high costs of obtaining justice, seem much the same as those used two decades earlier. The King's reply read as follows:

> My viceroy, president and judges of my *Audiencia Real* in Mexico City in New Spain: I, on behalf of the council, justice and regiment of that city and of Andrés de Loya de la Barrera, Bartolomé Cano, Francisco de Andenalguio, Domingo Cano, Antonio del Castillo y Diego Hurtado de Peñalosa, all from Mexico City, and the rest of the merchants from my kingdoms of Castile and provinces of Peru, the Philippine Islands and provinces of Yucatan, who have sent me a report: The report says that the commerce of merchandise and other things in the aforementioned kingdoms and provinces and islands and New Spain is so important that the lawsuits and disputes over accounts of companies, consignments, fleets, insurance, risk, damage to merchandise, losses, corruption, bankruptcies, and absences are many. Given the high costs and delays caused by solving these problems through justice, these might be better solved by setting up a merchant guild similar to those of Seville and Burgos.[13]

Hence in 1592 the King approved a royal decree authorising the creation of a merchant guild of Mexico City. Two years later, the new institution – whose organisation and ordinances were modeled after those of Seville's merchant guild – established its management, which was headed by a prior and two consuls. What had changed from 1560 to 1592 and induced the King to accept the founding of a merchant guild in Mexico? There were three primary factors.

---

13   "Mi virrey, presidente e oydores de mi audiencia Real que rreside en la ciudad de Mexico de la Nueva" Cited in Robert S. Smith, "Antecedentes del Consulado de México," *Revista de Historia de América* 15 (1942): 307–8.

First, the New Spanish economy had continued its growth during the 1570s and 1580s. The boom in New Spanish silver production during the 1580s and 1590s drove a flourishing trade between the Americas and Asia and also between New Spain and Peru.[14] Second, the development of trans-Pacific trade during the final two decades of the sixteenth century, in which the merchants of Castile did not take part, was necessary for Mexican wholesalers to be economically independent of their Sevillian counterparts. Third, international circumstances made the Crown more responsive to pressure from the Empire's socio-economic elite at the end of the sixteenth century than before. The declaration of war against England, along with the ongoing war in the Low Countries, led the Crown to increase financial pressure on the Empire's kingdoms. In the case of the Americas these income needs were satisfied by the growing remittances of money for the Royal Treasury from taxes on silver production and international trade. Because of their control over that production and over the trade with Peru and the Philippines, New Spanish merchants were essential to the Empire's economic life.[15]

The merchants of Mexico City had achieved their aim, but doing so had not been trouble-free. They had been supported in their goals by the city council of Mexico City; however, other groups of the viceroyalty were against the idea of an institution that damaged their interests. The *Real Audiencia* itself hindered the guild's establishment because it "was detrimental and damaging" and "could be problematic for royal jurisdiction."[16] The merchant guild's creation of a mercantile court external to the *Real Audiencia* meant eliminating a part of the royal prerogative of dispensing justice, although the viceroy was still entitled to appoint one of the three judges for appeals in that mercantile court. If the King acceded to severing part of the Crown's prerogative, it was only because of some compensation received. Such a concession fitted in perfectly with the competition between legal fora and jurisdictional fragmentation intrinsic to the composite nature of the Hispanic monarchy. The Crown's interest in extracting as much silver as possible was doubtless an integral part of the negotiation process and of the final concessions made to the American elite.[17] Furthermore, the Mexican wholesalers gained strategic position and wealth

---

14   Woodrow W. Borah, *Early Colonial Trade and Navigation between Mexico and Peru* (Berkeley, CA: University of California Press, 1954), 63–95.

15   Yun Casalilla, "The American Empire," 123–56; Guillermina del Valle Pavón, "Los Mercaderes de México y la Transgresión de los Límites al Comercio Pacífico en Nueva España," *Revista de Historia Económica – Journal of Iberian and Latin American Economic History* 23, no. 224 (2005): 223–24.

16   Smith and Ramírez Flores, *Los Consulados de Comerciantes*, 41.

17   Yun Casalilla, "Las Instituciones," 139–62.

with the commencement of the Manila Galleon trade, and this compelled the Crown to consider future financial support that could be obtained from the Mexican merchant guild.[18]

The foundation of Mexico's merchant guild was financially beneficial not only for the merchant classes of Mexico but also for the development of international trade, which was mainly controlled by those classes. The reason is that the guild eliminated some of the transaction costs associated with exchange. Medieval and early modern merchant guilds had different prerogatives and enjoyed different levels of trade control and jurisdiction depending on their location and the historical context. In the case of Mexico's merchant guild, some of its most important prerogatives were to administer the conditions of buying and selling in Mexico City and its hinterland, to finance such public construction projects as roads and ports in the viceroyalty, and to supervise tax collection (e.g., of the *alcabala* taxes). The guild also acted as a representative of the merchants, interceding with the King on behalf of wholesalers in the viceroyalty who infringed laws.[19] Perhaps the most financially beneficial element of the guild was likely the one merchants struggled most to obtain: the self-management of mercantile justice.

Scholarship has distinguished between "formal" and "informal" institutions that seek to assure trust in mercantile transactions and, in so doing, reduce transaction costs. Formal institutions consist of those involving state enforcement: public courts, merchant courts, written record keeping, a public notary system, and so forth. Informal institutions are those based on collective sanctions that depend on reputation concerns, coalitions, and membership in a particular family or "imagined community."[20] The focus here is on a specific

---

18   Del Valle Pavón, "Expansión," 540–41. Del Valle Pavón takes this hypothesis from Enrique-ta Vila Vilar's analysis of similar cases of financial support by the merchant guild of Seville to the King following its constitution in 1543. In other texts, Del Valle Pavón describes how the merchant guild of Mexico City provided the Crown with capital in order to deal with the Empire's warfare costs during the eighteenth century: Guillermina del Valle Pavón, "El Apoyo Financiero del Consulado de Comerciantes a las Guerras Españolas del Siglo XVIII," in *El Crédito en Nueva España*, ed. María P. Martínez López-Cano and Guillermina del Valle Pavón (México, D.F.: Instituto de Investigaciones Históricas, 1998), 131–50.

19   Rubén Ruiz Guerra, "El Consulado de Comerciantes de la Ciudad de México," in *Memoria del III Congreso de Historia del Derecho Mexicano*, ed. José L. Soberanes Fernández (México, D.F.: UNAM, 1983), 625–26.

20   Philip T. Hoffman, Gilles Postel-Vinay and Jean Laurent Rosenthal, *Priceless Markets. The Political Economy of Credit in Paris, 1660–1870* (Chicago: University of Chicago Press, 2000) 11–12; Yun Casalilla and Ramos Palencia, "El sur Frente al Norte," 19–20; Avner Greif, "Contract Enforceability and Economic Institutions in Early Trade: The Maghribi Traders' Coalition," *American Economic Review* 83, no. 8 (1993): 525–48; Avner Greif, *Institutions and the Path to the Modern Economy. Lessons from Medieval Trade* (Cambridge: Cambridge

"formal" institution – the mercantile court of the Mexico merchant guild – in order to show how this court (in concert with other institutions) helped reduce the costs of agency monitoring and contract enforcement.

There are many historical references to the high costs of lawsuits in early modern Castile.[21] Taking a case to court entailed enormous expenses and was, moreover, a huge waste of time owing to the lengthy duration of most lawsuits. Merchants normally tried to resolve matters through less expensive proceedings, such as arbitration.[22] It is hard to know exactly how much a lawsuit might cost in the *Real Audiencia* or in the court of Mexico's merchant guild; scholars have not yet attempted to quantify the cost of mercantile justice. However, there is general agreement that the diversion of judicial proceedings to the merchant guilds would have reduced the costs of processes considered expensive by merchants.[23] In the case of Castile, the tribunals and arbitration systems of the merchant guilds of Bilbao, Burgos, and Seville arrived at judicial resolutions quickly and increased the instances of agreement among guild members.[24] The same was true in Mexico City after establishment of the merchant guild there.

The justice administered by Mexico's merchant guild reduced the expenses of participants and hastened resolution when compared with the several avenues of ordinary royal justice. Guild courts prohibited the intervention of lawyers and limited the juridical formalisms characteristic of legal processes that would otherwise lead to indefinite delays. In this way, the parties tried to reach conciliation. If agreement could not be reached then the two parties had to present their cases in writing (after consultation with a lawyer). However, the presentations could not be written by lawyers and could not include any lengthy formalisms. After studying these presentations, the judges rendered their verdict. A last resort was the possibility of an appeal to the viceroy, who in such cases appointed an appellate judge to chair a new hearing; the litigant

---

University Press, 2006); Benedict R. Anderson, *Imagined Communities. Reflections on the Origin and Spread of Nationalism* (London: Verso, 1991).

21 Richard L. Kagan, *Pleitos y Pleiteantes en Castilla, 1500–1700* (Salamanca: Junta de Castilla y León, 1991), 62–63.

22 Kagan, *Pleitos y Pleiteantes*, 25; Manuel Olivencia Ruiz, *Arbitraje: Una Justicia Alternativa (Una Vision Histórica desde la Mueva Ley)* (Córdoba: Universidad de Córdoba, 2006), see 10–11 for references to the mercantile justice of the merchant guilds and the use of arbitration among merchants as a convenient means of conflict resolution.

23 One exception is Ogilvie, *Institutions and European Trade*, 250–314.

24 Yun Casalilla, *Marta contra Minerva*, 153–54; Antonio García-Baquero González, *La Carrera de Indias. Suma de Negociación y Océano de Negocios* (Sevilla: Algaida, 1992), 74–79.

merchants attended that hearing, which proceeded along the same lines as the original one.[25]

In Mexico City, the merchants justified their request to establish a merchant guild by arguing for the need to reduce mercantile costs and enforce commerce. Those arguments lend support to the notion the Mexico's merchant guild played a role in reducing transaction costs, which is corroborated by extant documents of its court. Most of the surviving documents from Mexico's merchant guild court of the late sixteenth and early seventeenth centuries are the front pages of lawsuits. Of 137 judicial documents of the merchant guild (dated from 1595 to 1641; see Figure 6), 113 are these front pages of judicial process and 24 include more of the lawsuit. Among the most significant judicial processes, there were processes concerning long-distance trade, which was (as in the case of Manila galleons) a relatively more expensive proposition. The front pages are useful for following the activity of this court because they contain the year, names of the plaintiff and of the accused, and the reason for the lawsuit. Although data are sparse, it is possible to glean some information that reveals the extent to which New Spain's merchants made effective use of the merchant guild's court. Through its proceedings, merchants were able to resolve their commercial disagreements. Merchants were taken to this court for various reasons, including breach of contract or fraud,[26] the non-payment of loans,[27] and (more rarely) theft.[28]

It is hard to determine how representative these documents are of overall judicial activity during the first half of the seventeenth century – or whether they indicate any trend in the mercantile court's activity. However, it is clear that Mexican merchants mainly used their guild's court as a means to resolve interparty disagreements. It is worth remarking that, of the documents that survive, the date for most (28) is the year immediately following the court's establishment: 1595. This finding is likely indicative of merchants' search for

---

25   Matilde Souto Mantecón, "Los Consulados de Comercio en Castilla e Indias: Su Establecimiento y Renovación (1494–1795)," *Anuario Mexicano de Historia del Derecho* 2 (1990): 241–42. See also Óscar Cruz Barney, *Historia del Derecho en México* (Oxford: Oxford University Press, 2004), 303–14.

26   AGN, *Indiferente Virreinal*, caja-exp.: 2854-017; AGN, *Acervo Histórico, Consulado*, vol. 47, exp. 1; AGN, *Indiferente Virreinal*, caja-exp.: 4671-012, *Filipinas*; AGN, *Indiferente Virreinal*, caja-exp.: 2013-023, *Consulado*; AGN, *Indiferente Virreinal*, caja-exp.: 3151-003, *Consulado*; AGN, *Indiferente Virreinal*, caja-exp.: 4992-021, *Consulado*; AGN, *Indiferente Virreinal*, caja-exp.: 4992-027, *Consulado*; AGN, *Indiferente Virreinal*, caja-exp.: 4992-029, *Consulado*.

27   AGN, *Acervo Histórico, Consulado*, vol. 131, exp. 3 and exp. 4; AGN, *Indiferente Virreinal*, caja-exp.: 2171-001, *Consulado*; AGN, *Indiferente Virreinal*, caja-exp.: 4779-039, *Consulado*; AGN, *Indiferente Virreinal*, caja-exp.: 4992-016, *Consulado*.

28   AGN, *Indiferente Virreinal*, caja-exp.: 0803-019, *Consulado*.

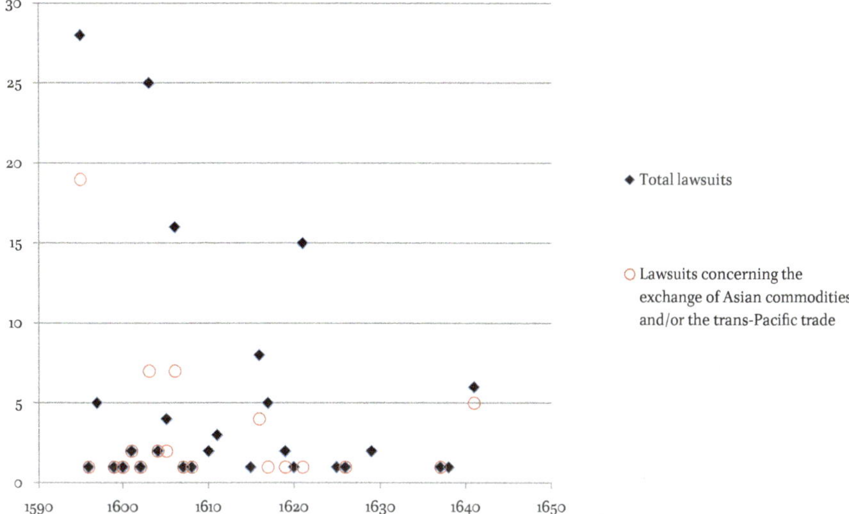

FIGURE 6   Lawsuits heard in the court of Mexico's merchant guild, 1595–1641 (N = 137).
SOURCE: APPENDIX A[8].

(and discovery of) cheaper judicial processes through the founding of a merchant guild. Adjudicated disputes were sometimes for surprisingly small sums of money. Of the 137 documents, 32 show the disputed value that motivated the opening of this court's judicial proceedings; see Table 3. Despite this small number of cases, the data are enlightening. The disputes processed in the merchant guild court concerned sums that averaged about 1,700 pesos. Yet there are cases involving barely 27 pesos, which for a trader was a small sum of money indeed. This fact strongly suggests that guild members could easily afford to litigate in the merchant court.[29]

It is noteworthy also that nearly half (59) of these 137 documents refer to conflicts concerning disagreements over the exchange of Asian goods and/ or the Manila Galleon trade.[30] These disagreements among merchants over

---

29   In 1620, the merchant Francisco Álvarez reported Father Francisco Martínez, prior of Saint John of God's monastery, to the guild court because the latter owed the former 27 pesos for the sale of merchandise: AGN, *Indiferente Virreinal*, caja-exp.: 1898-008, *Consulado*. There were other cases of merchants who opened judicial proceedings for small sums of money. In 1637, Pablo de Carrascosa (an *encomendero* in Acapulco) reported Juan Bautista de Paredes (a resident of Taxco) to the merchant guild court of Mexico City because Juan Bautista owed him 77 pesos for merchandise that Pablo had sold him on credit: AGN, *Indiferente Virreinal*, caja-exp.: 2171-001, *Consulado*.

30   AGN, *Indiferente Virreinal*, caja-exp.: 1786-054, *Consulado*; AGN, *Indiferente Virreinal*, caja-exp.: 2854-017, *Consulado*; AGN, *Indiferente Virreinal*, caja-exp.: 4629-056, *Consulado*; AGN, *Indiferente Virreinal*, caja-exp.: 4779-052, *Consulado*; AGN, *Indiferente Virreinal*,

TABLE 3   Sums of money disputed in the lawsuits of the court of Mexico's merchant guild,
             1591–1641 (in pesos of "pieces of eight")

Observations	Average	Median	Mode	Maximum	Minimum
32	1,732	600	2,000	12,000	27

SOURCE: SEE APPENDIX A[8].

the exchange of Asian goods and the trans-Pacific trade reflected problems of
trust. Such problems would be more severe with regard to trans-Pacific trade
and Asian goods, since monitoring commercial agents and contract commit-
ments was far more difficult in the case of long-distance trade (such as between the Philippines and New Spain) than for short-distance transactions. Of
the 24 judicial proceedings for which more than the frontispiece survives, 14
involved disagreements about the transaction of Asian goods or problems of
trust concerning Manila Galleon trade.[31]

Although in some cases it is difficult to know whether a party was a merchant or commercial agent residing in Manila, in other cases the documents
explicitly show conflicting parties who lived in Manila. For instance, in a lawsuit of 1599 the merchant Juan de León Plaza, residing in Mexico City, reported
that on his behalf Melchor de Molina had loaded 50 *cates* of floss silk (*seda
floxa*) from Gaspar de Maldonado, residing in Manila, instead of the 50 *cates*
of thrown silk (*seda torçida*) to which they had agreed – a substitution that
reduced the seller's cost.[32] In 1608, the Mexican merchant Domingo Ortiz de
Chago reported Doña Luisa de Carvajal, the wife and heiress of Blas Soto (from

---

caja-exp.: 5623-074, *Consulado*; AGN, *Indiferente Virreinal*, caja-exp.: 5623-076, *Consulado*;
AGN, *Indiferente Virreinal*, caja-exp.: 5623-077, *Consulado*; AGN, *Indiferente Virreinal*, caja-
exp.: 4992-027, *Consulado*.

31   AGN, *Indiferente Virreinal*, caja-exp.: 2854-017, *Consulado*; AGN, *Acervo Histórico, Consul-
ado*, vol. 131, exp. 1 and exp. 2; AGN, *Acervo Histórico, Consulado*, vol. 131, exp. 3 and exp. 4;
AGN, *Acervo Histórico, Consulado*, vol. 47, exp. 1; AGN, *Indiferente Virreinal*, caja-exp.: 4671-
012, *Filipinas* (the document contains only the reports of the witnesses); AGN, *Indiferente
Virreinal*, caja-exp.: 2013-023, *Consulado*; AGN, *Indiferente Virreinal*, caja-exp.: 3151-003,
Consulado; AGN, *Indiferente Virreinal*, caja-exp.: 2171-001, *Consulado*; AGN, *Indiferente
Virreinal*, caja-exp.: 4992-021, *Consulado*; AGN, *Indiferente Virreinal*, caja-exp.: 2095-003,
Consulado; AGN, *Indiferente Virreinal*, caja-exp.: 4992-016, *Consulado*; AGN, *Indiferente
Virreinal*, caja-exp.: 4992-027, *Consulado*; AGN, *Indiferente Virreinal*, caja-exp.: 4992-029,
Consulado.

32   AGN, *Indiferente Virreinal*, caja-exp.: 2854-017, *Consulado*.

Manila) because she did not return 600 pesos that he had sent to Blas Soto in Manila in 1604 to invest in merchandise.[33]

On the frontispieces of the judicial proceedings there are also examples of merchants from Manila who opened judicial proceedings in Mexico's merchant guild against Mexican merchants. The Manila merchants were able to do this through their representatives and confidants living in Mexico.[34] There are also cases of Mexican merchants who reported their commercial agents in Manila to the merchant court.[35] Common also were reports against the captains, masters, and crew of a galleon, and against the commercial agent responsible for taking care of the merchandise during the galleon's journey.[36] Finally, the *encomenderos* (commercial agents) of the port of Acapulco were also involved in lawsuits with Mexican merchants regarding the delivery of Asian merchandise or shipments of silver to Manila.[37]

The significance of long-distance trade is evident not only in the frontispieces of lawsuits and judicial processes concerning the Manila Galleon and Asian goods trade but also in those that refer to the trans-Atlantic trade. Besides merchants from other cities of the viceroyalty of New Spain (e.g., San Luis Potosí and Puebla de los Ángeles), there are judicial processes in which merchants from Veracruz, Cartagena de Indias, and even Lima and Seville were

---

33   AGN, *Indiferente Virreinal*, caja-exp.: 3151-003, *Consulado*.

34   AGN, *Indiferente Virreinal*, caja-exp.: 1786-054, *Consulado*); AGN, *Indiferente Virreinal*, caja-exp.: 4671-012, *Filipinas*; AGN, *Indiferente Virreinal*, caja-exp.: 2672-001, *Consulado*; AGN, *Indiferente Virreinal*, caja-exp.: 4680-042, *Consulado*; AGN, *Indiferente Virreinal*, caja-exp.: 5623-076, *Consulado*; AGN, *Indiferente Virreinal*, caja-exp.: 5623-077, *Consulado*; AGN, *Indiferente Virreinal*, caja-exp.: 5623-077, *Consulado*.

35   AGN, *Indiferente Virreinal*, caja-exp.: 1786-054, *Consulado*: AGN, *Indiferente Virreinal*, caja-exp.: 4629-056, *Consulado*; AGN, *Indiferente Virreinal*, caja-exp. 2854-017, *Consulado*); AGN, *Indiferente Virreinal*, caja-exp.: 5623-074, *Consulado*; AGN, *Indiferente Virreinal*, caja-exp.: 5623-074, *Consulado*AGN, *Indiferente Virreinal*, caja-exp.: 1876-022, *Consulado*.

36   AGN, *Acervo Histórico, Consulado*, vol. 131, exp. 1 and exp. 2; AGN, *Acervo Histórico, Consulado*, vol. 131, exp. 3 and exp. 4 (the document contains only the reports of the witnesses); AGN, *Indiferente Virreinal*, caja-exp.: 2013-023, *Consulado*; AGN, *Indiferente Virreinal*, caja-exp.: 4992-021, *Consulado*; AGN, *Indiferente Virreinal*, caja-exp.: 1786-054, *Consulado*; AGN, *Indiferente Virreinal*, caja-exp.: 4725-001, *Consulado*; AGN, *Indiferente Virreinal*, caja-exp.: 4725-001, *Consulado*; AGN, *Indiferente Virreinal*, caja-exp.: 5623-074, *Consulado*; AGN, *Indiferente Virreinal*, caja-exp.: 5623-076, *Consulado*; AGN, *Indiferente Virreinal*, caja-exp.: 2013-023, *Consulado*; AGN, *Indiferente Virreinal*, caja-exp.: 4992-021, *Consulado*; AGN, *Indiferente Virreinal*, caja-exp.: 6640-096, *Consulado*.

37   AGN, *Indiferente Virreinal*, caja-exp.: 5623-075, *Consulado*; AGN, *Indiferente Virreinal*, caja-exp.: 1876-022, *Consulado*; AGN, *Indiferente Virreinal*, caja-exp.: 2171-001, *Consulado*; AGN, *Indiferente Virreinal*, caja-exp.: 1786-054, *Consulado*.

involved. In these instances, as in the case of Manila, they needed representatives in Mexico City to participate in the lawsuit on their behalf.[38]

That merchants came to the merchant guild to solve their disagreements does not mean there were no other institutions available to enforce contracts and monitor commercial agents. To secure their businesses, Mexican wholesalers used different sets of institutions – whether formal or informal, public or private – along with the instruments offered by the merchant guild. For instance, Mexican merchants used their guild and also the public system of notaries and written record keeping to validate their contracts and agreements.[39] Moreover, there are cases of merchants who pursued lawsuits and, after using the merchant guild court, appealed to the viceroy and the *Real Audiencia* as a last resort.[40] Yet it was probably more common to resolve disagreements through the arbitration system offered by the guild.[41] That system was a means to resolve a disagreement quickly, cheaply, and amicably provided that the two parties agreed to appoint as referee a trustworthy person, relative, friend, or renowned merchant. Thus this system was a way to achieve resolution by merging formal entities (merchant courts) and informal means (amicable resolution by a referee).

Indeed, informal institutions were an essential means for Mexican merchants to enforce contracts and monitor their commercial agents. Partnerships or contracts with commercial agents of the same "nation" were ubiquitous among Mexican merchants.[42] The case of the Mexican merchant Santi Federighi is a good example. His family origins were in Florence, and his main commercial agent in Manila (Ascanio Guazzoni) was also Italian.[43] On the

---

38 AGN, *Indiferente Virreinal*, caja-exp.: 1786-054, *Consulado*); AGN, *Acervo Histórico, Consulado*, vol. 47, exp. 1; AGN, *Indiferente Virreinal*, caja-exp.: 6103-033, *Consulado*; AGN, *Indiferente Virreinal*, caja-exp.: 0761-006, *Consulado*; AGN, *Indiferente Virreinal*, caja-exp.: 6149-010, *Consulado*; AGN, *Indiferente Virreinal*, caja-exp.: 5623-077, *Consulado*; AGN, *Indiferente Virreinal*, caja-exp.: 1786-054, *Consulado*; AGN, *Indiferente Virreinal*, caja-exp.: 5303-008, *Consulado*; AGN, *Indiferente Virreinal*, caja-exp.: 4779-052, *Consulado*.

39 Louisa S. Hoberman, *Mexico's Merchant Elite, 1590–1660. Silver, State, and Society* (Durham, NC: Duke University Press, 1991), 127; AGN, *Indiferente Virreinal*, caja-exp.: 1876-016, *Consulado*, 19–29; ANotDF, Notario Juan Pérez de Rivera, Reg. 2007, Libro 4, 454; ANotDF, Notario Juan Pérez de Rivera, Reg. 3857, Libro 11, 165; ANotDF, Notario Juan Pérez de Rivera, Reg. 3900, Libro 11, 226.

40 AGN, *Indiferente Virreinal*, caja-exp.: 2145-011, *Consulado*.

41 AGN, *Indiferente Virreinal*, caja-exp.: 2854-017, *Consulado*; AGN, *Indiferente Virreinal*, caja-exp.: 0761-006, *Consulado*.

42 Here, "nation" is to be understood as an "imagined community" related to a common birthplace: Anderson, *Imagined Communities*.

43 Francisco Núñez Roldán, "Tres Familias Florentinas en Sevilla: Federighi, Fantoni y Bucarelli (1570–1625)," in *Presencia Italiana en Andalucía. Actas del III Coloquio*

other side of the Atlantic, Federighi's main partner in Seville was his brother-in-law, Antonio Maria Bucarelli, who was also of Florentine origin. Family companies worked similarly in the trans-Atlantic trade. Most of the wealthiest Mexican companies were family companies. The Portuguese of Mexico City also used their family networks to assure the smooth running of their long-distance businesses.[44] The arbitration system was likely also a system of trust assurance, which, like many other examples of mercantile "coalitions" in world history, guaranteed commitment through collective punishment against fraudsters.[45]

The availability of many sets of institutions to ensure trust, enforce contracts, and monitor long-distance trade does not imply that the merchant guild of Mexico City and its court was an inefficient guarantor of trust. It is actually hard to tell which institutions performed better in that capacity. Merchants turned to one institution or another to resolve setbacks depending on their specific commercial circumstances. Many of the aforementioned informal and formal institutions overlapped, and merchants used them at the same time or turned to different institutions when others did not work. For instance, in the conditions of early modern long-distance trade we might expect that merchants initially preferred kin and "national" networks for managing their businesses. Yet those relations were sometimes not enough to prevent fraud, non-payment of debts, or other problems, and in such cases merchants would have to utilize institutions of a more formal nature. I have found three cases of Mexican merchant families in this situation. The Mexican merchants Francisco de Alexandre, Matías del Castillo, and Pedro de la Sierra all reported their own brothers to the court of the merchant guild because they had not fulfilled their commercial contracts or had tried to cheat them.[46]

It has previously been mentioned how the merchants used the public system of written records (in addition to the guild's notary system) and, as last

---

Hispano-Italiano (Sevilla: CSIC, 1989), 23–50; José L. Gasch-Tomás, "Agents of globalisation: An approximation to Santi Federighi's commercial network, c. 1620-1643," in *Merchants and Trade Networks in the Atlantic and the Mediterranean, 1550-1800: Connectors of Commercial Maritime Systems*, ed. Manuel Herrero Sánchez and Klemens Kaps (London: Routledge, 2016), 130–144.

44   James C. Boyajian, *Portuguese Trade in Asia under the Habsburgs, 1580–1640* (Baltimore, MD: Johns Hopkins University Press, 1993), 74–85.

45   Avner Greif, "Contract Enforceability,": 525–48; Francesca Trivellato, *The Familiarity of Strangers. The Sephardic Diaspora, Livorno, and Cross-Cultural Trade in the Early Modern Period* (New Haven, CT: Yale University Press, 2009).

46   AGN, *Indiferente Virreinal*, caja-exp.: 5789-005, *Consulado*, 4; AGN, *Indiferente Virreinal*, caja-exp.: 0761-006, *Consulado*; AGN, *Indiferente Virreinal*, caja-exp.: 4992-013, *Consulado*.

resort, the public courts of law. Such behavior reflected the jurisdictional fragmentation that shaped the Spanish Empire. Furthermore, the merchant guilds were in many cases shaped by kin or other network types that were supported by ethnic, origin, or other cooperative relations.[47] Taking all this into account, it is probably better to view the foundation of the Mexico merchant guild as a general improvement of the economic institutions in New Spain from about 1560 onward, as was evident in Castile during the sixteenth century, and not in terms of merchant guilds "competing" with other informal, public, or law-making institutions.[48]

In short, Mexico's merchants petitioned the King and made use of the merchant guild (among other methods) in order to reduce transaction costs through the establishment of non-public justice, which reduced the costs of contract enforcement and long-distance monitoring. This was especially so when other institutions, such as family networks or collective action, did not work. Evidence for that claim may be garnered from looking at other commercial areas connected to Mexico City, such as the Philippines, where there was no merchant guild until 1769.[49] One can reasonably assume that the costs of mercantile justice were high in the *Real Audiencia* of Manila because some merchants in that city reported merchants of New Spain to the court of the Mexican merchant guild – even though doing so required that a representative open proceedings and act on their behalf in Mexico City, which entailed additional monetary and social capital costs. The merchants of Mexico City had achieved their goal of creating a merchant guild prior to the start of the seventeenth century. The empowerment of Mexico's merchants, which derived from their growing control of the rising silver production and the expansion of the Atlantic and trans-Pacific trades, enabled their successful negotiation with the Crown toward that end.

4.2　Mexican Merchant Strategies of Investing in the Manila Galleons

The decline of the Manila Galleon trade in the 1630s forced the merchants of New Spain to change some of their commercial strategies in the trans-Pacific trade. Bjork has documented that, even though some voices in Madrid's royal

---

47　Ibarra and Hausberger, *Comercio y Poder.*

48　This seems to be implied by Sheilagh Ogilvie's work, especially in Chapters 7 and 8 of *Institutions and European Trade.*

49　Carmen Yuste López, *Emporios Trans-Pacíficos. Comerciantes Mexicanos en Manila, 1710–1815* (México, D.F.: UNAM, 2007), 149–244.

circles were in favour of withdrawing Spanish troops and administration from the Philippines, the commercial interests of Mexico's merchants in preserving these islands within the Spanish Empire made it essential for the Crown to maintain its settlement in the Philippines.[50] However, doing so required changing some of the mechanisms for investing in Manila. Financial problems resulting from the strong dependence of New Spanish merchants on the arrival of the Atlantic fleets and the Pacific galleons were eventually solved by building a commercial system based on the exchange of credit and financing via commercial companies. This system, alongside silver, was indispensable for lubricating the commercial structure of New Spain.[51] The system was (not surprisingly) unstable, especially when the long-distance trade had more problems than usual or suffered periods of increased uncertainty. In the case of trans-Pacific trade, the system was similar to that governing Atlantic trade, but the uncertainty was higher owing to the constant attacks on Manila by enemies of the Spanish Empire and to the geographical difficulties faced by the galleons when sailing to the ocean from Manila. In addition, the financing of Manila's merchants depended on the silk-for-silver commercial circuit: the Mexican merchants' financing of Manila's merchants (on the one side) and of Chinese merchants and the Portuguese of Macao (on the other side).[52] In this context, the decrease in trade of the Manila galleons and the increasing diversion of Manila's trade westward – toward Dutch and English trade routes – had a negative effect on the businesses of Mexican merchants in the trans-Pacific trade. As a result of this situation, New Spain's merchants were forced to adapt their commercial strategies.

Here it is useful to consider the differentiation of Jeremy Baskes between risk and uncertainty when dealing with the dangers surrounding trade during the early modern era. According to Baskes, *risk* is "a quantity susceptible of measurement." Thus by calculating how the number of journeys and shipwrecks affected the probability of losing cargo, traders could reduce risk via a system of insurance that became more complex and efficient over time. In

---

50   Katharine Bjork, "The Link That Kept the Philippines Spanish: Mexican Merchant Interests and the Manila Trade, 1571–1815," *Journal of World History* 9, no. 1 (1998): 25–50.

51   María P. Martínez López-Cano, *La Génesis del Crédito Colonial en la Ciudad de México, Siglo XVI* (México, D.F.: UNAM, 2001); García-Baquero González, *La Carrera de Indias*, 237–67; Hilario Casado Alonso, "El Comercio de Nueva España con Castilla en la Época de Felipe II: Redes Comerciales y Seguros Marítimos," *Historia Mexicana* 61, no. 3 (2012): 935–93.

52   Some documents corroborate this dependence of the Philippine merchants not only on Mexican financing but also on Chinese financing; AGN, *Indiferente Virreinal*, caja-exp.: 3008-020, *Consulado*.

contrast, *uncertainty* is unmeasurable and therefore hard to monetise and pass on to a third party.[53] Of course, New Spanish merchants insured their transactions in the Manila galleons, as they did for the trans-Atlantic trade, to lower their risks.[54] But it can be shown that most of the Manila Galleon's trade uncertainty resulted from poor information, which hindered the planning and implementation of business. With the galleons, poor information derived from two sources. First, communication between New Spain and Manila was difficult, since only one fleet sailed across the Pacific each year – unlike the trans-Atlantic trade, for which two different fleets operated between Spain, one the one side, and New Spain and Tierra Firme, on the other. Second, military violence among European powers in Southeast Asia escalated during the early decades of the seventeenth century. From the late sixteenth century to the mid-seventeenth century, including the 1610s, war prevailed among the European powers in Southeast Asia. In times of war, it is natural for uncertainty to rise due to the growing volatility of market conditions. Hence it was difficult for Mexican traders to plan and execute their businesses in the Manila galleons, which in turn made it harder for potential insurers to assess their prospects.

We can understand these issues by matching up data from the clustering of court cases in Mexico's merchant guild (Figure 6) and the loss of galleons (Table 2): there seems to be correlations between (i) the loss of galleons and rise of violence at sea and (ii) the increase in uncertainty as proxied by the growth of activity in Mexico's merchant guild. For instance, three important episodes that point to growing uncertainty in the Manila Galleons trade – the shipwreck of a Manila galleon in 1603, occupation of the Maluku Islands by the Dutch and the recovery of those islands by the Spaniards and Portuguese in 1606, and construction of a new fortress in Acapulco to protect the port from Dutch and English attacks in 1615–1618 – nearly coincide with periods during which, in the court of Mexico's merchant guild, the most lawsuits were heard concerning the trans-Pacific trade: 1603–1606 and 1616.

In the Atlantic, some of the most frequently used strategies by merchants in times of war and privateering – apart from insuring their cargo, the premiums for which rose so high in wartime that many merchants were discouraged altogether from trade – were splitting the cargo between two or more vessels,

---

53   Jeremy Baskes, *Staying Afloat: Risk and Uncertainty in Spanish Atlantic World Trade, 1760–1820* (Stanford: Stanford University Press, 2013), 1–4.

54   Óscar Cruz Barney, *El Préstamo a la Gruesa Ventura o Riesgo Marítimo como Mecanismo de Financiación* (México, D.F.: Instituto de Investigaciones Jurídicas, 1998); Óscar Cruz Barney, *El Riesgo en el Comercio Hispano-Indio: Préstamos y Seguros Marítimos durante los Siglos XVI a XIX* (Mexico, D.F.: UNAM, 1998), 23–64.

loading cargo in ships of neutral nations, and shipping merchandise on war-ships.[55] Mexican merchants employed some of the strategies that had worked in the Atlantic, often splitting their cargo between the two or more galleons that sailed across the Pacific and loading their merchandise in warships (the Manila galleons actually were warships). Furthermore, the concentration of commercial investment in a few hands was more pronounced in the trans-Pacific than in the trans-Atlantic trade and served as a security mechanism against losses; a wealthy merchant was clearly better able to deal with setbacks than were small shippers.[56]

In order to deal with the uncertainty attendant upon concentrating more businesses and resources of the trans-Pacific trade in fewer hands, New Spanish merchants developed another commercial strategy consisting in diversifying investments in Southeast Asia by recruiting more commercial agents in Manila. The average number of commercial agents in Manila per Mexican merchant was 2.7 during 1590–1615, but this ratio rose to 3.6 in the period 1630–1639, when the trans-Pacific trade first began to show signs of stagnation (see Table 4). In other words, New Spanish wholesalers in the 1630s contracted more commercial agents to manage their businesses in Manila than were required at the turn of the century. The need for more a larger number of agents does not mean that costs raised, as commissions were paid according to a percentage of trade and costs would have remained constant. However, investors had to diversify the risks inherent in concentration of capital investment in trade in times of growing uncertainty.

There are few sources that can be used to support that conclusion; moreover, there are fewer sources for the years 1590–1615 than for 1630–1639.[57] Nonetheless, other sources can help illustrate these changing commercial strategies in response to declining trade volumes and rising uncertainty in the trans-Pacific trade. The business letters of merchants clearly indicate a trend of appointing more commercial agents to manage their businesses in Manila during the 1630s. The letters pertaining to Santi Federighi's commercial trans-Pacific trade network reveal the vicissitudes experienced at the end of the 1630s by Ascanio Guazzoni, who was Federighi's main agent in the Philippines. Guazzoni was ruined at the end of the 1630s, when the galleon trade suffered its greatest

---

55   Baskes, *Staying Afloat*, 151–74.

56   Hoberman, *Mexico's Merchant Elite*, 39–40. Nonetheless, such concentration was not so great that Mexican traders could monopolise trade and dictate prices in the trans-Pacific or the trans-Atlantic trade.

57   See Table 4 and Appendix A.

TABLE 4   Number of commercial agents in Manila per Mexican merchant, 1590–1639

	1590–1615	1630–1639
Average	2.7	3.6
Maximum	3	9
Minimum	1	1
No. of Mexican merchants	27	205
No. of agents in Manila	74	57

Notes: (1) The only surviving data are from the following years: 1590, 1597, 1598, 1599, 1603, 1604, 1608, 1609, 1613, 1615, 1630, 1634, 1635, 1636, 1637, 1638, and 1639. (2) Calculations *exclude* small shippers (i.e., merchants who invested less than 1,000 pesos in the Manila galleons). Since small shippers made small investments – and so would not require more than one commercial agent in Manila – and since the 1630–1639 sample is larger, it follows that excluding small shippers is a reasonable methodological precaution to weight the sample and thus avoid a bias stemming from the lower number of commercial agents in that latter sample.

SOURCES: FOR 1590–1615, REQUESTS OF LICENCES TO DISPATCH SILVER TO MANILA. FOR 1635–1639, *REPARTIMIENTO*. SEE APPENDIX A[11] FOR MORE DETAILS.

losses since 1580; Federighi's letters suggest that he responded by searching for new Philippine agents.

Ascanio Guazzoni joined the Federighi company around 1620. In 1621, Guazzoni was trading with Lisboan and Peruvian merchants in the Cádiz–Seville area, where he had arrived from Italy.[58] A year later, Guazzoni was trading with Santi Federighi, to whom he was shipping Castilian (and probably Italian) fabrics and clothes.[59] Sometime between 1624 and 1626, Guazzoni left Seville for New Spain, and soon thereafter he went to live in Manila as Federighi's agent.[60] Until 1640 there was another merchant, Luis de Arieta, who also acted as Federighi's agent in Manila, although Guazzoni seems to have been Federighi's main contact in the Philippines.[61] Around 1640, Ascanio Guazzoni's economic

58   AGN, *Indiferente Virreinal*, caja-exp.: 5078-011, *Consulado*; AGN, *Indiferente Virreinal*, caja-exp.: 5056-050, *Consulado*.

59   AGN, *Indiferente Virreinal*, caja-exp.: 1812-009, *Consulado*.

60   AGN, *Indiferente Virreinal*, caja-exp.: 4230-010, *Filipinas*, 1–4.

61   AGN, *Indiferente Virreinal*, caja-exp.: 5511-001, *Consulado*, 5. Only three of Luis de Arieta's letters to Santi Federighi have survived – one written on 17 July 1628 (when Luis de Arieta had just arrived in Manila), another on 12 August 1628, and another on 25 July 1640: AGN, *Indiferente Virreinal*, caja-exp.: 5078-011, *Consulado*, 1; AGN, *Indiferente Virreinal*, caja-exp.: 5511-001, *Consulado*, 5; and AGN, *Indiferente Virreinal*, caja-exp.: 5098-011, *Filipinas*.

situation, and the investments of Santi Federighi in the Manila Galleon trade, changed dramatically.

All the letters from Ascanio Guazzoni to Santi Federighi and to other Mexican merchants, as well as from other Philippine merchants to Santi Federighi, state that Guazzoni lost all his capital during the 1630s following several dramatic events. Guazzoni had severe financial problems triggered by the non-payment of several debts – in particular with Don Andrés Pacheco and Don Fernando del Hoyo y Azoca, the other two Mexican merchants for whom Guazzoni was an agent in Manila. Apparently, Ascanio Guazzoni owed Don Fernando del Hoyo 12,000 pesos; at the same time, Don Andrés Pacheco owed Ascanio Guazzoni 10,000 pesos. Moreover, Guazzoni had unspecified financial problems with the governor of the Philippines. He also suffered some losses of merchandise in the galleon trade during the 1630s.[62] In general, many letters of these and other merchants mention the bad situation of the trans-Pacific trade and the fall of Ascanio Guazzoni.[63] As an accurate and desperate testimony of his troubles, Guazzoni sent a "report of losses from 1631 to 1640" (*memoria de pérdidas entre 1631 y 1640*) to Santi Federighi; see Table 5. His losses in these years, which totalled 76,000 pesos, were strongly linked to the prevailing state of war among European powers in Southeast Asia. Of these 76,000 pesos, the considerable sum of 25,000 pesos was due to merchandise lost on cargo ships and to money paid in compensation for damaged merchandise during the journey (loss of the ship *Magdalena* in 1631, loss of the vessel which came from Taiwan in 1637, loss of a vessel that went to Japan in 1638, loss of a vessel which sank in the Mariana Islands in 1639, losses of vessels in Cagayan in 1640, and interest paid for damaged merchandise in 1640): in essence, losses caused by the war with the Dutch and uncertainty associated with Manila's unfavourable geographical and navigation conditions.

Guazzoni's letters are full of references to the dangers for trade caused by bad navigation conditions and external military menace. For instance, in 1628 he wrote to Federighi and declared that the galleons could not reach Manila because, although "anchored in Mindanao 30 leagues from here, for now they cannot come because the gales have been very strong."[64] In 1642 he wrote that, when the galleons arrived at the Philippines the previous year, they "had to

---

62 AGN, *Indiferente Virreinal*, caja-exp.: 6015-023, *Consulado*; AGN, *Indiferente Virreinal*, caja-exp.: 6015-023, *Consulado*; AGN, *Indiferente Virreinal*, caja-exp.: 5720-003, *Filipinas*; AGN, *Indiferente Virreinal*, caja-exp.: 6015-023, *Consulado*; AGN, *Indiferente Virreinal*, caja-exp.: 5720-002, *Filipinas*; AGN, *Indiferente Virreinal*, caja-exp.: 6015-023, *Consulado*.
63 AGN, *Indiferente Virreinal*, caja-exp.: 5098-011, *Filipinas*.
64 AGN, *Indiferente Virreinal*, caja-exp.: 5078-011, *Consulado*, 53.

TABLE 5   Economic losses from 1631 to 1640 reported in 1640 by Ascanio Guazzoni to Santi
Federighi

Year	Cause	Loss
1631	Loss of the ship *Magdalena*	12,000 pesos
1632	Unpaid deposits	9,000 pesos
1634	Losses of merchandise in the journey to Castile	20,000 pesos
1636	Payment to Don Pedro de Quiroga according to the "agreement" (*conçierto*) with him	4,000 pesos
1637	Loss of the *patache* (vessel) which came from *Isla Hermosa* (Taiwan)	1,000 pesos
1638	Losses in the levy on the buyo (a type of plant) and tobacco	0 pesos
1638	Loss of a vessel that went to Japan	2,000 pesos
1639	Loss of a vessel which sank in the *Ladrones Islands* (Mariana Islands)	3,000 pesos
1640	Losses of vessels in Cagayan (Luzon)	2,000 pesos
1640	Interest paid for damaged merchandise	5,000 pesos
1640	Expenses on sustenance	5,000 pesos
1640	Debts to pay to Don Juan Cerezo	3,000 pesos
1640	Debts from Don Andrés Pacheco	10,000 pesos
		76,000 pesos

SOURCE: "MEMORIA DE LAS PERDIDAS QUE YO ASCANIO GUAZONI, VEÇINO DE MANILA, HE TENIDO DESDE EL AÑO DE 1631 HASTA ESTE DE 1640": AGN, *INDIFERENTE VIRREINAL*, CAJA-EXP.: 5098-010, *FILIPINAS*.

hide in a bay, in the area of Maubán, and it is a miracle that the Dutch enemy have not found them, because they have been waiting for them for more than two months in the Embocadero Strait."[65] In this case the Spanish galleons were lucky, but the Dutch often accomplished their objectives and captured or sank Manila galleons. In 1628, Guazzoni wrote that "the Dutch enemy sank the flagship that went to Ternate with another ship to the aid of another flagship, and 25 Spaniards died in the skirmish."[66] Such references are constantly made in these business letters. In a commercial system such as that of the Manila

---

65   AGN, *Indiferente Virreinal*, caja-exp.: 6015-023, *Consulado*.
66   AGN, *Indiferente Virreinal*, caja-exp.: 5078-011, *Consulado*, 53.

galleons – which was highly dependent on galleons' journeys and the chains of credit – the accumulation of debts and the impossibility of paying them owing to excessive losses of merchandise and capital would prove to be financially disastrous. This is what happened to Ascanio Guazzoni and probably to many other merchants during the 1630s.

For the years 1642 and 1643 there are five letters from another five Philippine agents of Santi Federighi who (except for Luis de Arieta) had been away until that time. These five new commercial contacts in Manila were Fernando de Perona, Juan de Mendoza, Fray Domingo González, Juan Bautista Montalvo, and Gabriel Gómez del Castillo. Perhaps it is simply a problem of surviving sources, but the sudden appearance of these new Manila agents in Federighi's correspondence of the early 1640s must surely indicate Federighi's strategy of commercial diversification in the Philippine trade. Not only the presence but also the content of these five letters from different agents, which refer to their business with the Manila galleons and the bad circumstances of Ascanio Guazzoni, support this contention.[67] Santi Federighi's and Ascanio Guazzoni's situations in the 1630s contrast with those of other merchants from earlier periods – such as the Mexican merchant Cristóbal de la Plaza and his only commercial agent in Manila, Juan de la Cruz Godines, whose correspondence between 1608 and 1615 bears witness to prosperous commercial activity between Manila and Mexico City during those years.[68] Yet because Santi Federighi died in 1643, little more is known about his case and the fate of his agents in Manila.

In sum, the fall of the trans-Pacific trade in the 1630s, within a long-distance and risky commercial system dominated by exchange on credit and finance through commercial companies, may have been dramatic for many Philippine merchants. The case of Ascanio Guazzoni, given the significance of the Mexican merchant for whom he worked, is probably paradigmatic. The decline of trade between Manila and Acapulco during the 1630s would also have been severe for the wholesalers of Mexico – although these merchants had other sources of wealth because the internal markets of the Americas were

---

67   These letters are in AGN, *Indiferente Virreinal*, caja-exp.: 6015-023. Especially relevant is the case of Juan Bautista Montalvo. Althoug he had met Santi Federighi 20 years earlier, from his letter it can be deduced that he had played a token role in Federighi's businesses in Manila shortly before 1640. The letter from Gabriel Gómez del Castillo had been written in 1643 and was sent not to Santi Federighi but rather to Pedro López de Soto, since Santi Federighi had died that year and López de Soto was one of the executors of Federighi's properties: AGN, *Indiferente Virreinal*, caja-exp.: 5720-004, *Filipinas*.

68   Letters of 1612 between Cristóbal de la Plaza and his *encomenderos* in Acapulco (Francisco Pacheco, Martín de Arteaga, and Bernardino de Angulo) reveal that his business in the Manila Galleon trade was flourishing in the early 1600s: AGN, *Indiferente Virreinal*, caja-exp.: 1776-001, *Consulado*.

developing strongly during the first decades of the seventeenth century. In response to a series of negative events, Mexican merchants would have changed their investment strategies as necessary during the period when trade via the Manila galleons became riskier. The reduction (or, more accurately, the concentration in fewer hands) of Mexican merchants' investments in the Manila Galleon trade, the diversion of their capital to other, internal segments of the New Spanish market, and the use of more commercial agents for their businesses in Manila were all actions taken to counteract the negative events in the Pacific Ocean during the 1630s. The uncertainty associated with trans-Pacific trade was likely reduced following the Peace of Westphalia in 1648. By then, however, the Dutch and English were dominating ever greater proportions of Southeast Asian trade.

4.3   The Struggle for Silver and the Regulation of Trans-Pacific Trade

The shrinking trans-Pacific trade after several decades of growth took place alongside a series of economic and political problems that emerged within the Spanish Empire after the opening of the Manila Galleon route and then accelerated during the 1630s, when most agents of the Empire – especially those from the metropole – had begun to suffer the first signs of crisis in Castile. The trade between New Spain and the Philippines was a profitable enterprise for Mexican merchants, which led them to pressure the Crown into liberalising trans-Pacific trade to the greatest extent possible. However, the Manila Galleon trade also led to increasing amounts of American silver ending up in Southeast Asia; Sevillian merchants viewed this as an unacceptable trend because it meant that bullion was being diverted from the Atlantic trade to the Pacific, where the investment of Castilian merchants did not reach. Scholars such as Del Valle Pavón, Hoberman, Sales Colín and Bonialian (among others) have focused on some of these political conflicts within the Spanish Empire that brought the Hispanic elites into conflict, particularly the Mexican wholesalers and the Andalusian traders.[69] These conflicts are addressed in this section

---

69   Hoberman, *Mexico's Merchant Elite*, 214–22; Ostwald Sales Colín, "Una Coyuntura del Comercio Transpacífico: Fuentes Complementarias para la Visita de Pedro Quiroga en Acapulco, 1635–1640," in *Comercio Marítimo Colonial. Nuevas Interpretaciones y Últimas Fuentes*, ed. Carmen Yuste López (México, D.F.: Instituto Nacional de Antropología e Historia, 1997), 127–46; Del Valle Pavón, "Los Mercaderes de México,": 213–40; Mariano Ardash Bonialian, *El Pacífico hispanoamericano. Política y comercio asiático en el imperio español (1680-11784). La centralidad de lo marginal* (México, D. F.: El Colegio de México, 2012), 68–79.

by referring to some new sources and, above all, approaching them from the broad perspective of the Spanish Empire as a "composite monarchy" in its global context. In this way, it will be possible to identify the institutional changes that resulted from the political bargaining over the Manila Galleon trade and to demonstrate how such changes, after the years in which the establishment of a merchant guild in Mexico City benefited the Manila Galleon, affected the performance of trade in the opposite direction.

The diversion of bullion from the Atlantic to the Pacific Ocean triggered a political game involving pressure on the Crown and lengthy negotiation processes that resulted in several institutional changes and ad hoc norms that affected the trans-Pacific trade. The commercial elite of Seville were so concerned about their loss of privileges in the American markets that the Cardinal-Archbishop of Seville himself, Fernando Niño de Guevara (1601–1609), interceded with the King on behalf of the Sevillian oligarchies. In 1603, the Cardinal-Archbishop sent a letter to the King that contained the following text:

> This trade [*the trans-Atlantic trade*] has become so weak that if Your Majesty does not act quickly, in a few years this trade may collapse completely [...] The first [*reason*], which has to do with the Philippines, is the most damaging of all, because much money in reales is invested in those provinces, being exchanged for the worst and most useless things [...] The damages are great. Firstly, New Spain and Peru are so awash with silks and fabrics of so little value that when the fleets arrive at the Americas from Spain, there is no way to sell the merchandise and thus no one dares to load anything in the fleets. Secondly, given the abundant vineyards of Peru and the silks, fabrics, iron and other things provided by the Philippines, if the Indies can survive without Spain there is no sure way to keep them, since until now the Indies have been maintained because of their dependence on these kingdoms [*Castile*] and the trade with them.[70]

The Cardinal-Archbishop of Seville was denouncing the fact that that not only silk and textiles but even products such as iron were being introduced from the Philippines into the Americas. The rhetoric, though perhaps exaggerated to reflect the archbishop's interests, reveals how much the Manila Galleon trade was damaging the businesses of Seville's merchants. Although the Sevillian elites induced the King to restrict by law the volume of trans-Pacific trade, they felt that the problem

---

70   "Copia de carta original del cardenal arzobispo de Sevilla al rey sobre el remedio de la contratación de las Islas Filipinas con la Nueva España y el Perú" (28 October 1603), in *Colección de Documentos Inéditos para la Historia de España*, vol. 52 (Madrid, 1852), 565–72.

persisted. Trade between the Philippines and New Spain was on the agenda of several meetings of Seville's merchant guild, where traders manifested their uncertainties due to the growing trade between the Americas and the Philippines and the reduction of silver that this trade entailed for their Atlantic interests. The minutes of such meetings are full of merchants' declarations that argued for outright prohibiting trans-Pacific trade:

> Francisco Gallo de Escalada said that he is in the same situation. He gets no profit from the investments in the fleet of Tierra Firme [*bound for Panama/ Peru*], nor does he from the investments in the fleet of New Spain, where he has many businesses. The merchandise from Castile has no value there because of the considerable merchandise that comes there from China. This trade consumes the silver of New Spain. And much silver goes from Peru to New Spain, since no one there tries to invest silver in Spain, but [*rather*] in China via the Philippines. Because of the permission that His Majesty has given, more than three million in silver goes there every year. And if His Majesty does not remove that trade, [*then*] the Indies trade will be finished.[71]

Yet because the trade between Manila and Acapulco was neither forbidden nor sufficiently restricted for the Sevillian merchants' taste, they changed strategy: the elites of Seville proposed several times to open a direct commercial route from Seville to the Philippines – but this, too, was refused by the King.[72]

The Indies Council (*Consejo de Indias*) studied this economic clash between these two powerful elites of the Empire. The Indies Council asked Horacio Levanto, a Genoese merchant and naturalised Castilian who settled in Seville in 1610, to write a report (*memorial*) about the trade between China and New Spain. Levanto had amassed a great fortune as a merchant after having been in New Spain for fifteen years. In Seville, he bought several bureaucratic positions (*oficios*), including that of "high measurer" (*medidor mayor*) of the Seville corn exchange and "foundry manager" (*fundidor*) of Seville's mint.[73] Levanto carried out the task assigned and in 1621 sent the Indies Council his "Report on the Trade of China with New Spain and These Kingdoms" (*Memorial sobre el*

---

71   AGI, *Consulados*, L. 1 (21 May 1611).

72   In response to military threats in the Philippines, the King sent a fleet to Manila and permitted the merchants of Seville to load some merchandise; however, he did not allow commercial ships to return directly to the Iberian Peninsula without first passing through the Americas: AGI, *Consulados*, L. 1 (17 May 1616); AGI, *Consulados*, L. 1 (6 July 1616); AGI, *Consulados*, L. 1 (30 August 1616); AGI, *Consulados*, L. 1 (18 April 1619).

73   Lutgardo García Fuentes, *Los Peruleros y el Comercio de Sevilla con las Indias, 1580–1630* (Sevilla: Universidad de Sevilla, 1997), 205, 234.

Trato de la China con la Nueva España, y Estos Reynos).[74] This report confirmed the extreme competitiveness of Chinese silk in New Spanish markets. Levanto criticised in particular the great diversion of American silver to Southeast Asia as resulting from the actions of only a few merchants in Mexico City, Puebla de los Ángeles, Manila, and China. However, Levanto was less radical than the Cardinal-Archbishop and the Sevillian merchants, who had sought the closure of trans-Pacific trade and abandonment of the Philippines. Levanto proposed that the Indies Council prohibit only the trade of silk, which was the most competitive textile, while keeping open the trade of other textiles (e.g., cotton).[75]

The American merchant elites also pulled strings in favour of their own economic interests. The wholesalers of the merchant guild of Mexico proposed that the King relax the restrictions on trans-Pacific trade and so actually liberalise it.[76] The privileges of Mexico's merchants were so challenged by the pressure of Sevillian wholesalers that they did something unusual for the sixteenth century: Mexicans contacted not only Peruvian merchants but also some of the main institutions of Peru in order to stop the placement of limits on the Manila Galleon trade. Some of this correspondence has survived in Mexican archives. The following text is the fragment of a letter sent by the city council of Lima to that of Mexico City in 1599; in it, the Peruvians ask the Mexicans for help and mutual cooperation against the royal warrants that were limiting trade with Asia:

> In this city [*Lima*], the last decree of His Majesty has been published, as well as the information about efforts of the residents of the city of Seville to hinder the entry of merchandise from China to this kingdom, which is very damaging. As Your Honour [*the city council of Mexico City*] understands how damaging it may be for this city and kingdom, it has been requested to His Majesty that the judge who came to carry out the aforementioned decree not do so. For this, the city [*Lima*] has sent a representative and papers to solve this problem, which is common to both kingdoms [*New Spain and Peru*]. And this city asks Your Honour to help in finding the solution to this problem by entrusting it to the people

---

74   Horacio Levanto, "Memorial sober [sic] el Trato de la China con la Nueva España, y Estos Reynos": BN, R/17270 (6). Although this report is not dated, the report sent to the King by the *procurador general* of the Philippines in the 1620s dates Levanto's report to 1621: *Colección de Documentos Inéditos del Archivo de Indias*, vol. 6, 1866, Madrid, 478.

75   Levanto, "Memorial," 1–3.

76   Hoberman, *Mexico's Merchant Elite*, 214–17; Del Valle Pavón, "Los Mercaderes de México": 213–40.

whom Your Honour has in the Court and who are in contact with this city. At the service of Your Honour, whom Our Lord keeps and blesses.
Lima, October 18th 1599[77]

A few years later, the city council of Mexico dispatched one or two representatives to the King's Court of Madrid to negotiate over commercial restrictions on the trade with Manila. Their argument was based on the negative effects that those restrictions could have on maintaining the enclave of the Philippine Islands:

> Today [*the alderman*] Francisco Escudero de Figueroa said that it is widely known in this city [*Mexico City*] that the decrees made public under the king's command limit the consignments of money to China, which reduces the trade with that country. Given the problems of that kingdom [*the Philippines*], which he knows as a person who has been there at the service of His Majesty, the kingdom may be depopulated at a time when people are needed more than ever to keep the Philippines and the Maluku. Now there are more enemies than before, such as Dutch, Flemish and other nations who were already trading spices. Given the decline of trade, people are discouraged from going to that kingdom, because even though they go there with their wealth and without salary from His Majesty, once these people go there, they are bound to its defence. However, the people there are not wealthy and they cannot be maintained without the people here [*Mexico's merchants*], which implies many problems for those there and here. After being in touch with His Excellency the Viceroy Montesclaros he accepted, in light of wise advice, that one or two knights must go to the King's Court to ask His Majesty to keep that trade, which is very important for this kingdom. Furthermore, it is hardly credible that the trade of Castile would disappear, because it is very well supported. I ask Your Honour to discuss this issue.[78]

The Mexican merchants' interests in trans-Pacific trade were so extensive, the damage to the local interests of the Andalusian merchants was so threatening, and thus the potential for conflict was so great that even the highest authorities of New Spain (the viceroys) were involved in the tensions surrounding trade with Asia. The viceroys were the King's representatives in the American territories and, as such, were supposed to have no personal but rather only

---

77   AHAM, *Actas del Cabildo* (17 December 1599), vol. 353A.
78   AHAM, *Actas del Cabildo* (12 January 1607), vol. 16A.

state interests in these matters. However, the viceroys' initial opposition to trans-Pacific trade in the 1570s quickly dissipated with the emergence of growing and profitable businesses based on the Manila Galleon trade in the years 1580–1600. Before the trans-Pacific trade was well established – at a time when Manila and its hinterland had not completed the economic transition from a commercial agricultural economy to international trade – the Viceroy of New Spain (Martín Enríquez de Almansa, 1568–1580) was so against maintaining trade with China that he proposed to suspend it completely between New Spain and Manila:

> Up till now, this trade seems to be more damaging than beneficial, as I have written before, because nothing of value is brought here, because they trade with little money, and they only take *reales* away from this kingdom. I think they must have taken 40,000 *reales*, part of which is sold by the *encomenderos* and another part is sent to bring things from China and the Islands. There are processes to stop and prohibit this, but I have not dared employ them as those who live there are maintained by this trade, and many others wish to go there.[79]

Yet his successor, the Viceroy Count of La Coruña (1580–1583), came to support the trans-Pacific trade and stressed the great profits that the King could obtain from trading with China.[80] The Viceroy Marquis of Villamanrique (1585–1590) was even more explicit in his defence of such trade; in 1586 he sent a letter to the King in reply to a message in which the King seemed extremely critical of the trade between the New Spaniards and Asia. The King argued that "the silks and other things brought from China and the Philippine Islands to these kingdoms are very insignificant"; however, the viceroy used political, economic, and religious arguments to persuade the King that there were advantages to maintaining that trade. According to the Marquis of Villamanrique, the trade with China was indispensable "to maintain the grandeur of the Monarchy," crucial "in keeping the Philippine populations and Chinese merchants within the Christian fold," and also vital because all the silks and cloths from Asia were of better quality than those produced in New Spain.[81] Later, in the first decades of the seventeenth century, New Spanish viceroys gave total support to the merchants of Mexico against Sevillian merchants.

---

79   AGI, *México*, 20, N. 1.
80   "Cartas del Virrey Conde de la Coruña" (1 April 1581): AGI, *México*, 20, N. 60.
81   "Carta del Virrey Marqués de Villamanrique" (10 August 1586): AGI, *México*, 20, N. 35.

Besides the wholesalers and authorities from Seville, Mexico City, and Peru, the fourth party in this conflict was the elite of the Philippine Islands, who – although less powerful and further from the main Hispanic centres of power – had no qualms about pressuring the Crown to act on behalf of their own interests. The Philippine merchants, who did not have a guild until the second half of the eighteenth century and were highly dependent on Mexico's merchants, channelled their economic interests and political action through the main institutions of the archipelago: the city council, the *Audiencia Real*, the governor, and the bishop. In the 1610s and 1620s the Philippine elite, whose economy depended upon the strength of the trade with China and New Spain, participated in the conflict over the trans-Pacific trade. Sometime after 1620, Don Juan Grau y Monfalcón, who was a representative (*procurador general*) on Manila's city council, presented to the King and the Indies Council a long report addressing this issue and entitled "Report on the Claims of the City of Manila and Other Islands of the Archipelago in Their Trade with New Spain" (*Memorial sobre las Pretensiones de la Ciudad de Manila y Demas Islas del Archipielago en su Comercio con la Nueva España*).[82] The report acknowledged that some American silver escaped across the Pacific Ocean, but Grau y Monfalcón argued that this was due to excesses of the Mexican merchants who monopolised trade involving the Manila galleons. This point notwithstanding, on every page he defended the need for maintaining the trade for social and political-religious reasons as well as for reasons related to New Spain's demand for Chinese silks. According to Grau y Monfalcón, abandoning the Philippines would be a disaster for all Castilians who lived off trade in the archipelago, whereafter the Dutch would immediately take this strategic part of Asia. He also exaggeratedly pointed out that Chinese silks were less competitive in the American markets because they were consumed mainly by segments of the New Spanish population (e.g., indigenous peoples) who could hardly afford to buy the more expensive Castilian textiles – this claim by Grau y Molfancón was doubtless an exaggeration.[83] Overall, then, the economic tensions in a composite monarchy such as the Spanish Empire – within which the balance of power was the only guarantee of internal peace for the King – were leading to severe political and institutional conflicts.

The sources of the progressively tighter restrictions on trans-Pacific trade are to be found in these political conflicts, especially in the pressures put on the Crown by the Sevillian elite. When the Manila galleons first sailed,

---

82   *Colección de Documentos Inéditos del Archivo de Indias*, vol. 6 (Madrid, 1866), 364–484.
83   *Ibid.*, 471–79.

there were no limits on the trade between the Philippines and the Americas, and trade between Manila and Peru was also legal. In 1582, however, trade between the Philippines and Peru was forbidden. Later, the trade between Peru and New Spain was also prohibited, including all traffic between Acapulco and Callao, the port of Lima.[84] Hence trans-Pacific trade was confined to the ports of Manila and Acapulco, and restrictions were placed on the cargos, tonnages, and number of galleons. The royal restrictions on trans-Pacific trade applied mainly to the value (in pesos) of goods and of silver that investors were allowed to load. In 1593, a royal decree from Philip II limited the trade between the Philippines and New Spain to 250,000 pesos of merchandise from Manila to Acapulco and 500,000 pesos of silver from Acapulco to Manila. Furthermore, only two galleons of 300 tonnes each were allowed per year. This royal decree was renewed in 1604, 1606, 1619, and 1640 (see Table 6).

These royal limitations were problematic for those involved in the trans-Pacific trade, since a great deal of that trade involved smuggling. The successive renewals of trade limits between Acapulco and Manila appear to confirm the extent of smuggling in the trans-Pacific exchanges. Even viceroys took part in smuggling via the Manila Galleon trade: the Prince of Esquilache, Viceroy of Peru between 1614 and 1621, was prosecuted for (and convicted on) two counts of smuggling through this trade route.[85]

Smuggling was not a problem for the Mexican merchants if the King chose not to combat it, as was the case until the 1630s. Before then, royal intervention in the trans-Pacific trade was limited to the regulation of licences for exporting silver from New Spain to Manila; smuggling was seldom punished except with regard to trade between New Spain and Peru.[86] Mexican merchants traded above the legal limits in connivance with their agents in Acapulco and Manila and also with royal servants, who conveniently declined to open the boxes of merchandise in those ports.

However, the situation changed in the mid-1630s. The King, pressed by the merchants of Seville and the Crown's financial problems, sent the fraud inspector (*visitador*) Don Pedro de Quiroga – judge of the *Real Audiencia* of Valladolid – to investigate illegal trade in Acapulco in 1635. Don Pedro de

---

84   Borah, *Early Colonial Trade*, 116–27.

85   Antoni Picazo Muntaner, "El Comercio Sedero de Filipinas y su Influencia en la Economía de España en el Siglo XVII," in *La Declinación de la Monarquía Hispánica. VII[a] Reunión Científica de la Fundación Española de Historia Moderna*, ed. Francisco J. Aranda Pérez (Cuenca: UCLM, 2004), 508.

86   Del Valle Pavón, "Los Mercaderes de México:" 213–40.

TABLE 6   Maximum allowed value of trans-Pacific trade (in pesos of "pieces of eight"), 1593–1815

Year	Acapulco to Manila	Manila to Acapulco
1593	500,000	250,000
1604*	500,000	250,000
1606*	500,000	250,000
1619*	500,000	250,000
1640*	500,000	250,000
1697*	500,000	250,000
1702	500,000	300,000
1734	1,000,000	500,000
1779	1,500,000	750,000

Note: Asterisks (*) denote years during which previous restrictions were renewed.

SOURCES: JULIÁN DE PAREDES, *RECOPILACIÓN DE LEYES DE LOS REYNOS DE INDIAS*, T. 6, IV, MADRID, 1681; CARMEN YUSTE LÓPEZ, *EL COMERCIO DE LA NUEVA ESPAÑA CON FILIPI-NAS, 1590–1785*, MÉXICO, D.F.: INSTITUTO NACIONAL DE ANTROPOLOGÍA E HISTORIA, 1984, PP. 14–16; CARMEN YUSTE LÓPEZ: *EMPORIOS TRANS-PACÍFICOS. COMERCIANTES MEXICA-NOS EN MANILA, 1710–1815*, MÉXICO, D.F.: UNAM, PP. 34–38.

Quiroga took his task so seriously that he ordered boxes and bales of merchandise and silver to be opened in search of illicit shipments. His reports brought about a 1636 "agreement" (*concierto*), between the merchant guild of Mexico City and the royal representatives, whereby Mexican merchants paid 600,000 pesos to the King plus a "service" (*servicio*) to the Crown of 300,000 pesos.

The wording of this agreement is crucial for understanding that this payment of 900,000 pesos should be viewed in the context of a composite, "negotiated" monarchy in which merchant guilds were a cog in the Spanish Empire's imperial machine. The required payment was not strictly a fine for exceeding the limits of legal trade, as these were negotiated sums. Pressure from the Sevillian elites combined with the dire state of the Crown's finances led the King to increase his control over trans-Pacific trade. The financial context framing the royal decision to gain greater control over the trans-Pacific trade was marked by cash problems that stemmed from the war against the Dutch following rupture of the Twelve Years' Truce (1621), the Crown's bankruptcy in 1627, and especially the intervention by Spain in the Thirty Years' War and its direct war against France in 1635.[87]

The Spanish Crown made use of financial tools such as "loans" (*donativo*) and "services" (*servicio*) during the sixteenth, seventeenth, and eighteenth centuries.[88] The former was a mixture of extraordinary taxes and loans that the most powerful agents of the monarchy (e.g., nobles, cities, and merchant guilds) paid the King, which he returned with interest. Even the "donations and forced loans" (*donativo gracioso y préstamo*) had a strong contractual and collateral component. The "services" are more accurately described as an extraordinary tax paid by an agent of the monarchy to the Crown. These "services" were not a form of punishment but rather payments whose sums were the subject of bargaining with the Crown. In no case were these payments based on obligations imposed by the monarchy; instead, they were based on negotiations that depended upon the recognition of mutual rights and duties within the monarchical context.[89]

The 300,000 pesos paid to the Crown by the merchant guild of Mexico was a "service." The 600,000 pesos was neither a loan nor an extraordinary tax; it is defined in all the documents as an "agreement" (*concierto*) between Mexican merchants and royal representatives. Even though this sum was ostensibly a punishment for many years of illicit trade, the 600,000 pesos must be considered within a context of the monarchy's financial needs. The sums paid instead reflect a negotiated agreement between the merchant guild of Mexico and the royal inspector Pedro Quiroga, with the intervention of the viceroy:

> This merchant guild, in order to avoid the damages that the execution of the penalties imposed by the royal decrees would cause to the trade between the Philippines, Peru and other parts of the South Sea [*the Pacific Ocean*], tried to set out and agree this with the aforementioned Don

---

87 Carmen Sanz Ayán, *Estado, Monarquía y Finanzas. Estudios de Historia Financiera en Tiempos de los Austrias* (Madrid: Centro de Estudios Políticos y Constitucionales, 2004), 21–59.

88 The Hispanic Crown frequently tapped institutions – mostly the Cortes but also municipal institutions and merchant guilds of all its kingdoms (especially Castile) – for financial "services" during the early modern period; see Miguel Artola Gallego, *La Hacienda del Antiguo Régimen* (Madrid: Alianza, 1982).

89 Alejandra Irigoin and Regina Grafe, "A Stakeholder Empire: The Political Economy of the Spanish Imperial Rule in America," *Economic History Review* 65, no. 2 (2011): 627–31; Herbert S. Klein, *The American Finances of the Spanish Empire. Royal Income and Expenditures in Colonial Mexico, Peru, and Bolivia, 1680–1809* (Albuquerque, NM: University of New Mexico Press, 1998).

Pedro Quiroga. To this end, many committees and negotiations were made. With the authority of His Excellency the Marquis of Cadereyta, Viceroy of this New Spain, this guild, according to the agreement, had to pay His Majesty 600,000 pesos of silver pieces of eight, into the Royal Treasury of this city.[90]

In this incident, Mexican and Philippine merchants acted together in their common interests. The latter nonetheless secured an agreement from the King stating that only the Mexican merchants, through their guild, had to pay the "service" and "agreement" to the Crown. Mexico's merchant guild established a Committee of Distribution (*Junta de Repartimiento*) tasked with determining the quantities of cash that each merchant had to pay toward the total of 600,000 pesos, which was to be paid over a period of three years (i.e., 200,000 pesos per year). This committee opened complex proceedings through which the accountants (*contadores*), lawyers and notaries of the merchant guild had to establish how much those Mexican wholesalers who had traded with the Philippines between 1631 and 1635 ought to pay to the Crown. A huge mobilisation of resources was required to put this payment scheme into operation. The proceedings fostered frenetic activity in the merchant guild concerning how much to collect from each member and how best to collect it. Several pages would be needed even to outline the complexity of bureaucratic work and institutions created within the merchant guild to deal, for the first time in its history, with a payment to the monarchy like the "agreement" and "service" of 600,000 and 300,000 pesos. Much of this complexity resulted from creating a new committee (and subcommittees) to deal with merchant payments. After several discussions about the criteria for distributing payment and the implementation of some projects, it was decided that each merchant should pay four-and-a-half per cent of the value of merchandise he had traded between 1631 and 1635. Although it is hard to know what the profit margins of merchants were in the Manila Galleon trade, this four-and-a-half per cent was likely viewed as a low tax because it was charged in addition to the *alcabala* tax, which was jointly managed by the merchant guild and the city council.[91] Notwithstanding the negotiated character of these payments, they could hardly have improved the performance of trans-Pacific trade when it was already in decline.

---

90   AGN, *Indiferente Virreinal*, caja-exp.: 3855-003, *Filipinas*, 9.

91   See details in José L. Gasch-Tomás, "Mecanismos de funcionamiento institucional en el imperio hispánico. El Comercio de los Galeones de Manila y el Consulado de Comerciantes de México en la década de 1630," *Revista Jerónimo Zurita* 90 (2015): 56-74.

As it turned out, the trans-Pacific trade was re-established after Quiroga's death in 1639. By royal prerogative, the King agreed to maintain the trade as it was prior to 1635, which is to say he would not prosecute illegal trade.[92] The merchants of Mexico City had thus overcome the restrictions and confiscations. The Hispanic Crown kept the trade between New Spain and the Philippines at pre-1635 conditions, and the Mexican and Philippine merchants enjoyed a pre-1635 legal framework until the eighteenth century. There was what could be described as legislative passivity in regard to the Manila Galleon trade from 1640 until the early eighteenth century. However, the eighteenth century saw renewed conflict between the Mexican and Andalusian elites over the Manila galleons.[93] This renewal of tensions demonstrated the conflict's structural nature and also the monarchy's inability to balance market expansion both in the Atlantic and the Pacific while relying on the same sources of silver or to balance the interests of its own various commercial agents.

This episode, the institutional changes that resulted, and the bargaining processes between different powers of the empire must all be understood in reference to the composite character of the Hispanic monarchy and the importance of the merchant powers within it. The royal concession to establish merchant guilds reduced wholesale traders' transaction expenses, not only because it allowed the merchants to institute and use faster and cheaper mercantile courts but also because it entailed a form of collective action that guaranteed Crown's commitment and facilitated trade expansion.[94] The way in which the trans-Pacific trade crisis of 1636–1639 was solved exemplifies the process of collective action by Mexican merchants. A ruler (in this case, the King) finally agreed to restore the Manila Galleon trade system to its operational status quo over the previous 40 years. The Mexican merchant guild had gained the privilege of collecting commercial taxes such as the *avería* and the *alcabala* – in some cases along with the city council – through contracts that were similarly

---

92   The prerogative of 19 September 1639 stated that "the customs and norms extant before Pedro Quiroga will be kept" (*se guarde la constumbre, y estilo que havia antes de Pedro Quiroga*) and "ordered, regarding the assessments and registers, not to open bales, nor to weigh the boxes of the Philippine Islands' ships that arrived in Acapulco, unless there were denunciations' (*mandó que en cuanto a las evaluaciones y registros, no abriese los fardos, ni pesase los cajones de las naos de las yslas Filipinas, que llegase a Acapulco, si no fuese precediendo las denunciaciones*). Quoted in Sales Colín, *El Movimiento Portuario*, 129–30.

93   Bonialian, *El Pacífico Hispánico*, 68–9 and 131–40; Yuste López, *Emporios Transpacíficos*, 360–4.

94   Avner Greif, Paul Milgro, and Barry R. Weingast, "Coordination, Commitment, and Enforcement: The Case of the Merchant Guild," *Journal of Political Economy* 102, no. 4 (1994): 745–77; Avner Greif, "Securing Property Rights from the Grabbing Hand of the State. The Merchant Guild," in Greif, *Institutions*, 91–123.

negotiated among the city council, the guild, and the Crown.[95] The merchants were aware, however, that these advantages came at a price: the payment of future compensation to the ruler. Financial support of the Crown's military needs – by way of loans from the Mexican and other merchant guilds of the Spanish Empire – was an ongoing cost of business.[96] The payment of 900,000 pesos agreed to in the arrangement of 1636 fell within this framework.

On the other side of the Atlantic, the Sevillian and Castilian merchants managed to impose legal restrictions on the trans-Pacific trade, which rendered exchanges between Manila and Acapulco less secure owing to the danger of punishment for smuggling. These conflicts gave rise to legal measures and bargaining games that allowed the King not only to raise cash for his European wars but also to keep the various conflicting parties satisfied, thereby avoiding a rupture of the political system upon which the empire was based.

4.4   Conclusions

The growth of trade between New Spain and China via Manila was – alongside production of silver, diversification of investment and the existence of cheap labour in the Americas – a part of the changes that contributed to the growing economic autonomy of the Americas during the seventeenth century. However, development of the trans-Pacific trade triggered interests both for and against it in distant parts of the Empire. The playing out of these conflicting interests and bargaining processes, in which the Crown was a key actor, defined new legal frameworks that affected institutions. Although the conflicts of interests and bargaining processes between elites and the Crown did not aid economic growth in the long term, they were crucial to preserving the Empire's political system, including the American territories. The political conflict over the trans-Pacific trade (and its resolution) is a vivid example of that importance. There are also reasons to suppose that – in some historical moments,

---

95   Robert S. Smith, "Sales Taxes in New Spain, 1575–1770," *Hispanic American Historical Review* 28, no. 1 (1948): 2–37.

96   Del Valle Pavón, "El Apoyo Financiero," 131–50; Irigoin and Grafe, "A Stakeholder Empire," 647–49. Seville's merchant guild, for instance, provided several "loans" (*donativos*) to the Crown after its foundation in 1543. In exchange, that guild was awarded progressively more power and privileges: determining the volume of ships, collecting some local taxes, establishing prices of merchandise, and regulating the "naturalisation" of foreigners (which was indispensable for participating in the Indies trade). See José M. Oliva Melgar, *El Monopolio de Indias en el Siglo XVII y la Economía Andaluza. La Oportunidad que Nunca Existió* (Huelva: Universidad de Huelva, 2004), 18–19.

geographical areas, and economic fields – negotiation between elites and the Crown resulted in institutional changes that favoured economic growth. At the end of the sixteenth century, contributions made by increased silver production, strengthening of internal markets, and developing trans-Atlantic and trans-Pacific trade to the creation of Mexico City's merchant guild, after decades of fruitless requests, illustrate the significance of colonial elites in institutional change. These institutional changes were ultimately favourable for these groups and for the development of international trade generally. The role of the guild (along with many other formal and informal institutions) in reducing transaction costs – through such methods as the enforcement of collective action for Mexican merchants and the establishment of a non-public and more efficient system of mercantile justice – can hardly be denied, especially in light of the improving economic situation between 1590 and 1630 in New Spain.

In the 1630s the monarchy's financial needs, the enter of Dutch and English in Iberian commercial circuits of Southeast Asia, and the decline of the trans-Pacific trade combined to alter the political equilibrium of the Spanish Empire. These changing circumstances aggravated tensions between the most powerful wholesalers of the monarchy, who formed guilds and other local institutions while watching their trading profits and surpluses decline because of a seemingly permanent state of international war. In the context of political conflicts between the elites of this empire, the Crown acted much as a referee – although, of course, always focusing on its finances and its income from taxes on international trade. Against this backdrop of financial need, international hostility, and Seville's pressure on the Manila Galleon trade, the King sent the fraud inspector Don Pedro Quiroga to Acapulco. The subsequent political negotiations of 1636–1639 between the merchant guild of Mexico and the royal authorities in New Spain resulted in an agreement under which Mexican merchants would pay the Crown 900,000 pesos charged on trans-Pacific commerce, whereafter the trans-Pacific trade resumed in accord with pre-1636 laws. The payment was devised within the monarchy's political bargaining mechanisms and was based on the price that merchants were willing to pay in exchange for advantages derived from the foundation of their guild.

The Manila Galleon trade continued for almost another 200 years, albeit with some changes after the 1630s. In the 1620s and especially during the political and economic turmoil of the 1630s, the trade via Manila galleons – which had always been risky – became progressively weaker and even less safe. Many Mexican merchants withdrew their capital from the galleons and diverted it to economic activities other than international trade, particularly internal American commerce. The Manila Galleon trade was likely less profitable in the 1630s than it was around 1600 because of the growing uncertainty, the worldwide convergence of silver's value and the likely oversupply of Asian goods in the New Spanish markets. Only the richest merchants of Mexico City could continue trading across the Pacific Ocean, but using new commercial strategies. These merchants both diversified and increased the number of their commercial agents in Manila as a means to reduce commercial risk, for otherwise the Manila Galleon trade would not have been a viable enterprise.

Now that we have taken trans-Pacific trade into the account of economic restructuring of New Spain and the Spanish Empire's seventeenth-century decline in the trans-Pacific trade, the picture becomes more complete. Many elements played a part in that decline: the weaknesses of the Spanish trade against its rivals; the falling American silver production at the end of the 1630s; the growing politico-economic isolation of Japan in the 1630s; the Chinese crisis of the 1640s; the expansion of the English and Dutch empires in the Atlantic and their success to gain more sources of trade in Asia than the Portuguese Empire, which got its independence from the king of Spain in 1640; the higher danger and uncertainty associated to the Manila Galleon trade than to the Atlantic trade; and the politico-economic contradictions derived from the rise of the trans-Pacific trade from the 1580s to *circa* 1630 within the Spanish Empire. That dominance was made possible by the development of Atlantic trade in American foodstuffs and slaves, the migration of thousands of people across the ocean, and the spread of the northern European companies' trade from the Atlantic to Asia. There were also consequences felt on the other side of the world: the rise of the Atlantic economy, in terms of trade volume, finally removed trans-Pacific and other interregional trade as significant players in the global game during the eighteenth century. This decline notwithstanding, the entry of Asian products in the Spanish Empire had long-term consequences in the spheres of craftsmanship production and consumption.

CHAPTER 5

Impact of the Manila Galleon Trade on Hispanic Production of Manufactured Goods

In our age of globalisation, in which cultural interaction can be found almost everywhere, historians are discovering the potential of using approaches that emphasise imitation, exchange, intersection, translation, and transformation of artefacts and practices in the making of history.[1] In this view, cultural relations and commercial exchanges between Europe and Asia in history are now being understood from viewpoints that move away from the Eurocentric perspectives used previously and that stress the processes of transformation resulting from such exchanges.[2] Within the histories of consumption and demand, studies show how the expansion of trade and the taste for Asian products – such as Chinese porcelain and Indian cottons – fostered processes of imitation, innovation, and even technical transfer from Asia to Europe. In addressing product innovation, Styles focused on seventeenth- and eighteenth-century London and described how, in the context of imports from abroad and the development of new tastes for new goods, many products were copied, adapted, reinvented, and then put on sale in the English markets.[3] Berg showed that taste and aesthetics were essential to product imitation, which influenced consumer markets and manufacturing innovation during the eighteenth century. Examples include the development of "import substitution" industries, which imitated and reinvented Asian products such as Chinese porcelain and played a role in some transformations prior to British industrialisation.[4] Interaction with the East, innovation in production, and the development of new aesthetics were linked in the British case to the creation of new consumer goods.[5] Knowledge, techniques, and skill transfers from Asia to

---

1 Peter Burke, *Cultural Hybridity* (Cambridge: Polity Press, 2009).

2 Michael North, ed., *Artistic and Cultural Exchanges between Europe and Asia* (Farnham: Ashgate, 2010); Madelaine Herren, Martin Rüesch and Christiane Sibille (*Transcultural History. Theories, Methods, Sources*, Heidelberg: Springer, 2012).

3 John Styles, "Product Innovation in Early Modern London," *Past and Present* 168 (2000): 124–69.

4 Maxine Berg, "From Imitation to Invention: Creating Commodities in Eighteenth-Century Britain," *Economic History Review* 55, no. 1 (2002): 1–30; Maxine Berg, "In Pursuit of Luxury: Global History and British Consumer Goods in the Eighteenth Century," *Past and Present* 182 (2004): 85–142.

5 Maxine Berg, *Luxury and Pleasure in Eighteenth-Century Britain* (Oxford: Oxford University Press, 2005), 85–110.

Europe were present in this expansion of consumer markets and in the imitation and transformation of manufactures.[6] Similar processes transpiring a century earlier can be detected in other areas of the world. A taste for Asian goods fostered new consumer markets and transformed fashions in the main cities of the early seventeenth-century Americas, as will be shown in Chapter 6. Furthermore, as in Britain and other European countries in the eighteenth century, the commercial interaction of New Spanish traders with Asia propelled cultural exchanges and product innovations that affected the production of local manufactured goods.

A change of perspective from the European to the Spanish American viewpoint makes other aspects of the interaction, during the early modern era, between Asia and the Atlantic World more visible to the historian's eye. Through the pages of this chapter the reader will gain insight into how New Spain became a protagonist in receiving transfers of the materials and skills needed to produce Asian-like products as soon as the early decades of the seventeenth century. Note that the following pages choose not to use the term "hybridity" to define the product of transfers of materials and skills needed to produce Asian-like products in colonial New Spain. Hybridity is a construction which depends on its historical context. Hybridity, which is to say mixture, in the colonial Spanish American context was strongly related to hierarchy. Hierarchy was in the very nature of the *casta* organisation of the colonial American society, where race and culture were not easily distinguishable but they socially classified people. *Chino* was among the categories of the *casta* society – by *chino* Spanirds meant whoever looked like Asian. However, Asian products and Asian-like products produced in New Spain were not easily attached to any social category – the New Spanish society and New Spanish craftsmen likely would not have perceived Asian-like products as hybrids, less in the modern sense of hybridity.[7]

Section 5.1 addresses the growing presence of Chinese silk in both New Spain and Castile. The form of this expansion illustrates the problematic and contradictory nature of the emergence, in the Spanish Empire, of a new product with such a high degree of cultural particularity. The circulation of Chinese silk was not culturally and economically desirable for all classes of Hispanic society, and Hispanic traders and producers responded differently, depending on their businesses' scope and the markets they controlled, to its increasing

---

6   Giorgio Riello, "Asian Knowledge and the Development of Calico Printing in Europe in the Seventeenth and Eighteenth Centuries," *Journal of Global History* 5 (2010): 1–28.

7   Carolyn Dean and Dana Leibsohn, "Hybridity and Its Discontents: Considering Visual Culture in Colonial Spanish America," *Colonial Latin American Review* 12, no. 1 (2003): 5-35.

presence in the Empire's networks. Conflicting interests regarding silk led to some areas of the Empire receiving more woven and semi-manufactured silk from China than raw silk, which had multiple consequences.

Section 5.2 describes how craftsmen of New Spain became interested in making Asian-like products using the same techniques and materials as those used in Asia. As in other parts of the world, in New Spain the successful production of imitations and transformations of such Asian luxury and semi-luxury goods as Chinese porcelain and Chinese and Japanese furniture depended on creating new products that accommodated the tastes of local consumers. Another important factor was how adequately the requisite knowledge and skills could be transferred from China and Japan to New Spain. This chapter explores the evolution of such transfers after the opening of Manila Galleon trade.

5.1 The Impact of Chinese Silk on Castilian and New Spanish Industries

There was a long tradition of silk production in the Iberian Peninsula before the early modern period, especially in areas with a strong Islamic background and Italian influence such as Valencia, Murcia, Cordoba, and especially Granada.[8] This tradition was extended to the Americas after the conquest. However, the conquest of the Americas by the Castilians at the end of the sixteenth century triggered contradictory processes. It entailed the establishment on the "new" continent of forms of producing goods that were already produced in the Iberian Peninsula as well as the opening up of new markets, which was seen as an economic opportunity for Iberian producers to sell their goods. Silk production provides an example. The silk craftsmen in Granada and Seville hoped to export some of their textiles via the Atlantic fleets bound for the Americas; however, once the conquest and colonisation had succeeded, Spanish settlers and entrepreneurs sought to establish silk production within those new territories. After some fruitless attempts to grow silkworms in the Caribbean and Florida, the New Spanish authorities achieved to plant mulberry trees and raise silkworms in the areas around Mexico City, Antequera de Oaxaca,

---

8   Luca Molà, *The Silk Industry of Renaissance Venice* (Baltimore, MD: Johns Hopkins University Press, 2000), 21–22; Miguel A. Ladero Quesada, "La Producción de Seda en la España Medieval. Siglos XIII–XVI," in *La Seta in Europa, Secc. XIII–XX,* ed. Simonetta Cavaciocchi (Florence: Le Monnier, 1993), 125–39; Germán Navarro, *El Despegue de la Industria Sedera en la Valencia del Siglo XVI* (Valencia: Generalitat Valencia, 1992), 29–38; Manuel Garzón Pareja, *La Industria Sedera en España. El Arte de la Seda en España* (Granada: Archivo de la Real Chancillería, 1972), 243–352.

and above all Puebla de los Ángeles in the 1540s and 1550s.[9] Puebla, which had been founded in 1531, soon became one of the most important re-exportation centres of Castilian and European textiles – mainly silks and wools, as well as linens and cottons – in New Spain. Moreover, this city developed a dye production industry that flourished in parallel with the silk industry's rise, since the widespread presence of cochineal in the region of Tlaxcala facilitated the production of dyes. By the second half of the sixteenth century, Puebla had become the main textile production centre of New Spain and a serious competitor of Mexico City's silk industry owing to the low prices of Puebla's manufactured silk.[10] However, this situation changed upon the commercial opening of the Pacific Ocean.

In the late sixteenth century, the increasing exports of silk from China to New Spain via Manila contributed to the dramatic fall in New Spanish production of silk by 1600. Reports of merchandise possessed by Mexican traders establish that the main Asian textile imported to New Spain from the Philippines was Chinese silk; see Figure 7. In comparison, only negligible quantities of calicoes were shipped from India to Manila and then to the Americas. The competitiveness of Chinese silk caused both sericulture and the silk industry of Puebla to contract so much that the city was forced to shift its textile production to wool. The city did not recover its previous economic power, and in the seventeenth century it ceased to be an economic challenge to the merchants and silk artisans of Mexico City.[11]

The reasons for the decline in Puebla of two of its main economic sectors, sericulture and silk craftsmanship, were related to the nature of the silk imports in New Spain from the Philippines. Unlike in Seville, where such imports were mainly in the form of raw silk (see Figure 8), in New Spain the imports of Chinese silks arriving via Manila galleons consisted mainly of woven silks. These were usually semi-manufactured fabrics such as taffetas, satins, *gorgoranes*, velvets, *sinabafas*, and damasks. Furthermore, raw silk and silk in the form of yarn – which included thrown silk (*seda torcida*), bundled silk (*seda en mazo*), floss silk (*seda floja*), long-pile silk (*seda de pelo*), and silk in wefts (*seda de tramas*) – made up a large part of the imports of Asian textiles to New Spain

---

9   Woodrow W. Borah, *Silk Raising in Colonial Mexico* (Berkeley, CA: University of California Press, 1943), 1–14; William B. Taylor, "Town and Country in the Valley of Oaxaca, 1750–1812," in *Provinces of Early Mexico. Variants of Spanish American Regional Evolution*, ed. Ida Altman and James Lockhart (Los Angeles: University of California Press, 1976), 66–69.

10   Jan Bazant, "Evolución de la Industria Textil Poblana (1544–1845)," *Historia Mexicana* 13, no. 4 (1964): 473–84; Peter Boyd-Bowman, "Spanish and European Textiles in Sixteenth Century Mexico," *The Americas* 29, no. 3 (1973): 334–58.

11   Borah, *Silk Raising*, 85–101; Bazant, "Evolución de la Industria," 483.

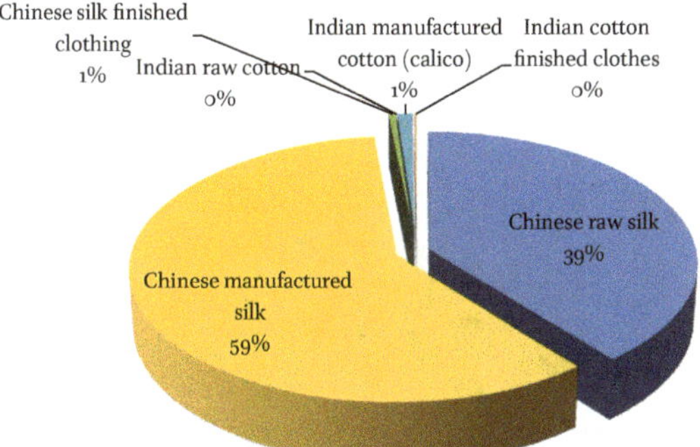

FIGURE 7   Percentage of Asian textile values (by type of textile) arriving in New Spain from
the Philippines, *ca.* 1600–1640.
SOURCE: APPENDIX A[2].

from Asia. Much rarer were imports of finished clothes (silk shirts, stockings, sleeves, shoes, etc.), which typically were exported to New Spain in the form of gifts and personal orders. An even more pronounced version of this same pattern can be traced in the probate inventories of Mexican storekeepers and shop accounts found in the Mexican archives and dated in the late sixteenth and early seventeenth centuries. For such storekeepers with Chinese textiles, most retail Chinese silks were semi-manufactured silks and fabrics.[12] These data reveal that some of the retailed semi-manufactured silk had already passed through Mexican workshops.

The decline of sericulture in New Spain followed naturally from the decision of Mexico City's craftsmen and tailors (i.e., those with enough capital) to access directly the Philippine sources of cheaper Chinese silk. Probate data related to the Mexican tailor Manuel Tinoco (died 1591) contains two reports of commercial agreements made by Tinoco and Bartolomé de Ocaña, another tailor, with Lorenzo Murientes, a merchant who operated in Manila on behalf of the two tailors. These reports include requests for Asian goods, most of them raw silk and silk fabrics, which Lorenzo Murientes carried from the Philippine Islands to Mexico City. Tinoco ordered several pieces of taffeta and damask worth 71 pesos in addition to several *cates* of thrown silk valued at 8.5 pesos. De Ocaña's request consisted of 218 pesos worth of semi-manufactured silks – taffetas, damasks, and *sinabafas* – as well as 28 pesos worth of thrown and floss

---

12   ANotDF, Notario Juan Bautista Moreno (375), vol. 2483, 199–205; ANotDF, Notario Andrés Moreno (374), vol. 2467, 465–78; AGI, *Contratación*, 517, N. 2, R. 1, 108–10; AGN, *Indiferente General*, caja-exp.: 1818-006, *Consulado*; AGN, *Indiferente General*, caja-exp.: 5012-011, *Industria y Comercio.*

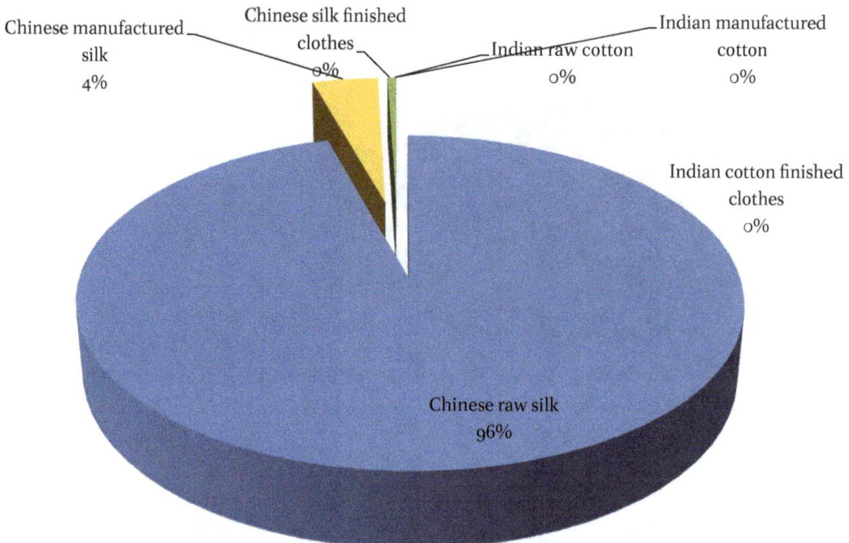

FIGURE 8   Percentage of Asian textile values (by type of textile) arriving in Seville from New
            Spain, *ca.* 1600–1640.
            SOURCE: APPENDIX A[1].

silk.[13] Other documents show that silk fabrics, and not raw silk, dominated the
orders place by Mexican artisans for materials from the Philippines. This was
the case of Isabel Villalobos, a Mexican craftswoman (died 1591) who also had
direct commercial links with the Philippines that supplied her with silks.[14] In
the list of goods of the tailor Alonso del Riego, who died in 1603, Chinese fabrics (mainly satins and taffetas) likewise predominated over Chinese raw silk.[15]
These cases illustrate why sericulture in New Spain declined. For the tailors and
weavers of Mexico City it was cheaper to buy Chinese silk through merchants
who travelled to Manila than to buy the silk produced natively in Puebla.

By 1600, the New Spanish sericulture crisis was widespread. Silk production
suffered another blow in 1634, when the Crown prohibited maritime contact
between New Spain and Peru (i.e., the destination of many New Spanish textiles). New Spain's silk industry did not recover until the eighteenth century. In
these circumstances, there was no way for "import substitution" – or of imitation industries involving silk – to develop.

---

13   AGI, *Contratación*, 242, N. 1, R. 5.

14   AGI, *Contratación*, 487, N. 1, R. 25.

15   AGI, *Contratación*, 274A, N. 1, R. 11.

The re-exportation of Chinese silk from New Spain to Seville did not have the same effects on the silk industries of Castile as in the case of New Spain because the nature of that re-exportation was different. According to the "inward registers of merchandise," about 96 per cent of all Asian textiles coming in to Seville from New Spain was raw Chinese silk (see Figure 8), mainly in the form of thrown silk, bundled silk, floss silk, and long-pile silk. In contrast to the Manila galleons, the Atlantic fleets that sailed from New Spain to Castile seldom contained Chinese semi-manufactured silk fabrics. Pre-eminence of raw Chinese silk reflected the competitiveness of Chinese silks in American markets, which led to conflicts of interest among Sevillian traders, Mexican merchants, and Castilian silk craftsmen.

Sevillian merchants pressured the Crown to close the Manila Galleon trade not only because a part of American silver was diverted to this route but also because the trans-Pacific trade was stealing some of the American clothing market, which they viewed as their own. Sevillian traders had been sending Castilian and European linens, wools, and silks to American markets since the opening of the trade between Castile and the New World.[16] There was only limited American demand for imported textiles and probably much less than anticipated by Castilian artisans and merchants at the start of colonisation.[17] Hence there developed conflicts between Sevillian merchants, who saw how the already limited American demand for import textiles being reduced further by the entry of Asian textiles, and Mexican wholesalers, who were flooding American markets with semi-manufactured, raw, and even finished Chinese silks from the Philippines.[18] Annual textile exports from Seville to the Americas were valued at some 43 million *maravedís* (equivalent to about

---

16   Boyd-Bowman, "Spanish and European Textiles," 334–58; Eufemio Lorenzo Sanz, *Comercio de España con América en la Época de Felipe II. Tomo I: Los Mercaderes y el Tráfico Indiano* (Valladolid: Diputación Provincial de Valladolid, 1986), 289–423.

17   By 1570 there were 150,000 Creoles and Spaniards in the Americas, a number which equalled around 2 per cent of population in Spain. Yun Casalilla estimates that the annual value of exports from Seville to the Americas was equivalent to the annual value of trade in a city like Cordoba: Bartolomé Yun Casalilla, "The American Empire and the Spanish Economy: An Institutional and Regional Perspective," *Revista de Historia Económica – Journal of Iberian and Latin American Economic History* 16, no. 1 (1998): 130–31.

18   Guillermina del Valle Pavón, "Los Mercaderes de México y la Transgresión de los Límites al Comercio Pacífico en Nueva España," *Revista de Historia Económica – Journal of Iberian and Latin American Economic History* 23, no. 224 (2005): 213–40; Antoni Picazo Muntaner, "El Comercio Sedero de Filipinas y Su Influencia en la Economía de España en el Siglo XVII," in *La Declinación de la Monarquía Hispánica. VII\ª Reunión Científica de la Fundación Española de Historia Moderna,* ed. Francisco J. Aranda Pérez (Cuenca: UCLM, 2004), 501–4.

158,000 pesos in "pieces of eight") at the end of the sixteenth century.[19] Exports of Asian merchandise to the Americas from the Philippines were legally limited to a maximum of 250,000 pesos per year, although this figure does not reflect the value of contraband. In other words, Chinese silk imported to New Spain from the Philippines gained ground on the amount of textiles imported from Castile by the viceroyalty to the extent that some textiles exported from Seville to the Americas were returned to Seville because they could not be sold in American markets.[20] Letters from merchants who lived in Mexico City to their relatives and partners in Castile also acknowledged the limited competitiveness of Castilian fabrics in the viceroyalty.[21]

The clash between the economic interests of Castilians and New Spaniards with respect to the importation of Chinese silk in Spanish America was so bitter that it reached the highest political spheres of the Empire. In his "Report on the Trade of China with New Spain and These Kingdoms" sent to the Indies Council in 1621, Horacio Levanto confirms the damage that imported Asian textiles in New Spain did to the production of New Spanish textiles and to the export of Andalusian textiles to the Americas. Hoping to alarm the Council, he pointed out that the low prices of Asian textiles made them affordable not only for the Spanish and Creole elites but even for the indigenous American populations.[22]

More hostile to the Manila Galleon trade is the report entitled "Reasons for Not Allowing Trade with China" (*Razones para No Admitir el Comercio con China*), sent to the King and the Indies Council in 1628; it was written by Juan Velázquez Madridejos, probably a merchant from the area of Seville or Granada. In his text, Velázquez Madridejos asked the Crown to ban the trade between New Spain and China not only because of the flight of New Spanish silver to the East but also because "the entry of silk in the Indies and Spain from China and its trade is very pernicious." He claimed that, in the Americas, "people buy less merchandise from Spain than they used to, and they would buy more if there were not merchandise from China. This means that Spain consigns half the products that were shipped in the past." He stated further that Chinese silk imports causes "such great damage, especially to the producers of silk, that every day the production of silk decreases." This, he warned,

19   Antonio García-Baquero González, *La Carrera de Indias. Suma de Negociación y Océano de Negocios* (Sevilla: Algaida, 1992), 206–7.

20   AGI, *Contratación*, 1800, 32–35; AGI, *Contratación*, 1805, 69–72; AGI, *Contratación*, 1841, 2221–24; AGI, *Contratación*, 1850, 473–75.

21   AGN, *Indiferente Virreinal*, caja-exp.: 1812-009, *Consulado*.

22   BN, R/17270 (6), 1.

would have disastrous consequences for the Royal Treasury, since the fall in silk production would lead to reduced tax revenues collected (as from the *alcabala*) in silk-raising centres such as Granada.[23]

Some authors have argued that the competitiveness of Chinese silk against European textiles was due to the former's low price; others have claimed that Chinese silk was competitive because of its high ratio of quality to price.[24] In any case, the encroachment of Chinese silks on New Spain's market was a source of conflict between Mexican and Sevillian wholesalers, which was far from finished in the seventeenth century. In the eighteenth century this conflict gained a global dimension when other European merchants – especially French, English, and Dutch, all of whom also exported European (and even Asian) textiles to the Americas – joined forces with Iberian merchants against the interests of Mexican merchants.[25]

There was another social group involved in this conflict of interests: silk craftsmen from several Castilian cities, especially Seville and Granada. The silk industry in Castile enjoyed continual growth during the sixteenth century thanks to technical and productive improvements, growing demand, processes of specialisation in different fabrics, the growth of urban areas in the country, and better access to new dyes (e.g., cochineal dye and indigo) by way of international and Spanish American markets.[26] In this context, Granada enjoyed a monopoly on exporting silk to the relatively small American market from

---

23   AGI, *Filipinas*, 40, N. 5, 1–4.

24   Lorenzo Sanz, *Comercio de España*, 442–43; Picazo Muntaner, "El Comercio Sedero," 502; Del Valle Pavón, "Los Mercaderes de México," 519; Mariano Ardash Bonialian, *China en la América Colonial. Bienes, Mercados, Comercio y Cultura del consumo Desde México hasta Buenos Aires* (México, D. F.: Instituto Mora, 2014), 111–117. The first two of these authors claim that Chinese silks were cheaper than European textiles in the Americas but do not offer any data on pricing. Lorenzo Sanz reports that the quality of Chinese silk was higher than that of European silk, but Picazo Muntaner claims that Chinese silk was of low quality. Bonialian also argues that although there was Chinese silk of good quality, most of the Chinese silk that circulated in the Americas was of medium or low quality. I have analysed new sources and confirmed that Chinese silk was on average cheaper than Castilian silk not only in New Spain but also in Seville: José L. Gasch-Tomás, "Transport costs and prices of Chinese silk in the Spanish empire, c. 1571-1650" *Revista de Historia Industrial* 60 (2015): 15-47.

25   Mariano Ardash Bonialian, *El Pacífico Hispanoamericano. Política y Comercio Asiático en el Imperio Español (1680–1784). La Centralidad de lo Marginal* (México, D.F.: El Colegio de México, 2012), 198–207.

26   Bartolomé Yun Casalilla, *Marte contra Minerva. El Precio del Imperio Español* (Barcelona: Crítica, 2004), 166–68; José I. Fortea Pérez, *Córdoba en el Siglo XVI: Las Bases Demográficas y Económicas de una Expansión Urbana* (Córdoba: Monte de Piedad y Caja de Ahorros de Córdoba, 1981), 312–34.

1569 to 1591. This monopoly actually ran counter to the interests of Sevillian merchants and craftsmen. Seville's merchants and textile guilds had been introducing Castilian and European textiles (mainly wool and linens) into American markets since the early sixteenth century.[27] Yet they must have had difficulties to enter the American silk market from 1569 to 1591, when it was controlled by the silk producers of Granada and, to an increasing extent, by the silk workshops (*obrajes*) of New Spain, which had risen to prominence during the second half of the sixteenth century. Seville's wholesalers put pressure on the Crown to eliminate the privilege of Granada's craftsmen. These Sevillian traders were finally able to break Granada's monopoly on exporting silk to the Americas in 1591,[28] but it was too late. By 1600, the Philippines were already supplying America with silks that were preferred over those that the Europeans could supply.

At this point it becomes even more important to distinguish between *sericulture*, whose main competitor was imported raw silk and silk in yarn, and *silk craftsmanship*, which could benefit from the importation of semi-manufactured silk fabrics. This distinction is key to understanding why the Spanish Empire's importation of Chinese silk is a story of comparative disadvantages and advantages.

It is a story of disadvantages for the planters of mulberry trees and silkworm breeders from Puebla, who could not compete with Chinese raw silk and silk in yarn. Sericulture had also declined in the Iberian Peninsula, especially in the centres of Valencia and Murcia, but Chinese silk likely was not responsible because the decline in Iberian sericulture transpired in the late sixteenth century, before China could have become a competitor.[29] Moreover, the importation of Chinese raw silk might actually have benefited Iberian silk craftsmen and tailors, especially in Granada, and hence delayed the crisis that affected other economic sectors of Castile.

There was no crisis in the silk industries of Castile until the seventeenth century.[30] In Toledo, for instance, the silk industry crisis was not severe until the 1660s, when the number of looms began to decrease.[31] In Valencia, the silk industry manifested symptoms of exhaustion after its expansion of the

---

27   Antonio M. Bernal, Antonio Collantes Morán and Antonio García-Baquero González, "Sevilla: De Los Gremios a la Industrialización," *Estudios de Historia Social* 5, no. 6 (1978): 78.

28   Lorenzo Sanz, *Comercio de España*, 440–41.

29   Garzón Pareja, *Industria Sedera*, 259; Fortea Pérez, *Córdoba en el Siglo XVI*, 320–6.

30   Yun Casalilla, "American Empire," 132.

31   Hilario Rodríguez de Gracia, "El Negocio Sedero Toledano en la Segunda mitad del Siglo XVII," in *Declinación*, ed. Aranda Pérez, 525–27.

sixteenth century. Even so, Valencia's silk industry appeared to have overcome that decline by 1620 (although documentation for the period 1630–1690 is sketchy).[32] In the case of Córdoba the seventeenth-century crisis of its silk and textile manufacturers clearly resulted from their poor adaptation to changes in demand.[33] The stagnation of silk manufacturers in Granada was related to problems of competitiveness within the Iberian Peninsula itself, especially with silks woven in Murcia and Toledo.[34] So why, within an overall decline in sericulture, did the silk industry of Castile suffer from this crisis later than did other areas of the economy? Part of the answer lies in the above-mentioned arrival of Chinese raw silk from New Spain. The mercantile registers of Seville's port confirm that the final destination of some of the Chinese raw silk arriving in Seville was silk manufacturing centres, such as those in Toledo and Granada. The silk craftsmen in these cities considered Chinese (and also Italian) raw silk to be a good substitute for native silk.[35] In this context, Granada's producers of silk perhaps became even more competitive in the production and trade of silk by reducing input prices – nonetheless, this cannot be proved because of the absence of price series for silk in Granada or data on production costs in any other Castilian city in the first decades of the seventeenth century, neither of which I have been able to find. To sum up, the reason that there was a relative balance between raw and semi-manufactured silks among the Chinese silk imported in New Spain from the Philippines, that raw silk and silk in the form of yarn – rather than semi-manufactured silks and fabrics – dominated the Chinese silk sent to Seville from New Spain, and the effects of the different composition of Chinese silk imports in New Spain and Castile on the sericulture and silk craftsmanship the two kingdoms, can be found in this tangled web of interests concerned with the production and trade of silk in the Spanish Empire.

---

32   Ricardo Franch Benavent, "La Evolución de la Sedería Valenciana durante el Reinado de Felipe II," in *Felipe II y el Mediterráneo*, vol. 1, ed. Ernest Belenguer Cevriá (Madrid: Sociedad Estatal para la Conmemoración de los Centenarios de Felipe II y Carlos V, 1999), 289–310; Ricardo Franch Benavent, "El Artesanado Sedero Valenciano en el Siglo XVII," in *Declinación*, ed. Aranda Pérez, 511–13.

33   José I. Fortea Pérez, "La Industria Textil en el Contexto General de la Economía Cordobesa entre Fines del Siglo XVII y Principios del XVIII: Una Reactivación Fallida," in *Actas II Coloquio Historia de Andalucía. Andalucía Moderna* (Córdoba: Monte de Piedad y Caja de Ahorros de Córdoba, 1983), 445–46; Molà, *Silk Industry*, 241–60.

34   Garzón Pareja, *Industria Sedera*, 259–65.

35   AGI, *Contratación*, 1795, 7–8; AGI, *Contratación*, 1806, 285–86.

5.2   Knowledge Transfer and "Import Substitution" Industries in New Spain

Ever since the Cape route was opened by the Portuguese in the late fifteenth century, the presence of European missionaries and proto-scientists in China fostered knowledge transmission from East to West. The settlement of Spaniards in the Philippines in 1565 was to add another route for knowledge and technical transfers related to the taste for Asian goods from Asia to the Atlantic World during the early modern era.[36]

Of all the scholars who lived in the Philippines at the end of the sixteenth century, Hernando de los Ríos Coronel (1559–1624) was one of the most important. He was a soldier, naval pilot, representative of the Philippines at the King's Court of Madrid, and – toward the end of his life – a priest. Although he is known primarily for his research on navigation and for creating an astrolabe, he was interested in many issues related to mathematics, astronomy, and engineering.[37] De los Ríos Coronel was also interested in geography and in the political organisation of the Philippines; see illustration 4. His interest in geography led him to draw maps of the Philippines area, including Taiwan and the coast of China, which he sent to the King at the end of the sixteenth century.[38]

De los Ríos Coronel's interests in agriculture and attempts to transplant Chinese mulberry trees and produce silkworms in Europe are less known. In 1609 he sent the King a report about the production of silk in China, along with a mulberry tree seed, with the aim of convincing the monarch to produce, in Spain, silk of the quality found in China:

> Hernando de los Ríos Coronel, representative of the Philippines, in order to serve Your Grace and this republic declares the following. A fertile seed of silk which is produced in China may be taken to Spain. From this seed, the silkworms make cocoons as big as this one I send you, which is bigger than hundreds of the cocoons produced here. This seed is produced there, in Lanquin, which is a land 40 degrees in longitude and with a similar climate to Spain. It will be easy to take this seed there by sending it

---

36   Elisabetta Corsi, ed., *Órdenes Religiosas entre América y Asia. Ideas para Una Historia Misionera de los Espacios Coloniales* (México, D.F.: Colegio de México, 2008).

37   John N. Crossley, *Hernando de los Ríos Coronel and the Spanish Philippines in the Golden Age* (Burlington, VT: Ashgate, 2011).

38   AGI, "Mapas y Planos," *Filipinas*, 6.

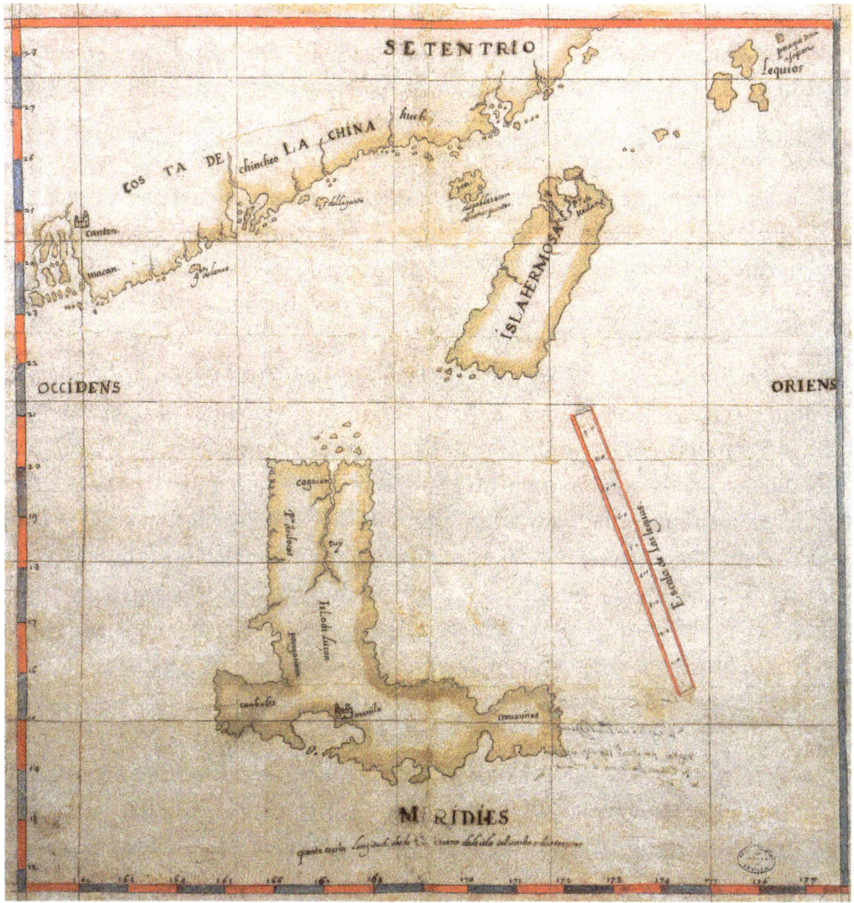

ILLUSTRATION 4   Map of Luzon, Taiwan and the coast of China, by Hernando de los Ríos Coronel (1597).

SOURCE: MINISTERIO DE EDUCACIÓN, CULTURA Y DEPORTE (SPAIN). ARCHIVO GENERAL DE INDIAS, "MAPAS Y PLANOS," *FILIPINAS*, 6

to the governor of the Philippines along with the instructions to raise it. This silk is finer than that of Spain, and this seed will be very useful for the kingdom [...] The governor must be asked to ship a seed to test it in Spain.[39]

---

39   AGI, *Filipinas*, 27, N. 72. According to Sugaya, Lanquin was likely a port in Fujian province: Nariko Sugaya, "Spanish Colonial Manila in Transition: Trade and Society at the Turn of the Nineteenth Century," 愛媛大学法文学部論集. 人文学科編 36 (2014): 30.

The governor of the Philippines effectively issued the order to send the mulberry tree seed from China to Spain.[40]

Some years earlier, in 1581, Gonzalo de las Casas – who had been a landowner in Yahuitlán (Oaxaca) – published "New Art of Silk Production" (*Arte Nuevo para Criar Seda*); in that text, the author explained how to plant mulberry trees and raise silkworms in New Spain. He did not mention Chinese silk, which indicates that Chinese silk was not yet a significant problem for New Spanish sericulture.[41] However, in less than the three decades that elapsed between the publishing of De las Casas's work and the account sent by Hernando de los Ríos Coronel to Madrid, Chinese silk had become a central concern of silk producers and scholars of the empire. De los Ríos Coronel's decision to consign a mulberry tree seed from China to Iberia and to try persuading the King to plant Chinese mulberry trees (in the conviction that they were of better quality than the mulberry trees of New Spain and Spain) must be understood in the context of the events that transpired during that interim. The circulation and trade of Chinese silks had spread in New Spain during the last quarter of the sixteenth century. The raising of silkworms and the production of raw silk in New Spain almost collapsed around 1600. The wholesalers of Andalusia, with whom De los Ríos Coronel may have been in contact as a representative at the King's Court – De los Ríos Coronel was from Andalusia –,[42] were already struggling against the competition of Asian textiles carried by the Manila galleons to New Spain. In this context, De los Ríos Coronel's proposal of producing silk of a similar quality to Chinese silk by sending seeds of Chinese mulberry trees to Europe was an opportunity to weaken the New Spanish elites' demand for silk acquired via trans-Pacific trade.

De los Ríos Coronel's attempt to transplant Chinese mulberry trees to Spain was an idea that most likely never came to fruition: there is no evidence of that plan being implemented in the Iberian Peninsula. Nonetheless, his endeavour suggests how the transfer of knowledge and skills from Asia to the Spanish Atlantic World was related to the development of the trans-Pacific trade and new consumer markets in the Americas.

In contrast to the case of Chinese silkworms and cocoons, there was a successful transfer from China to New Spain of some dye products (via the Manila

---

40   AGI, *Filipinas*, 329, L. 2, 118.

41   Gonzalo de las Casas, *Arte Nuevo para Criar Seda* (edited by Antonio Garrido Aranda) (Granada: Universidad de Granada, 1996 (first published in 1581)). See also Woodrown W. Borah, "El Origen de la Sericultura en la Mixteca Alta," *Historia Mexicana* 13, no. 1 (1963): 1–17.

42   Crossley, *Hernando de los Ríos Coronel*, 25–26.

galleons) and of the skills and techniques needed to decorate porcelain. There exists a vast literature on the global expansion of blue-and-white Chinese porcelain during the early modern era and on how it influenced earthenware production all over the world. This phenomenon is one of the best examples of the cultural and economic entanglements that developed at a global level before the modern era, as Chinese porcelain was the most imitated and re-created product in the world before the nineteenth century.[43] From the 1560s to the 1640s, the Chinese porcelain for which demand was greatest in the Atlantic World was *kraak* porcelain, which was characterised by its blue-and-white colouration and rich decorations featuring flora, fauna, landscape scenes, and panelled borders. It was produced in Jingdezhen (Jiangxi) and reached, along with other types of blue-and-white porcelain products, the most important civilisations of the world from Japan through Turkey and from Safavid Iran to Italy and Portugal.[44] The earliest European imitations of this porcelain style were produced in Italy and Portugal, although the most internationally successful were those crafted in Delft, the Netherlands.[45]

The development of porcelain imitations in New Spain was parallel to that in Europe. In Spanish America, Puebla de los Ángeles was the most notable location where imitation Chinese porcelain industries developed. After the fall of sericulture and the silk industry in Puebla at the end of the sixteenth century, an economic field for which the city became renowned was the production of glazed tiles and ceramics. The deposits of clay around the city made the area an ideal place to produce earthenware. In the seventeenth century, Puebla became the foremost producer of pottery on the American continent and the main exporter of glazed earthenware from New Spain to South America and the Caribbean. The high volume in New Spain of imported Chinese porcelain, whose consumption was so widespread in the viceroyalty, led Puebla's artisans

---

43 Robert Finlay, "The Pilgrim Art: The Culture of Porcelain in World History," *Journal of World History* 9, no. 2 (1998): 141–87

44 Anne Gerritsen, "Ceramics for Local and Global Markets: Jingdezhen's Agora of Technologies," in *Cultures of Knowledge. Technology in Chinese History*, ed. Dagmar Schäfer (Leiden: Brill, 2012), 161–84; Stacey Pearson, "The Movement of Chinese Ceramics: Appropriation in Global History," *Journal of World History* 23, no. 1 (2012): 9–39.

45 Anne E. McCants, "Exotic Goods, Popular Consumption, and the Standard of Living: Thinking about Globalization in the Early Modern World," *Journal of World History* 18, no. 4 (2007): 459–60; Berg, *Luxury and Pleasure*, 80–81; Teresa Canepa, "The Portuguese and Spanish Trade in Kraak Porcelain in the Late 16th and Early 17th Centuries," in *Proceedings of the International Symposium: Chinese Export Ceramics in the 16th and 17th Centuries and the Spread of Material Civilization* (City University: Hong Kong, 2012), 257–85; John Carswell, *Blue and White. Chinese Porcelain and Its Impact on the Western World* (Chicago: University of Chicago Press, 1985), 37–40.

to appropriate the decorative style, motifs, techniques, and – unlike the case of early seventeenth-century Europe – also the dye products of Chinese potters.[46]

Initially, Puebla's potters closely followed the production techniques and patterns of Castile. In the mid-sixteenth century, many artisans moved to Puebla from the great ceramic centre of Talavera de la Reina in Castile. They brought with them their techniques and styles, which is why Puebla's ceramics were popularly known as "talaveras" in New Spain. In the late sixteenth and seventeenth centuries, Puebla's potters produced the same type of earthenware as that produced in Talavera. These were ceramics glazed with white varnish obtained from tin oxide and quartz sand that, following Muslim and *mudéjar* patterns, were decorated with geometric figures and geometric plants.[47] The pottery production of Puebla gained such importance that a potters' guild was officially established there in 1653.[48]

Alongside the production of Castilian-like ceramics, the potters of Puebla began to create Chinese-like ceramics around 1600; see illustrations 5 and 6. Although some copies of Chinese porcelain items could have been produced in Venice, Genoa, Lisbon, or Delft and then imported, most of them were produced in Puebla.[49] As the Manila Galleon trade expanded and more Chinese porcelain came to New Spain, the presence of Chinese motifs became more common in the pottery of Puebla. Archaeologists have identified Chinese porcelain objects at several sites in Puebla de los Ángeles and Mexico City that are dated to the seventeenth century. The imitation of Chinese porcelain was manifest in the use of themes that were doubtless of Chinese inspiration, such as oriental gardens, chrysanthemums, lotus flowers, and birds. That being said,

---

46   Margaret Connors McQuade, "La Talavera Poblana: Cuatro Siglos de Producción y Coleccionismo," *Mesoamérica* 40 (2000): 118–40; María Bonta de la Pezuela, *Porcelana China de Exportación para el Mercado Novohispano: La Colección del Museo Nacional del Virreinato* (Mexico, D. F.: UNAM, 2008), 131–33.

47   Francisco Pérez de Salazar Verea, "Talavera de Puebla," in *Talaveras de Puebla. Cerámica Colonial Mexicana, Siglos XVII a XXI*, VVAA, (Barcelona: Museu de Ceràmica de Barcelona, 2007), 55–57.

48   Efraín Castro Morales, "Puebla y la Talavera a Través de los Siglos," *Artes de México* 3 (2002): 20–29; Leonor Cortina and Alejandra Peón Soler, *La Talavera de Puebla* (México, D.F.: Comermex, 1973); Jessica M. Tolentino Martínez and Rocío Rosales Ortega, "La Producción de Talavera de Puebla y San Pablo del Monte, Tlaxcala: Un Sistema Productivo Local en Transformación," *Revista Pueblos y Fronteras* 6, no. 11 (2011): 209–10.

49   Ana Ruiz Gutiérrez, "Influencias Artísticas en las Artes Decorativas Novohispanas," in *Cruce de Miradas, Relaciones e Intercambios*, ed. Pedro San Ginés Aguilar (Granada: Universidad de Granada, 2010), 335–37; Alfonso Pleguezuelo, "Cerámicas de Ida y Vuelta. Castilla, América y Asia," in *Talaveras de Puebla*, VVAA, 31–33.

ILLUSTRATION 5   Blue-and-white "talavera" from Puebla with Chinese-like motifs
(seventeenth century).
SOURCE: MÉXICO, D. F. MUSEO FRANZ MAYER, MEXICO CITY (MEXICO)

Chinese motifs were most often transformed and adapted to Creole taste – that is, merged with European and pre-Hispanic themes by the Puebla producers.[50]

Seventeenth-century Puebla ceramics could hardly have replaced Chinese porcelain in New Spanish markets because, among other reasons, the trans-Pacific trade was strong enough to keep the economic interests of the viceroyalty's most powerful merchants very much concentrated on both the trans-Pacific trade and Chinese porcelain. Nevertheless, Puebla's industry of imitating Chinese porcelain shared some characteristics with "import substitution" industries and constituted an early and notable effort to produce Chinese-like porcelain in the Atlantic World. The importing of Chinese pottery and the producing of imitations in New Spain was accompanied not only by a better knowledge of the consumer market of porcelain in early modern Spanish America but also by an adaptation in the American arena of technological

---

50   Florence C. Lister and Robert H. Lister, "The Potters' Quarter of Colonial Puebla, Mexico," *Historical Archeology* 18, no. 1 (1984): 99–100; George Kuwayama, *Chinese Ceramics in Colonial Mexico* (Honolulu, HI: University of Hawaii Press, 1997), 20–22.

processes developed in China.[51] Puebla's potters learnt the technique used by the Chinese to decorate their ceramic with blue and imported the substance (cobalt oxide) needed for such decoration directly from China.

Cobalt oxide was the mineral used by Chinese potters of Jingdezhen to stamp the strong blue colour onto their ceramics; that colour was obtained after painting the ceramic with a liquid derived from cobalt and then firing the piece.[52] If recent works are correct in their interpretation, it was not until the early eighteenth century that Europeans first became aware of using cobalt oxide to create the blue decoration of blue-and-white Chinese porcelain.[53] In contrast, the potters of Puebla used cobalt to decorate their pottery in the Chinese fashion a full century earlier.

These potters regularly bought cobalt in Manila through their intermediaries in Acapulco and Manila from the late sixteenth century onward. Thereafter, they discovered that cobalt could be obtained from the mines of Tepotztlán in New Spain. Although the potters from Puebla exerted less quality control than did the Chinese when producing blue dye from cobalt – which likely meant that the New Spanish dye was inferior – they did manage to produce it.[54] They used dense concentrations of the mineral, which stamped the figures with a blue colour that was darker than that seen on porcelain from China, and Chinese-like ceramics ended up being the most expensive among all the wares produced by the potters of Puebla.[55]

Lacquerwork was the other field in which skill transfers from Asia to the Americas took place in concert with the expanding New Spanish taste for Chinese and Japanese goods. This was a field in which skills and decorative styles from China, Japan, American pre-Hispanic cultures, and Iberia converged. Decorating and finishing pieces of furniture with lacquer had a long tradition

---

51 The concept of "import substitution" should not be understood here in the sense of twentieth-century import substitution industries – that is, as industries linked to policies of high tariffs on imports – but rather in the sense of import substitution industries of the early modern era. Early modern import industries were related to the development of a better knowledge of markets and the adaptation of technological processes in response to the increasing demand for consumer goods: Berg, "In Pursuit of Luxury," 87, 99–104.

52 Bonta de la Pezuela, *Porcelana China*, 63.

53 Anne Gerritsen and Stephen McDowall, "Material Culture and the Other: European Encounters with Chinese Porcelain, ca. 1650-1800," *Journal of World History* 23, no. 1 (2012): 100.

54 Emma Yanes Rizo, "La Loza Estannífera de Puebla. De la Comunidad Original de Loceros a la Formación del Gremio (1550–1653)" (PhD thesis, México, D. F.: UNAM, 2013), 118–19, 128–30.

55 Carswell, *Blue and White*, 52; Kuwayama, *Chinese Ceramics*, 10–14; Ruiz Gutiérrez, "Influencias Artísticas," 335–37.

ILLUSTRATION 6   Tin-glazed basin with landscape in Chinese style (Puebla de los Ángeles),
attributed to the Workshop of Diego Salvador Carreto, c. 1650–1700.

both in Asia and in the pre-Hispanic Americas. In China, lacquerwork had
made great progress during the Han dynasty (206 BC–220 AD) and the Tang
dynasty (618–907), when the use of animals, birds, and flowers carved in gold
and silver into the surface of lacquered wood pieces made them coveted luxuries among the rich of Chinese society. During the Ming dynasty (1368–1644),
lacquerwork was – like other crafts – strongly promoted by the state.[56] In Japan, the shellac paint known as *makie* was introduced from abroad, along with

56   Hang Jian and Guo Qiuhui, *Chinese Arts and Crafts* (translated by Zhou Youruo and Song
Peiming) (Beijing: China Intercontinental Press, 2006), 54–58.

Buddhism, in 552. This craft underwent considerable development in subsequent centuries, and *makie* began to be applied together with *urushi* lacquer to decorative and functional items.[57] In pre-Hispanic America, the ability of natives to lacquer objects was noted by their Spanish conquerors in chronicles written during the first half of the seventeenth century. The production of furniture in New Spain was strongly influence at the outset by both Iberian and indigenous American heritages. Spanish American marquetry of the sixteenth century followed the Iberian *mudéjar* models of decoration and used raw materials such as tortoiseshell, ivory, and nacre as well as local woods. Craftsmen from Campeche and Oaxaca produced lacquer from a bituminous paste of burned lime and black plant dye extracted from dyewood (*palo*), which was then applied to the lines grooved in the wood.[58]

After the opening of the Manila Galleon route, the richest pieces of wooden furniture received in Spanish America from Asia came from Japan; these were items varnished with *urushi* lacquer using the *makie* technique and following the patterns of *namban* art: *horror vacui* decoration, linear perspective of figures, and the use of gold or silver dust and pigments of red, yellow, or green in the *urushi* engravings. For the New Spanish elites, folding screens (*biombos*) became the most well known and desirable lacquered pieces. These products, like the rest of *namban* works of art commissioned by Western foreigners, were produced exclusively for exportation – mostly by the artisans of Kyoto. However, there was no lasting influence of *namban* furniture on lacquerwork production in early modern Spanish America. In 1625, Japan closed its borders to the Christian Iberians; immediately afterward, other types of lacquered works became imitated.[59]

When New Spaniards started avidly acquiring pieces of furniture lacquered in black and golden colours from Japan (and even more colourful ones from China) that were shipped via Manila galleons in the seventeenth century,

---

57 Kaizo Kanki, "Artes Industriales Namban," *Archivo Español de Arte* 196 (1976): 455–67; Barbara Brennan Ford, "Japan," in *East Asian Lacquer. The Florence and Herbert Irving Collection*, VVAA (New York: Metropolitan Museum of Art, 1991), 150–73.

58 María Paz Aguiló Alonso, *El Mueble en el Siglo XVIII: Nuevas Aportaciones a Su Estudio* (Barcelona: Associació per a l'Estudi del Moble, 2008), 19; VVAA, *El Mueble Mexicano. Historia, Evolución e Influencias* (Mexico, D. F.: Fomento Cultural Banamex, 1985); Paz Aguiló Alonso, *El Mueble*, 22–24.

59 Yayoi Kawamura, "Coleccionismo y Colecciones de la Laca Extremo Oriental en España desde la Época del Arte Namban hasta el Siglo XX," *Artigrama* 18 (2003): 211–30; María Paz Aguiló Alonso, "Via Orientalis 1500–1900. La Repercusión del Arte del Extremo Oriente en España en Mobiliario y Decoración," in *El Arte Foráneo en España: Presencia e Influencia*, ed. Miguel Cabañas Bravo (Madrid: CSIC, 2005), 525–38.

Asian influence was already making itself felt in the furniture craftsmanship of New Spain; see illustration 7.[60] Unlike the case of cobalt, which was imported from Asia to reproduce blue decoration in Chinese-like ceramics from Puebla, there was no transfer of materials used to decorate furniture in the craftsmanship of New Spain; instead, craftsmen sought to obtain the same decorative results seen in Chinese and Japanese lacquered furniture while using locally produced materials. Michoacán was the area in which the Asian influence on furniture production was greatest. In Michoacán, the inlaying technique used to finish a product was similar to the technique of inlay mastered by Japanese artisans. This was a technique transmitted from Japan to Europe and also to the Americas. In Michoacán, as in Japan, furniture artisans decorated objects with a single colour, which was usually black or some other dark shade. A drawing was then traced on the object by scratching with a sharp tool, and finally the grooves of the drawing were decorated with different colours. Although the decorative result was similar, Asian woodworkers used a plant lacquer extracted from the *sumack* tree whereas New Spanish woodworkers used a shellac (*maque*) paste made of both plant and animal components. The most important of these ingredients was *axe*, the fat of an insect. These imitations were also produced in Europe – especially in the eighteenth century, when they became quite popular – although the resins used were of lower quality than those used in China and Japan.[61]

Whether unsuccessuful, like De los Ríos Coronel's attempts to transplant Chinese mulburrey trees in Spain, or successful, like the use of Japanese techniques to inlay furniture, the transmission of manufacturing techniques became a new horizon for the Spanish Empire. Successful producers imported not only techniques but also materials when seeking to imitate Asian goods, as when cobalt oxide was used to produce Chinese-like ceramic. These possibilities, perhaps dreamed of by seamen and explorers who sought new routes from Europe to East Asia before 1492, were realized a century later. But the protagonists were not merchants and artisans from Europe but rather traders and craftsmen who had been born and lived in Spanish America.

---

60   Paz Aguiló Alonso, "Via Orientalis," 525–38.

61   Sonia Pérez Carrillo, "Imitación de la Laca Oriental en Muebles Novohispanos del Siglo XVIII," *Cuadernos de Arte Colonial* 3 (1987): 51–78; Ruiz Gutiérrez, "Influencias Artísticas," 338–40; Berg, *Luxury and Pleasure*, 81–82; María Soledad García Fernández, "Muebles y Paneles Decorativos de Laca en el Siglo XVIII," *Oriente en Palacio. Tesoros Asiáticos en las Colecciones Reales Españolas*, vvaa (Madrid: Patrimonio Nacional, 2003), 338–44.

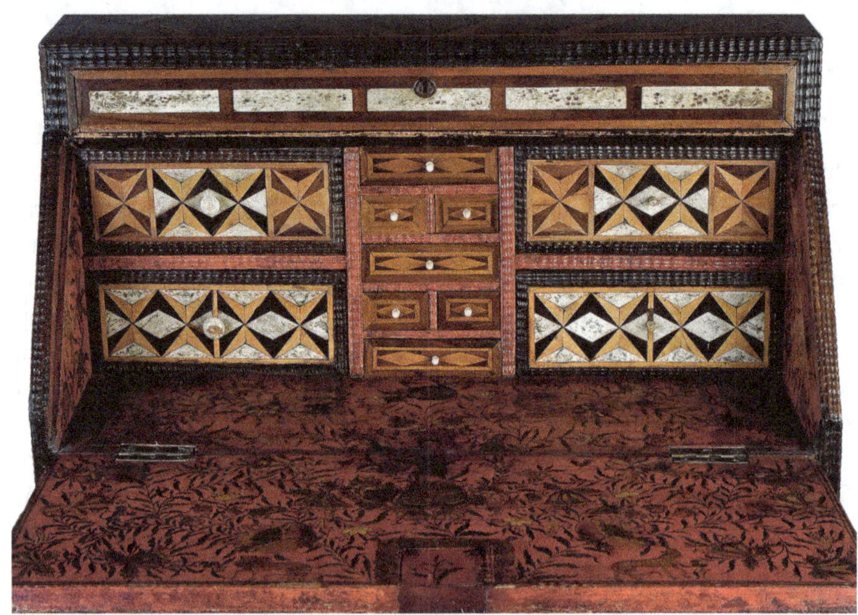

ILLUSTRATION 7   Escritoire with Chinese flower decoration (New Spain, seventeenth century).
SOURCE: MÉXICO, D. F. MUSEO FRANZ MAYER, MEXICO CITY (MEXICO)

5.3   Conclusions

Persistent political tension was triggered by the expansion of trade, by the circulation in New Spain of Chinese silk and porcelain (and Japanese lacquered furniture) pieces from Japan and China, and by their re-exportation to Iberia. This political tension destabilised the Empire and led to changes in the Crown's political economy regarding the Americas, which was also affected by the Manila Galleon's place in the international arena. Imports of Asian goods also played a part in the economic transformations occurring in some areas of the Spanish Empire, which were fuelled by producers' search for the raw materials used in Asian manufacturing processes. Although similar dynamics played out in other areas of the world, in the Spanish Empire they resulted not only as a reaction to new inputs from Asia (as changes were driven by the Manila Galleon trade) but also as the way in which conflicting interests among different trading and producing agents of the Empire evolved.

The spread of Chinese silk in New Spain led to a series of changes that extended beyond the decline of silk production in New Spain. Changes were especially dramatic in Puebla and Oaxaca, as classic historiography has shown. A focus on the nature of the silk trade, both Pacific and trans-Atlantic, helps to account for the evolving reactions (and conflicts) of Hispanic traders and producers of luxuries and semi-luxuries. Silk tailors and weavers from Mexico City changed their supply sources of silk from Puebla and Oaxaca to Manila. They imported, occasionally through their own agents in Manila, raw silk and silk yarns as well as semi-manufactured fabrics. Wholesalers and silk producers from Castile reacted strongly because their American market for textiles shrank precipitously once the Manila Galleon trade developed. The competitiveness of Chinese silk was such that, even in Castile, Sevillian traders imported it from New Spain in raw and yarn form. Precisely because the main share of Chinese silk imports in Castile from New Spain were in raw and yarn form, instead of fabrics, they were enthusiastically taken up by the silk tailors, weavers, and workshops in such production centres as Granada, which was the final destination for much of the Chinese raw silk arriving in Seville. The tangle of interests embroiled in the importing of Chinese silk in the Spanish Empire meant that its impact depended on the economic sector involved and the perspective of the Empire's relevant social groups.

The Spanish Empire's reception of other products, such as Chinese porcelain and lacquered furniture from China and Japan, did not trigger such conflicting reactions because the quantity imported via the Manila Galleon trade was lower than that of silk. One of the most notable consequences of the expansion of the Manila Galleon trade, especially from the 1580s to the 1610s, was the transfer of skills from one continent to another. The potters from Puebla assayed to copy the blue colour of Chinese porcelain by identifying and obtaining, first via the galleons and later domestically, the substance used by Chinese artisans to decorate their pottery. Both the importing of cobalt oxide from Asia and its application in Puebla ceramics resulted from a search for and transmission knowledge driven by the circulation Chinese blue-and-white porcelain. In the case of lacquerwork, carpenters and designers from regions such as Michoacán were not able to identify the Asian source of *makie* in Asia, but even so they managed to imitate its effects in their own wood furniture using dyes that were indigenous to America. The response of New Spanish manufacturers to the increasing circulation of Asian goods in the viceroyalty was to initiate a transfer of knowledge, skills, and particular techniques from Asia to Spanish America. These transfers were contemporaneous with – and in some cases (e.g., the use of cobalt to decorate ceramics) occurred earlier than – similar transfers from Asia to Europe. Nonetheless, circulation and trade did not by themselves create the conditions under which these transfers of manufacturing skills, techniques, and materials could take place; those conditions were mediated by the increasing taste, among New Spain's elites, for Asian goods. The spread of consumer preferences for Chinese silk and other Asian products, which helped alter the social and cultural realities and elite representations of the wealthiest people of New Spain, played an essential role in facilitating this cultural transfer. That topic is addressed in the following chapter.

CHAPTER 6

Consumption Habits, Fashions, and Taste for Asian Manufactured Goods among Elites in Mexico City and Seville

After the opening of the Manila Galleon route – and, above all, following Manila's definitive commitment to international trade in the 1580s – Asian manufactured goods started to become a part of the Hispanic elites' culture on both sides of the Atlantic Ocean. Goods from Asia such as Chinese silk and porcelain, Japanese furniture, folding screens and fans, and other minor products transported in the Manila galleons, such as Indian calico and Japanese porcelain, introduced new material realities into the cultural plurality of the Spanish Empire.[1] However, this incorporation of Asian material culture, which ended up fostering imitations and new products in New Spanish, was not immediate, and neither was the cultural pattern of integration the same in all segments of Hispanic society. There were asymmetries in the reception and forms of using and consuming Asian manufactured goods that depended on economic, geographic, and socio-cultural factors. Owing to the dispersion of markets that dominated global trade in the late sixteenth and early seventeenth century, it was cheaper to ship Asian goods from the Philippines to Spanish America than to transport them from Asia to Castile. As a result, Asian manufactured goods cost less in Spanish America than in Castile.[2]

Cheaper prices and family networks closer to Asia favoured an easier access to Asian goods by the elites of Spanish America than by the elites of Castile. However, price and distribution methods were not the only elements that regulated access to Asian novelties in the Spanish Empire. Taste preferences, which were determined by the shape of different identities and practices, affected the demand for Asian manufactures among the Empire's elite. In the Spanish Empire, being a member of the elite of New Spain did not have the same social and cultural connotations as being a member of the elite of a Castilian city. And in Spanish America, those of the so-called *peninsular* or Iberian elite (i.e.,

---

1 Cinta Krahe, *Chinese Porcelain in Habsburg Spain* (Madrid: Madrid, CEEH, 2016); Carmen Yuste López, "Un Océano de Intercambios," *El Galeón de Manila. Catálogo*, VVAA (Madrid: Ministerio de Educación, 2000).

2 José L. Gasch-Tomás, "Transport Costs and Prices of Chinese Silk in the Spanish Empire. The Case of New Spain, c. 1571–1650," *Revista de Historia Industrial* 60 (2015): 15-47.

rulers who had been born in Castile or Portugal) were socially advantaged in comparison with Creoles (i.e., those of New Spaniard or Peruvian ancestry or of European ancestry yet born in the Americas). Furthermore, within the elite groups of both American and Castilian societies, mid-level elites such as rich artisans and civil servants lived in different cultural, social, and aesthetic environments than those of the rich nobles and wholesalers – notwithstanding their common economic superiority over most members of their societies. The different significance that Asian manufactured goods held according to the diverse social and cultural environments in which they were integrated, and the different ways of using such goods in their respective social spheres, meant that the Creole elites of the Americas and certain social groups of Castile and New Spain were relatively more receptive to Chinese silk and porcelain, lacquered furnishings from Japan, and other Asian manufactured goods. Social, symbolic, and cultural mechanisms determined the tastes, uses, and forms of consumption of Asian manufactured goods by the elites of New Spain and Castile. The cities of Mexico and Seville and their elites and probate inventories offer a good perspective on such differences.

6.1 Identification of the Elites of Seville and the Creole and Iberian Elites of Mexico City

The Spanish Empire was a political power presiding over socially and culturally heterogeneous societies. This diversity was evident among the common people of two main areas of the Spanish Empire, Castile and the Americas. In 1600, the subaltern populations of Castile differed sharply from indigenous Americans despite the cultural, religious, and political impositions of Castilian power over the latter. Differences between the dominant groups and rulers of Castile and those of the Americas were naturally less than those between the two continents' majority populations. Creole elites of the Americas stemmed from Castilian conquerors or Castilian emigrants – or, in fewer cases, from pre-Hispanic rulers who had been thoroughly "Hispanised" –, and both Castilian and Creole elites shared common political and cultural backgrounds and occasionally even came from similar family branches. During the early modern era, however, the elites of Castile and of the Americas ended up identifying themselves and representing their powers through different discourses and material artefacts.

In the following pages I frequently employ the terms "elite." Furthermore, I use the term "identification," instead of "identity." Both "elite" and "identity" have been overused in common speaking and in social science publications, which has undermined their intended meaning. This book follows Mill's classic approach, according to which the *elite* is composed of people "whose positions enable them to transcend the ordinary environments of ordinary men and women," which is to say that "they are in positions to make decisions having major consequences." Elite comprises a minority of people of the higher circles who "may also be conceived as members of a top social stratum," who feel themselves to be and are felt by others to be an upper inner circle and who form a more or less compact social and psychological entity.[3] In the context of the early modern hierarchical Americas, Creoles (a word stemming from the Portuguese *crioulo*) were settlers of European ancestry born in the Americas. Thus the Creole elite in New Spain comprised a heterogeneous group of individuals who shared two features: born to Europeans but in the Americas, and "members of a top social stratum" whose positions and decisions had major consequences – in particular, rulers of principal American institutions (e.g., the viceroyalty administration, city councils, Mexico City's mint), wealthy members of religious orders, rulers of guilds, wealthy merchants, and rich artisans and landowners.

Creole elite raised in New Spain competed with the peninsular (Iberian) elite,[4] and Creole elite is identified here in opposition to the *peninsulares*. These considerations lead us to the term "identity." Following Brabuker and Cooper, I prefer to use *identification* when referring to affinities, affiliations, forms of belonging, and experiences of communality; doing so distinguishes between the agent who identifies and the identified group (in this case, Creoles). Recall that Creoles usually self-identify as such. Thus Creoles are here identified as an emerging group in the sixteenth- and seventeenth-century Americas. Even while stressing the complex process by which the Creoles as a group emerged, we must bear in mind that the Creole group was heterogeneous in its composition. Following this approach facilitates to gauge the role played by the consumption of Asian goods in the identification – and self-identification – of Creole elites.

In this chapter I argue that the link between such an identification of the Creole elite and consumption of Asian goods matters for two reasons. The first reason concerns one of the most debated questions in the studies of consumption: the agency of consumers, or *why* consumers purchase what they

---

3   C. Wright Mills, *The Power Elite* (Oxford: Oxford University Press, 2000 (originally published in 1956)), 2–4, 11. Although Mills focused on the American elite of his time, the definition is broad enough to define the elite of other places and eras.

4   Ralph Bauer and José Antonio Mazzotti, eds., *Creole Subjects in the Colonial Americas. Empires, Texts, Identities* (Chapel Hill: University of North Carolina Press, 2009), 3–7.

purchase.[5] By linking the identification of the Creole elite – and their emergence as a (howsoever heterogeneous) group whose members had common political objectives and similar cultures – with their desire to consume Chinese silk and porcelain and other Asian goods, we can explain why Creole elites in Mexico City purchased more Asian goods than did their Iberian counterparts from Seville (and from Mexico City). In line with Smith's definitions of *cultural contexts* and *cultural meaning*,[6] the next pages argue that Asian goods had more meaning in the cultural context of the Creole elite than in the peninsular elites' cultural context for both material and behavioural reasons. In the first place, Asian goods were better adapted to the material plurality and family backgrounds of the Creole elite. Second, one of this book's main arguments is that the link between identification of a Creole elite and consumption of Asian goods helps to disentangle the cultural, economic, and social processes – set in motion by the trans-Pacific trade with Spanish America – that eventually triggered some transformations in the Atlantic World. Thus the following pages illustrate and analyse how the Creole elites, despite being essentially European, changed over time to represent themselves differently from the European standard; for example, they acquired non-Castilian social and cultural practices earlier than their Castilian counterparts. The focus will be on how, within the divergent yet connected Euro-American and Castilian elite cultural contexts, Asian objects served as cultural capital in different ways and sometimes regardless of whether they had any practical use.

Seville and Mexico City were two of the largest and most influential cities of the Spanish Empire, and home for Creole and Iberian elites, and Castilian elites, respectively. They had institutional and political similarities, but their social and cultural components – as well as their demographic composition – made them two very different urban spaces. Unlike Mexico City, which had been created practically *ex novo* from Tenochtitlan, Seville had a long history

---

5   Maxine Berg, *Luxury and Pleasure in Eighteenth-Century Britain* (Oxford: Oxford University Press, 2005); Jan de Vries, *The Industrious Revolution: Consumer Demand and the Household Economy, 1650 to the Present* (Cambridge: Cambridge University Press, 2008); Amanda Vickery, *Behind the Closed Doors. At Home in Georgian England* (New Haven: Yale University Press, 2009); Woodruff D. Smith, *Consumption and the Making of Respectability, 1600–1800* (London: Routledge, 2002).

6   Smith, *Consumption and the Making*, 9–21. A cultural context can be defined as an assembly of factors or traits that make *sense* as an ensemble to the people living in a particular time and area, which is to say as elements of their world *meaningfully* linked to one another. *Meaning* in this framework is defined as a phenomenon observable in human thought and behaviour that is essential to – and perhaps arises from – the interaction of humans with each other and to the negotiation of their physical environment: *ibid.*, 13, 19–20.

that included undergoing many changes during the sixteenth century, its century of splendour. Seville was the only Spanish *entrepôt* that could legally trade with the Americas. It thus became a city whose vibrancy and level of commercial activity were unprecedented in Castile, and its only contemporary European rivals in that respect were Lisbon and Antwerp. An important consequence of this status was the presence in Seville of many foreign merchants who traded there and made the city one of the most cosmopolitan of all Europe.[7] That being said, Seville remained a city in which the noble medieval values still played a significant role in social and institutional life, undeterred by the emergence of powerful mercantile classes. The importance of elements like "purity of blood" (i.e., not having Jewish ancestors) in Seville's society, combined with the high number of nobles in comparison with other Castilian cities, made Seville a city with many social and cultural barriers. This does not mean that Seville and its elites were isolated from the main cultural currents of their time. On the contrary, as with other Andalusian aristocrats, the Sevillian noblemen used the cultural platform of the Renaissance and Humanism to renew linguistic and artistic ways of representing their power. Besides the older and medieval modes of power expression, such as the coat of arms, sixteenth-century Castilian aristocrats used the new languages of the Renaissance to exhibit their power and social status. Among some nobles there was a cultural interest in the new customs of Humanism, which included a taste for lectures and music as well as interest in Ancient Greek and Roman civilisations, scientific curiosities, and natural oddities. One of the main expressions of such novel cultural trends was the collecting of rarities and natural objects from faraway places, although it is often difficult to distinguish true scientific interest from the mere display of power among the possessions of noble families.[8]

The social context of sixteenth-century Sevillian elites was characterised by the combining of new mercantile classes, which emerged and grew as a result of profitable trans-Atlantic trade, with the old noble families who maintained the highest status in the city. Many Sevillian nobles invested in trade, but not publicly given the non-noble values associated with commerce. However, the main socio-economic trend among Sevillian elites was investment in land, though wealthy merchants were likely to invest also in cultural capital (e.g., falsifying and

7   Antonio Domínguez Ortiz, *Orto y Ocaso de Sevilla* (Sevilla: Universidad de Sevilla, 1981).

8   Enrique Soria Mesa, *La Nobleza en la España Moderna. Cambio y Continuidad* (Madrid: Marcial Pons, 2007), 268–70; Antonio Urquízar Herrera, " 'Masserizia' y Mayorazgo: La Recepción Andaluza de las Ideas Italianas sobre la Casa del Noble y Su Adecuación Social," in *El Modelo Italiano en las Artes Plásticas de la Península Ibérica durante el Renacimiento*, ed. María J. Redondo Cantera (Valladolid: Universidad de Valladolid, 2004), 195–207.

"ennobling" their lineages).[9] These social and cultural changes in Sevillian society, especially those involving the elites, had an extraordinary influence on the forms of elite consumption of Asian manufactured goods in the Andalusian city.

On the other side of the Atlantic, Mexico City encapsulated the post-1500 new world era within its walls even better than did Seville. Besides the native peoples subjugated by the Spanish conquerors, there were European immigrants, African slaves, and also Asian peoples who travelled, lived, and worked in Spanish America and Mexico City.[10] Tenochtitlan, as Mexico City was known in pre-Hispanic times, was conquered by the Spaniards in 1521. Despite the epidemics that annihilated thousands of *mexicas* and the rest of the native population, the Spaniards and their descendants were always a minority, the ruling elite. Initially the Spaniards lived in the centre of Mexico City, while the indigenous Americans lived in the neighbourhoods and fields (*encomiendas*) around the centre. Nonetheless, miscegenation occurred early on. The natives entered Spanish areas, usually looking for work, and the original three-category ethnic scheme of Spaniard, Black, and Indian was soon complicated by racial integration; the categories of *mestizo, mulato,* and so forth were added. Miscegenation was accompanied by cultural changes leading to a multi-dimensional cultural web wherein the "latinisation" of *naturales* (natives) by religious orders was the main but not the only component. Moreover, Spanish and Creole elites adopted native customs (e.g., the consumption of chocolate) and aesthetic practices.[11] Mexico, like other American cities, was governed by a hierarchical ideology and social structure with racial, religious, cultural, economic, and occupational foundations. Despite these European impositions, Mexico became a new city with a new society that was likely more open to cultural and social change than were Castilian and many other European cities. Peoples, beliefs, goods, ideas, and languages mixed together in Mexico City. In fact, since Mexico was a capital and one of the most populated cities of the Americas, the plurality of cultures was greater there than in other areas of the continent.[12]

---

9   Enriqueta Vila Vilar, *Los Corzo y los Mañara. Tipos y Arquetipos del Mercader con Indias* (Sevilla: Escuela de Estudios Hispano-Americanos, 1991).

10   Edward S. Slack, "The *Chinos* in New Spain: A Corrective Lens for a Distorted Image," *Journal of World History* 20, no. 1 (2009), 35–67; Tatiana Seijas, *Asian Slaves in Colonial Mexico. From Chinos to Indians* (Cambridge: Cambridge University Press, 2015).

11   James Lockhart and Stuart B. Schwart, *Early Latin America. A History of Colonial Spanish America and Brazil* (Cambridge: Cambridge University Press, 1983), 129–30; Arnold J. Bauer, *Goods, Power, History: Latin America's Material Culture* (Cambridge: Cambridge University Press, 2001).

12   Louisa S. Hoberman and Susan S. Socolow, *Ciudades y Sociedad en Latinamérica Colonial* (México, D.F.: Fondo de Cultura Económica, 1993), 7–28; Serge Gruzinski, *Las Cuatro Partes*

In New Spanish society, those who held the highest positions in the viceroyalty – viceroys, archbishops, *corregidores*, and the main members of the *Real Audiencia* – were the *peninsulares* (Iberians). Their numbers were few and so, given how the monarchy had directed the conquest, there were not many groups of titled aristocratic families in Mexico City, especially when compared to Seville. This control by the *peninsulares* (most appointed by the King himself) of the viceroyalty's important positions was in contrast to the Creole majority of the New Spanish elites in America. Indeed, scholars have identified this period – the late sixteenth and early seventeenth centuries – with a "Creolisation" or the birth of a Creole self-identification, which was based on their sense of voicelessness and discrimination within the Empire and which matured in the eighteenth century to become essential to the independence processes of the early nineteenth century. Yet this rise of a Creole identification did not, in the seventeenth century, translate into a desire for political rupture.[13] The focus here is on the shaping of a Creole self-identification and identification in the viceroyalty of New Spain, although reference will be made to parallel processes that transpired in Peru.

Brading and Cañizares-Esguerra have defined the dynamics that shaped American Creole identification during the seventeenth and eighteenth centuries as Creole patriotic discourses; these arose as a reaction of conqueror descendants to their loss of economic privileges and were later nourished by conflicts of power between the Creoles and Iberians of the New Spanish and Peruvian viceroyalties. The negative image of the Americas that was pronounced in Castile by metropolitan learned scholars (*letrados*) and other elites, in many cases expressed in written texts, triggered Creole reaction at the turn of the century.[14] In contrast with metropolitans' image of the Americas, which was viewed as both culturally and environmentally degenerate, Creole apologists touted a positive image based on religious, social, pseudo-historical, and even

---

del Mundo. Historia de una Mundialización (México, D.F.: Fondo de Cultura Económica, 2010), 97–123.

13   The focus here is on the shaping of a Creole identity in the viceroyalty of New Spain, although reference will be made to parallel processes that transpired in Peru. For the Peruvian Creole consciousness, see Bernard Lavallé, *Recherchers sur l'Apparition de la Conscience Créole dans la Vice-Royauté du Pérou. L'Antagonisme Hispano-Créole dans les Orders Religieuses (XVIe–XVIIe Siècles)* (Lille: Université de Lille, 1982); and José A. Mazzotti, "La Heterogeneidad Colonial Peruana y la Construcción del Discurso Criollo en el Siglo XVII," in *Asedios a la Heterogeneidad Cultural. Homenaje a Antonio Cornejo Polar*, ed. José A. Mazzotti and U. Juan Zevallos Aguilar (Philadelphia, PA: Asociación Internacional de Peruanistas, 1996), 173–96.

14   David A. Brading, *The Origins of Mexican Nationalism* (Cambridge: Centre of Latin American Studies, 1985).

racial discourses. The main points of this incipient Creole self-identification discourse can be found in at least three elements: the merging of the Iberian heritage with a positive view of the pre-Hispanic civilizations and rulers; the creation of a Creole mythology; and the existence of a capital city (Mexico City in New Spain, Lima in Peru) wherein the virtues of Creole society converged.

Seventeenth-century Creole self-identification was an Iberian and European discourse that incorporated Aztec and Inca images in (respectively) New Spain and Peru. European elements arose from Iberian, Catholic, and Renaissance language. One point that clearly demonstrated the connection between Iberian culture and the Creole self-identification was the cultural and political importance given by the Creoles to the conquest of America. Within the genre of epic stories about that conquest written during the sixteenth century, Creoles viewed themselves as natural descendants of the conquerors, set against the *peninsulares* and their contemporary Iberian counterparts. Written in 1610, the epic poem *Historia de la Nueva España* (History of New Spain) by the captain Gaspar Pérez de Villagrá (1555–1620) clearly reflects the Iberian and European foundations of the Creole mind. Its author was a Humanist in the Italian Renaissance mold: a "soldier-poet" or man of arms and letters. In Homeric–Virgilian and Christian idioms, Pérez de Villagrá celebrated the conquest and colonisation of the Pueblo Indians in 1596 by Juan de Oñate (1550–1626). The author blamed the difficulties enountered in colonising New Spain at that time on the nature of the Iberian newcomers. He contrasted the Creole with the Peninsular nature by using Castilian discourses and values while adapting them to Creole society. According to Pérez de Villagrá, the Iberian newcomers – unlike Oñate's old Christian blood and consequent willingness to countenance hardships in the northern frontiers – were likely *conversos* (Jewish converts or descendants) and not brave enough to conquer the Pueblo Indians.[15] The Creole elites of the early seventeenth century were building an identification of themselves distinct from that of their Peninsular counterparts, but its motifs remained Peninsular and European.

The poem by Pérez de Villagrá extols another characteristic of the Creole identification and self-identification: its connection with pre-Hispanic nobles. His text presents Oñate as a great-grandson of Moctezuma, which is at odds with the discourses created in Castile about the pre-Hispanic past of the Americas. In Castile, the Aztec and Inca civilisations were characterised as degenerate and ruined; however, the *mestizo*, Creoles, and some missionary servants

---

15   *Ibid.*, 425–26; Jorge Cañizares-Esguerra, "Racial, Religious, and Civic Creole Identity in Colonial Spanish America," *American Literary History* 17, no. 3 (2005): 425–27.

(born in Castile but raised in the Americas) developed narratives praising the societies conquered by Cortés and Pizarro.[16] The debates between Creole and Castilian scholars over characterisation of pre-Hispanic civilisations and natives of the Americas, especially Bartolomé de las Casas's texts, were important because they were – along with Franciscan (and other missionary) texts and codices in native American languages – essential references for two works that profoundly marked the Creole discourses about the Americas until the end of the eighteenth century. These works were the *Comentarios Reales* (Royal Commentaries), published in 1609 by Gómez Suárez de Figueroa (1539–1616), a.k.a. the Inca Garcilaso de la Vega, and the *Monarquía Indiana* (Monarchy of the Indies), published in 1615 by the Franciscan Juan de Torquemada (1557–1624).

The *Comentarios Reales* by Garcilaso, a *mestizo* son of the leading conqueror and mayor (*corregidor*) of Cuzco, Sebastián Garcilaso de la Vega, and the Inca princess Isabel Chimpu Occllo, was written with the aim of exalting both the Castilian and Inca ancestors of the writer. The *Monarquía Indiana* was produced by Juan de Torquemada, a Franciscan born in Castile and raised in New Spain, to defend and glorify Franciscans. It was a text dominated by the Franciscan vision of pre-Hispanic Indians: although controlled by the Devil (as demonstrated by Aztec rites), natives were pure in soul and prudent in justice. These two texts had many notable differences, but they played similar roles in the two viceroyalties of the Americas. Both Torquemada and especially Garcilaso described the Indians in a favourable light, viewing the native people as those who followed "natural" law. In this context of glorifying pre-Hispanic civilisations and nobles, many Creole grandees claimed noble Indians as their biological ancestors.[17]

This rising Creole self-identification in the seventeenth-century Americas, which was based on both European and Iberian cultural heritage and also on a positive valuation of pre-Hispanic civilisations and rulers, took form alongside new American myths. Most of these myths featured essential Creole components, which made it easier for them to reach a wide audience. In New Spain, the myth of Our Lady of Guadalupe (*Virgen de Guadalupe*) was the most important. Unlike Our Lady of Los Remedios (*Virgen de los Remedios*), the most

---

16   David A. Brading, *The First America. The Spanish Monarchy, Creole Patriots, and the Liberal State, 1492–1867* (Cambridge: Cambridge University Press, 1991), 25–101.

17   Jorge Gurría Lacroix, "Aprovechamiento de la *Monarquía Indiana* en los Siglos XVI, XVII, XVIII, XIX y XX," in *Monarquía Indiana*, Juan de Torquemada (edited by Miguel León-Portilla) (México, D.F., 1973–1985), 433–35. Cañizares-Esguerra, "Racial, Religious, and Civic Creole Identify," 423; Jorge Cañizares-Esguerra, "New World, New Stars: Patriotic Astrology and the Invention of Indian and Creole Bodies in Colonial Spanish America, 1600–1650," *American Historical Review* 104, no. 1 (1999): 33–68.

celebrated image in Mexico City, Our Lady of Guadalupe became a reference point for the whole viceroyalty of New Spain and, over time, for modern Mexico. Other Mexican myths, such as the identification of St. Thomas with the Indian hero-god Quetzalcóatl, similarly served as a catalyst for New Spanish Creole discourses.[18]

The last component of the rising Creole self-identification in the late sixteenth and early seventeenth centuries was one for which the connection of New Spain with China and the trade of Asian manufactured goods in the Americas was essential: the rise of the capital city as emblematic of the virtues and power of the Creole elite. The Creole spirit was essentially urban and was shaped in the two viceroyal capitals: Lima in Peru and Mexico City in New Spain were each conceived by Creoles as the crossroads of the monarchy if not of the world itself. This image of the two cities was built up through literary texts and paintings that were produced starting at the end of the sixteenth century. Mexico City and Lima were praised by the elites of New Spain and Peru for their heroic stories, beauty, and power – and also for their roles as Christian centres (on a continent with a pagan past) and as economic and commercial powers. The Peruvian Creoles viewed Lima as a metaphor for themselves, describing the city as a place full of wealth and as an enormous market whose walls circumscribed elements of the entire world;[19] the Mexican Creoles held similar views about Mexico City.

Paintings of seventeenth- and eighteenth-century Mexico City show it playing a central role in both history and Christendom. The representation of the city as a commercial emporium and a space where products from all over the world converged was recurrent in descriptions of Mexico City and also of Lima. According to the Creole elites of New Spain, commercial power was one of the key elements that made Mexico City magnificent. This belief is manifest in the treatises about the city written in the eighteenth century. Two exemplary texts are the 1768 *Exacta Descripción de la Magnífica Corte Mexicana, Cabeza del Nuevo Mundo* (Exact Description of the Magnificent Mexican Court, Head of the New World) by Juan Manuel de San Vicente (?–1778) and the 1777 *Breve Compendiosa Narración de la Ciudad de México, Corte y Cabeza*

---

18   David A. Brading, *Mexican Phoenix, Our Lady of Guadalupe: Image and Tradition across Five Centuries* (Cambridge: Cambridge University Press, 2001); see also Brading, *The First America*, 343–61; Brading, *Origins*, 12.

19   Sonia V. Rose, "¿Un Lima Mercurial? Toma de Poder y Autoimagen de la Elite Criolla," in *Des Merchands entre Deux Mondes. Pratiques et Représentations en Espagne et en Amerique (XVe–XVIIIe Siècles)*, ed. Béatrice Pérez and Jean-Pierre Clément (Paris: PUPS, 2007), 267–85.

de Toda la América Septentrional (Brief Narrative Compendium of Mexico City, Court and Head of All Northern America) by Juan de Viera (1719–1780). In both treatises, a review of the history of Tenochtitlan/Mexico and its main buildings is accompanied by a description of the merchandise that converged in the capital of the viceroyalty.[20] Viera described the central square of Mexico in the following terms: "The *Parian* has the form of a citadel or castle [...] Inside and outside is full of all types of merchandise from Europe, Asia and this land. There are infinite varieties of china, precious stones, silver goods, dress trimmings, etc., which are valued at more than 30 million [...] Unique curiosities of sheets, clocks, glasses, and thousands of silver things are sold; swords, ceremonial swords, firearms, trappings, books, niches, images, mirrors, etc. [...] Footwear for rich and poor alike. There is a lot of Moroccan leather of many colours, and embroidered satins, velvets and rich fabrics."[21] San Vicente delineated the main square of Mexico City in similar terms.[22]

Perhaps the text that most clearly depicts Mexico City as a cosmopolitan centre and mercantile haven is the early poem "Grandeza Mexicana" (*Mexican Splendour*) (1602) by Bernardo de Balbuena (1562–1627). This ode is about a hero in the form of a city. De Balbuena's text summarises the natural history and geography of Mexico, and it praises the capital of New Spain as unique because riches from all over the globe converged there. Accordingly, Mexico's splendour arises from three features that make it incomparable: a heroic history, an excellent climate, and a market that situates the city at the world's centre:[23]

> This is the richest and most opulent city,
> with more trade and treasures
> of the North and the South.
> Silver from Peru and gold from Chile
> come here, and fine cloves
> from Ternate, and cinnamon from Tidore.

---

20   Antonio Rubial García, ed., *La Ciudad de México en el Siglo XVIII (1690–1780). Tres Crónicas* (México, D.F.: Consejo Nacional para la Cultura y las Artes, 1990).

21   Juan de Viera (1990 [1778]), *Breve Compendiosa Narración de la Ciudad de México, Corte y Cabeza de Toda la América Septentrional*, in *Ciudad de México*, ed. Ruibal García, 214.

22   Juan M. de San Vicente (1990 [1768]), *Exacta Descripción de la Magnífica Corte Mexicana, Cabeza del Nuevo Mundo*, in *Ciudad de México*, ed. Ruibal García, 172.

23   Bernardo de Balbuena, *Grandeza Mexicana* (México, D.F.: Sociedad de Bibliófilos Mexicanos, 1927 (first published in 1602)), 76–77; Bárbara Fuchs and Yolanda Martínez-San Miguel, "*La Grandeza Mexicana* de Balbuena y el Imaginario de Una 'Metrópolis Colonial,'" *Revista Iberoamericana* 75, no. 228 (2009): 678–79.

Fabrics from Cambray, treasures from Quinsay,
coral from Sicily, tuberose from Syria,
incense from Arabia, garnets from Ormuz;
diamonds from India, and rubies
and fine emeralds from the gallant Scythian,
ivory from Goa, dun ebony from Siam.
The finest things from Spain and the Philippines,
the most precious objects from Macao,
riches from the two Javas.
Fine porcelain from the Chinese,
rich martens from the Scythes,
myrrh from the Troglodyte [sic];
amber from Malabar, pearls from Idaspes,
drugs from Egypt, scents from Pancaya,
carpets from Persia, jaspers from Etolia.
From the great Chinese colourful silks,
bezoar stones from the Andes,
stamps from Rome, delicacies from Milan.
All the clocks from Flanders,
fabrics from Italy, and trinkets
carved in Venice.[24]

The poem is obsessed with viewing Mexico City as a crossroads, an obligatory stop on the routes between Europe, the West Indies, and Asia (and thereby displacing Europe as the centre of commerce). Thus the value of Mexico City stems not only from its moral and aesthetic value but also from its material wealth: the accumulation within the city of merchandise and other objects produced in the Americas, Europe, and China:

These are the most important goods,
these are by far
the great cares of the world and its delicacies.
India produces ivory, Arabia perfumes,
Vizcaya iron, Dalmatia gold,
Peru silver, Melaka spices.
Japan produces silk, the South Sea treasures
of rich pearls, Chinese mother-of-pearl,

24	Balbuena, *Grandeza Mexicana*, 76–77.

Tiro purpura, and Moorish dates [...].
You bring together Spain and China,
Italy and Japan, and finally
the whole world in trade and discipline.
The greatest treasures of the West
and the finest products of the East are enjoyed within you.
Silver is the least of the riches here,
because it is incredibly abundant
and very cheap.[25]

The cultural practices and material culture, including Asian manufactured goods, of the Creole elites in Mexico and of the Castilian elites in Seville need to be understood within the framework of these discourses.

6.2 Social Aspects of the Consumption of Asian Manufactured Goods in Mexico City and Seville

Some works mention that, during the early modern era, Asian manufactured goods had long been present among the possessions of wealthy Spanish Americans.[26] Other studies have analysed the occurrence of Asian goods in Spanish American probate inventories; they show that the consumption of Asian goods extended southward beyond New Spain and Lima toward Tucumán and Buenos Aires in the eighteenth century.[27] Furthermore, archaeology documents has provided evidence of use of Chinese silk and porcelain in areas as far north as present-day New Mexico and Chihuahua as soon as the early seventeenth century.[28] More recent studies have employed more refined statistical methods

25   Balbuena, *Grandeza Mexicana*, 89–90.
26   John E. Elliot, "España y América en los Siglos XVI y XVII," in *Historia de América Latina. 2. América Latina Colonial: Europa y América en los Siglos XVI, XVII, XVIII*, ed. Leslie Bethell (Barcelona: Crítica, Barcelona), 3–44; Gustavo Curiel, " 'Al Remedo de la China': El Lenguaje 'Achinado' y la Formación de un Gusto dentro de las Casas Novohispanas," in *Orientes-Occidentes. El Arte y la Mirada del Otro*, ed. Gustavo Curiel (México, D.F.: UNAM, 2007), 299–317.
27   Mariano Ardash Bonialian, "Tejidos y Cerámica de China en la Gobernación de Tucumán y Buenos Aires, Siglo XVIII. Apuntes Sobre su Circulación y Consumo," *Anuario de Estudios Americanos* 71, no. 2 (2014): 631–60; Mariano Ardash Bonialian, *China en la América Colonial. Bienes, Mercados, Comercio y Cultura del Consumo desde México hasta Buenos Aires* (México, D.F.: Instituto Mora, 2014), 119–84.
28   Donna Pierce, "Popular and Prevalent: Asian Trade Goods in Northern New Spain, 1590–1850," *Colonial Latin American Review* 25, no. 1 (2016): 77-97.

and several metrics to indicate that the presence of Asian goods in Mexico City increased from twice to ten times that observed in Seville during the late sixteenth and early seventeenth century.[29] However, the works cited in this paragraph have not assessed the consumption of Asian goods from both a geographic and a social perspective. A look into the consumption of Asian manufactures as inferred from the stocks of accumulated Asian goods (according to probates of Mexico City's and Seville's elites) should yield further information about the social and cultural mechanisms behind the desire to consume Asian goods in New Spain and Castile.

When sorted by wealth group, the stocks of Asian goods reveal further information about the use and consumption of Asian goods relative to social classes at the turn of the century. Table 7 illustrates what common sense tells us: the richer the probate inventories, the more frequently they contain Asian goods; see Appendix A [3] for the sample of probates. However, the comparison between Mexico City and Seville offers more information than can be gleaned from the data pertaining to either city alone. The breakdown by wealth group (i.e., by the total value of goods and estates collected in the inventories) shows more clearly that the ownership of Asian goods extended among broader social groups in Mexico City than it did in Seville. In Mexico City, most of the inventories valued at more between 50,000 and 1,000,000 *maravedís* and all valued at more 1,000,000 *maravedís* contain Asian products; in Seville, not even half the inventories valued at more than 1,000,000 *maravedís* had any Asian products. Only the very richest of society would have probate inventories worth more than 1,000,000 *maravedís*. In Mexico City, such estates belonged to individuals in the highest positions of the viceroyal administration, members of the *Audiencia Real* or the city council, the city's wholesale merchants, and the highest religious elites. In Seville, inventories valued at more than 1,000,000 *maravedís* belonged to the city's highest nobles and richest merchants. Inventories worth more than 5,000,000 *maravedís* in Seville were those not only of rich people but also of such city notables as aldermen (*caballeros veinticuatro*) and wholesale merchants who held positions in the merchant guild.

Nearly 83 per cent of the inventories in Mexico City that were valued between 100,000 and 1,000,000 *maravedís* contained Asian goods. Indeed, some of these inventories are fairly brimming with items manufactured in Asia. In Seville, however, only about 20 per cent of the inventories in this value range

---

29   José Luis Gasch-Tomás, "Asian Silk, Porcelain and Material Culture in the Definition of
      Mexican and Andalusian Elites," in *Global Goods and the Spanish Empire, 1492–1824. Cir-
      culation, Resistance and Diversity*, ed. Bethany Aram and Bartolomé Yun-Casalilla (Lon-
      don: Palgrave Macmillan, 2014), 157–8.

TABLE 7   Asian products in probate inventories of Mexico City and Seville by wealth group (as indicated by total value), 1580–1630

Inventory value in *maravedís*	Mexico City inventories			Seville inventories		
	Total (*N*)	With Asian goods (*N*)	With Asian goods (%)	Total (*N*)	With Asian goods (*N*)	With Asian goods (%)
≤ 50,000	28	4	14.3	11	1	9.0
50,001 to 100,000	17	13	76.5	8	1	12.5
100,001 to 1,000,000	58	48	82.8	34	7	20.6
1,000,001 to 5,000,000	13	13	100.0	36	15	41.6
> 5,000,000	6	6	100.0	42	15	35.7
TOTAL	122	84	68.9	131	39	29.8

Notes: Inventory values are deflated using prices of maize and wheat in Mexico and Seville, respectively, and using the value of *maravedí* in silver; the base period is 1606–1610. See Appendix B for additional details.

SOURCE: SEE APPENDIX A[3].

contained any Asian items. This group included less wealthy or mid-level elites and also people who simply lived well, such as craftsmen and bureaucrats from either city. In Seville, a mere 10 per cent of inventories valued at 100,000 *maravedís* or less contained any Asian products,[30] yet in Mexico City, most inventories valued in the range of 50,000 to 100,000 *maravedís* had at least one item from Asia. The demarcation between those with and without Asian products appears to be lower on the social scale in Mexico City than in Seville. In the New Spanish capital, that cutoff level is the group whose inventories were valued at less than 50,000 *maravedís*, among which few Asian goods appear. This wealth group encompassed the majority of Seville's entire population and the majority of Mexico City's white population. In other words, these values

---

30   The true percentage is likely to be smaller given that, for Seville, the sample contains only eight inventories valued between 50,000 and 100,000 *maravedís* and only eleven valued at less than 50,000 *maravedís*.

indicate a greater penetration of Asian manufactured goods within Mexican versus Sevillian society.

If we consider only Creoles and Iberians – that is, the people most likely to employ notaries – then the percentage of those consuming Asian goods was quite high in Mexico City, given that almost all probate inventories valued at more than 50,000 *maravedís* contain Asian goods. This means that in Mexico City Asian goods were consumed not only by the highest elites and mid-level elites, but also by some poor white people who could have acquired any of these products in Mexico City. However, if we consider the entire Mexican population then it cannot be reasonably claimed that *mestizos*, mulattoes, and indigenous Americans typically owned products of Asian manufacture because members of these subgroups rarely employed a notary to compile probate inventories. Hence we must refer to other, non-quantitative sources for clues about the penetration of Asian goods into indigenous American groups and the racial minorities who lived in Mexico. Thomas Gage, an English Dominican friar who travelled around Mexico and Guatemala between 1625 and 1637, wrote this about the clothing of mulattas:

> Nay a blackamoor or tawny young maid and slave will make hard shift but she will be in fashion with her neck-chain and bracelets of pearls, and her ear-bobs of some considerable jewels. The attire of this baser sort of people of blackamoors and mulattoes (which are of a mixed nature, of Spaniards and blackamoors) is so light, and their carriage so enticing, that many Spaniards even of the better sort (who are too too [*sic*] prone to venery) disdain their wives for them. Their clothing is a petticoat of silk or cloth, laced with gold or silver, bound with a broad double ribband of a different colour, with long taggs [*sic*] of gold and silver hanging down before to ground and the like behind; their jackets are made tight like bodice, with shirts likewise laced with gold or silver, without sleeves, and a girdle about their body of great value, stuck with pearls and knots of gold (if they happen to be favourites) they then put on sleeves made of *Holland* or fine *China* linen, wrought some with coloured silks, some with silk and silver, and some with silk and gold.[31]

In 1621, Horacio Levanto pointed out in his "Report on the Trade of China with New Spain and These Kingdoms" that indigenous Americans bought

---

31   Thomas Gage (1603?–1656), *The Traveller. Part I. Containing a Journal of Three Thousand Three Hundred Miles, through the Main Land of South-America* (New Jersey, NJ: printed and sold by James Parker, 1758), 45–46.

Asian goods, especially cottons (likely produced in the Philippines Islands) exported to New Spain:

> My Lord, the business between China and the city of Manila, which is the head of Luzon island, is great. Many Chinese lived and arrived in Manila with ships full of cotton and silks, which the residents of Manila send to New Spain. These silks are so well-liked and cheap in New Spain that sometimes they are shipped to this city of Seville from New Spain, because the profits obtained are large. The Indians also use cotton, to the extent that they prefer it to the linen fabrics sent from this kingdom [...] And in New Spain rich and poor alike consume the silks from China, because although these textiles are sold at a great profit, they are cheap.[32]

And in his "Report about the Claims of the City of Manila and the Rest of Islands of the Archipelago on Its Trade with New Spain," also written in the 1620s, Don Juan Grau y Monfalcón similarly remarked on how indigenous Americans and even the black populations of New Spain consumed cheap Asian (likely Philippine) cottons in preference to other, Castilian fabrics:

> The products traded on this island are of six types. First, silk in yarn, bundled silk and raw silk. Second, woven silks. Third, woven cottons. Fourth, fruits of this island. Fifth, the other trinkets and things which come here. Of all these types of goods, the latter is scant and does not damage the trade of Spain because they are curiosities. Regarding the fourth type of product, the shipment of fruits must be permitted by justice, because no province can be prohibited from selling its fruits. Regarding the third type of goods, the cottons are so cheap that even if these were prohibited in New Spain, they would not be replaced by other fabrics. The Indians and blacks only want fabrics from China and the Philippines, and if they do not find them they prefer not to use other similar fabrics because they do not have money to pay eight *reales* for something which is worth one-and-a-half reales [...] New Spain is not heavily populated by Spaniards, and those who are there are so poor that they have the same attitude as the Indians to cotton textiles, that is to say that the Spaniards use textiles from China if they can find them, and prefer not to use any if they cannot.[33]

---

32   Horacio Levanto, "Memorial sober [sic] el Trato de la China con la Nueva España, y Estos Reynos," BN, R/17270 (6), 1–2.

33   *Colección de Documentos Inéditos del Archivo de Indias*, vol. 6 (Madrid, 1866), 475–76.

Although these references do not in themselves indicate the precise extent to which Asian textiles circulated among the indigenous American, mixed-race, and African populations of Mexico and must be understood in the political and economic context described in Chapter 4, they do contribute to a picture of early modern Spanish America in which cultural plurality and mixture was not only a discourse but also an actuality.[34] It is probable that certain segments of New Spain's subaltern populations, especially those who were servants of Creoles and Iberians, had access to Asian luxuries and semi-luxuries such as Chinese porcelain. The wide range of types of Asian manufactured goods in Mexico City points to this great presence of Asian products in the households of Mexican elites and also certain subaltern populations. For instance, in some Mexican inventories there are goods as common as household equipment – pots (*peroles*), caldrons (*calderos*), saucepans (*caçerolas*), and mortars (*almireçes*) – which came from China.[35]

This level of consumption of Asian goods in Mexico City was unattainable in Seville.[36] Even so, by the start of the seventeenth century there were high noblemen, extraordinarily rich clergymen, and wholesalers whose possessions were valued at more than 5,000,000 *maravedís* who had purchased Asian goods in the Andalusian city. They had the grandest houses and palaces in the city. Also some artisans, small-scale merchants, civil servants, and other Sevillian mid-level elites began to buy Asian durables in the first decades of the seventeenth century. Their houses and dresses were not as rich as those of the nobles and wholesale merchants, but some of these individuals owned porcelain and/or garments of Chinese silk.

Tables 8–11 detail just how much the different socio-economic groups of these cities invested in two specific types of Asian manufactured goods – textiles and furnishings – in relative terms (i.e., with respect to their total investment in non-Asian products of the same sort). These tables establish that elite

---

34   Gruzinski, *Cuatro Partes*, 97–123.

35   AGI, *Contratación,*487, N.1, R.25, 5; AGI, *Contratación*, 259B, N.2, R.3, 4 and 16; ANotDF, Notario: Andrés Moreno (374), Vol. 2467, 1–26; ANotDf, Notario: Andrés Moreno (374), Vol. 2467, 465–78.

36   That there were more Asian goods in colonial America than in Iberia is well known in historiography. However, no one has ever carried out a systematic comparison of the possession and use of Asian goods between both areas of the Hispanic Atlantic World. Some preliminary ideas contained in the following pages can be seen in Gasch-Tomás, "Asian Silk," 153–173.; and José L. Gasch-Tomás, "Textiles asiáticos de importación en el mundo hispánico, c. 1600. Notas para la historia del consumo a la luz de la nueva historia trans-'nacional,'" in *Comprar, vender y consumir. Nuevas aportaciones a la historia del consumo en la España moderna*, ed. Daniel Muñoz Navarro (Valencia: Publicacions de la Universitat de València, 2011), 55-76.

TABLE 8   Percentage of value in probate inventories attributable to Asian textiles, by
            category and wealth group (as indicated by total inventory value): Mexico City,
            1580–1630 (*N* = 122)

Inventory value in *maravedís*	Non-finished	Garments	Accessories	Foot-wear	Bed-clothes	Home decorations	Other
≤ 50,000 (28)	0.0	1.2	0.0	0.0	5.1	24.6	0.0
50,001–100,000 (17)	1.1	21.4	3.2	15.0	3.7	0.0	0.0
100,001–1,000,000 (58)	11.2	13.5	4.5	0.0	33.3	10.7	2.5
1,000,001–5,000,000 (13)	30.7	8.9	4.5	0.0	57.1	27.4	0.0
> 5,000,000 (6)	1.4	4.4	1.4	3.8	26.1	1.6	0.0

Notes: The number of inventories is given in parentheses. Percentages are of the total value (in constant *maravedís*) of textiles contained within the same category. Values are deflated using prices of maize and the Spanish American value of *maravedí* in silver grammes (see Appendix B); the base period is 1606–1610.

SOURCE: SEE APPENDIX A[3].

consumption of Asian goods in Mexico City was less restricted than in Seville and also that, in both cities, the consumption of Chinese silk and porcelain was not led by the richest of the elites. These patterns are evident from the value of Asian textiles by product category and wealth groups in Mexico City as reported in Table 8. Despite the elitist nature of such consumption, the leading consumers of Asian textiles, most of which were Chinese silks, in Mexico City were not the city's richest citizens; instead, the ownership of Asian textiles was dominated by groups with patrimonies ranging between 100,000 and 5,000,000 *maravedís*. These groups purchased relatively more Asian textiles than the groups whose wealth exceeded 5,000,000 *maravedís*. Note also that the greater acquisition of Asian textiles exhibits an even more (socially) downward pattern in the categories of garments and decorative household textiles.

TABLE 9   Percentage of value in probate inventories attributable to Asian textiles, by
           category and wealth group (as indicated by total inventory value): Seville, 1580–
           1630 (*N* = 131)

Inventory value in *maravedís*	Non-finished	Garments	Accessories	Footwear	Bedclothes	Home decorations	Other
≤ 50,000 (11)	0.0	0.0	0.0	0.0	0.0	0.0	0.0
50,001–100,000 (8)	0.0	0.0	0.0	0.0	0.0	0.0	0.0
100,001–1,000,000 (34)	2.3	0.0	0.0	0.0	8.2	0.2	0.0
1,000,001–5,000,000 (36)	16.9	2.2	0.0	0.0	11.7	8.5	0.0
> 5,000,000 (42)	0.8	2.1	0.0	0.0	12.2	3.0	0.0

Notes: The number of inventories is given in parentheses. Percentages are of the total value (in constant *maravedís*) of textiles contained within the same category. Values are deflated using prices of wheat and the Castilian value of *maravedí* in silver grams (see Appendix B); the base period is 1606–1610.

SOURCE: SEE APPENDIX A[3].

For instance, the groups who invested relatively more in garments of Chinese silk were not in the range of 100,000 to 1,000,000 *maravedís* but rather in the range of 50,000 to 100,000 *maravedís* of estate value. In no category were those with patrimonies of more than 5,000,000 *maravedís* the principal investors in textiles of Asian manufacture.

That the wealthiest elites of Mexico City, who could purchase whatever they liked, devoted less of their income than did other (less wealthy) groups to purchasing Asian versus other textiles is indicative of two facts: as compared with those other social groups, (i) their purchases of consumer durables were relatively more diverse and (ii) their taste for Asian textiles was relatively less pronounced. This limited enthusiasm of the city's richest elites for Asian textiles – in comparison with that of less wealthy elites (e.g., artisans, bureaucrats, shopkeepers, and professionals) – is especially marked as regards not only non-finished textiles (since the wealthiest elites were less likely to produce garments at home) but also garments and decorative textiles. This finding reflects the different tastes of the various social groups. For instance, it is not surprising that the nobles and richest groups of Mexico did not consume as many Chinese silks in the form of draperies, wall hangings, and Asian carpets to decorate their homes; these groups were more inclined to invest in silken coats of arms and Flemish tapestries and carpets, which were extraordinarily expensive and rarely consumed by those with patrimonies of less than 5,000,000 *maravedís*. The wealthiest elites had well-established tastes that were little affected by the Chinese novelties entering the market. For instance, they usually owned several exclusive *reposteros* (hangings adorned with the heraldic symbols of his family), and wall hangings from Brussels and Flanders.[37] Just as "trickle-down" emulation does not explain the social expansion of novelty consumption in eighteenth-century Britain,[38] it was the New Spanish mid-level elites and not the richest of society who were pioneers in acquiring (and developing tastes for) Asian goods such as Chinese silk.

This pattern of consumption – in which the city's richest residents did *not* lead in the purchase of Asian goods – appears to be present also in Seville, although it is more difficult to draw additional conclusions given both the more pronounced elitist consumption of Asian goods and the low numbers of such goods contained in the probate inventories of that Andalusian city; see Table 9. As in the case of Mexico City, the wealthiest elites of Seville invested in a diverse array of products. The dowries of the richest women reveal that Seville's richest families acquired great quantities of dresses made of non-Chinese silks and decorated with gold yarns and pearls;[39] this reduced the proportion of textiles made from Chinese silk in their wardrobes and bedchambers.

The stocks of Asian furnishings in probate inventories reveal patterns of consumption that are unmistakably elitist in both Mexico and Seville (see Tables 10 and 11). One exception is Chinese tableware. In both cities, mid-level elites purchased more Chinese tableware (i.e., porcelain) than did the richest groups. Especially significant is the case of Seville, where the *least* prosperous groups invested relatively more in Chinese porcelain than did the richest elites.

---

37   AGN, *Indiferente Virreinal*, caja-exp.: 4808-031, *Intestados*; ANotDF, Notario José Rodriguez (555), vol. 3837, 13–16, 49–51. Other examples may be found in ANotDF, Notario Andrés Moreno (374), vol. 2471, 298–305.

38   Ben Fine and Ellen Leopold, *The World of Consumption* (London: Routledge, 1993); Lorna Weatherill, *Consumer Behaviour and Material Culture in Britain, 1660–1760* (London: Routledge, 1996).

39   Francisco Núñez Roldán, *La Vida Cotidiana en la Sevilla del Siglo de Oro* (Madrid: Sílex, 2004), 51–70.

TABLE 10 Percentage of value in probate inventories attributable to Asian furnishings, by category and wealth group (as indicated by total inventory value): Mexico City, 1580–1630 (*N* = 122)

Inventory value in *maravedís*	Table-ware	Household equipment	Tables & chairs	Escritoires	Beds
≤ 50,000 (28)	1.4	0.0	0.0	0.0	0.0
50,001–100,000 (17)	0.0	0.0	0.0	0.0	0.0
100,001–1,000,000 (58)	3.9	0.0	0.0	6.1	0.0
1,000,001–5,000,000 (13)	0.6	0.0	13.2	13.7	40.9
> 5,000,000 (6)	0.6	10.0	68.4	9.2	12.9

Notes: The number of inventories is given in parentheses. Percentages are of the total value (in constant *maravedís*) of furnishings contained within the same category. Values are deflated using prices of maize and the Spanish American value of *maravedí* in silver grams (see Appendix B); the base period is 1606–1610.

SOURCE: SEE APPENDIX A[3].

TABLE 11 Percentage of value in probate inventories attributable to Asian furnishings, by category and wealth group (as indicated by total inventory value): Seville, 1580–1630 (*N* = 131)

Inventory value in *maravedís*	Table-ware	Household equipment	Tables & chairs	Escritoires	Beds
≤ 50,000 (11)	6.5	0.0	0.0	0.0	0.0
50,001–100,000 (87)	0.6	0.0	0.0	0.0	0.0
100,001–1,000,000 (34)	0.0	0.0	0.0	0.0	0.0
1,000,001–5,000,000 (36)	0.0	0.0	0.0	0.0	0.0
> 5,000,000 (42)	0.7	0.0	6.2	1.2	8.1

Notes: The number of inventories is given in parentheses. Percentages are of the total value (in constant *maravedís*) of furnishings contained within the same category. Values are deflated using prices of wheat and the Castilian value of *maravedí* in silver grams (see Appendix B); the base period is 1606–1610.

SOURCE: SEE APPENDIX A[3].

This lower investment in porcelain by the wealthiest elites in each city can be attributed partly to their tastes and partly to the lower intrinsic value of porcelain in comparison with similar silver products. The wealthiest in Mexico City and Seville made large purchases of silver objects for their tableware kitchenware. Silver cutlery, which was extremely expensive, was preferred by the rich when dressing their tables. This explains the relatively low stocks of Chinese porcelain tableware in the estates of Mexican and Sevillian elites. Asian furniture (e.g., tables, chairs, escritoires, and especially beds) were more exclusive and luxurious than Chinese silks and porcelain. Only the richest of Seville's society owned pieces of furniture manufactured in Asia, for which the markets were less competitive than those for textiles.

The wider range and more socially widespread presence of Asian goods in Mexico City than in Seville is of interest also because it speaks to epistemic processes of the discovery of Asia as a continent with several countries and cultures in the Spanish Empire. Notaries and appraisers who drew up probates in Mexico City recorded that most of these goods came from China, followed by Japan and India. Doubtless most Asian manufactured products consumed in the Americas did come from China, but probably not as many as these inventories suggest. China was regarded as a distant, unknown country for most sixteenth-century residents of both Spain and New Spain – so much so that it was common to confuse China with the rest of Asia. Even the Philippines were usually referred to simply as "China."[40] As early as in the 1580s, the assessors who assisted notaries in preparing probate inventories would likely not have distinguished China clearly from the rest of Asia. This hypothesis is supported by the categorisation as "Chinese" of some clearly Japanese objects, such as *katanas*, and of Philippine objects such as ivory sculptures. Over time, Mexican notaries and appraisers grew more skilled at distinguishing the different origins of inventoried objects. By the 1600s – and increasingly so in the 1610s and 1620s – the growing number of products from India or Japan reported in Mexican inventories reflects not only the expanding trade with those regions but probably also a better knowledge of Asian geography. Such knowledge was the result of greater numbers of missionaries going to China and Japan from New Spain and the Philippines,[41] the publication of new books about Asia – a prime example is the *Historia del Gran Reino de la China* (History of the Great

---

40   Juan Gil, *La India y el Lejano Oriente en la Sevilla del Siglo de Oro* (Sevilla: Ayuntamiento de Sevilla, 2011), 51–60.

41   Manel Ollé, *La Empresa de China. De la Armada Invencible al Galeón de Manila* (Barcelona: Acantilado, 2002), 121–64; Juan Gil, *Hidalgos y Samurais. España y Japón en los Siglos XVI y XVII* (Madrid: Alianza, 1991).

Kingdom of China) by Juan González de Mendoza (Rome, 1585) –, increased commercial contacts with Asia, and the circulation of Asian manufactured goods throughout the Americas.

The situation was similar in Seville, but not only because most Asian products coming in to that Andalusian port were considered Chinese. In one Sevillian inventory, products classified as American (*de las Indias*) seem rather to have been Asian.[42] This mistake reveals the contemporary Castilian geographical ignorance about Asia as well as the extent to which, in the late sixteenth century, Asian manufactured goods were viewed there as being related to American goods. Such imprecision would naturally have been corrected over time as information from and about Asia improved; indeed, after 1600 it is hard to find instances of confusion between Asian and American items. Moreover, Sevillian inventories after 1600 more clearly distinguish Chinese from Japanese and Indian goods, which indicates that Asian manufactured goods were better identified as such. This improvement is evident in the 1600s, when the few fabrics of Indian cotton present in probate inventories are clearly labeled as Indian and not as Chinese.[43] American elites paved the way for these epistemic advances in the Spanish Empire: the perception of Asia as a region with more countries than just China is evident earlier in Mexican than in Sevillian inventories.

6.3   Asian Material Culture in the Spanish Empire

The image that the Castilian elites had of themselves and the discourses that shaped the self-identification of the Creole elites were accompanied by cultural practices to which some objects of material culture adapted better than others. The particular material spaces and cultural contexts of the elite on both sides of the Spanish Atlantic grew increasingly distant from each other over the early modern era. Asian material culture and objects were an identifiable component in this process of divergence. In New Spain, the material and cultural contexts to which Asian goods were more adaptable than in Seville (and

---

42   This is the case of the probate inventory of the captain Gaspar de Guadalche (1600), which contains two gourds from the Indies (*dos chicaras de Yndias*) that are nevertheless described, in the report of the public auction of his goods, as bowls from China (*escudillas de China*): AHPS, *Protocolos*, Leg. 16138, 292–94. In the few cases of confusions such as these, I have considered the products as Asian in the tabulated calculations.

43   AHPS, *Protocolos*, Leg. 8476, 1039–47.

other large European centres) were dress fashions, public spaces in the city, and domestic household areas. These contexts will be addressed in turn.

Clothing is a human necessity, but culturally speaking it is more than that. The dominant social order in the early modern Western world was the stratum (*estamental*) one, which was built on the concepts of rank and appearance. This is especially important for a visual culture like that of the Baroque. The distinction between social strata was a matter not only of rank but also of appearance: honour and decorum were intimately related, because decorum demands a strict correlation between *being* an honourable person and *appearing* to be so. That is why conspicuous consumption and dress became a powerful instrument of social differentiation in the early modern world, a social instrument in the hands of noble elites.[44]

In Spain and Spanish colonial America, like in most of the early modern world, textiles and clothes were a language used to communicate status in public. In order to control the sumptuary consumption of goods that were considered noble, the Hispanic elite employed two methods of discouraging common people from dressing like aristocrats: through sumptuary laws and, in a more complex manner, through fashion.[45] Although fashion expanded as a regulator of taste, sumptuary laws gained a renewed importance in the seventeenth century, as crisis drove many once-rich families to hide their impoverishment with excess in dress.[46] The dress culture and use of Chinese silk in the seventeenth-century Hispanic world is an extraordinary example of how Hispanic elites, depending on the identification they constructed for themselves and their cultural contexts, associated these Asian fabrics to ostentation and prestige, incorporated them into their material culture, and prevented common people's access to them through fashion and sumptuary laws.

Sumptuary laws that controlled the use of Chinese silk, alongside other rich objects and expensive products, were a notable feature of the Spanish Empire.

---

44   Amanda Vickery, *Behind the Closed Doors. At Home in Georgian England* (New Haven: Yale University Press, 2009); Antonio Álvarez-Ossorio Alvariño, "Rango y Apariencia. El Decoro y la Quiebra de la Distinción en Castilla (ss. XVI–XVIII)," *Revista de Historia Moderna* 17 (1998/99): 264–66;

45   Arjun Appadurai, "Introduction: Commodities and the Politics of Value," in *The Social Life of Things. Commodities in Cultural Perspective*, ed. Arjun Appadurai (Cambridge: Cambridge University Press, 1986), 3–63; Igor Kopytoff, "The Cultural Biography of Things: Commoditization as Process," in Appadurai, *Social Life of Things*, 64–91.

46   Amanda Wunder, "Dress (Spain)," in *Lexikon of the Hispanic Baroque. Transatlantic Exchange and Transformation*, ed. Evonne Levy and Kenneth Mills (Austin, TX: University of Texas Press, 2013), 106-110.

This is evident in Seville, though the continual affirmation and renewal of such laws in 1573, 1578, 1590, 1593, 1600, 1602, and 1611 suggests that they were not especially effective.[47] According to the royal prerogative of 1600, which severely punished excess in the consumption and display of silks and jewels by non-noble groups, many plebeians had to declare their luxury goods in the presence of a notary. Some of those declarations remain in the archives. There are declarations of silk garments, damasked textiles, golden or silver threaded carpets, golden rings, lavish necklaces, precious stones, and also Asian objects in Seville's archives.[48] For instance, the artisan Hernando de Oviedo had to declare a black satin doublet from China with a small ribbon before a royal civil servant on 8 November 1600.[49] The doctor Alonso Núñez declared a gold damask mantilla from China with blue-and-crimson braid, lined with pinkish taffeta, all from China on 2 November 1600.[50] The resident Baltasar de Valdés declared a green-and-yellow taffeta shirt from China with golden braids on 17 November 1600.[51]

Although in late sixteenth-century and early seventeenth-century Mexican sources appear less consistently than they do in Seville, excess – which is to say good (according to elite) taste – was severaly punished against those groups who did not belong to dominant social groups. This, in the case of New Spain, left out the vast majority of non-white people.[52]

Fashion was a more effective way of controlling the taste for Chinese silk in the Hispanic world. Around the year 1600, the dominant fashions and dress customs of the New Spanish elite were in essence the same as those of Castile. Dress fashions on both sides of the Atlantic followed the "court custom" (*uso cortesano*) as defined by contemporary texts. The Spanish dress custom had spread to the Spanish American territories by 1600 and had also influenced the

---

47   Juan Sempere y Guarinos, *Historia del Luxo y de las Leyes Suntuarias en España*, vol. 2 (Alicante: Biblioteca Virtual Miguel de Cervantes, 2006 (first published 1788)), 93–94, 98–103.

48   AHPS, *Protocolos*, Leg. 5437, 603–26; AHPS, *Protocolos*, Leg. 10852, no page.; AHPS, *Protocolos*, Leg. 14437, no page; AHPS, *Protocolos*, Leg. 3565, no page; AHPS, *Protocolos*, Leg. 9314, 724.

49   AHPS, *Protocolos*, Leg. 5437, 603.

50   *Ibid.*, 605.

51   *Ibid.*, 619.

52   Rebecca Earle, " 'Two Pairs of Pink Satin Shoes!!': Clothing, Race and Identity in the Americas, 17th–19th Centuries," *History Workshop Journal* 52 (2001): 175–95; Gridley McKim-Smith, "Dress (Spanish America)," in *Lexikon of the Hispanic Baroque. Transatlantic Exchange and Transformation*, ed. Evonne Levy and Kenneth Mills (Austin, TX: University of Texas Press, 2013), 111–115.

court garb of most European countries.[53] Moreover, the other social groups in Spain took their basic dress references from court fashions, which were imitated to the extent allowed by social, economic, and political resources. The Spanish noble fashion was basically a Castilian fashion characterised by the evolution of medieval dress customs with Muslim and other European influences on some existing garments. Castilian clothes were linked to a precise set of moral codes. Most of these clothes had military origins and tended to imprison bodies, reduce mobility, and keep the head upright. This gave the aristocratic people who wore such clothes a calm and proud figure. The clothing of commoners was similar, but clothes worn by plebeians fit more loosely and were made of plainer fabrics and fewer pieces. What were the main features of Spanish-style clothing?

On the one hand, Spanish male fashions (see illustration 8) were stable from the second half of the sixteenth century until the mid-seventeenth century. The main changes concerning male dress during the first decades of the seventeenth century involved the accentuation of some of its principal components. Spanish male garb was characterised by being tight, though garments below the waist tended to puff out. The main items of the male dress were the doublet (*jubón*), which was a sort of padded but firm undergarment shirt, lending the aspect of a cuirass to the wearer's torso; the upper hose or breeches (*calzas* or *muslos*) and the nether hose or stockings (*medias calzas* or *medias*), which by the first decade of the seventeenth century became extremely puffed out; the jerkin (*coleto* or *cuera*), which was a garment that had passed from military to civilian dress and, in the early seventeenth century, men used to wear it open; the shirt (*ropa* or *ropilla*), which was larger than the jerkin and covered part of the hose; and different types of layers (*capas*), caps and hats. One of the most famous Spanish garments of the period was the enormous ruff (*cuellos*), also known as *lechugillas*. As with the hose, ruffs became bigger during the last decades of the sixteenth century, to the extent that they resembled huge bowls reaching up over the ears. *Lechuguillas* were replaced by replaced by *golillas*, collars that were both smaller and plainer.With respect to footwear, the most characteristic Spanish shoes were the *borceguíes*. Of Moorish origins, these were made of flexible leather and were dyed in different colours.[54]

---

53   Lena Rangtröm, "Suecos en Traje Español," in *El Quijote en sus Trajes*, VVAA (Madrid: Ministerio de Cultura, 2005), 59–73; José Luis Colomer and Amalia Descalzo, eds., *Vestir a la Española en las Cortes Europeas (Siglos XVI y XVII). Volumen I* (Madrid: CEEH, 2014).

54   Carmen Bernis, *Trajes y Modas en la España de los Reyes Católicos. II. Los Hombres* (Madrid: CSIC, 1979); Carmen Bernis, *Indumentaria Española en Tiempos de Carlos V* (Madrid: CSIC, 1962), 32–41; Carmen Bernis, "La Moda en la España de Felipe II a Través del Retrato de Corte," *Alonso Sánchez Coello y el Retrato en la Corte de Felipe II*, VVAA

ILLUSTRATION 8   Rodrigo de Villandrano, *El príncipe Felipe y el enano Soplillo*(1620).
SOURCE: MINISTERIO DE EDUCACIÓN, CULTURA Y DEPORTE (SPAIN).
MUSEO DEL PRADO, MADRID (SPAIN)

On the other hand, Spanish female dress (see illustration 9) also maintained its key elements during the late sixteenth century and the beginning of the seventeenth century. As with male dress, changes in female dress mainly involved

____

(Madrid: Museo del Prado, 1990), 66–88; Carmen Bernis, *El Traje y los Tipos Sociales del Quijote* (Madrid: Ediciones el Viso, 2001), 138–200; Maribel Bandrés Oto, *La Moda en la Pintura. Usos y Costumbres del Siglo XVII* (Pamplona: Eunsa, 2002), 53–65.

exaggerations of previous characteristics and small changes in ruffs, sleeves, and other accessories. The female dress consisted of a petticoat (*faldellín* or *manteo*) serving as underwear, a skirt (*saya*) or a matching doublet (*jubón*) and skirt (*basquiña*) over the petticoat, a ruff that followed the style patterns of the ruffs worn by men, a sort of large shirt (*ropa* or *galera*) worn over the entire dress, and a large cloak (*manto*) that was worn only in public. Unlike the plebeian *saya*, which was a skirt that began at the waist, the aristocratic *saya* began at the neck or chest and consisted of two parts: a body (*cuerpo*) similar to the male doublet, and a large skirt with a train. The sleeves of the *sayas* were most often richly adorned. The alternative to the *saya* was the ensemble of doublet and *basquiña* skirt, which had the same colour but might be woven with different fabrics. Unlike the *saya*, the *basquiña* was fuller at the front than at the back. These two garments are only partially visible in paintings of the period, since they were typically covered by a gown (*galera* or *ropa*). When outdoors in public, women – especially the wealthier ones – wore big cloaks (*mantos*) that covered their heads. The most common footwear among women were *chapines*, shoes made from several thin layers of cork or leather, which made them seem taller and were decorated according to a woman's wealth.[55]

These were the main garments constituting the male and female dress fashions of the Spanish elites around the turn of the century. The Creole elites of the Americas were not immune to the influence of these styles. In fact, Creole elites' dress fashions were basically aristocratic and Castilian in form. The main garments that appear in the probate inventories of Mexicans are the same as in those of Sevillians. It is worth asking what the main differences between New Spanish and Castilian elites' fashions were in the first decades of the seventeenth century. An inordinate use of Chinese fabrics and ornaments, in conjunction with some pre-Hispanic garments, played the most important role in these differences.

An obvious element in the different clothing of New Spanish versus Sevillian elites was the far greater popularity of Chinese silk among the former. It seems that, in the early seventeenth century, Chinese silk had not yet been adopted by the dress fashions and tastes of either the noble elites of Seville or the Iberian elites (*peninsulares*) of Mexico. These groups were apparently reluctant to wear Chinese silks and preferred other fabrics, in particular Castilian and Italian fabrics. Italian materials, garments, and influences were

---

55 Carmen Bernis and Amalia Descalzo, "El Vestido Femenino en la época de los Austrias," in *Vestir a la Española en las Cortes Europeas (Siglos XVI y XVII). Volumen I*, ed. José Luis Colomer and Amalia Descalzo (Madrid: CEEH, 2014), 39–75; José Deleito y Piñuela, *La Mujer la Casa y la Moda en la España del Rey Poeta* (Madrid: Espasa-Calpe, 1966), 151–70.

ILLUSTRATION 9   Diego Velázquez, *Isabel de Borbón* (1632).
SOURCE: AUSTRIA. KUNSTHISTORISCHES MUSEUM, KHM-
MUSEUMSVERBAND, VIENNA (AUSTRIA)

hardly present in Mexico in comparison with Seville, as indicated by the relative absence of Italian clothes in Mexican probate inventories. Moreover, those
Mexican inventories with greater quantities of Castilian and Italian garments
belonged to elites who were likely powerful *peninsulares* with strong links to
Castile. Let us consider three examples. These are three inventories of people
who died in Mexico City but had strong Castilian backgrounds – judging by

their political positions, which were traditionally held by *peninsulares*: Don Alonso Fernández Bonilla, Archbishop of Mexico City, who died in 1600; Don Francisco Muñoz de Monforte, *corregidor* (mayor appointed by the Crown) of Mexico City, who was born in Pasarón (Extremadura, Spain) and died in 1607; and Don Francisco Ortiz de Navarrete, personal doctor of the Viceroy of New Spain – the Marquis of Gelves –, who was born in Seville and died in 1624. These three important figures of the viceroyalty were unsurpassed in the inventories of Mexico City as regards the possession of clothing made from Castilian and Italian fabrics.

Don Alonso Fernández Bonilla, Archbishop of Mexico City, had 61 garments and clothing accessories among his goods. Of these, only one was made of Chinese silk: a satin doublet from China with buttons. Yet he possessed five items or accessories either from Castile or made of Castilian fabrics: a black *gorgorán* cloth of Castile, two new wool birettas from Castile, and two pairs of gloves from Ciudad Real, Castile. It is especially relevant that he had more Castilian than Asian garments, which is unusual among the Mexican inventories.[56] Don Francisco Muñoz de Monforte, *corregidor* of Mexico City, had 28 garments and dress accessories; among these, one was from Spain and another from Italy. The former item was a damask cap from Castile, and the latter was a *raja* rain cloak from Florence with a gold and silver stripe.[57] Finally, the doctor of the Viceroy of New Spain, Don Francisco Ortiz de Navarrete, had 41 garments and accessories, among which four were Castilian, two were Italian, and two Chinese. There was a blue damask doublet and upper hose from China. The Castilian clothes were an embroidered shirt from Vizcaya and a complete brownish-grey wool set of clothes from Castile consisting of upper hosiery, cloth, and a cloak. The Italian clothes were a *gorgorán* layer and cassock that were lined with taffeta.[58]

The main differences between garments made from Chinese versus Castilian fabrics were manifest in the colour, motifs, and type of dress ornaments of their designs. Creoles of New Spain wore more garments of Chinese silk, so their dress colours were more varied (and not as dark) as those worn in Castile during the first decades of the seventeenth century. Chinese silks featured blues, greens, reds, yellows, oranges, pinks, and other strong colours. Inventories rarely describe garments in detail but do usually mention their colour,

---

56   ANotDF, Notario Andrés Moreno (374), vol. 2467, 1–26.
57   Muñoz de Monforte also had seven garments from China: AGI, *Contratación*, 375A, N. 4; AGI, *Contratación*, 375B, N. 4.
58   AGI, *Contratación*, 543, N. 1, R. 3.

and the strong colours of Chinese silks were enthusiastically taken up by Creole elites in New Spain. This colourful variety in Asian fabrics was compatible with the multi-coloured pre-Hispanic and indigenous American clothing and arts, which New Spanish Creoles, unlike many Iberian scholars, admired. Furthermore, the Chinese and Asian motifs were another feature that the New Spanish elites' clothing borrowed from Asia. Alongside floral motifs, such as peonies, carnations, pine cones, lotus flowers, chrysanthemums, and small peach flowers, Chinese gauzes, satins and velvets were stamped, embroidered and brocaded with motifs which symbolized such Chinese religions as Taoism, which was strongly connected to an interest in nature. In fact, many of the Chinese representations reflected Chinese cosmology and religious ideas. For instance, the blue dragon, the phoenix, the white tiger, and the turtle-snake symbolised the four seasons, the cardinal points, and the four periods of life in China.[59] Despite offering few descriptions of the motifs of Asian fabrics, some Mexican inventories describe Chinese silks as being decorated with flora and fauna. For instance, the presbyter Pedro Martínez Gómez Buytrón, who died in 1596, possessed several Chinese silks featuring birds.[60] Other Mexicans had Chinese silks decorated with coloured flowers.[61]

Closely related to motifs were dress ornaments and accessories. The clothing of the wealthiest people of New Spain and Castile was often abundantly decorated. Common adornments were (inter alia) silk ribbons and buttons, trimmings, backstitches, and decorative fastenings. Occasionally these ornaments were made of silver and gold threads. Other accessories included ruffs, sleeves, cuffs, and linings. Small accessories in New Spanish elite clothing might well feature Asian patterns, which was not the case in Castile. Creole dresses were often decorated with mantillas and golden buttons from China; ruffs and headscarves of Chinese fabric; veils of Chinese taffeta; and caps (*monteras*), sleeves, and scapulars of Chinese damask.[62] In describing the dress of New Spanish *mulatas* in the first third of the seventeenth century, Thomas Gage himself

---

59	Gasch-Tomás, "Asian silk," 159-160; Virginia Armella de Aspe, "Artes Asiáticas y Novohispanas," in *El Galeón del Pacífico. Acapulco-Manila. 1565–1815*, ed. Javier Wimer (México, D.F.: Instituto Guerrerense de Cultura, 1992), 223–30; Gonzalo Obregón, "El Aspecto Artístico del Comercio con Filipinas," *Revista Artes de México* 143 (1971): 74–97.

60	ANotDF, Notario Andrés Moreno (374), vol. 2464, 105–56.

61	ANotDF, Notario Juan Pérez de Rivera (497), vol. 3360, 796–807.

62	AGI, *Contratación*, 259B, N. 2, R. 3; AGI, *Contratación*, 503B, N. 13, 79; ANotDF, Notario José Rodriguez (555), vol. 3837, 13–16, 49–51; AGI, *Contratación*, 375A, N. 4, 29; ANotDF, Notario Andrés Moreno (374), vol. 2466, 51–55; AGI, *Contratación*, 298, N. 1, R. 5; ANotDF, Notario Juan Pérez de Rivera (497), vol. 3360, 796–807; ANotDF, Notario José Rodriguez (555), vol. 3838 (cuarto cuadernillo a y d), no page; AGI, *Contratación*, 371A, N. 4.

pointed out the presence of coloured ribbons, laces, and sleeves made of cloth from China in its design.[63]

For all these reasons, Chinese and other Asian fabrics (especially silks) affected the attire of New Spanish elites, especially Creole elites, more strongly than that of Sevillian and Castilian elites. Although it would be an exaggeration to say that Chinese silks had transformed the fashions of New Spanish elites by 1600, it is evident that Chinese silks introduced new colours, motifs, and ornaments that made Creole clothing noticeably different from the dominant aristocratic garb of Castilian elites and Iberian elites living in New Spain. In the second half of the seventeenth century and the eighteenth century, when the Creole identification and self-identification as a social group was better established, Chinese silks and ornaments played an even larger part in New Spanish Creole fashion. For example, Chinese silks were instrumental in the late seventeenth-century Mexican women's fashions that consisted of heavy damasks, brocades, and ripped velvet for wide skirts or smocks. Accessories, such as small silver or blue cloth cloaks, were Chinese and had been commonly used by women in China and India.[64]

European designs, pre-Hispanic colours, and Asian fabrics merged in the attire of the New Spain elites much more than in Castile. These three elements, properly codified, formed part of the cultural context and material world of the rising Creole elites of New Spain. Chinese silk did not codify into the racial categories of Spanish colonial America, but into the Western clothing categories, which related sumptuousness to wealth, power and prestige. Creole elites of New Spain, who in the early seventeenth century dressed and displayed Asian textiles in public as in no other elite in the Atlantic World – including Europe –, were a powerful group of the Spanish Empire. This was actually corroborated by the fact that they wore expensive, colourful and Chinese fabrics in the streets and public squares of Mexico City.

---

63   Gage, *Traveller*, 46.

64   Virginia Armella de Aspe, "La Influencia Asiática en la Indumentaria Novohispana," in *La Presencia Novohispana en el Pacífico Insular. Actas de las Segundas Jornadas Internacionales Celebradas en la Ciudad de México del 17 al 21 de Septiembre de 1990*, ed. María C. Barrón (México, D.F.: Universidad Iberoamericana, 1992), 58–59. For additional information on types of clothes (but with fewer details about fashions), see Ivonne Mijares, "El Abasto Urbano: Caminos y Bastimentos," in *Historia de la Vida Cotidiana en México. II: La Ciudad Barroca*, ed. Antonio Rubial García (México, D.F.: Colegio de México, 2005), 109–16. See also Virginia Armella de Aspe, "El Traje Civil," in *La Historia de México a Través de la Indumentaria*, ed. Virginia Armella de Aspe, Teresa Castelló Yturbide and Ignacio Borja Martínez (México, D.F.: Inversora Bursátil, 1988), 77–78; and Armella de Aspe, "Artes Asiáticas," 58–59.

The second sphere in which the social value of Asian goods, especially Chinese silks, became apparent in Mexico City during the first decades of the seventeenth century was public feasts and celebrations. There is a large body of literature on the cultural significance of such events as rituals and means of social control in the early modern period.[65] The interest here in public celebrations is related to the objects that – from a cultural perspective – gave meaning to these rituals, in which virtually the entire population took part. Mexico City, as capital of the viceroyalty of New Spain, was the clearest example. The public festivities, whose ultimate aim was the legitimisation of the system of power distribution, became a collective space for the New Spanish elites and the ordinary people. More importantly, these frequent and familiar parties served to mark the rhythm of the civil and religious calendar. The displays in such popular festivities were magnificent and sumptuous. People wore their best clothes, and the streets and squares were decorated with the most beautiful ornaments.[66]

One of the most memorable festivities that took place in Mexico City around 1600 was the procession and celebration organised to welcome Fray García Guerra, Archbishop of Mexico, who was proclaimed viceroy in 1611. The city council devoted nearly three months, starting in April, to the organisation of the civic reception of the Archbishop Viceroy on 17 June.[67] Besides the difficulties in financing the reception, the city council discussed in detail how the procession should evolve, the position of every authority, the clothes they should wear, the decoration of the streets, and all the elements that would make the celebration as perfect as the event deserved to be. The street decorations and the clothes of public officials were made of rich fabrics from Castile containing silver and gold threads, images, and so on. The sheen and quality of the Chinese silks, as well as their reasonable price in comparison with other imported silks, also made them indispensable in a celebration as lavish as the welcoming ceremony for the Archbishop Viceroy:

---

65   Edward Müir, *Fiesta y Rito en la Europa Moderna*, Madrid: Editorial Complutense, 2001; Laura R. Bass and Amanda Wunder, "Moda y Vistas de Madrid en el siglo XVII," in *Vestir a la Española en las Cortes Europeas (Siglos XVI y XVII). Volumen I*, ed. José Luis Colomer and Amalia Descalzo (Madrid: CEEH, 2014), 363-384.

66   María D. Bravo, "La Fiesta Pública: Su Espacio y Su tiempo," in *Historia de la Vida Cotidiana*, ed. Rubial García, 435-61.

67   AHAM, *Actas del Cabildo* (11 April 1611), vol. 357A; AHAM, *Actas del Cabildo* (15 April 1611), vol. 357A; AHAM, *Actas del Cabildo* (19 April 1611), vol. 357A; AHAM, *Actas del Cabildo* (20 April 1611), vol. 357A; AHAM, *Actas del Cabildo* (21 April 1611), vol. 357A; AHAM, *Actas del Cabildo* (7 May 1611), vol. 357A; AHAM, *Actas del Cabildo* (11 May 1611), vol. 357A; AHAM, *Actas del Cabildo* (20 May 1611), vol. 357A; AHAM, *Actas del Cabildo* (27 May 1611), vol. 357A; AHAM, *Actas del Cabildo* (6 June 1611), vol. 357A; AHAM, *Actas del Cabildo* (10 June 1611), vol. 357A.

And likewise the *correo mayor* [*postmaster*] was entrusted with ordering the clothing and ceremonial robes as follows: 12 *varas* of crimson velvet from Castile and eight *varas* of coloured satin from Castile, in sufficient quantities, and seven *varas* of black *azabachado* from Castile for the hose and jerkins, and three *varas* of linen for hosiery, and a piece of fabric for doublets similar in needlework and colour to the hosiery, and a pair of silk stockings, a pair of black velvet shoes from Castile, and a black velvet cap from Castile with a ribbon and white feathers.[68]

And similarly [*the alderman*] Don Francisco de Trejo is entrusted with ordering two velvet dresses from China and black woollen cloaks from this land and hats, and to dress two Spanish footmen who will take the horse to His Grace on the day of welcome.[69]

Today the city agrees to give two velvet hoses from China, and white cordovan boots, and satin sleeves from China, to the two porters who have to accompany the people during the day that His Grace enters the city.[70]

The prevalence of Chinese silks in such an important celebration is not the only example highlighting the importance of Asian fabrics in the public life and celebrations of Mexico City. The discussions of the city council in 1617 regarding the organisation of a party in honour of St. Hippolyte are even more meaningful as pertaining to the public uses of Chinese silk in Mexico's scenography. Such use is significant because it reflects a change with respect to traditions of the metropole. Its liquidity problems notwithstanding, the Mexican city council considered it necessary to celebrate the game of canes (*juego de cañas*) during the St. Hippolyte party. Along with the bullfights, the game of canes was one of the most popular events celebrated in Hispanic cities. "Canes" was a game of Muslim origins in which a group of men formed eight squads, where a squad had from four to eight cavalrymen. The squads all moved to different sides of the enclosure, and every cavalryman brandished a cane in his right hand. Then each squad would charge at the one located at the opposite side and throw their canes at the opposing cavalrymen, who protected themselves with shields. It was an impressive spectacle for the public.[71] Not only did this

---

68   AHAM, *Actas del Cabildo* (14 May 1611), vol. 357A.
69   *Ibid.*
70   AHAM, *Actas del Cabildo* (27 May 1611), vol. 357A.
71   Milena Cáceres Valderrama, *La Fiesta de Moros y Cristianos en el Perú* (Lima: PUCP, 2005) 124.

ILLUSTRATION 10 Juan de la Corte, *Fiestas en la Plaza Mayor* (1623).
SOURCE: AYUNTAMIENTO DE MADRID (SPAIN). MUSEO DE HISTORIA
DE MADRID (SPAIN)

game have Muslim origins, participants also wore Moorish attire (*a la morisca*) consisting of *marlotas* (a sort of Moorish riding smock that was worn tightly) and *capellares* (Moorish cloaks); see illustration 10.[72]

In 1617, the council of Mexico City decided to organise a feast and a game of canes in honour of St. Hippolyte. In order to maintain the sumptuousness of the event while avoiding excessive cost, the council agreed to produce the participants' liveries (*libreas*) with silk from China, although not of gold-coloured silk:

> Today Don Alonso Tello, *corregidor* of this city, declared that riding is so important in the republics that the cities of Spain make sure that it is preserved [...] and so the cavalrymen who know this art should not let it be forgotten. They also use this art for feasts and rejoicing, which is very important for the people, who very much enjoy the public feasts [...] Because of all this, he begs this city to organise the St. Hippolyte feast and the game of canes with rejoicing but as cheaply as possible, I mean, with easy livery and without spending money on cloaks and caps.

---

72   Bernis, *El Traje*, 60–61.

> [*The alderman*] Mr. Alonso de Valdez said that his vote and opinion is to
> organise bullfights and game of canes with liveries of taffeta from China,
> although not gold-coloured, in order to save money. As there is money in
> this city to pay for the silk, he thought of taking it from the propios [*mu-*
> *nicipal rented assets*] to pay for the silk for the liveries, in order to continue
> the custom of celebrating Glorious Saint Hippolyte's feast in this city.[73]

This quote shows the extent to which the combination of material culture in
Mexico City had proceeded in the first decades of the seventeenth century.
A Catholic feast with a game of canes, in which the main participants wore
Moorish garb, was part of the Creole culture in Mexico – as in any other Hispanic city. Yet in the New Spanish capital, the clothing, which was surely also of
a Moorish style, was made of Chinese taffeta for this 1617 feast. The perception
of Mexico City as a city in the middle of four continents, as captured in Bernardo de Balbuena's ode, fits well with this description of the game of canes in
Moorish dress made of Chinese silks.

The domestic household areas is the final cultural context in which Asian
objects achieved more cultural meaning in Mexico City than in Seville. The
idea of private life is a creation of the medieval and early modern eras, where
the division of common household spheres (such as parlours) and private
spaces (such as personal chambers), as well as male versus female spaces,
took form – especially in the houses of the wealthiest classes. Domesticity is
a space where the history of power, family, privacy, consumerism, design, and
decorative arts converge.[74] Castilian and American Creole households were no
exceptions to this trend. Within the context of common and private spheres
of the house, people displayed household material culture in order to transmit
an image of themselves and of the social group to which they belonged, either
through the meaning of the objects as decorative items or through their uses
associated with cultural practice. The focus here will be on Mexican elite houses and palaces, given that Asian objects were far more prevalent in Mexican
than in Sevillian elite material culture.

The size, material, quality, number of rooms, and decoration of a house in
Mexico City depended on its inhabitants' economic and social group. However,
there were some common patterns in Mexican home construction. The city's
quadrangular design was full of squares and rectangular houses, most of which

---

73   AHAM, *Actas del Cabildo* (24 July 1617), vol. 360A.
74   Vickery, *Behind the Closed Doors*, 1–2; Jacques Ravel et al., "Forms of Privatization," in
      A History of Private Life. Passions of the Renaissance, ed. Roger Chartier (Cambridge,
      MA: Harvard University Press, 1989), 161–395, 399–445.

had two or three floors, vaults for storage, and courtyards around which the rooms were arranged. The most powerful white elites had houses with many rooms, a private chapel, garages for coaches and horses, and colourful patios. This was the Andalusian model of a house, one that applied also to most homes of the Sevillian elite. The wealthiest houses of the Creole elite exhibit a richness and variety of objects as well as their tastes as a group. Creole houses were full of fine hardwood furniture, paintings, sculptures, and carpets in addition to tapestries and wall hangings of gold and silver yarns, silk, and other rich materials.[75] The most expensive objects in such homes were jewels and, above all, silver tableware, the presence of which was a reliable indicator of wealth. Together with the silver tableware and candlesticks, the most expensive and valued objects were those imported from Europe and Asia. Except for tapestries from Flanders, which were extremely expensive and valued, it seems that the most treasured imported products in Creole Mexican parlours were Asian objects. Probate inventories indicate that, apart from silk cushions, Castilian objects were less significant than Asian goods in Creole homes. Asian objects liberally decorated Creole parlours, which featured carpets and wall hangings made in Asia (mainly China), porcelain items, folding screens, and ivory sculptures carved in Manila or Macao. Again, the peninsular elites appeared to have fewer Asian (and more Castilian) household objects than did the Creole elites.[76]

Exotic objects from Asia, such as Chinese porcelain, were common in the collections, cabinets, and special rooms of sixteenth-century European monarchs.[77] In Castile, Asian goods were often part of the so-called chambers of wonders (*cámaras de las maravillas*) and in the collections of rarities of kings and nobles during the sixteenth century. One of the cultural manifestations of Renaissance and Humanism was the "scientific" interest in newly discovered lands, especially the Americas, and their objects, animals, and plants. Considering the difficulties of travel – to see the wonders of the world with one's own

75   Martha Fernández, "De Puertas para Adentro: La Casa Habitación," in *Historia de la Vida Cotidiana*, ed. Rubial García, 49–56; Núñez Roldán, *Vida Cotidiana*, 40–44; Gustavo Curiel, "Ajuares Domésticos. Los Rituales de lo Cotidiano," in *Historia de la Vida Cotidiana*, ed. Rubial García, 82–90.

76   A good example is the aforementioned case of Don Alonso Fernández Bonilla, Archbishop of Mexico City, who had carpets, tablecloths, wall hangings, and chairs from Alcaraz (Castile): ANotDF, Notario Andrés Moreno (374), vol. 2467, 1–26; AGI, *Contratación*, 375A, N. 4; AGI, *Contratación*, 375B, N. 4; AGI, *Contratación*, 543, N. 1, R. 3.

77   Annamarie Jordan Gschwend and Almudena Pérez de Tudela, "*Exotica Habsburgica*. La Casa de Austria y las Colecciones Exóticas en el Renacimiento Temprano," in *Oriente en Palacio. Tesoros Asiáticos en las Colecciones Reales Españolas*, ed. Marina Alfonso Mola and Carlos Martínez Shaw (Madrid: Patrimonio Nacional, 2003), 27–32.

eyes – that interest and curiosity were translated into the alternative of importing and collecting the rarities and natural objects of distant places. These chambers of wonders and collections were full of rhinoceros horns, Egyptian idols,
coral, shells, and American plants, among other items. Kings, queens, aristocrats, and Humanist scholars also had objects from China and Japan in their collections. The sixteenth-century Court of the Medici in Florence is an illustrative
example. That Philip II had 57 objects from China and India among his most
prized possessions is indicative of the place held by Asian goods in this custom
of accumulating objects in the sixteenth century. Asian objects appeared also
in the collections of powerful individuals: Philipp II's mother (Isabella of Portugal), his aunt Catalina of Austria, and aristocrats such as the Duke of Medina
Sidonia and the Duke of Lerma. Chinese porcelain was frequently among the
exotica collections of nobles from other countries, including England.[78] These
cultural trends, which originated in the Renaissance, extended also to Mexico.[79]
In New Spain, however, some of these Asian products had spread and transformed into other forms of consumption that by 1600 were far removed from
collecting "exotica." The case of Chinese porcelain is paradigmatic.

Chinese porcelain was culturally significant in American households in
part because it merged with cultural practices of pre-Hispanic origins, such as
the consumption of chocolate; see illustration 11. By the seventeenth century,
chocolate had already been adopted as a social dining ritual by the elites of
the Americas, who liked to drink it mixed with water, sugar, cinnamon, vanilla,
or spices in the parlours of Mexican houses.[80] This practice, which reflected

---

78   Peter Mason, "From Presentation to Representation: *Americana* in Europe," *Journal of the
      History of Collections* 6, no. 1 (1994): 1–20; José M. Morán and Fernando Checa, *El Colec-
      cionismo en España. De la Cámara de las Maravillas a la Galería de Pinturas* (Madrid: Cáte-
      dra, 1985), 74; Yayoi Kawamura, "Coleccionismo y Colecciones de la Laca Extremo Oriental
      en España desde la Época del Arte Namban Hasta el Siglo XX," *Artigrama* 18 (2003): 211–13;
      Stacey Pierson, "The Movement of Chinese Ceramics: Appropriation in Global History,"
      Journal of World History 23, no. 1 (2012): 18–19.
79   Elías Trabulse Atala, "La Ciencia en el Convento. La Vida Cotidiana de un Científico Novo-
      hipano en el Siglo XVII," i, *Historia de la Vida Cotidiana*, ed. Rubial García, 193–219; Perla
      Chinchilla Pawling, "La Invención de lo Cotidiano, ¿Una Empresa del Barroco?," in *Histo-
      ria de la Vida Cotidiana*, ed. Rubial García, 589–93.
80   Gustavo Curiel, "Customs, Conventions, and Daily Rituals among the Elites of New
      Spain: The Evidence from Material Culture," in *La Grandeza del México Virreinal: Teso-
      ros del Museo Franz Mayer*, VVAA (México, D.F.: Museo Franz Mayer, 2002), 29; William
      G. Clarence-Smith, "The Global Consumption of Hot Beverages, c. 1500 to c. 1800," in
      Food and Globalization. Consumption, Markets and Politics in the Modern World, ed. Frank
      Trentmann and Alexander Nützandel (Oxford: Berg, 2008), 37–55; Irene Fattacciu, "Across
      the Atlantic: Chocolate Consumption, Imperial Political Economies and the Making of a
      Spanish Imaginary (1700–1800)" (PhD thesis, European University Institute, 2011).

ILLUSTRATION 11   Blue-and-white porcelain bow from China (probably Jiangxi, 1573–1619).
SOURCE: MINISTERIO DE EDUCACIÓN, CULTURA Y DEPORTE (SPAIN).
MUSEO NACIONAL DE ARTES DECORATIVAS, MADRID (SPAIN)]

the acquisition and transformation of "alien" habits for ritual by the Creole elites, was well established in New Spain as early as the 1620s – according to the memoirs of Dominican friar Thomas Gage, who visited Veracruz in 1625 and met the prior of the city:

> Father *Calvo* presented his Dominicans to the prior of the cloister of *St. Dominick*, who entertained us very kindly with sweetmeats and chocolate; after which a most stately dinner was provided both of fish and flesh [...] After dinner he conducted us to his apartment [...] His chamber was richly dress'd, and hung with many pictures and hangings of cotton wool, and colour'd leathers of *Mechoacan*; his tables covered with carpets of silk, his cupboards adorned with several sorts of *China* cups and dishes, and stored within with sundry dainties of sweetmeats and conserves.[81]

The letter sent from Manila in 1631 by Ascanio Guazzoni to Santi Federighi's wife, Teresa Setin, is even more enlightening about the remarkable growth of Chinese porcelain as vessels for consuming chocolate in New Spain. In this letter, which was accompanied by objects from Asia (among them, bowls from China), he wrote: "I also send you another little box from Japan, which is covered by a blanket and is entitled "For Your Honour"; the box contains bowls of fine china from Macao, which nowadays are used to drink chocolate."[82]

---

81   Gage, *Traveller*, 15.
82   AGN, *Indiferente Virreinal*, caja-exp.: 5887-014, *Industria y Comercio*, 5.

The popularity of Chinese porcelain among the elite of New Spain is especially relevant because their decorative patterns clearly departed from the most celebrated ceramics produced in other centres of the empire: Talavera de la Reina in Castile and Puebla de los Ángeles in New Spain. As already mentioned, the Chinese porcelain export *par excellence* was "blue-and-white" porcelain. The decorative motifs of Chinese porcelain were directly related to Chinese cosmology and religious belief – even more so than textiles because, unlike silk, porcelain always arrived in New Spain as a finished product. Chinese wares usually depicted one or more elements that, according to Chinese imagery, made up the universe: water, fire, wood, metal, and earth. Also popular were animal and anthropomorphic motifs, such as birds and children playing in gardens, which were all closely related to the Taoist worldview. Nonetheless, the Chinese ended up adapting to European and Euro-American demand by also producing porcelain with Western motifs.[83]

The interior decoration of houses owned by the Mexican Creole elite also followed patterns that began to diverge from the interiors of the Andalusian elite, in which Asian objects played a role. This divergence was visible in the use of decorative items and of items that were at least partly functional. On the one hand, houses and palaces of the Castilian elite were richly decorated with silver cutlery, Flemish tapestries, paintings, sculptures, wall hangings, and cushions with Moorish and Turkish motifs – which followed the strong Islamic background and social customs (e.g., sitting on cushions) of many elites from Iberia, especially southern Iberia. These residences also had escritoires and furnishings originating in places as distant from Iberia as Germany and Russia. On the other hand, houses and palaces of the Mexican elite – judges, rich artisans, priests, and so forth – also contained silver cutlery, Flemish tapestries, paintings, and sculptures typically owned by elites in Seville and in the rest of the Hispanic world.[84] The novelties of Creole Mexican houses included Filipino sculptures, Japanese folding screens, Chinese fans, and Japanese mother-of-pearl and lacquer (*makie*) chests, which decorated and were used in chambers designed for social meetings (see illustration 12), and bedclothes of Chinese silk, which were patterned with Oriental elements and added cultural value

---

83 Armella de Aspe, "Artes Asiáticas," 213–17, 235–37; María Bonta de la Pezuela, *Porcelana China de Exportación para el Mercado Novohispano: La Colección del Museo Nacional del Virreinato* (México, D.F.: UNAM, 2008), 51–65; Lucia Caterina, ed., *Museo nazionale della ceramica "Duca di Martina" di Napoli. Catalogo de la porcellana cinese di tipo bianco e blu* (Roma: Poligrafo de los Stato, 1986), 25.

84 AGI, *Contratación*, 259B, N.2, R.3; ANotDF, Notario José Rodriguez (555), vol. 3837, 704–8; ANotDF, Notario Juan Pérez de Rivera (497), Libro Protocolos 11, 13–20; ANotDF, Notario Andrés Moreno (374), vol. 2471, 298–305, 306–9.

ILLUSTRATION 12   Folding screen depicting a view of Mexico City. Diego Correa, *La muy noble y leal Ciudad de México* (*ca.* 1690).
SOURCE: INSTITUTO NACIONAL DE ANTROPOLOGÍA E HISTORIA (INAH) (MEXICO). MUSEO NACIONAL DE HISTORIA, MEXICO CITY (MEXICO)

to bedchambers, beds and canopies. Furthermore, the Creole elites of Mexico had among their possessions goods that were, in the early seventeenth century, rare in the material culture of the Atlantic World; examples include sunshades (*quitasoles*) and combs from China.[85] The divergence in use of such decorative items as Moorish and Turkish decorative textiles (which were absent from Creole Mexican houses but profusely decorated Castilian palaces) and Chinese and Japanese objects (common in Creole palaces but rare in Castilian ones) marked a difference not only between Creole and Castilian elites,[86] but also between the Creole and Iberian (*peninsulares*) elites who lived in Mexico City. Iberian elites who lived in Mexico City yet maintained strong relations with Castile were more likely to own items that exhibited the Castilian decorative forms of Muslim influence. The aforementioned example of Don Alonso Fernández Bonilla, the Archbishop of Mexico City, is persuasive because his probate inventory reflects – to a greater degree than any others that were analysed – a taste for Hispanic-Muslim decorations. He possessed three large Turkish carpets, a small worn Moorish carpet, a rich Moorish decorative tablecloth, another fine Moorish decorative tablecloth with crimson silk fringes, and yet another Moorish decorative tablecloth made of silk.[87] At this point the

---

85   Gasch-Tomás, "Asian Silk," 161–6.

86   AGI, *Contratación*, 259B, N.2, R.3, 16; AGI, *Contratación*, 503B, N.13, 77 and 5; AGI, *Contratación*, 503B, N.13, 31; ANotDF, Notario Hernando de Arauz (4), Vol. 7, 13–16; AGI, *Contratación*, 354, N.2.

87   ANotDF, Notario Andrés Moreno (374), vol. 2467, 1–26.

Archbishop appears to be following more the taste of elites on the other side of the Atlantic than of their Creole counterparts.

To recap, like Chinese silk in the case of dress, Chinese porcelain and Asian pieces of furniture, which decorated the interiors of houses and palaces, became an essential part of Creole's consumer culture in New Spain around 1600. Objects from Asia codified into the old European concept of sumptuousness and prestige by renewing that concept – the new Creole consumer culture of New Spaniards shaped in expressions of novelty, surprise and comfort, in which Chinese porcelain, Chinese fans, Japanese lacquer chests and Chinese silk bedclothes, among other goods, were a driving force.

6.4   Conclusions

In the early seventeenth century, Hispanic elites and institutions – Castilian and especially American – owned Chinese fabrics as part of their clothing and lived in homes containing Asian pieces of furniture and porcelain. The fabrics, furniture, and porcelain from Asia were better adapted to the tastes of American Creole elites than to those of Castilian elites. By the end of the sixteenth century, Creoles were already identifying themselves with discourses and historical references differed from those of their Castilian counterparts; likewise, their Castilian counterparts and Iberian elites living in Spanish America also started identifying Creoles as a distinct group. Asian products played a role in the genesis of this process of identification. In New Spain, Asian silks and furnishings (along with their motifs) merged with other European and American products. Chinese silk had a place in Creole wardrobes and clothes, along with Castilian silk and indigenous American clothes such as *huipiles*; in Mexican parlours, Japanese escritoires and folding screens shared spaces with furnishings from Michoacán and Flanders; and the silver tableware sets and earthenware manufactured in Puebla de los Ángeles (New Spain) and Talavera de la Reina (Castile) were accompanied by Chinese porcelain. Moreover, Asian objects such as porcelain soon became material means for engaging in such indigenous American habits as drinking chocolate, which became fashionable in Europe several decades after its adoption in New Spain. Other practices, such as the consumption of *pulque* (a pre-Hispanic wine produced from cacti), were more associated with common people than with elites. The various foreign objects and cultural practices fostered mixed cultural mores among the elites of the Americas; because their identification as a group was still being formed, they were more open to incorporating Asian products and aesthetics from all over the world than were the Empire's European elites. The identification politics of the Spanish American elites, and especially the discourse related to the capital cities of Mexico and Lima as cosmopolitan centres where material richness from all the continents converged, more aptly framed the adaptation of Asian objects than did the aristocratic, medieval, and Renaissance discourses of the Castilian elites.

The cultural contexts and self-identification of the Creole elites, Iberian elites of New Spain, and Castile's elites were different. Hence the integration, forms of consumption, and uses of Asian manufactured products also differed among these groups and held various cultural meanings according to the context. Chinese silks, because of their colours and motifs, were not easily integrated into the dress fashions of Castilian elites. In contrast, Creole and colonial American elites did not hesitate to use Chinese silks in their garb. A similar process took place with other Asian objects, such as porcelain and furniture. In Mexico City, the possession of objects such as Chinese silk and porcelain was widespread among elites, and the use of these items was driven by utility, market, fashion, and cultural practices such as public gatherings and drinking beverages with peers; in Castile, the possession of Asian objects was not associated with any such cultural practices. At the turn of the century, Asian goods were integral to home decoration in Mexico and also in Castile, although in Europe these goods also appeared – alongside other foreign items – in collections of unique objects. This form of consumption, which was related more to accumulation for display purposes than to any practical activity, has been labeled by Bayly as an "archaic" form of consumption because it was based on pre-modern ideologies that linked the reputation and rarity of objects to conspicuous consumption. In Spanish America, Asian goods such as porcelain were valued for reasons related to their actual use and became part of new socio-cultural practices. Their *raison d'être* had to do with use, convenience, comfort and fashion. This was a different, "modern" form of consumption in which an item's value did not depend solely on its rarity and geographical origin.[88]

Social and cultural innovations related to the consumption and use of Asian goods in the early seventeenth-century Spanish Empire were not pioneered by elites of medieval backgrounds – such as aristocratic nobles, which included the *peninsulares* of sixteenth-and early seventeenth-century America – but instead by other social classes and groups who were born in early modern times. The identification and self-identification of the new elites was forged in the plurality of worlds that were being explored and shaped in the sixteenth

---

88   Christopher A. Bayly, " 'Archaic' and 'Modern' Globalization in the Eurasian and African Arena, c. 1750–1850," in *Globalization in World History*, ed. Antony G. Hopkins (London: Pimlico, 2002), 50–52.

century. These groups, such as American Creoles and other non-noble elites (e.g., mid-scale merchants and bureaucrats), arose in the new global societies of early modern American and Atlantic cities and straddled two cultures. They hoped still to ennoble their names and families, but at the same time they were building social and cultural spaces that differed from those of the nobility. Asian goods were an important part of those new spaces.

CHAPTER 7

The Manila Galleons – An American Bridge from Asia to Europe

Prior to the eighteenth century, globalisation was not a single process led by Europe but rather a consequence of many processes originating in various locales. The years from 1500 to 1700 witnessed a chain of events involving the circulation and diffusion of capital, goods, knowledge, and skills in different areas of the globe. The Atlantic World and the Euro-Asian exchange via the Cape route were spaces in which interconnection – and, in some cases, integration – intensified. In fact, the Atlantic World ended up as the globalising space *par excellence* in the eighteenth and nineteenth centuries. In the sixteenth and seventeenth centuries, however, this outcome did not seem inevitable. The history of the Atlantic World and the new global approach to history are helping us recognize the important role played by regions beyond Europe in the intensification of economic, cultural, and political relations during the early modern era. This book has described how the Pacific Ocean and the Manila Galleon route, alongside and connected to the Atlantic World, constituted another globalising arena of the early modern era; it also demonstrates that processes considered by historiography since the 1970s as pre-eminently northwestern European actually derived from developments in non-European areas.

The opening of the Manila Galleon route between Spanish America and Southeast Asia propelled a new line of globalisation that contributed to interaction between the Atlantic World and Asia in the early modern era. Spanish American cities and elites were the main agents in this connection via the Pacific Ocean. The trade growth of the Manila galleons and the reception of Asian manufactured goods by the elites of Spanish America at the end of the sixteenth century placed America at the very centre of the Atlantic–Asian encounter. New Spanish cities and elites became agents in the emergence of markets of Asian goods in the Spanish Empire, including its European territories.

The contribution of trade across the Pacific to increasing global interdependence was based on more than the Spanish Empire and its American elites. In particular, it reflected a convergence of the New Spanish elites' strengthened position, both economic and political, with other phenomena. These other factors include: the orientation of Manila's economy toward international trade, in which a key element was the commerce of Filipinos with Chinese merchants that was driven by the former's need for resources to pay their tributes in cash to the Spanish administration; the strong commitment of the Chinese economy to silver; and importance in Manila's trade of Portuguese commercial houses in Southeast Asia. The eventual decline of the Manila Galleon trade, an outcome that weakened the link between Southeast Asia and the Atlantic World across Spanish America, was not caused by a deficient New Spanish economy (which actually grew during the seventeenth century); it was rather caused by the convergence of another set of factors.

Perhaps one of the main limits of the global approaches developed in the historiography of the last decade is their focus on the ebb and flow of people, goods, ideas, flora, and fauna to the exclusion of more violent components underlying processes of connection among continents and of possible limits to increasing global interdependence. Indeed, it is now commonplace for the media to report on resistance to globalisation (with reference to fundamentalism, nationalism, or economic crisis) and on the development of "de-globalisation" processes in some areas of the world. In the early modern era, there was also resistance (albeit of a different nature) to increasing global connections. Processes of global connection among areas of the world in the early modern era were not fluent and instead were marked by adoptions, adaptations, and frequent rejections. In the case of the exchanges between Pacific Ocean and the Atlantic World, resistance to globalisation was characterised by geographical motivations, dynamics of power and dialectics between markets and politics within global empires, and the loss of Iberian hegemony in both the Atlantic World and Southeast Asia. The resistance derived from these historical processes was ultimately greater than the forces that originally drove interdependence by way of the Pacific Ocean; as a result, trade was displaced from the Manila Galleon route to the Cape route.

The weakening of this trans-Pacific trade cannot be understood without accounting for the delicate balance of powers within the Spanish Empire, which was large and also rife with conflicting interests. During the first quarter of the seventeenth century, the trans-Pacific trade's increasing importance (as against the Atlantic trade) to the New Spanish economy triggered a series of tensions between the elites of the Empire that in turn had a negative effect on the trade between Asia and the Americas. From the 1580s to the 1630s, the growing diversion of American silver and commercial operations from the Atlantic to the Pacific alarmed the Sevillian merchant elites, who were confronted with an unexpected commercial rival in their own empire. Although the rise of the trans-Pacific trade contributed to reducing transaction costs and controlling volatility of market conditions through a commercial system which resembled the fleet system of the Atlantic under favorable economic circumstances (so much that the merchant elites of Mexico were empowered to establish a merchant guild at the turn of the century), this advantage dissipated when economic conditions worsened. The political system of the Spanish Empire had mechanisms for addressing the economic rivalries that arose between the American and the Sevillian merchant elites, and solutions were devised to preserve the balance of power between them. The political benefits to the Crown of the Hispanic monarchy's "composite" mechanisms are exemplified by the return, after complex negotiations between the Crown and the opposed merchant groups, to the status quo regulation of trans-Pacific trade that had prevailed before the contretemps resulting from the royal fraud inspector's actions in the late 1630s. This is not to say that such solutions were immune to episodes of economic tension or that they always guaranteed security in transactions, since the Manila Galleon trade during this period clearly shows otherwise. The trans-Pacific trade had increasingly become unsafe over time, and Mexican merchants needed to adapt their commercial strategies to the new, less favourable situation. The less safe the Manila Galleon trade became, the more the Mexican shippers needed to diversify their sources of investment in Manila. The navigation difficulties around Manila and on the long route that connected the Philippines with Acapulco were a drag on the performance of trans-Pacific trade – even more than in the Atlantic trade. Furthermore, the economic and political conflict of interests between the New Spanish traders and Andalusian traders did not disappear in the 1630s. Although it cooled down for decades, conflict struck the empire with renewed force in the eighteenth century.

From the late sixteenth century to the mid-seventeenth century, the importance of the Pacific Ocean as a globalising arena was manifest also in the development of imitation industries of Asian-like products – such as the Chinese-style porcelain produced in Puebla de los Ángeles – which in some aspects resembled the "import substitution" industries of eighteenth-century Europe. In addition, globalising influences can be seen in the transfer, from Asia to the Americas, of skills and technology for the manufacture and finishing of products (e.g., furniture varnishing techniques) assembled in New Spain; a notable example was the import of cobalt oxide and techniques to produce Chinese-like ceramics. Yet these transfers did encounter some resistance. Some agents of the empire, especially Castilian traders and silk producers, managed to prevent the importation of such certain types of Chinese silk as semi-manufactured fabrics. The development of imitation industries in New Spain were linked to an expanding market for Asian goods, which adapted better to the cultural contexts of the Spanish American elite than to those of the Castilian elite or of the Iberians who lived in the Americas. At this point, a global perspective clarifies the entanglement between the cultural and the economic aspects of this dynamic. The taste for Asian goods did not result solely from the commercial import of Asian goods in New Spain; it also reflected the circulation of Asian goods through commercial and family networks, whose interweaving contributed to expansion in the trade of Asian goods across the empire. The circulation of goods through several means, the adaptation of Asian artisans to Euro-American taste, and the transformation of local goods were trends that overlapped in a complex process that radiated from New Spain's trans-Pacific trade.

The fall of that oceanic trade during the 1630s – and the subsequent rise of the Cape route as the main Atlantic-Asia trade axis – resulted from a combination of several factors: the aforementioned clashes of interests among elites of the Empire concerning the Manila Galleon trade, which hindered development of an effective connection between the trans-Pacific and trans-Atlantic markets as well as (and more generally) between the development of international markets and the interests of all the Spanish Empire's merchant classes; the global convergence of silver values in the late 1630s and 1640s, which reduced the profits from exporting silver to China; what was likely an oversupply of Asian goods in the New Spanish market, owing to several decades of constant importation and the limited size of Spanish American markets; the decline in New Spanish silver output between 1640 and 1670, during which time the Dutch found alternative sources of silver in Japan; the hostility and wars among various European empires; the Hispanic Crown's difficulties in defending Manila (and the Manila galleons) from its enemies; and the reduced profits from the Manila Galleon trade from the 1630s onward. The decline of the Manilla Galleon route and rise of the Cape route were connected by the diversion of trade from the former to the latter, and they reflected a general change of the economic cycle in which Spanish American elites were involved. The international commercial cycle of sixteenth-century Europe, which was characterised by dominance of the Spanish and Portuguese in the Atlantic and in the main *entrepôts* of Asia, began shifting toward northwestern Europe by the first decades of the seventeenth century. The flourishing sixteenth-century Castilian economy and its Spanish American territories did not possed the political and economic mechanisms needed to overcome the international tensions arising from the expansion of global markets in the seventeenth century. To an increasing extent, the Dutch (and later the English) controlled markets and perhaps most importantly the silver produced in America over the seventeenth century; this trend weakened the Spanish trade and also the Spanish Empire itself in the Atlantic. This process was connected to the Portuguese loss of ground against the Dutch and such Asian powers as Safavids and Burmese in the Asian commercial arena.

To conclude: Given that Asian goods were consumed in large quantities by the Mexican elites, and in light of the power of the Manila Galleon trade and the re-exportation and diffusion of Asian goods from the Americas to Seville, we can gauge the extent to which the trans-Pacific commercial route was an early space of globalisation and also the extent to which Creole elites of the Americas served as a bridge between the Atlantic and Asia. The Pacific Ocean as a globalising space, and the influence of American Creole elites as agents who filled the gap between two worlds – the Atlantic World and East Asia –, weakened over time due to the rise of trade via the Cape route as the main avenue of exchanges between East and West. History changed when the Atlantic economy strengthened hand-in-hand with the Dutch and English empires over the seventeenth century, but that is another story. Four centuries ago, the agents who connected the Atlantic World and Asia were not only in Europe but above all in places far from the Continent – in Southeast Asia and Spanish America.

Survey of Primary Sources

This appendix describes the main primary sources referred to when writing the text.
[1] *Ship Registers*. Several sets of sources were used to study the diffusion of Asian goods across the Spanish Empire. There are no official reports or lists of merchandise transported in the Manila galleons. For trans-Pacific trade, the monarchy did not gather lists of merchandise, as it did for trade passing through the Atlantic ports of Veracruz, Nombre de Dios-Portobelo, and Seville. With respect to ships sailing across the Pacific Ocean, the monarchy simply collected the *avería* tax and the *almojarifazgo* tax. Collection of the former tax was soon managed by the merchant guild of Mexico. Documents related to the latter tax, although managed by royal servants in collaboration with the merchants of Acapulco, do not contain detailed lists of merchandise – only totals of the tax sums collected. For this reason I used private merchant reports of merchandise, which the commercial agents of Manila sent to Mexico City's wholesalers along with the merchandise itself, to analyse the exporting and diffusion of Asian goods from the Philippines to Castile. These private merchant reports of merchandise are guarded in the *Archivo General de la Nación* (AGN) of Mexico.

The export of Asian goods from New Spain to Castile (figure 2) and the prices of silk in Veracruz (figure 3) were analysed using more well-known sources: the so-called inward registers to Seville from New Spain (*registros de venida de la Nueva España*) and the registers of the *avería* tax. I ruled out other mercantile sources – for instance, the catalogue of ship registers (*catálogo de registros de barcos*), which shows only the dates of entry in the Americas and of return to Seville for the ships along with their main characteristics (tonnage, captains and masters, ports of reference, etc.). Also excluded were the outward registers to New Spain (*registros de ida a la Nueva España*) because they are not relevant to the issues discussed in this book. The two sources that were used (i.e., the inward registers to Seville and the registers of the *avería* tax) are both located in the *Archivo General de Indias* (AGI) of Seville and do not contain exactly the same information.

The inward registers have been used previously as a reference by other authors – including Pierre and Huguette Chaunu, Antonio Garcia-Baquero, and Lutgardo García Fuentes – who have described the sources in detail, especially Pierre and Huguette Chaunu.[1] These registers of ships returning to Seville from New Spain are the

---

1 Pierre and Huguette Chaunu, *Seville et l'Atlantique (1504-1650)*, 8 vols. (Paris: SEVPEN, 1955–1960); Lutgardo García Fuentes, *El Comercio Español con América, 1650–1700* (Sevilla: Diputación Provincial de Sevilla, 1980); Antonio García-Baquero González, *Cádiz y el Atlántico (1717–1778)*, 2 vols. (Cádiz: CSIC, 1988). García Fuentes has in other work used as a

individual registers of each ship of every fleet that sailed annually from Veracruz to Seville with a stopover in Havana. The fleets consisted of one to three warships (*naos capitanas y almirantas*) and several smaller vessels. The warships were larger than the rest and, despite their defensive function, carried most of the merchandise. The registers of each ship are organised into three parts. The first part contains all the information regarding the administrative proceedings that the ship's officials needed to complete before sailing: the license requested by the ship's master to load the merchandise, a declaration of the ship's stowage, and the certification issued by the relevant royal office to allow the journey. Note that, unlike the outward registers from Seville to the Americas, the inward registers contain no description of the ship(s). The second part of the document contains the registers of the merchandise, which were made by the ship's master in the presence of a notary and witnesses; this list ran to hundreds and sometimes thousands of pages for each load and included the type and quantity of merchandise, the name of the merchants who shipped and received the goods, and the *avería* tax paid for transportation. The margin of each register contains the *avería* tax to be paid and the sums made to calculate it, along with the type and quantity of the merchandise; from these figures one can infer the total value of the merchandise. The document was written in the Americas. However, some corrections were made in Seville by the civil servants of the House of Trade (*Casa de Contratación*) with regard to the quantity and value of the merchandise (and hence to the *avería* tax due). These corrections probably reflect anti-fraud efforts, given that the bales and boxes were rarely opened by agents of the House of Trade. When these corrections have appeared, I recorded the highest quantity and value. Finally, the third part of a ship's register contains a declaration listing the passengers as well as the names of those who died during the journey.

I processed only the information contained in the second part of the inward registers, which describe the merchandise loaded and the *avería* tax paid, for the years 1587–1641; these registers are located in the *Contratación* section of the *Archivo General de Indias*, files 1793 to 1929B. Processing of all data in each register would have been impracticable – and also unnecessary, given the aim of this research. Silver was pre-eminent among the merchandise transported from New Spain to Seville. Most registers describe mainly silver shipments. The second leading export from New Spain was cochineal dye, the intense red dye made in New Spain from a small insect raised in prickly pears and for which European demand was great. Other products imported from New Spain included other dyes, such as indigo (*añil*), Brazil wood (*palo de Brasil*

---

main reference source the registers of the outward journey to Tierra Firme: Lutgardo García Fuentes, *Los Peruleros y el Comercio de Sevilla con las Indias, 1580–1630* (Sevilla: Universidad de Sevilla, 1997).

or *Brasilete*), and Campeche wood (*palo de Campeche*). Less frequently shipped were products like chocolate. I processed the data from only three types of registers: registers of silk (whether raw or semi-manufactured, whether Chinese or non-Chinese), registers of the rest of Asian manufactures, and registers of gifts. In some cases, these three items constitute the entire inward register. For each shipment entry, I recorded the merchants involved in the transaction and the product: its precise description, quantity, and value.

The "registers of the *avería* tax" record the payments of this tax, which was used by the Crown to finance its defence of the trans-Atlantic fleets from pirates and enemies of the monarchy. Each entry in these registers includes information on merchandise shipments and also records the merchant owner, quantity of the loaded merchandise, and tax payment.[2] I analysed all the *avería* tax registers that contained data on silk imports and other Asian products to Seville from New Spain for the period 1600–1642 (AGI, *Contratación* section, files 4408 to 4467). These documents are less complex than the inward registers. For instance, the *avería* tax registers do not record all merchants involved in the shipment of merchandise but only the lading merchant; neither do they detail the types of product inside the bales or boxes. The registers of the *avería* simply group the merchandise into such categories as "silver," "cochineal dye," "Chinese silk," and so forth; they do not specify, for instance, the precise type of silk. These registers are concentrated in only a few books; this makes them easier to analyse because data on exports are more simplified and more reliable than those of the inward registers, which consist of hundreds of books (some of which have disappeared). Both types of sources refer solely to legal commercial operations; for obvious reasons, fraud and smuggling are not recorded.

[2] *Private Reports of Merchandise*. Mexican merchants usually received merchandise from their commercial agents in Manila along with business letters and reports of the merchandise consigned to them. I consulted documents of this type for the years between (approximately) 1600 and 1640.[3] These reports, which are guarded in the *Archivo General de la Nación* of Mexico, are patchy and so do not allow for the construction

---

2   An analysis of the *avería* tax from a legal perspective can be found in Guillermo Céspedes del Castillo, "La Avería en el Comercio de Indias," *Anuario de Estudios Americanos* 2 (1945): 515–698. An economic analysis of this tax that includes references to the registers housed in the AGI is provided by Pierre and Huguette Chaunu, *Séville et l'Atlantique (1504–1650)*. *Tome Premier: Introduction Méthodologique* (Paris: SEVPEN, 1955), 169–238.

3   AGN, *Indiferente Virreinal*, caja-exp.: 2111-020, *Consulado*, 3–4; AGN, *Indiferente Virreinal*, caja-exp.: 2926-008, *Consulado*, 5; AGN, *Indiferente Virreinal*, caja-exp.: 0535-014, *Filipinas*, 20–21; AGN, *Indiferente Virreinal*, caja-exp.: 4259-026, *Filipinas*, 5; AGN, *Indiferente Virreinal*, caja-exp.: 0535-014, *Filipinas*, 28–30; AGN, *Indiferente Virreinal*, caja-exp.: 0535-014, *Filipinas*, 32–39; AGN, *Indiferente Virreinal*, caja-exp.: 4976-006, *Filipinas*; AGN, *Indiferente Virreinal*, caja-exp.: 3465-012, *Consulado*, 1–4; AGN, *Indiferente Virreinal*, caja-exp.: 0535-014,

of a series of imports to New Spain from the Philippines. However, the documents are useful insofar as they give information about the type of Asian products that were sent across the Pacific and about the merchants who managed the trade of Asian goods in Manila and Mexico City. This source has been useful to know approximate percentage of Asian textile values (by type of textile) arriving in New Spain from the Philippines [figure 7].

[3] *Probate Inventories.* The main source used to develop comparisons between Mexico and Seville with regard to levels and patterns of elite consumption of Asian manufactures during the period 1580–1630 is a type of notarial record: probate (postmortem) inventories. The types of probate inventories vary in accordance with their nature and the aims for which they were written; hence there are diverse types of inventories that yield different sorts of information. In conducting the research for this book, I used four types of inventories. For Mexico City, I used mainly the "Goods of Deceased" (*Bienes de Difuntos*) collection, which is located at the *Archivo General de Indias* of Seville. The *Bienes de Difuntos* collects the proceedings opened in the Americas, when people from Castile died in the colonies, with the aim of sending their goods to their heirs (and/or heiresses) in the places of origin of the deceased.[4] For information on

<hr>

Filipinas, 40–43; AGN, *Indiferente Virreinal*, caja-exp.: 4259-012, *Filipinas*; AGN, *Indiferente Virreinal*, caja-exp.: 0535-014, *Filipinas*, 44–48; AGN, *Indiferente Virreinal*, caja-exp.: 0535-014, *Filipinas*, 49–50; AGN, *Indiferente Virreinal*, caja-exp.: 0535-014, *Filipinas*, 51–52; AGN, *Indiferente Virreinal*, caja-exp.: 0535-014, *Filipinas*, 53–55; AGN, *Indiferente Virreinal*, caja-exp.: 0535-014, *Filipinas*, 56–59; AGN, *Indiferente Virreinal*, caja-exp.: 6477-019, *Consulado*, 7; AGN, *Indiferente Virreinal*, caja-exp.: 6477-019, *Consulado*, 8–9; AGN, *Indiferente Virreinal*, caja-exp.: 3338-002, *Consulado*; AGN, *Indiferente Virreinal*, caja-exp.: 5511-001, *Consulado*; AGN, *Indiferente Virreinal*, caja-exp.: 5078-011, *Consulado*, 4–5; AGN, *Indiferente Virreinal*, caja-exp.: 5078-011, *Consulado*, 6; AGN, *Indiferente Virreinal*, caja-exp.: 5078-011, *Consulado*, 14; AGN, *Indiferente Virreinal*, caja-exp.: 1388-033, *Consulado*; AGN, *Indiferente Virreinal*, caja-exp.: 1388-034, *Consulado*; AGN, *Indiferente Virreinal*, caja-exp.: 4779-088, *Consulado*; AGN, *Indiferente Virreinal*, caja-exp.: 4829-041, *Consulado*; AGN, *Indiferente Virreinal*, caja-exp.: 6179-032, *Consulado*; AGN, *Indiferente Virreinal*, caja-exp.: 4004-028, *Consulado*; AGN, *Indiferente Virreinal*, caja-exp.: 6449-046, *Consulado*; AGN, *Indiferente Virreinal*, caja-exp.: 4829-042, *Consulado*; AGN, *Indiferente Virreinal*, caja-exp.: 5710-034, *Filipinas*; AGN, *Indiferente Virreinal*, caja-exp.: 5922-069, *Industria y Comercio*; AGN, *Indiferente Virreinal*, caja-exp.: 6590-004, *Industria y Comercio*.

4   Annie Molinié-Bertrand, "Bienes de Difuntos et Liens Familiaux en Espagne et en Amérique (XVIe–XVIIIe Siècles)," in *Familles, Pouvoirs, Solidarités. Domaine Méditerranéen et Hispano-Américain (XVe–XXe Siècles)*, ed. Marie-Catherine Barbazza and Carlos Heusch (Montpellier: Université de Montpellier, 2002), 393–96; Antonio J. López Gutiérrez, "Los Expedientes de Bienes de Difuntos del Archivo General de Indias y Su Aportación a la Historia del Arte," in *Actas del III Congreso Internacional del Barroco Americano. Territorio, Arte, Espacio y Sociedad*, 2001 (via http://www.upo.es/depa/webdhuma/areas/arte/actas/3cibi/documentos/008f.pdf).

the consumption of Asian goods in Mexico City, I processed data from simple probate inventories as well as public auctions; the latter record the goods sold in street auctions after their owner's death. These inventories and auctions are guarded in the *Archivo de las Notarías del DF* (ANotDF). Although some of the inventories were consulted in the *Protocolos* section of this archive, others were consulted in the edited versions of these documents published by the *Universidad Nacional Autónoma* of Mexico (UNAM). Several of these inventories, along with other notarial records, have been edited by Ivonne Mijares and published in three (digital) volumes. The notarial records that have been edited and compiled in this fashion are those belonging to the notaries *Gaspar Calderón (1554–1555) and Antonio Alonso (1557–1581) in volume I; Juan Pérez de Rivera (1582–1631) and Juan Pérez de Rivera Cáceres (1632–1651)* in volume II; and *Antonio del Águila (1578–1579), Luis de Aguilera (1598), Martín Alonso (1564–1586), Diego de Ayala (1551–1553), Luis de Basurto (1589–1594), Juan de Lerín Caballero (1689), and Cristóbal Ramírez de Heredia (1596)* in volume III.[5] Inventories not compiled in these volumes were consulted in the archive itself.

For Seville, the sources referred to are probate inventories, public auctions of goods, and divisions (*particiones*) of patrimony between heirs and heiresses. The most exhaustive of the three are the divisions, all of which are located in the *Archivo Histórico Provincial* of Seville (AHPS). For the research reported here I followed the archive's catalogue of "signatures" of notarial records as well as the volume edited by Jesús Aguado de los Reyes and published in 1996, which collects such signatures for hundreds of Sevillian probate inventories between 1600 and 1650.[6]

[4] *Other Notarial Records.* Besides probate inventories, other notarial records were essential to the development of some chapters – especially those that focus on the trade and circulation of Asian goods across both the Pacific and the Atlantic Ocean. Among these other protocols, the testaments of New Spanish inhabitants and Castilian immigrants in New Spain played an essential role. Some of these testaments can be found inside the summaries of *Bienes de Difuntos* (Goods of Deceased) of the *Archivo General de Indias*, but most are found in the *Protocolos* section of the *Archivo de las Notarías del DF*. Unlike the probate inventories of Mexico City, some of which were consulted at the archive, all the testaments cited in the book were taken from

---

5 Ivonne Mijares, ed., *Catálogo de Protocolos del Archivo General de Notarías de la Ciudad de México. Volumen I (México, D.F.: UNAM, 2005)*; Ivonne Mijares, ed., *Catálogo de Protocolos del Archivo General de Notarías de la Ciudad de México. Volumen II (México, D.F.: UNAM, 2005)*; Ivonne Mijares, ed., *Catálogo de Protocolos del Archivo General de Notarías de la Ciudad de México. Volumen III (México, D.F.: UNAM, 2006). These volumes have been published in CD format along with an introduction in book format.*

6 Jesús Aguado de los Reyes, *Fortuna y Miseria en la Sevilla del Siglo XVII* (Sevilla: Ayuntamiento de Sevilla, 1996).

the digital volumes published by Mijares.[7] Other records besides inventories and testaments were also used as sources in some parts of the text; examples include receipts for payment and other mercantile documents such as bills of exchange and reports of merchandise. Some of these are located in the *Archivo de las Notarías del DF*, but others are found in the *Consulado* and *Filipinas* sections of the *Archivo General de la Nación* of Mexico.

[5] *Official Correspondence.* The letters of New Spain's viceroys and of public officials in the Philippines – for example, the governor of Manila – were useful in describing the conditions and diverse social interests that influenced the trans-Pacific trade. Letters of the Archbishop of Manila and of other religious missionaries in Southeast Asia are part in this official correspondence, which was usually addressed to the King and the Castilian authorities. The *Filipinas* section of the *Archivo General de Indias* of Seville contains many letters of this sort.

[6] *Business Letters and Reports of Merchandise.* Along with the aforementioned documents of merchants, the *Consulado* and *Filipinas* sections of the *Archivo General de la Nación* of Mexico contain many business letters of Mexican merchants and reports of merchandise sent to Mexican merchants from commercial agents in Manila. These documents, as like most of the documents in these sections of the *Archivo General de la Nación*, are dispersed and not always well organised in the boxes of documents. Much additional effort was required to effect some semblance of organisation. There are hundreds of letters of merchants who wrote and received the documents in these sections. Yet as explained in Chapter 1, my focus was primarily on those letters associated with the Mexican merchant Santi Federighi because, for unknown reasons, many more of these documents have survived than of those associated with other merchants. I focused also on the letters of other merchants that were related to trans-Pacific trade and business involving Manila, Acapulco, and Mexico City. The main group of analysed documents comprises 98 letters, all of which concern the trans-Pacific trade. Of these, 41 belonged to the mercantile network of Santi Federighi; some were sent between Federighi's commercial agents, but most were addressed to Federighi himself. There are 20 letters associated with the network of another important Mexican merchant, Cristóbal de la Plaza; of these, about half were sent by his commercial agent in Manila, the cleric Juan de la Cruz Godines, with the rest sent from agents in Acapulco. Another 20 letters were from Manila and Acapulco, addressed to the merchant Lorenzo de Aguirre during 1633 and 1634; the remaining letters were associated with other merchants; see figure 9.

[7] *Minutes of the City Council* (Cabildo) *of Mexico and the Merchant Guild of Seville.* The minutes of the meetings of the city council of Mexico City and the merchant guild

---

7   Ivonne Mijares, ed., *Catálogo de Protocolos del Archivo General de Notarías de la Ciudad de México* (México, D.F.: UNAM, 2005–2006).

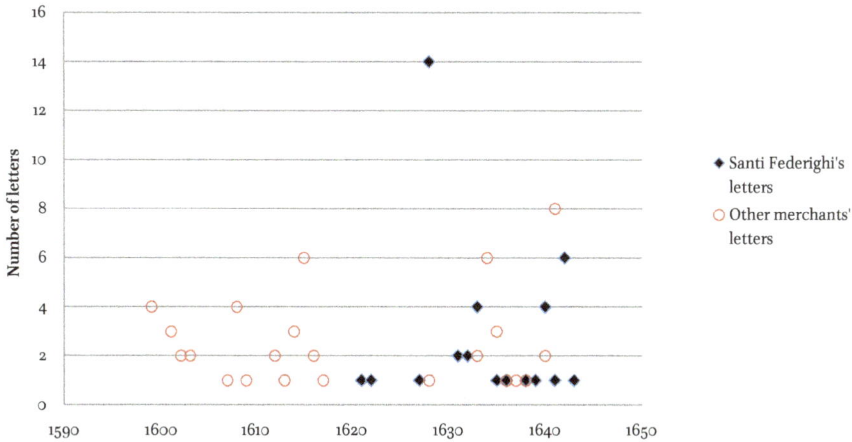

FIGURE 9   Number of merchant letters per year (1595–1643).
SOURCE: APPENDIX 6[A].

of Seville were important sources for identifying the interests and views of New Spanish and Castilian traders regarding trans-Pacific trade and the trade of Asian products. It would have been ideal to examine the minutes of Mexico City's merchant guild for evidence of discussions in the guild about the royal regulations of that trade. However, those minutes were not be be found in the *Consulado* section of the *Archivo General de la Nación*. As the next-best alternative, I consulted the minutes of the *city council* of Mexico City, which was strongly linked to the merchant guild there. The minutes of the city council of Mexico City for the years 1580–1640 (approximately) were consulted in the *Archivo Histórico del Ayuntamiento de México* (AHAM), which houses the original minutes of the city council's meetings as well as the copies of those minutes that were made in the nineteenth century. Only nineteenth-century copies, which are guarded in the *Actas del Cabildo* section, are accessible. For Seville, I consulted all the minutes of that city's merchant guild from 1596 to 1647; these are located in the *Consulados* section, books 1 to 4, of the *Archivo General de Indias*. Although the merchant guild of Seville was founded in 1543, I am aware of no minutes dated prior to 1596 that have survived or are available in the *Archivo General de Indias*.

[8] *Lawsuits Heard in the Court of the Merchant Guild of Mexico.* Chapter 4 uses a reference source consisting of a set of documents from the *Consulado* section – and, to a lesser extent, the *Filipinas* section – of the AGN: the frontispiece summaries of judicial processes between merchants that were administered by the tribunal of justice of the merchant guild of Mexico City. I use the term "frontispiece summary" because in most cases all that has survived is the lawsuit's front page. Such a summary is, of course, less useful than a record of the entire judicial process. That being said, these frontispieces give information that complements the arguments given

in the chapter text: names of the plaintiff and the defendant, the lawsuit's raison
d'être, and sometimes the amount of funds in dispute. Moreover, some of the court
transcripts have survived *in toto*. The merchant guild of Mexico City was established
in 1592 and organised during the period 1592–1594. I have identified and analysed 131
frontispieces and transcripts dating from 1595 to 1641. Of those 137 documents, 24
consist of either a complete account or a substantial portion of the lawsuit (i.e., not
just the front page).[8]

[9] *Documentation of the Royal Treasury of Acapulco.* The Royal Treasuries (*Cajas
Reales*) were royal offices in charge of collecting taxes. The monies collected were used

---

8   The following signatures give the locations of the front pages (or more) of lawsuits referred to
    in the text. For 1595: AGN, *Indiferente Virreinal*, caja-exp.: 1786-054, *Consulado*; AGN, *Indiferente
    Virreinal*, caja-exp.: 1838-028, *Consulado*; AGN, *Indiferente Virreinal*, caja-exp.: 4629-056, *Con-
    sulado*; AGN, *Indiferente Virreinal*, caja-exp.: 4725-001, *Consulado*. For 1596: AGN, *Indiferente
    Virreinal*, caja-exp.: 4779-052, *Consulado*. For 1597: AGN, *Indiferente Virreinal*, caja-exp.: 4571-
    044, *Consulado*; AGN, *Indiferente Virreinal*, caja-exp.: 4779-036, *Consulado*; AGN, *Indiferente
    Virreinal*, caja-exp.: 4779-037, *Consulado*; AGN, *Indiferente Virreinal*, caja-exp.: 4779-038, *Con-
    sulado*; AGN, *Indiferente Virreinal*, caja-exp.: 4779-039, *Consulado*. For 1599: AGN, *Indiferente
    Virreinal*, caja-exp.: 2854-017, *Consulado*. For 1600: AGN, *Indiferente Virreinal*, caja-exp. 2854-
    017, *Consulado*. For 1601: AGN, "Acervo Histórico," vol. 131, exp. 1 and exp. 2, *Consulado*; AGN,
    "Acervo Histórico," vol. 131, exp. 3 and exp. 4, *Consulado*. For 1604: AGN, "Acervo Histórico,"
    vol. 47, exp. 1, *Consulado*; AGN, *Indiferente Virreinal*, caja-exp.: 5789-005, *Consulado*; AGN,
    Indiferente Virreinal, caja-exp.: 4671-012, *Filipinas*. For 1605: AGN, *Indiferente Virreinal*, caja-
    exp.: 5623-075, *Consulado*. For 1606: AGN, *Indiferente Virreinal*, caja-exp.: 4680-040, *Consul-
    ado*; AGN, *Indiferente Virreinal*, caja-exp.: 4680-041, *Consulado*; AGN, *Indiferente Virreinal*,
    caja-exp.: 4680-042, *Consulado*; AGN, *Indiferente Virreinal*, caja-exp.: 5623-076, *Consulado*.
    For 1607: AGN, *Indiferente Virreinal*, caja-exp.: 2013-023, *Consulado*. For 1608: AGN, *Indiferente
    Virreinal*, caja-exp.: 3151-003, *Consulado*. For 1610: AGN, *Indiferente Virreinal*, caja-exp.: 6103-
    033, *Consulado*; AGN, *Indiferente Virreinal*, caja-exp.: 6182-027, *Consulado*. For 1611: AGN, *Indif-
    erente Virreinal*, caja-exp.: 0761-006, *Consulado*; AGN, *Indiferente Virreinal*, caja-exp.: 6149-011,
    Consulado. For 1615: AGN, *Indiferente Virreinal*, caja-exp.: 2145-011, *Consulado*. For 1616: AGN,
    Indiferente Virreinal, caja-exp.: 1876-020, *Consulado*; AGN, *Indiferente Virreinal*, caja-
    exp.: 1876-021, *Consulado*; AGN, *Indiferente Virreinal*, caja-exp.: 1876-022, *Consulado*; AGN,
    Indiferente Virreinal, caja-exp.: 2672-001, *Consulado*. For 1617: AGN, *Indiferente Virreinal*, caja-
    exp.: 6149-010, *Consulado*. For 1619: AGN, *Indiferente Virreinal*, caja-exp.: 5303-008, *Consulado*;
    AGN, *Indiferente Virreinal*, caja-exp.: 5623-077, *Consulado*. For 1620: AGN, *Indiferente Virreinal*,
    caja-exp.: 1898-008, *Consulado*. For 1621: AGN, *Indiferente Virreinal*, caja-exp.: 5623-077, *Con-
    sulado*. For 1625: AGN, *Indiferente Virreinal*, caja-exp.: 4922-004, *Consulado*. For 1626: AGN,
    Indiferente Virreinal, caja-exp.: 6640-096, *Consulado*. For 1629: AGN, *Indiferente Virreinal*,
    caja-exp.: 1876-016, *Consulado*; AGN, *Indiferente Virreinal*, caja-exp.: 1876-016, *Consulado*.
    For 1637: AGN, *Indiferente Virreinal*, caja-exp.: 2171-001, *Consulado*. For 1638: AGN, *Indiferente
    Virreinal*, caja-exp.: 0803-019, *Consulado*. For 1641: AGN, *Indiferente Virreinal*, caja-exp.: 2095-
    003, *Consulado*; AGN, *Indiferente Virreinal*, caja-exp.: 4992-013, *Consulado*; AGN, *Indiferente
    Virreinal*, caja-exp.: 4992-016, *Consulado*; AGN, *Indiferente Virreinal*, caja-exp.: 4992-021, *Con-
    sulado*; AGN, *Indiferente Virreinal*, caja-exp.: 4992-027, *Consulado*; AGN, *Indiferente Virreinal*,
    caja-exp.: 4992-029, *Consulado*.

first to pay for the institutional expenses associated with carrying out their duties in America's main provinces. The funds that remained were sent to the Royal Treasury of the viceroyalty (in the case of New Spain, this was the treasury of Mexico City) and from there to Castile. The documents of the Royal Treasuries are organised into two parts, charges and discharges (*cargo y data*); the former records tax revenues and the latter records administrative expenses. The documents of the Royal Treasury of Acapulco for the period 1592–1692 are located in the *Contaduría* section of the *Archivo General de Indias*, dossiers 897 to 906B. I consulted these documents for the years 1592 to 1650, which are in the dossiers with signatures 897–905A. I analysed in particular the parts of this documentation that report the Royal Treasury's income sources or are related to the Manila galleons that sailed from the Philippines to Acapulco. Although this source does not account for fraud (e.g., smuggling) and is woefully non-specific when referring to merchandise (which is listed simply as "bales" and "boxes"), documents from the Royal Treasury of Mexico do indicate the value of merchandise and silver loaded on the galleons. The information that I have collected from the Royal Treasury of Acapulco is the same as the collected by Pierre Chaunu several decades ago (see figure 1).[9]

[10] *Letters of Castilian emigrants to the Americas and the Philippines*. These letters are contained in two sets of edited sources that include the private letters of immigrants who settled in New Spain from Castile – and in the Philippines from the Americas – during the sixteenth and seventeenth centuries. Most of the letters were written by people who were not wealthy, so they offer an alternative perspective on material from some of the aforementioned sources. More specifically, I searched these letters for complementary references to the circulation and uses of Asian objects in the Americas. The letters that I examined were edited by Enrique Otte (in 1983) and by Rocío Sáchez Rubio and Isabel Testón Núñez (in 1999). The former included emigrants' letters found in the *Archivo General de Indias*, and the latter collected letters contained within archives of the Inquisition of New Spain.[10]

[11] *Requests for Licenses to Dispatch Silver to the Philippines and the Repartimiento of 1635–1639*. Dispersed among boxes located in the *Consulado* and *Filipinas* sections of the *Archivo General de la Nación* of Mexico is a set of documents that proved useful for reconstructing the commercial relations between the Philippines and New Spain – namely, the requests of licenses to dispatch silver to Manila and the distributions

---

9   Pierre Chaunu, *Les Philippines et le Pacifique des Iberiques (XVIe. XVIIe. XVIIIe siècles). Introduction Méthodologique et Indices d'activité* (Paris: SEVPEN (6th edition), 1960).

10 Enrique Otte, ed., *Cartas Privadas de Emigrantes a Indias, 1540–1616* (México, D.F.: Fondo de Cultura Económica, 1996); Rocío Sánchez Rubio and Isabel Testón Núñez, eds., *El Hilo Que Une. Las Relaciones Epistolares en el Viejo y el Nuevo Mundo (Siglos XVI–XVIII)* (Mérida: Universidad de Extremadura, 1999).

(*repartimientos*) of rights among the Spanish and American Creole inhabitants of the Philippines to consign merchandise to New Spain. The requests and *repartimientos* are incomplete, but as a whole they contain valuable information. These documents were processed by the Office of the Chamber (*Secretaría de Cámara*) of the viceroy of New Spain. Licenses to dispatch silver to the Philippines were requested by Mexican merchants seeking to consign silver to their Philippine agents in exchange for Asian goods.

The *repartimientos* that I analysed for this book are not the distribution lists that were compiled annually by colonial institutions in the Philippines. According to the system established by the Castilian authorities, only the Spanish and American Creole inhabitants of the Islands could trade with the Manila galleons. Their names were registered in a Book of Distribution (*Libro de Repartimiento*) and administered by a Committee of Distribution (*Junta de Repartimiento*). Unfortunately, I have found no clues concerning the survival of any Book of Distribution for the sixteenth or seventeenth century.[11] The *repartimiento* analysed here is the distribution of trade licenses that were conceded as a grant (*merçed*) by the Count-Duke de Olivares to the merchants of the Philippines, during 1635–1639, in the context of the trade crisis between Manila and Acapulco.

The two sets of documents share some common elements. Both the requests to ship silver from New Spain and the *repartimiento* contain the names of those Mexicans and merchants living in Manila who traded by way of the Manila galleons as well as the quantity of silver that the former sent to the latter in exchange for merchandise consigned. The following table summarizes the years, merchant names, and silver quantities shipped from New Spain to the Philippines as documented in these sources.

---

11   Yuste Lóprez analyses the *Libros de Repartimiento* of 1723, 1730, and 1753: Carmen Yuste López, *Emporios Transpacíficos. Comerciantes Mexicanos en Manila, 1710–1815* (México, D.F: UNAM, 2007), 78–84 (and appendices).

TABLE 12   Licenses to dispatch silver to the Philippines and *Repartimiento*, 1590–1639

MEXICAN MERCHANTS	LICENCE	PHILIPPINE MERCHANTS
1590		
Alonso Fernández de Flandes	3,000 pesos	Juan de la Guardia
1597		
Diego de Torres Navarro	10,000 pesos	Antonio de Espinosa
		Juan de Anteada
Diego de Velasco	2,500 pesos	Gaspar de los Reyes Plata
	600 pesos	Cristóbal Min
1598		
Juan de Castilla Calderón	2,000 pesos	Lucas de Castro
Francisca Paredes	20,000 pesos	Diego Muñoz
Francisco Espino Figueroa	1,600 pesos	Capitán Juan Juárez Gallinato
1599		
Catalina Agúndez	5,000 pesos	Juan Maldonado
Capitán García de Cuadros	2,000 pesos	Francisco de Herrera
Licenciado Miguel de Chaves	4,000 pesos	Antonio de Chaves
Pedro Fernández Segura	15,000 pesos	Juan Bautista Bocanegra
		Juan Bravo de Lagunas
		Rodrigo de Salinas
Capitán Diego de Molina Padilla	16,800 pesos	Juan de Zamudio
	6,750 pesos	Capitán Vargas Pachuca
	10,000 pesos	Capitán Gómez de Padilla
Juan de Astudillo	14,000 pesos	Sebastián Ochoa de Villafranca
		Doña Maria del Castillo
		Luis de Heredia
		Capitán Francisco de Flores
		Isabel Cornejo
		Pedro Sarmiento
Luis de Herrera	4,000 pesos	Enrique de Herrera
Sebastián de Barreda	16,000 pesos	Juan de Ortiz
Juan Rodríguez de Figueroa	24,000 pesos	Andrés Duarte de Figueroa
1603		
Francisco Palao	14,000 pesos	Francisco Ruiz de Avendaño
	6,000 pesos	Francisco Franco

TABLE 12   (*con't*)

MEXICAN MERCHANTS	LICENCE	PHILIPPINE MERCHANTS
1604		
Martin de Ynarra	14,500 pesos	Juan de Artosa
	11,000 pesos	Juan de Ortiz
	3,200 pesos	Pedro Ortega
	3,000 pesos	Pedro y Miguel de Medrano
	2,000 pesos	Rodrigo de Quillestegui
	2,000 pesos	Pedro de Llano Sander
Juan de Paraya	5,200 pesos	Juan de Marrón Alvarado
	600 pesos	Capitán Ezgarra
	5,000 pesos	Doña Catalina Rodriguez
	4,000 pesos	Capitán Ruiz de Ycoaga
Pedro Ruiz de Ahumada	15,000 pesos	Diego de Quevedo
		Miguel Crespo
		Rodrigo de Quevedo
1608		
Juan Castillete	8,920 pesos	Lucas de Carvajal
1609		
Tomás Salucio	1,500 pesos	Sancto de Cabra
(resident in Manila)	5,500 pesos	
1613		
Alonso Ortiz	3,750 pesos	Juan de Mujica
	468 pesos	Gonzalo Leal
Diego Alonso	937.5 pesos	Juan de Morales
Alexandre Federique	187.5 pesos	Gabriel González
	187.5 pesos	Melchor de los Reyes
	1,406 pesos	Lucas de Vergara
Juan de Barrientos	375 pesos	Ana de Vega Cavallos
	750 pesos	Don Diego de Baeza
	375 pesos	Juan Arias Girón
	281 pesos	Juan González Tomellin
Rodrigo de León	4,687.5 pesos	Pedro de Chaves
	937 pesos	Pedro de Vera
	468 pesos	Diego de León
	562.5 pesos	Juan Venegas

MEXICAN MERCHANTS	LICENCE	PHILIPPINE MERCHANTS
1615		
Juan Hurtado de Leyba	2,000 pesos	Bartolomé Vallejo
	600 pesos	Alonso Crespo
Tomás de Suaznabar y Aguirre	2,000 pesos	Pedro Martinez de Meabe
	6,000 pesos	Alonso de Guillestegui
	4,000 pesos	Capitán Pedro de Chaves
	4,000 pesos	Capitán Lucas de Manozca
	4,000 pesos	Martin de Esquivel
	2,000 pesos	Don Fernando Centeno Maldonado
	3,000 pesos	Pedro de Anciondo
	1,000 pesos	Juan de Arana
	1,000 pesos	Francisco de Bidaurre
	1,000 pesos	Juan de Arriola
	3,000 pesos	Don Rodrigo de Alvarado
	3,000 pesos	Doña Isabel de Alvarado
	2,000 pesos	Doña María de Alvarado
	2,000 pesos	Juan Antonio de Beas
	2,000 pesos	Francisco Martínez de Morales
Capitán Domingo Ortiz de Chagoru	1,000 pesos	Andrés de Chagoya
	800 pesos	Francisco López Patiño
1630		
Esteban de Alcázar (vecino de Manila)	12,000 pesos	Esteban de Alcázar (vecino de Manila)
1634		
Francisco Pacheco	6,400 pesos	n.a.
Domingo de Barayca	2,000 pesos	Gaspar Méndez
Santi Federighi	5,000 pesos	Alonso Tarancón
	10,000 pesos	Ascanio Guazzoni
	5,000 pesos	Luis Alonso de Roa
Doña Valeriana y doña Jerónima de Camargo	2,000 pesos	n.a.
Sebastián de Barreda	2,000 pesos	Don Lorenzo de Olaso
		Doña Constancia Gómez
		Diego Diaz
		Domingo Martin
		Don Francisco de Figueroa

TABLE 12   *(con't)*

MEXICAN MERCHANTS	LICENCE	PHILIPPINE MERCHANTS
Don Fernando Carrillo	1,000 pesos	n.a.
Pedro de Armendariz	2,000 pesos	Luis de Tovar Godinez
		Capitán Gregorio de Lizarralde
Don Antonio Urrutia Vergara	4,000 pesos	n.a.
1635		
Juan Maldonado de Paz	1,000 pesos	n.a.
Jerónimo Sanz de Santa Marina	1,500 pesos	Manuel Suárez de Olivera
Don Tomás Velázquez de la Cueva	1,000 pesos	Diego León de Rivera
Nicolás de Bonilla	2,500 pesos	Don Juan de Arceo
	2,000 pesos	Vasco Gutiérrez Mendoza
	1,000 pesos	Francisco de Araujo
	1,000 pesos	Lucas de Castro
	1,000 pesos	Pedro de Riva
	1,000 pesos	Bernabé Martinez
	1,500 pesos	Alonso de Tarancón
	500 pesos	Juanes de Galcagorta
	1,000 pesos	Capitán Hernández Machado
Antonio de Recil	500 pesos	Francisco de Castejón
Gabriel del Villar	1,500 pesos	Bartolomé Rodriguez de Soto
	1,000 pesos	Enrique Flores
	1,500 pesos	Andrés Martin
Don Juan de Montemayor	4,000 pesos	Capitán Josepe de Zornosa
	4,000 pesos	Don Jusepe de Montemayor
	4,000 pesos	Juan de Aldazo
	4,000 pesos	Gaspar de Pastrana
	4,000 pesos	Francisco de Salinas
Clemente de Valdés	500 pesos	Don Diego de Baeza
	1,000 pesos	Juan Ortuño
	1,000 pesos	Cristóbal de Mercado
	3,000 pesos	Capitán Marcos Zapata
Gonzalo de Francia	1,000 pesos	Domingo Ramirez
	1,500 pesos	Hernán Garcia

MEXICAN MERCHANTS	LICENCE	PHILIPPINE MERCHANTS
Tomé de Acuña	500 pesos	Racionero Pablo Raminez
	6,000 pesos	Don Juan Claudio de Veraztegui
	1,500 pesos	Antonio de Calcedo
Jaime Calcedo	2,000 pesos	El deán de Manila
	1,500 pesos	Pedro Bañuelos
	6,000 pesos	Capitán Juan López de Acaldegui
	500 pesos	Alonso Gutiérrez de los Rios
	1,000 pesos	Antono de Mesinas
	500 pesos	Andrés de Angulo
	1,000 pesos	Capitán Andrés Navarro
	500 pesos	Antonio Alfonso
	3,000 pesos	Antonio de Espinosa
	1,000 pesos	Alonso Baeza
	3,000 pesos	General Alonso Martin
	1,000 pesos	Capitán Agustin
	1,500 pesos	Doña Ana de Castilla
	1,500 pesos	Doña Beatriz Cornejo
	1,000 pesos	Doña Catalina de Aguirre
	1,500 pesos	Doña Catalina de Guzmán
	500 pesos	Diego Serrano
	2,000 pesos	Diego Diaz el Viejo
	2,000 pesos	Alférez Domingo Ruiz
	500 pesos	Diego Sánchez de Elorriaga
	1,000 pesos	Don Diego de Guillestigui
	2,000 pesos	Diego Bernal
	100 pesos	Don Diego Baranda
	500 pesos	Diego Jiménez
	3,000 pesos	Doña Francisca Leal
	1,500 pesos	Francisco López Montenegro
	3,000 pesos	General don Fernando de Ayala
	1,000 pesos	Francisco Carrasco
	1,000 pesos	Francisco Ezquerra
	1,000 pesos	Francisco de Larrea

TABLE 12   *(con't)*

MEXICAN MERCHANTS	LICENCE	PHILIPPINE MERCHANTS
Juan López de Olaiz	1,500 pesos	Bartolomé y Francisco de Carvajal
	500 pesos	Francisco de la Torre
	2,500 pesos	Almirante Jerónimo Enriquez
	1,000 pesos	Licenciado Gabriel de Mújica
	1,000 pesos	Capitán Gregorio Lisaral
	5,000 pesos	Don Gonzalo Ronquillo
	2,500 pesos	Capitán Gabriel Carranza
	6,000 pesos	Capitán Juan de Olaez
	2,500 pesos	Capitán Juan López de Andoain
	1,500 pesos	Capitán Jusepe de la Cueva
	1,500 pesos	Capitán Juan Fernández Aparicio
	6,000 pesos	Capitán Don Juan de Sarmiento
	4,000 pesos	General Don Juan de Alcaraz
	7,000 pesos	Jusepe de Naveda
	1,000 pesos	Capitán Juan de Castañeda
	1,500 pesos	Sargento Juan de Bahamonte
	1,500 pesos	Capitán Juan de Herrera
	1,000 pesos	Juan de Zambrano
	2,000 pesos	Capitán Juan López de Olaez
	1,500 pesos	Juan Bautista Estaño
	1,000 pesos	Juan Bautista de Zubiaga
	2,000 pesos	Doña Jusepa Girón
	2,000 pesos	Capitán don Luis de Vela
	4,000 pesos	Capitán Luis Alonso de Roa
	1,500 pesos	Doña Luisa de Cozar
	16,000 pesos	Don Lorenzo de Olazo
	500 pesos	Capitán Lucas de Acevedo
	1,500 pesos	Luis Coria de Mora
	1,000 pesos	Maria de Jesús
	1,000 pesos	Doña Maria de Aguirre
	1,000 pesos	Doña Maria de Illescas
	1,000 pesos	Doña Maria de Salazar

MEXICAN MERCHANTS	LICENCE	PHILIPPINE MERCHANTS
	500 pesos	Doña MAria de Figueroa
	500 pesos	Martin de Ribera
	1,000 pesos	Doña Maria de Saldaña
	2,000 pesos	Licenciado Nicolás Antonio
	1,000 pesos	Sargento Nicolás González
	500 pesos	Capitán Pascual Caseros
	1,500 pesos	Sargento don Pedro de Jara
	500 pesos	Pedro de la Fuente
	1,000 pesos	Pedro de Leitona
	1,500 pesos	Don Pedro Manuel de Bahamonte
	1,500 pesos	Doña Potenciana Ezquerra
	3,000 pesos	Capitán Pedro de Rojas
	5,000 pesos	Capitán don Pedro Gómez
	3,500 pesos	Sargento don Pedro de Mendiola
	1,000 pesos	Capitán Pedro de Alcaraz
	500 pesos	Pedro Yañez
	2,000 pesos	Pedro de la Mata
	500 pesos	Pedro del Mazo
	1,000 pesos	Capitán don Pedro Sarmiento
	1,000 pesos	Capitán Pedro Zambrano
	5,000 pesos	Capitán Santiago de Gastezu
	500 pesos	Cristóbal de León
	6,000 pesos	Don Diego de Azqueta
Jerónimo de Aresti	3,000 pesos	Alférez Francisco de Olmos
	4,000 pesos	Canónigo Juan de Miranda
Clemente de Valdés	3,000 pesos	Almirante Gabriel de la Rúa
	7,500 pesos	Capitán Juan de Castañeda
	4,000 pesos	Mayordomo de la Mesa de la Misericordia
Don Nicolás de Bonilla	3,000 pesos	Capitán Tomás de Vertiz
	3,000 pesos	Don Luis de Bastida
	2,000 pesos	Alonso Tarancón
Francisco Martinez de Guadiana	3,000 pesos	Capitán Lope Osorio

TABLE 12 *(con't)*

MEXICAN MERCHANTS	LICENCE	PHILIPPINE MERCHANTS
1636		
Bernardo de Balboa	500 pesos	Damián Calvo
1637		
Alonso López de Cobarrubias	2,000 pesos	Francisco López de Montoya
Diego Garcia Montenegro	4,000 pesos	Manuel Piñero
Cristóbal de Zuleta	4,000 pesos	Francisco de Aguirre
	4,000 pesos	Doña Maria de Saldaña
Tomás Treviño de Sobremonte	4,000 pesos	n.a.
Capitán Bernardo de Bernardo de Cuéllar	15,000 pesos	n.a.
Francisco Martinez de Guadiana	4,000 pesos	Capitán Pedro de Alcaraz
Capitán Antonio de Regil	6,000 pesos	n.a.
Licenciado Francisco Roldán	1,000 pesos	Alonso de Leyba
1638		
Jerónimo de Areizti	1,000 pesos	Don Atanasio de Legazpi
	1,000 pesos	Juan Bautista Estanoli
	500 pesos	Don Esteban de Somoza
	500 pesos	Domingo de Vitoria
	1,500 pesos	Don Francisco de Ezquerra
	2,000 pesos	General Don Juan de Ezquerra
	1,000 pesos	Diego Diaz el Viejo
Almirante Don Juan de Brahamante	1,000 pesos	Licenciado Nicolás Antonio
	1,000 pesos	Don Pedro Diaz de Mendoza
Capitán Juan de Echevarria	1,000 pesos	Miguel Garcia Mesón
Contador Andrés de Zárate	1,000 pesos	Andrés de Zárate
	1,500 pesos	Sargento Don Pedro de Jara
	2,000 pesos	Don Alonso López de Cózar
	1,000 pesos	Doña Luisa de Cocai
Bernardo de Cuéllar	1,000 pesos	Maria de Herrera

MEXICAN MERCHANTS	LICENCE	PHILIPPINE MERCHANTS
Pedro Sánchez Lobato	500 pesos	Deán Miguel Garcetas
	1,000 pesos	Sargento Pedro Bañuelos
Bartolomé Cardoso	2,000 pesos	Luis Arias de Morados
	1,000 pesos	Doctor Mora
Antonio de Regil	500 pesos	Alférez Juan de Miraval
	500 pesos	Juan Bautista de Espinosa
Juan Páez	2,000 pesos	Doña Catalina de Guzmán
Juan Yllan	500 pesos	Benito Tavares
	1,500 pesos	Almirante Pedro de Zárate
Francisco Martinez Guadiana	1,000 pesos	Licenciado Manuel Suárez
Juan Suárez de Sande	500 pesos	Don Fernando Suárez
Lorenzo de Aguirre	1,000 pesos	Capitán Tomás de Vertiz
Simón de Haro	1,000 pesos	Marcos Pestaño de Gordejuela
	1,000 pesos	Lucas de Porras
	1,000 pesos	Hernando del Castillo
	1,000 pesos	Capitán don Juan de Salinas
Don Pedro López de Covarrubias	1,500 pesos	Doña Constanza Gómez
	1,000 peso	Manuel Piñeiro
Capitán Andrés de Briones	1,000 pesos	Capitán Andrés de Briones
n.a.	1,000 pesos	Capitán Alonso de Aranda
n.a.	1,000 pesos	Capitán Alonso López de Vizcaya
n.a.	1,000 pesos	Don Diegode Vitoria
n.a.	1,000 pesos	Francisco de Pastrana
n.a.	1,000 pesos	Francisco Montañez
n.a.	1,000 pesos	Felipe Hernández Machado
n.a.	1,000 pesos	Jerónimo de Fuentes Cortés
n.a.	1,500 pesos	Capitán Don Juan de Arezo
n.a.	2,000 pesos	Capitán Juan Bautista de Medina
n.a.	1,000 pesos	Capitán Juan Bautista de Zubiaga
n.a.	3,500 pesos	Capitán Martin de Aduna

TABLE 12   *(con't)*

MEXICAN MERCHANTS	LICENCE	PHILIPPINE MERCHANTS
Alférez Cristóbal Romero	1,000 pesos	Francisco de la Haya
Francisco Rodriguez de Ribadeneyra	500 pesos	Francisco Rodriguez
n.a.	500 pesos	Alonso de Trujillo
n.a.	500 pesos	Damián Calvo
n.a.	500 pesos	Doña Francisca de Mendoza
n.a.	1000 pesos	Almirante don Fernando Galindo
n.a.	1,000 pesos	Almirante Francisco Diaz de Montoya
n.a.	1,000 pesos	Almirante Francisco López de César
n.a.	500 pesos	Gaspar de Almonacid
n.a.	500 pesos	Juan de Herrera
n.a.	1,000 pesos	Juan Diaz de Mendoza
n.a.	1,000 pesos	Juanes de Calzacorta
n.a.	1,000 pesos	Capitán Jusepe de la Cueva
n.a.	500 pesos	Juan de Uclés
n.a.	2,000 pesos	General Don Juan Francisco Hurtado
n.a.	500 pesos	Jusepe de Mataya
n.a.	500 pesos	Doña Luisa de León
n.a.	500 pesos	Doña Leocadia de Illescas
n.a.	1,000 pesos	Doña Leonor de Velasco
n.a.	1,500 pesos	Capitán don Mateo de Arceo
n.a.	1,500 pesos	Pedro Quintero
n.a.	500 pesos	Don Pedro Monroy
n.a.	1,500 pesos	Capitán don Pedro Gómez Cañete
n.a.	500 pesos	Pedro Cadenas
n.a.	500 pesos	Alonso Baeza del Rio
n.a.	1,000 pesos	Ascanio Guazzoni
n.a.	1,000 pesos	Francisco de Navarrete
n.a.	500 pesos	Alférez Francisco Gutiérrez
n.a.	500 pesos	Francisco de la Torre Sarmiento

MEXICAN MERCHANTS	LICENCE	PHILIPPINE MERCHANTS
n.a.	500 pesos	Francisco de Castrejón
n.a.	500 pesos	Doña Francisca de Perea
n.a.	500 pesos	Don Juan de Ledo
n.a.	500 pesos	Capitán don Lorenzo Gómez Cañete
n.a.	500 pesos	Doña Maria de Aguirre
n.a.	500 pesos	Pedro de Gainza
n.a.	1,000 pesos	Capitán don Pedro Sarmiento
n.a.	1,000 pesos	Capitán don Pedro de Monreal
n.a.	500 pesos	Alférez don Critóbal de Neyra
1639		
Jerónimo de Areizti	500 pesos	Domingo de Vitoria
	1,000 pesos	Don Francisco de Ezquerra
	1,000 pesos	General Don Juan Ezquerra
	2,000 pesos	Almirante Don Pedro Zárate
	500 pesos	Juan Garcia
Almirante Don Juan de Brahamante	1,000 pesos	Don Pedro Diaz de Mendoza
	1,000 pesos	Don Atanasio de Legazpi
Capitán Juan de Echevarria	1,000 pesos	Miguel Garcia Mesón
Contador Andrés de Zárate	1,000 pesos	Andrés de Zárate
	1,000 pesos	Sargento Don Pedro de Jara
	1,000 pesos	Don Alonso López de Cózar
	1,000 pesos	Doña Luisa de Cocai
Bernardo de Cuéllar	500 pesos	Doña Catalina de Gaona
	1,500 pesos	Doña Constanza Gómez
Pedro Sánchez Lobato	1000 pesos	Deán Miguel Garcetas
	2,000 pesos	Sargento Pedro Bañuelos
Antonio de Regil	500 pesos	Juan Bautista de Espinosa
	500 pesos	Diego Ruiz de Galarza
	500 pesos	Alférez Juan de Miraval
Juan Páez	1,000 pesos	Doña Catalina de Guzmán
Correo Mayor Don Pedro Diaz de la Barrera	500 pesos	Sebastián Guerra
Capitán Santi Federighi	500 pesos	Capitán Pedro de Mendoza
	1,000 pesos	Ascanio Guazzoni

TABLE 12   *(con't)*

MEXICAN MERCHANTS	LICENCE	PHILIPPINE MERCHANTS
Capitán Lope Osorio	500 pesos	Capitán Don Esteban de Somoza
Capitán Andrés de Briones	1,000 pesos	Capitán Andrés de Briones
n.a.	1,000 pesos	Capitán Alonso de Aranda
n.a.	1,000 pesos	Capitán Alonso López de Vizcaya
n.a.	1,000 pesos	Don Diego de Vitoria
n.a.	1,000 pesos	Diego León de Rivera
n.a.	1,000 pesos	Francisco de Pastrana
n.a.	500 pesos	Francisco de Vivero
n.a.	500 pesos	Francisco de Cervigón
n.a.	500 pesos	Francisco de Pastrana
n.a.	1,000 pesos	Felipe Hernández Machado
n.a.	1,000 pesos	Jerónimo de Fuentes Cortés
n.a.	2,000 pesos	Capitán Don Juan de Arezo
n.a.	1,000 pesos	Capitán Don Juan de Frias
n.a.	2,000 pesos	Capitán Juan Bautista de Medina
n.a.	1,000 pesos	Capitán Juan Bautista de Zubiaga
n.a.	2,000 pesos	Capitán Martin de Aduna
n.a.	500 pesos	Capitán Pascual Raseros
n.a.	1,000 pesos	Capitán Tomás de Vertiz
Juan Antonio de Caravallo	1,000 pesos	General don Antonio de Leos
	1,000 pesos	General don Fernando de Ayala
Alférez Cristóbal Romero	500 pesos	Francisco de la Haya
	500 pesos	Capitán Pedro Romero
Francisco Rodriguez de Ribadeneyra	500 pesos	Francisco Rodriguez
Marcos Rodriguez Zapata	500 pesos	Sargento Marcos Zapata Carvajal
n.a.	500 pesos	Alonso de Trujillo
n.a.	1,000 pesos	Antonio de Mesina
n.a.	500 pesos	Benito Tavares
n.a.	500 pesos	Damián Calvo

MEXICAN MERCHANTS	LICENCE	PHILIPPINE MERCHANTS
n.a.	1,000 pesos	Capitán don Diego de Morales
n.a.	1,000 pesos	Capitán Diego Núñez Crespo
n.a.	500 pesos	Castellano Diego Feliz
n.a.	500 pesos	Doña Francisca de Mendoza
n.a.	500 pesos	Almirante don Fernando Galindo
n.a.	500 pesos	Almirante Francisco Diaz de Montoya
n.a.	500 pesos	Almirante Francisco López de César
n.a.	500 pesos	Gaspar de Almonacid
n.a.	1,500 pesos	Arcediano don Gregorio Ruiz de Escalona
n.a.	500 pesos	Juan de Herrera
n.a.	1,000 pesos	Juan Diaz de Mendoza
n.a.	500 pesos	Juan de Uclés
n.a.	500 pesos	Juan Bautista Sánchez
n.a.	1,000 pesos	Juan Fernández de Ledo
n.a.	500 pesos	Juan Diaz de Yela
n.a.	500 pesos	Alférez Juan de Montoya
n.a.	1,000 pesos	Capitán Don Juan de Salinas
n.a.	500 pesos	Jusepe de Mataya
n.a.	1,000 pesos	Juan Fernández de León
n.a.	500 pesos	Juan de Arrida
n.a.	500 pesos	Juan de Torres Sarmiento
n.a.	500 pesos	Juan de Silva
n.a.	500 pesos	Juan de Morales Nebro
n.a.	500 pesos	Doña Luisa de León
n.a.	500 pesos	Doña Leocadia de Illescas
n.a.	1,000 pesos	Doña Leonor de Velasco
n.a.	500 pesos	Don Luis Castillo
n.a.	500 pesos	Don Luis Ferández Flores
n.a.	1,000 pesos	Doña Maria de Saldaña
n.a.	1,000 pesos	Marcos Pestaño Gondejuela
n.a.	1,000 pesos	Doña Magdalena Gaona

TABLE 12   *(con't)*

MEXICAN MERCHANTS	LICENCE	PHILIPPINE MERCHANTS
n.a.	1,000 pesos	Capitán don Mateo de Arceo
n.a.	500 pesos	Doña Maria de Parada
n.a.	500 pesos	Doña Potenciana Ezquerra
n.a.	1,000 pesos	Pedro Quintero
n.a.	1,000 pesos	Don Pedro Monroy
n.a.	1,000 pesos	Capitán don Pedro Gómez Cañete
n.a.	500 pesos	Presbítero don Pedro de Artusa
n.a.	500 pesos	Pedro Cadenas
n.a.	500 pesos	Alonso Baeza del Rio
n.a.	100 pesos	Capitán don Pedro de Monreal

SOURCES: AGN, INDIFERENTE VIRREINAL, CAJA-EXP.: 3543-025, CONSULADO; AGN, INDIFERENTE VIRREINAL, CAJA-EXP.: 3543-027, CONSULADO; AGN, INDIFERENTE VIRREINAL, CAJA-EXP.: 4431-026, CONSULADO; AGN, INDIFERENTE VIRREINAL, CAJA-EXP.: 2926-008, CONSULADO; AGN, INDIFERENTE VIRREINAL, CAJA-EXP.: 4327-027, CONSULADO; AGN, INDIFERENTE VIRREINAL, CAJA-EXP.: 4431-027, CONSULADO; AGN, INDIFERENTE VIRREINAL, CAJA-EXP.: 4431-029, CONSULADO; AGN, INDIFERENTE VIRREINAL, CAJA-EXP.: 6720-025, CONSULADO (1599); AGN, INDIFERENTE VIRREINAL, CAJA-EXP.: 5393-032, CONSULADO; AGN, INDIFERENTE VIRREINAL, CAJA-EXP.: 6477-019, CONSULADO; AGN, INDIFERENTE VIRREINAL, CAJA-EXP.: 3216-019, CONSULADO; AGN, INDIFERENTE VIRREINAL, CAJA-EXP.: 2821-006, CONSULADO; AGN, INDIFERENTE VIRREINAL, CAJA-EXP.: 2365-029, FILIPINAS; AGN, INDIFERENTE VIRREINAL, CAJA-EXP.: 2436-001, FILIPINAS; AGN, INDIFERENTE VIRREINAL, CAJA-EXP.: 4312-034, FILIPINAS; AGN, INDIFERENTE VIRREINAL, CAJA-EXP.: 1355-030, FILIPINAS; AGN, INDIFERENTE VIRREINAL, CAJA-EXP.: 3027-002, FILIPINAS; AGN, INDIFERENTE VIRREINAL, CAJA-EXP.: 4371-021, FILIPINAS; AGN, INDIFERENTE VIRREINAL, CAJA-EXP.: 4601-021, FILIPINAS; AGN, INDIFERENTE VIRREINAL, CAJA-EXP.: 6027-012, FILIPINAS; AGN, INDIFERENTE VIRREINAL, CAJA-EXP.: 3855-001, FILIPINAS; AGN, INDIFERENTE VIRREINAL, CAJA-EXP.: 4259-013, FILIPINAS; AGN, INDIFERENTE VIRREINAL, CAJA-EXP.: 4259-023, FILIPINAS; AGN, INDIFERENTE VIRREINAL, CAJA-EXP.: 4259-011, FILIPINAS; AGN, INDIFERENTE VIRREINAL, CAJA-EXP.: 0130-025, FILIPINAS; AGN, INDIFERENTE VIRREINAL, CAJA-EXP.: 1355-031, FILIPINAS; AGN, INDIFERENTE VIRREINAL, CAJA-EXP.: 2949-022, FILIPINAS; AGN, INDIFERENTE VIRREINAL, CAJA-EXP.: 3052-007, FILIPINAS; AGN, INDIFERENTE VIRREINAL, CAJA-EXP.: 5922-004, FILIPINAS; AGN, INDIFERENTE VIRREINAL, CAJA-EXP.: 6511-061, FILIPINAS; AGN, INDIFERENTE VIRREINAL, CAJA-EXP.: 6561-056, FILIPINAS; AGN, INDIFERENTE VIRREINAL, CAJA-EXP.: 6657-030, FILIPINAS; AGN, INDIFERENTE VIRREINAL, CAJA-EXP.: 3538-039,

FILIPINAS; AGN, INDIFERENTE VIRREINAL, CAJA-EXP.: 4230-007, FILIPINAS; AGN, IN-
DIFERENTE VIRREINAL, CAJA-EXP.: 5710-034, FILIPINAS; AGN, INDIFERENTE VIRREINAL,
CAJA-EXP.: 1451-014, FILIPINAS; AGN, INDIFERENTE VIRREINAL, CAJA-EXP.: 3640-017, FIL-
IPINAS.

Note: "n.a." = not available.

Conversion from Current to Constant Values

Most values and prices in the Philippines and New Spain are expressed in *pesos de oro común* (pesos of 8 pieces) or in *tomines/reales* (1 peso = 8 *tomines/reales*).[1] In contrast, for Seville the preferred currency is either *maravedís*, *reales*, or *ducados*. In all cases, values have been transformed into the common currency of the Spanish Empire, the *maravedí*. In the Philippines and New Spain, 1 peso = 272 *maravedís* and so 1 *tomín/real* = 34 *maravedís*. In Seville, 1 *real* = 34 *maravedís* and 1 *ducado* = 374 *maravedís*.

In figure 1, adjusted values for Manila are deflated using China's rice prices published by Peng Xinwei (via http://gpih.ucdavis.edu); adjusted values for Acapulco are deflated using New Spain's maize prices collected by Richard L. Garner; the base period is 1616–1620. Correcting for the effects of inflation on figure 2 and the values of inventories (table 7 to table 11) required two operations. First, in order to adjust the samples for general inflation over time, I deflated them using price indices of basic goods: wheat for Seville and maize for Mexico City. Prices for Seville's wheat are those collected by Manuel González-Mariscal at the Hospital of Santa Clara, who has kindly provided them for this book. González-Mariscal's wheat prices are strongly similar to the Andalusian wheat prices reported by Hamilton, though the former are more complete.[2] Mexico's inventories were deflated using the maize prices in New Spain published by Richard L. Garner.[3] However, Garner's list of maize prices are missing some years. In re-publishing these prices, the Institute of Social History filled in the "gap" years with the price of the most recent previous year for which data is available. I have followed that IISH approach except with respect to those gap years (1597, 1598, 1605, 1607, 1615, 1616, 1623, 1624, and 1641) that could be filled with data from other sources.[4]

Second, in order to adjust the samples for inflation of the *vellón* money (copper and silver alloy) in Castile, I also deflated values using two indices: an index of the value of

---

1 Rarer are the *pesos de oro de minas* (each equal to 450 *maravedís*).

2 Earl J. Hamilton, *El Tesoro Americano y la Revolución de los Precios en España, 1501–1650* (Barcelona: Crítica, 2000 (first published in 1934)).

3 These prices are available at his website (http://www.insidemydesk.com/hdd.html). The Institute of Social History (IISH) has published an augmented version of Garner's maize prices (http://www.iisg.nl/hpw/data.php#southamerica).

4 In particular: Charles Gibson, *The Aztecs under the Spanish Rule. History of the Indians of the Valley of Mexico, 1519–1810* (Stanford, CA: Stanford University Press, 1964), 453–54; letters to the King from viceroys reporting on the economic situation of New Spain (AGI, "México," 28, N. 32, 1–2); and notarial records of commercial transactions (ANotDF, Notario Juan Pérez de Rivera, vol. 5090, 316–345; ANotDF, Notario Juan Pérez de Rivera, vol. 2594, 8–9; ANotDF, Notario Juan Pérez de Rivera, vol. 3012, 63; ANotDF, Notario Juan Pérez de Rivera, vol. 4185, 28–29).

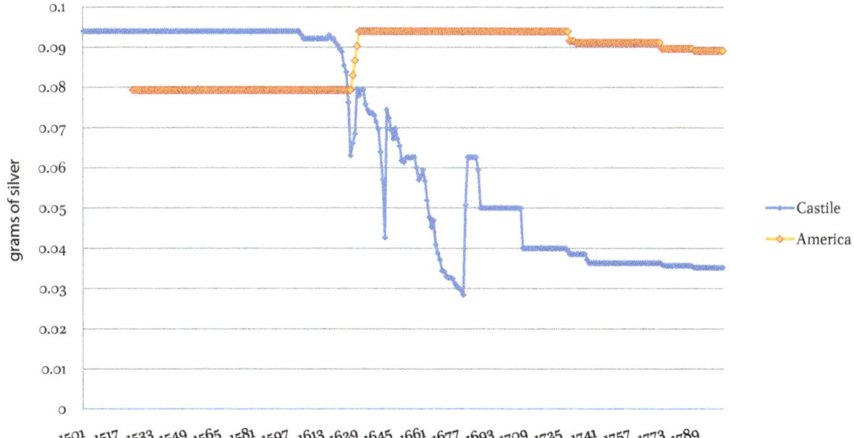

FIGURE 10   Value of the *maravedí* in grams of silver: Castile and the Americas (1500–1800).
SOURCE: SEE NOTES 5 AND 6 OF APPENDIX B.

maravedí accounting unit in grams of silver in Castile to deflate the values of Sevillian inventories,[5] and another index of the value of *maravedí* in grams of silver in the Americas to deflate the values of Mexican inventories.[6] The reason for these adjustments is that the *vellón*'s intrinsic value was not constant because the monarchy reduced, on a frequent basis in the first half of the seventeenth century, the quantity of silver to which *vellón* (and *maravedí*) were equivalent in Castile. In the Americas, the monarchy did not destabilize currency in this way. In fact, the monetary policies applied in the Americas by the Crown ran counter to those developed in Castile. In 1627, 1628, 1629, and 1630, the main American currency – the peso of 8 pieces (*peso de oro común*), which in principle was equivalent to 272 *maravedís* – increased slightly in value (i.e., in equivalent quantity of silver). Although the *maravedís* currency had the same nominal value in the Americas as in Castile (1 peso of 8 pieces = 272 *maravedís*; 1 *real* = 34 *maravedís*), the respective monetary policies followed on the two continents resulted in the intrinsic value of the *maravedí* being higher in the Americas than in Castile. In order to compensate for these distortions in the *maravedí*'s worth, I have adjusted the value of inventories and Asian goods using indices of the currency's intrinsic value as just described.

5   Hamilton, *El Tesoro Americano*, 108. The Global Price and Income History Group has compiled Hamilton's "premiums" per *maravedí* in a data file (http://gpih.ucdavis.edu/files/Spain_1351-1800.xls).
6   Leticia Arroyo Abad, 2005, database of the IISH website (http://www.iisg.nl/hpw/data.php#-southamerica). Humberto Burzio, "El Peso Plata Hispanoamericano", *Historia* 3 (1958), 21–52.

Glossary of Fabrics, Garments, and Textiles

This glossary consists mostly of terms that refer to the fabrics, garments, and units of measure described in the text. Also included are some lesser-known general terms as well as geographical names given by the Spaniards to cities and regions of China and Southeast Asia.[1]

almática – white tunic (worn by Catholic priests) with short, wide sleeves and decorations of purple colour

bundled silk (*seda en mazo*) – raw silk piled up in rolls

capellar – cloak of Muslim style worn in early modern Spain

capichola – thin fabric made of silk in the form of lace

cate – weight measure used in the early modern Philippines; it was equal to one tenth of 1 *chinanta*, to 1 pound and 6 ounces, and to 632.63 grammes (cf. *chinanta*)

chaúl – Chinese silk woven with little shine and usually of blue colour

chinanta – weight measure used in the early modern Philippines; it was equal to one tenth of 1 *pico* and to 6.326 kilogrammes (cf. *cate*)

cordovan (*cordobán*) – goatskin leather

damask – patterned silk of high quality, woven (usually in drawings) with only one warp and with wefts woven using yarns of the same thickness and colour

espolín – strong fabric made of silk or cotton and patterned with drawings of flowers

floss silk (*seda floja*) – silk that has not been twisted

gorgorán – piping silk

holanda – fine linen

huipiles – low sleeveless tunics embroidered with bright colours of Aztec origin

lampote – cotton fabric produced in the Philippines

Lanquin – according to Alfonso Mola and Martínez Shaw, this is the city of Nanking (in Jiangsu province, China); according to Sugaya, this is a port in the province of Fujian (China).

long-pile silk (*seda de pelo*) – silk fabric typically used in embroideries, laces, ribbons, plaits, fringes, and other dress ornaments

---

1 Term descriptions were checked against the following sources: *Diccionario de la Real Academia de la Lengua Española*, 22nd ed.; Sebastián de Covarrubias, *Tesoro de la Lengua Castellana o Española* (Madrid: Luis Sánchez, 1611); and Rosa M. Dávila Corona, Montserrat Duran Pujol and Máximo García Fernández, *Diccionario Histórico de Telas y Tejidos. Castellano-Catalán* (Salamanca: Junta de Castilla y León, 2004).

manípulo – holly ornament similar to (but shorter than) priest's stole

marlota – Muslim tight dress of medieval origin

mudéjar – art style, characterised by the use of Christian and Muslim ornaments, that flourished in the Iberian Peninsula from the thirteenth to the sixteenth centuries

medriñaque – Philippine fabric made of abaca, buri, and other vegetal fibres

pico – weight measure used in the early modern Philippines; it was equal to 10 *chinantas* and to 63.262 kilogrammes

raja – cotton fabric of high quality; in the early modern period, the *rajas* from Florence were renowned for their sumptuousness

raw silk (*seda cruda*) – silk (in skeins) that has been spun but not dyed

reposteros – decorative cloth for homes that was patterned with the owner's coat of arms

satin – fabric made of fine, smooth, and shiny silk

sinabafa – fabric made of fine linen; similar to *holanda*

tabí – silk fabric with patterned motifs in the form of waves resembling water

taffeta – silk that is fine, dense, closely woven, and glossy

thrown silk (*seda torcida*) – raw silk of twisted yarns

vara – length measure used in early modern Spain; it was equal to 0.836 metres

velvet – silk fabric that is rough on one side and smooth on the other side

weft silk (*seda de tramas*)[2] – either a variant of or a synonym for thrown silk (*seda torcida*)

wimple – a cloth covering for women that was worn over the head and around the neck and chin

---

2   This term does not appear as an entry in any of the dictionaries consulted.

Sources and Bibliography

[1]   Edited Primary Sources

Balbuena, Bernardo de, *Grandeza Mexicana*, México D. F.: Sociedad de Bibliófilos Mexicanos, 1927 (originally published 1602).

Casas, Gonzalo de las, *Arte nuevo para criar seda*, edited by Antonio Garrido Aranda, Granada: Universidad de Granada, 1996 (first published in 1581).

Colección de Documentos Inéditos del Archivo de Indias, vol. 6, 1866, Madrid.

Colección de Documentos Inéditos para la Historia de España, vol. 52, Madrid, 1852.

Covarrubias, Sebastián de, *Tesoro de la lengua castellana o española*, Madrid: Luis Sánchez, 1611.

Gage, Thomas (1603?–1656), *The Traveller. Part I. Containing' a journal of three thousand three hundred miles, through the main land of South-America*. New Jersey, NJ: Printed and sold by James Parker, 1758.

Mijares, Ivonne, ed., *Catálogo de protocolos del Archivo General de Notarías de la Ciudad de México*, 3 volumes, México D.F.: UNAM, 2005–2006.

Morga, Antonio de, *Sucesos de las Islas Filipinas*, Madrid: Polifemo, 1997 (first published in 1609).

Morga, Antonio de, *Sucesos de las Islas Filipinas*, Francisca Perujo, ed., México D. F.: Fondo de Cultura económica, 2007 (first published in 1609).

Paredes, Julián de, *Recopilación de leyes de los reynos de India*, T. 6, IV, Madrid, 1681.

Otte, Enrique, ed., *Cartas privadas de emigrantes a Indias, 1540–1616*, México, D. F.: Fondo de Cultura Económica, 1996 [first published in 1983].

Recopilación de Leyes de los Reynos de Indias – Tomo III, 3rd edition, 1791.

Sánchez Rubio, Rocío, and Testón Núñez, Isabel, eds., *El hilo que une. Las relaciones epistolares en el Viejo y el Nuevo Mundo (siglos XVI–XVIII)*, Mérida: Universidad de Extremadura, 1999.

San Vicente, Juan M. de, *Exacta descripción de la magnífica Corte mexicana, cabeza del Nuevo Mundo*, 1768, in Rubial García, Antonio ed., *La Ciudad de México en el siglo XVIII (1690–1780). Tres crónicas*. Mexico, D. F.: CNCA, 1990.

Sempere y Guarinos, Juan, *Historia del Luxo y de las Leyes Suntuarias en España*. Vol. 2, Alicante: Biblioteca Virtual Miguel de Cervantes, 2006 (originally published 1788).

Torquemada, Juan de, *Monarquía Indiana* (edited by Miguel León-Portilla), Mexico, D. F., 1973–1985.

Viera, Juan de, *Breve compendiosa narración de la ciudad de México, corte y cabeza de toda la América septentrional*, 1977, in Rubial García, Antonio ed., *La Ciudad de México en el siglo XVIII (1690–1780). Tres crónicas*. Mexico, D. F.: CNCA, 1990.

[2] Bibliography

Acemoglu, Daron, Johnson, Simon, and Robinson, James A. "Atlantic Trade, Institutional Change, and Economic Growth." *American Economic Review* 95, no. 3 (2005): 546–79.

Adamson, Glenn, Riello, Giorgio, and Teasley, Sarah, ed. *Global History Design*. London: Routledge, 2011.

Aguado de los Reyes, Jesús. *Fortuna y Miseria en la Sevilla del Siglo XVII*. Sevilla: Ayuntamiento de Sevilla, 1996.

Aguiló Alonso, María Paz. *El Mueble en el Siglo XVIII: Nuevas Aportaciones a Su Estudio*. Barcelona: Associació per a l'Estudi del Moble, 2008.

Alfonso Mola, Marina, and Martínez Shaw, Carlos, ed. *Oriente en Palacio. Tesoros Asiáticos en las Colecciones Reales Españolas*. Madrid: Patrimonio Nacional, 2003.

Allen, Robert C. *The British Industrial Revolution in Global Perspective*. Cambridge: Cambridge University Press, 2009.

Alonso Álvarez, Luis. "Don Quijote en el Pacífico: La Construcción del Proyecto Español en Asia, 1591–1606." *Revista de Historia Económica – Journal of Iberian and Latin America Economic History* 23 (2005): 241–74.

Alonso Álvarez, Luis. *El Costo del Imperio Asiático. La Formación Colonial de las Islas Filipinas bajo Dominio Español, 1565–1800*. A Coruña: Universidade da Coruña, 2009.

Alston, Lee J., Eggertson, Thráinn, and North, Douglass C. eds. *Empirical Studies in Institutional Change*. Cambridge: Cambridge University Press, 1996.

Altman, Ida, and Lockhart, James, ed. *Provinces of Early Mexico. Variants of Spanish American Regional Evolution* . Los Angeles: University of California Press, 1976.

Alva Rodríguez, Inmaculada. *Vida Municipal en Manila (Siglos XVI–XVII)*. Córdoba: Universidad de Córdoba, 1997.

Álvarez-Ossorio Alvariño, Antonio. "Rango y Apariencia. El Decoro y la Quiebra de la Distinción en Castilla (ss. XVI–XVIII)." *Revista de Historia Moderna* 17 (1998/99): 263–70.

Anderson, Benedict R. *Imagined Communities. Reflections on the Origin and Spread of Nationalism*. London: Verso, 1991.

Appadurai, Arjun, ed. *The Social Life of Things, Commodities in cultural perspective*. Cambridge: Cambridge University Press, 1986.

Aram, Bethany, and Yun-Casalilla, Bartolomé, ed. *Global Goods and the Spanish Empire, 1492–1824. Circulation, resistance and Diversity*. New York, NY: Palgrave, 2014.

Aranda Pérez, Francisco J., ed. *La Declinación de la Monarquía Hispánica. VII^a Reunión Científica de la Fundación Española de Historia Moderna*. Cuenca: UCLM, 2004.

Ardash Bonialian, Mariano. *El Pacífico Hispanoamericano. Política y Comnercio Asiático en el Imperio Español (1680–1784). La Centralidad de lo Marginal*. México, D.F.: El Colegio de México, 2012.

Ardash Bonialian, Mariano. "Tejidos y Cerámica de China en la Gobernación de Tucumán y Buenos Aires, Siglo XVIII. Apuntes Sobre su Circulación y Consumo". *Anuario de Estudios Americanos* 71, no. 2 (2014): 631–60.

Ardash Bonialian, Mariano. *China en la América Colonial. Bienes, Mercados, Comercio y Cultura del Consumo desde México hasta Buenos Aires*. México, D.F.: Instituto Mora, 2014.

Armella de Aspe, Virginia, Castelló Yturbide, Teresa, and Borja Martínez, Ignacio, ed. *La Historia de México a Través de la Indumentaria*. México, D.F.: Inversora Bursátil, 1988.

Armitage, David and Braddick, Michael J., ed. *The British Atlantic World*. New York, NY: Palgrave, 2002.

Artola Gallego, Miguel. *La Hacienda del Antiguo Régimen*. Madrid: Alianza, 1982.

Aston, Trevor H., and Philpin, Charles H., eds., *The Brenner Debate. Agrarian Class Structure and Economic Development in Pre-Industrial Europe*. Cambridge: Cambridge University Press, 1985.

Atwell, William S. "International Bullion Flows and the Chinese Economy circa 1530–1650." *Past and Present* 95 (1982): 68–90.

Bailey, Gauvin A. "A Mughal Princess in Baroque New Spain. Catarina de San Juan (1606–1688): the china poblana." *Anales del Instituto de Investigaciones Estéticas de la Universidad Nacional Autónoma de México* 71 (1997), 37–73.

Bailyn, Bernard. *Atlantic History: Concept and Contours*. Cambridge, MA.: Harvard University Press, 2005.

Bandrés Oto, Maribel. *La Moda en la Pintura. Usos y Costumbres del Siglo XVII*. Pamplona: Eunsa, 2002.

Barbazza, Marie-Catherine, and Heusch, Carlos, eds. *Familles, Pouvoirs, Solidarités. Domaine Méditerranéen et Hispano-Américain (XVe–XXe Siècles)*. Montpellier: Université de Montpellier, 2002.

Baskes, Jeremy. *Staying Afloat: Risk and Uncertainty in Spanish Atlantic World Trade, 1760–1820*. Stanford, CA: Stanford University Press, 2013.

Bakewell, Peter. *Silver Mining and Society in Colonial Mexico. Zacatecas, 1546–1700*. Cambridge: Cambridge University Press, 1971.

Balbuena, Bernardo de. *Grandeza Mexicana*. México, D.F.: Sociedad de Bibliófilos Mexicanos, 1927 (first published in 1602).

Barrón, María C., ed. *La Presencia Novohispana en el Pacífico Insular. Actas de las Segundas Jornadas Internacionales Celebradas en la Ciudad de México del 17 al 21 de Septiembre de 1990*. México, D.F.: Universidad Iberoamericana, 1992.

Bauer, Arnold J. *Goods, Power, History: Latin America's Material Culture*. Cambridge: Cambridge University Press, 2001.

Bauer, Ralph, and Mazzotti, José Antonio, eds. *Creole Subjects in the Colonial Americas. Empires, Texts, Identities*. Chapel Hill: University of North Carolina Press, 2009.

Bayly, Christopher A., Beckert, Sven, Connelly, Matthew, Hofmeyr, Isabel, Kozol, Wendy, and Seed, Patricia. "AHR Conversation: On Transnational History." *American Historical Review* (111, no. 5, 2006): 1441–65.

Bazant, Jan. "Evolución de la Industria Textil Poblana (1544–1845)." *Historia Mexicana* 13, no. 14 (1964): 473–516.

Belenguer Cevriá, Ernest, ed. *Felipe II y el Mediterráneo*, vol. 1. Madrid: Sociedad Estatal para la Conmemoración de los Centenarios de Felipe II y Carlos V, 1999.

Berg, Maxine. "From Imitation to Invention: Creating Commodities in Eighteenth-Century Britain." *Economic History Review* 55, no. 1 (2002): 1–30

Berg, Maxine. "In Pursuit of Luxury: Global History and British Consumer Goods in the Eighteenth Century." *Past and Present* 182 (2004): 85–142.

Berg, Maxine. *Luxury and Pleasure in Eighteenth-Century Britain*. Oxford: Oxford University Press, 2005.

Bernabéu Albert, Salvador, and Martínez Shaw, Carlos, ed. *Un Océano de Seda y Plata: El Universo Económico del Galeón de Manila*. Sevilla: CSIC, 2013.

Bernabéu Albert, Salvador, Mena García, Carmen, and Luque Azcona, Emilio J., ed. *Filipinas y el Pacífico: Nuevas miradas, nuevas reflexiones*. Sevilla: Universidad de Sevilla, 2017.

Bernal, Ignacio. *Historia General de México*. México, D.F.: Colegio de México, 2000.

Bernal, Antonio M., Collantes Morán, Antonio, and García-Baquero González, Antonio, "Sevilla: De Los Gremios a la Industrialización," *Estudios de Historia Social* 5, no. 6 (1978): 7–307.

Bernis, Carmen. *Indumentaria Española en Tiempos de Carlos V*. Madrid: CSIC, 1962.

Bernis, Carmen. *Trajes y Modas en la España de los Reyes Católicos. II. Los Hombres*. Madrid: CSIC, 1979.

Bernis, Carmen. *El Traje y los Tipos Sociales del Quijote*. Madrid: Ediciones el Viso, 2001.

Bethell, Leslie, ed. *Historia de América Latina. 2. América Latina Colonial: Europa y América en los Siglos XVI, XVII, XVIII*. Barcelona: Crítica, 1990.

Bjork, Katharine. "The Link That Kept the Philippines Spanish: Mexican Merchant Interests and the Manila Trade, 1571–1815." *Journal of World History* 9, no. 1 (1998): 25–50.

Blondé, Bruno, Briot, Eugénie, Coquery, Natacha, and van Aert, Laura, ed, *Retailers and Consumer Changes in Early Modern Europe. England, France, Italy and Low Countries*. Tours: Presses Universitaires François-Rabelais, 2005.

Blondé, Bruno, Stabel, Peter, Stobart, Jon, and van Damme, Ilja, ed. *Buyers and Sellers. Retail Circuits and Practices in Mediaeval and Early Modern Europe*. Turnhout: Brepols, 2006.

Bonta de la Pezuela, María. *Porcelana China de Exportación para el Mercado Novohispano: La Colección del Museo Nacional del Virreinato*. México, D. F.: UNAM, 2008.

Borah, Woodrow W. *Silk Raising in Colonial Mexico*. Berkeley, CA: University of California Press, 1943.

Borah, Woodrow W. *New Spain's Century of Depression* . Berkeley, CA: University of California Press, 1951.

Borah, Woodrow W., *Early Colonial Trade and Navigation between Mexico and Peru*. Berkeley, CA: University of California Press, 1954.

Borah, Woodrow W., and Cook, Sherburne F. *The Population of Central Mexico in 1548. An Analysis of the Suma de Visitas de Pueblos*. Berkeley, CA: University of California Press, 1960.

Borah, Woodrown W. "El Origen de la Sericultura en la Mixteca Alta." *Historia Mexicana* 13, no. 1 (1963): 1–17.

Borah, Woodrow W., and Cook, Sherburne F. *Essays in Population History. Mexico and the Caribbean*, 3 vols. London: University of California Press, 1971, 1974, and 1979.

Borao, José E. "The Massacre of 1603 Chinese Perception of the Spanish in the Philippines." *Itinerario* 22, no. 1 (1998): 22–40.

Böttcher, Nikolaus, Hausberger, Bernd, and Ibarra, Antonio. *Redes y Negocios Globales en el Mundo Ibérico*. Madrid: Publicaciones del Instituto Ibero-Americano, 2011.

Boxer, Charles R.. "A Note on the Triangular Trade between Macao, Manila, and Nagasaki, 1580–1640." *Terrae Incognitae* 17 (1985): 51–59.

Boxer, Charles R. "The Portuguese and Spanish Rivalry in the Far East during the Seventeenth Century." *Journal of the Royal Asiatic Society* 3 (1946): 150–64.

Boyajian, James C. *Portuguese Bankers at the Court of Spain, 1626–1650*. New Brunswick, NJ: Rutgers University Press, 1983.

Boyajian, James C. *Portuguese Trade in Asia under the Habsburgs, 1580–1640*. Baltimore, MD: Johns Hopkins University Press, 1993.

Boyd-Bowman, Peter. "Spanish and European Textiles in Sixteenth Century Mexico." *The Americas* 29, no. 3 (1973): 334–58.

Brading, David A. *The Origins of Mexican Nationalism*. Cambridge: Centre of Latin American Studies, 1985.

Brading, David A. *The First America. The Spanish Monarchy, Creole Patriots, and the Liberal State, 1492–1867*. Cambridge: Cambridge University Press, 1991.

Brading, David A. *Mexican Phoenix, Our Lady of Guadalupe: Image and Tradition across Five Centuries*. Cambridge: Cambridge University Press, 2001.

Brewer, John, and Trentmann, Frank, ed. *Consuming Cultures, Global Perspectives: Historical Trajectories, Transnational Exchanges*. Oxford: Berg, 2006.

Bulmer-Thomas, Victor, Coatsworth, John H., and Cortés Conde, Roberto ed. *The Cambridge Economic History of Latin America*, vol. 1. New York: Cambridge University Press, 2006.

Burke, Peter. *Cultural Hybridity*. Cambridge: Polity Press, 2009.

Cabañas Bravo, Miguel, ed. *El Arte Foráneo en España: Presencia e Influencia.* Madrid: CSIC, 2005.

Cabañas Moreno, Pilar. "Una Visión de las Colecciones de Arte Japonés en España." *Artigrama* (18, 2003): 107–24.

Cabrero, Leoncio. *España y el Pacífico. Legazpi,* vol. 2. Madrid: Sociedad Estatal de Conmemoraciones Culturales, 2004.

Cáceres Valderrama, Milena. *La Fiesta de Moros y Cristianos en el Perú.* Lima: PUCP, 2005.

Cachero Vinuesa, Montserrat. "Should we trust? Explaining trade expansion in early modern Spain: Seville, 1500–1600". PhD Thesis, European University Institute: Florence, 2010.

Canepa, Teresa. "The Portuguese and Spanish Trade in *Kraak* Porcelain in the Late 16th and Early 17th Centuries." in *Proceedings of the International Symposium: Chinese Export Ceramics in the 16th and 17th Centuries and the Spread of Material Civilization* (Hong Kong: City University of Hong Kong, 2012), 257–85.

Cañizares-Esguerra, Jorge. "New World, New Stars: Patriotic Astrology and the Invention of Indian and Creole Bodies in Colonial Spanish America, 1600–1650." *American Historical Review* 104, no. 1 (1999): 33–68.

Cañizares-Esguerra, Jorge. "Racial, Religious, and Civic Creole Identity in Colonial Spanish America." *American Literary History* 17, no. 3 (2005): 425–27.

Cañizares-Esguerra, Jorge, and Seeman, Eric R., ed. *The Atlantic in Global History, 1500–2000.* Upper Saddle River, NJ: Pearson, Prentice Hall, 2007.

Carswell, John. *Blue and White. Chinese Porcelain and Its Impact on the Western World.* Chicago: University of Chicago Press, 1985.

Casado Alonso, Hilario. "El Comercio de Nueva España con Castilla en la Época de Felipe II: Redes Comerciales y Seguros Marítimos." *Historia Mexicana* 61, no. 3 (2012): 935–93.

Castro Morales, Efraín. "Puebla y la Talavera a Través de los Siglos." *Artes de México* 3 (2002): 20–29.

Caterina, Lucia, ed. *Museo nazionale della ceramica "Duca di Martina" di Napoli. Catalogo de la porcellana cinese di tipo bianco e blu.* Roma: Poligrafo de los Stato, 1986.

Centenero de Arce, Domingo. and Terrasa Lozano, Antonio. "El Sudeste Asiáticos en las Políticas de la Monarquía Hispánica. Conflictos Luso-Castellanos entre 1580–1621." *Anais de História de Alem-Mar* 9 (2008): 289–332.

Céspedes del Castillo, Guillermo. "La Avería en el Comercio de Indias." *Anuario de Estudios Americanos* 2 (1945): 515–698.

Chartier, Roger, ed. *A History of Private Life. Passions of the Renaissance.* Cambridge, MA: Harvard University Press, 1989.

Chaunu, Pierre and Chaunu, Huguette, *Seville et l'Atlantique, 1504–1650,* 8 vols. Paris: SEVPEN, 1955–1960.

Chaunu, Pierre. *Seville et l'Atlantique (1504–1650)*. *Partie Statistique: Tome VI-2, Table Statistiques*. Paris: SEVPEN, 1956.

Chaunu, Pierre and Chaunu, Huguette. *Seville et l'Atlantique (1504–1650)*. *Partie Interpretative. La Conjoncture, Tome VIII* Paris: SEVPEN, 1960.

Coase, Ronald H. "The Nature of the Firm," *Economica* 4, no. 16 (1937): 386–405.

Coffman, D' Maris, Leonard, Adrian, and Neal, Larry, eds. *Questioning Credible Commitment. Perspectives on the Rise of Financial Capitalism*. Cambridge: Cambridge University Press, 2013.

Colomer, José Luis, and Descalzo, Amalia, eds., *Vestir a la Española en las Cortes Europeas (Siglos XVI y XVII)*. *Volumen I*. Madrid: CEEH, 2014.

Connors McQuade, Margaret. "La Talavera Poblana: Cuatro Siglos de Producción y Coleccionismo," *Mesoamérica* 40 (2000): 118–40.

Conrad, Sebastian, *What is Global History?*. Princeton and Oxford: Princeton University Press, 2016.

Corsi, Elisabetta, ed. *Órdenes Religiosas entre América y Asia. Ideas para Una Historia Misionera de los Espacios Coloniales*. México, D.F.: Colegio de México, 2008.

Cortina, Leonor, and Peón Soler, Alejandra. *La Talavera de Puebla*. México, D.F.: Comermex, 1973.

Cavaciocchi, Simonetta, ed. *La Seta in Europa, Secc. XIII–XX*. Florence: Le Monnier, 1993.

Crossley, John N. *Hernando de los Ríos Coronel and the Spanish Philippines in the Golden Age*. Burlington, VT: Ashgate, 2011.

Cruz Barney, Óscar. *El Préstamo a la Gruesa Ventura o Riesgo Marítimo como Mecanismo de Financiación*. México, D.F.: Instituto de Investigaciones Jurídicas, 1998.

Cruz Barney, Óscar. *El Riesgo en el Comercio Hispano-Indio: Préstamos y Seguros Marítimos durante los Siglos XVI a XIX*. México, D.F.: UNAM, 1998.

Cruz Barney, Óscar. *Historia del Derecho en México*. Oxford: Oxford University Press, 2004.

Curiel, Gustavo, ed. *Orientes-Occidentes. El Arte y la Mirada del Otro*. México, D.F.: UNAM, 2007.

Cushner, Nicholas P. "Merchants and Missionaries. A Theologian's View of Clerical Involvement in the Galleon Trade." *Hispanic American Historical Review* 47, no. 3 (1967): 360–69.

Dávila Corona, Rosa M., Duran Pujol, Montserrat, and García Fernández, Máximo. *Diccionario Histórico de Telas y Tejidos. Castellano-Catalán*. Salamanca: Junta de Castilla y León, 2004.

Dean, Carolyn, and Leibsohn, Dana. "Hybridity and Its Discontents: Considering Visual Culture in Colonial Spanish America." *Colonial Latin American Review* 12, no. 1 (2003): 5–35.

Del Valle Pavón, Guillermina. "El Consulado de Mercaderes de la Ciudad de México, 1594–1827. Historiografía y fuentes sobre su historia." *América Latina en la Historia Económica* 9, no. 17 (2002): 11–21.

Del Valle Pavón, Guillermina. "Expansión de la Economía Mercantil y Creación del Consulado de México." *Historia Mexicana* 51, no. 3 (2002): 517–557.

Del Valle Pavón, Guillermina. "Los Mercaderes de México y la Transgresión de los Límites al Comercio Pacífico en Nueva España." *Revista de Historia Económica – Journal of Iberian and Latin American Economic History* 23, no. 224 (2005): 214–40.

De Morga, Antonio. *Sucesos de las Islas Filipinas*. Madrid: Polifemo, 1997 [first published in 1609].

De Sousa, Lucio. *The Early European Presence in China, Japan, and the Philippines and Southeast Asia (1555–1590): The Life of Bartolomeu Landeiro*. Macao: Macao Foundation, 2010.

De Sousa Pinto, Paulo Jorge. "Manila, Macao and Chinese networks in South China Sea: adaptive strategies of cooperation and survival (sixteenth-to-seventeenth centuries)." *Anais de História de Além-Mar*, XV (2014): 79–100.

Dessì, Roberta, and Ogilvie, Sheilagh. "Social Capital and Collusion: The Case of Merchant Guilds." *Cambridge Working Papers in Economics* 417 (2004): 1–40.

De Paula Solano Pérez-Liria, Francisco, ed. *El Extremo Oriente Ibérico. Investigaciones Históricas: Metodología y Estado de la Cuestión*. Madrid: CSIC, 1989.

De Vries, Jan. *European Urbanization, 1500–1800*. Cambridge, MA: Harvard University Press, 1984.

De Vries, Jan. *The Economy of Europe in an Age of Crisis, 1600–1750*. Cambridge: Cambridge University Press, 1976.

De Vries, Jan. *The Industrious Revolution: Consumer Demand and the Household Economy, 1650 to the Present*. Cambridge: Cambridge University Press, 2008.

Díaz Rodríguez, Antonio J. "Sotanas a la Morisca y Casullas a la Chinesca: El Gusto por lo Exótico Entre los Eclesiásticos Cordobeses, 1556–1621." *Investigaciones Histórica* 30 (2010): 31–48.

Domínguez Ortiz, Antonio. *La Sociedad Americana y la Corona Española en el Siglo XVII*. Madrid: Asociación Francisco López de Gomara, 1996.

Domínguez Ortiz, Antonio, ed. *Historia de España. La Crisis del Siglo XVII*. Barcelona: Planeta, 1988.

Domínguez Ortiz, Antonio. *Orto y Ocaso de Sevilla*. Sevilla: Universidad de Sevilla, 1981.

Drelichman, Mauricio. "The Curse of Moctezuma: American Silver and the Dutch Disease." *Explorations in Economic History* 42 (2005): 349–80.

Earle, Rebecca. " 'Two Pairs of Pink Satin Shoes!!': Clothing, Race and Identity in the Americas, 17th–19th Centuries." *History Workshop Journal* 52 (2001): 175–95.

Elisseeff, Vadime. ed. *The Silk Roads. Highways of Culture and Commerce*. Paris: UNESCO, 1998.

Elizalde Pérez-Grueso, María D. *Las Relaciones entre España y Filipinas. Siglos XVI–XX*. Madrid: CSIC, 2002.

Elliot, John H. "A Europe of Composite Monarchies." *Past and Present* 137 (1992): 48–71.

Elliot, John H. *Empires of the Atlantic World: Britain and Spain in America, 1492–1830*. New Haven: Yale University Press, 2007.

Elliot, John H. "The Decline of Spain." *Past and Present* 20 (1961): 52–75.

Epstein, Stephan R. *Freedom and Growth. The Rise of States and Markets in Europe, 1300–1750*. London: Routledge, 2000.

Fattacciu, Irene. "Across the Atlantic: Chocolate Consumption, Imperial Political Economies and the Making of a Spanish Imaginary (1700–1800)". PhD thesis, European University Institute, 2011.

Fine, Ben, and Leopold, Ellen. *The World of Consumption*. London: Routledge, 1993.

Finlay, Robert. "The Pilgrim Art: The Culture of Porcelain in World History." *Journal of World History* 9, no. 2 (1998): 141–87.

Flynn, Dennis O., and Giráldez, Arturo. "Arbitrage, China, and World Trade in the Early Modern Period." *Journal of Economic and Social History of the Orient* 38, no. 4 (1995): 429–48.

Flynn, Dennis O., and Giráldez, Arturo. "Born with a 'Silver Spoon'. The Origin of World Trade in 1571." *Journal of World History* 6 (1995): 201–21.

Flynn, Dennis O., and Giráldez, Arturo. "Cycles of Silver: Global Economic Unity through the Mid-Eighteenth Century," *Journal of World History* 13, no. 2 (2002): 391–427.

Flynn, Dennis O., Giráldez, Arturo, Glahn, Richard von, ed. *Global Connections and Monetary History, 1470–1800*. Burlington, VT: Ashgate, 2003.

Fortea Pérez, José I. *Córdoba en el Siglo XVI: Las Bases Demográficas y Económicas de una Expansión Urbana*. Córdoba: Monte de Piedad y Caja de Ahorros de Córdoba, 1981.

Friedman, Jonathan, ed. *Consumption and Identity*. Amsterdam: Harwood, 1990.

Fuchs, Bárbara, and Martínez-San Miguel, Yolanda. "*La Grandeza Mexicana* de Balbuena y el Imaginario de Una 'Metrópolis Colonial' ". *Revista Iberoamericana* 75, no. 228 (2009): 675–95.

García-Abásolo, Antonio, ed. *España y el Pacífico*. Córdoba: Asociación Española de Estudios del Pacífico, 1997.

García-Baquero González, Antonio. *Cádiz y el Atlántico (1717–1778)*, 2 vols. Cádiz: CSIC, 1988.

García-Baquero González, Antonio. *La Carrera de Indias. Suma de Contratación y Océano de Negocios*. Sevilla: Algaida, 1992.

García Fuentes, Lutgardo. *El Comercio Español con América, 1650–1700*. Sevilla: Diputación Provincial de Sevilla, 1980.

García Fuentes, Lutgardo. *Los Peruleros y el Comercio de Sevilla con las Indias, 1580–1630*. Sevilla: Universidad de Sevilla, 1997.

García Hernán, David, ed. *La historia sin complejos. La nueva visión del Imperio español.* Madrid: Actas, 2010.

Gasch-Tomás, José L. "Globalisation, market formation and commoditisation in the Spanish Empire. Consumer demand for Asian goods in Mexico City and Seville, c. 1571–1630." *Revista deHistoria Económica – Journal of Iberian and Latin American Economic History* 32, no. 2 (2014): 189–221.

Gasch-Tomás, José L. "Transport costs and prices of Chinese silk in the Spanish empire, c. 1571–1650." *Revista de Historia Industrial* 60 (2015): 15–47.

Gasch-Tomás, José L. "Mecanismos de funcionamiento institucional en el imperio hispánico. El Comercio de los Galeones de Manila y el Consulado de Comerciantes de México en la década de 1630." *Revista Jerónimo Zurita* 90 (2015): 56–74.

Garzón Pareja, Manuel. *La Industria Sedera en España. El Arte de la Seda en España.* Granada: Archivo de la Real Chancillería, 1972.

Gerritsen, Anne, and McDowall, Stephen. "Material Culture and the Other: European Encounters with Chinese Porcelain, ca. 1650–1800." *Journal of World History* 23, no. 1 (2012): 87–113.

Gibson, Charles. *The Aztecs under the Spanish Rule. History of the Indians of the Valley of Mexico, 1519–1810*. Stanford, CA: Stanford University Press, 1964.

Gil, Juan. *Hidalgos y Samurais. España y Japón en los Siglos XVI y XVII*, Madrid: Alianza, 1991.

Gil, Juan. *Los chinos en Manila. Siglos XVI y XVII*. Lisboa: Centro Científico e Cultural de Macau, 2011.

Gil, Juan. *La India y el Lejano Oriente en la Sevilla del Siglo de Oro*. Sevilla: Ayuntamiento de Sevilla, 2011.

Glete, Jan. *War and the State in Early Modern Europe. Spain, the Dutch Republic and Sweden As Fiscal-Military States, 1500–1660*. London: Routledge, 2002.

Grafe, Regina. *Distant Tyranny: Markets, Power, and Backwardness in Spain, 1650–1800*. Princeton: Princeton University Press, 2012.

Grafe, Regina. *Entre el mundo ibérico y el atlántico. Comercio y especialización regional, 1550–1650*. Bilbao: Diputación Foral de Bizkaia, 2005.

Grafe, Regina, and Gelderblom, Oscar. "The Rise and Fall of the Merchant Guilds: Re-Thinking the Comparative Study of Commercial Institutions in Premodern Europe." *Journal of Interdisciplinary History* 40, no. 4 (2010): 477–511

Greengrass, Mark. *Conquest and Coalescence: The Shaping of the State in Early Modern Europe*. London: Edward Arnold, 1991.

Greif, Avner. "Contract Enforceability and Economic Institutions in Early Trade: The Maghribi Traders' Coalition". *American Economic Review* 83, no. 8 (1993): 525–48.

Greif, Avner. *Institutions and the Path to the Modern Economy. Lessons from Medieval Trade.* Cambridge: Cambridge University Press, 2006.

Greif, Avner, Milgro, Paul, and Weingast, Barry R.. "Coordination, Commitment, and Enforcement: The Case of the Merchant Guild." *Journal of Political Economy* 102, no. 4 (1994): 745–77.

Gruzinski, Serge. *Las Cuatro Partes del Mundo. Historia de Una Mundialización.* México, D.F.: Fondo de Cultura Económica, 2010.

Gruzinsky, Serge. "Les monde mêles de la Monarchie Catholique et autres 'connected histories'." *Annales HSS* 1 (2001): 85–117.

Guo Ping, Jin, and Zhiliang, Wu. *Revisitar os primórdios de Macau: para uma nova abordagem da história.* Macau: Instituto Português do Oriente, 2007.

Hamashita, Takeshi. *China, East Asia and the Global Economy. Regional and historical perspectives.* London: Routledge, 2008.

Halikowski, Stephan S. " 'Profits Sprout Like Tropical Plants': A Fresh Look at What Went Wrong with the Eurasian Spice Trade, c. 1550–1800." *Journal of Global History* 3 (2008): 389–418.

Hamilton, Earl J. *El Tesoro Americano y la Revolución de los Precios en España, 1501–1650.* Barcelona: Crítica, 2000.

Helpman, Elhanan, ed. *Institutions and Economic Performance.* Cambridge: Cambridge University Press, 2008.

Herren, Madelaine, Rüesch, Martin, and Sibille, Christiane. *Transcultural History. Theories, Methods, Sources.* Heidelberg: Springer, 2012.

Herrero Sánchez, Manuel. "La Política de Embargos y el Contrabando de Productos de Lujo en Madrid (1635–1673). Sociedad Cortesana y Dependencia de los Mercados Internacionales." *Hispania* 201 (1999): 177–91.

Herrero Sánchez, Manuel, and Kaps, Klemens, ed., *Merchants and Trade Networks in the Atlantic and the Mediterranean, 1550–1800: Connectors of Commercial Maritime Systems.* London: Routledge, 2016.

Hoberman, Louisa S. *Mexico's Merchant Elite, 1590–1660. Silver, State, and Society.* Durham, NC: Duke University Press, 1991.

Hoberman, Louisa S. and Socolow, Susan S. *Ciudades y Sociedad en Latinamérica Colonial.* México, D.F.: Fondo de Cultura Económica, 1993.

Hoffman, Philip T., Postel-Vinay, Gilles, and Rosenthal, Jean Laurent. *Priceless Markets. The Political Economy of Credit in Paris, 1660–1870.* Chicago: University of Chicago Press, 2000.

Hobsbawm, Eric J. "The Overall Crisis of the European Economy in the Seventeenth Century." *Past and Present* 5 (1954): 33–53.

Hopkins, Antony G., ed. *Globalization in World History.* London: Pimlico, 2002.

Howell, Martha C. *Commerce before Capitalism in Europe, 1300–1600.* Cambridge: Cambridge University Press, 2010.

Ibarra, Antonio, and Hausberger, Bernd, eds. *Comercio y Poder en la América Colonial. Los Consulados de Comerciantes, Siglos XVII–XIX*. México, D.F.: Colegio de México, 2003.

Inikori, Joseph E. "Africa and the Globalization Process: Western Africa, 1450–1850." *Journal of Global History*, 2 (2007): 63–86.

Irigoin, Alejandra, and Grafe, Regina. "A Stakeholder Empire: The Political Economy of the Spanish Imperial Rule in America." *Economic History Review* 65, no. 2 (2011): 609–51.

Irigoin, Alejandra, and Grafe, Regina. "Bargaining for Absolutism: A Spanish Path to Nation-State and Empire Building." *Hispanic American Historical Review* 88, no. 2 (2008): 173–209.

Irigoin, Alejandra, and Grafe, Regina. "The Spanish Empire and Its Legacy: Fiscal Redistribution and Political Conflict in Colonial and Post-Colonial Spanish America." *Journal of Global History* 1, no. 2 (2006): 241–67;

Irving, Leonard A. *La Época Barroca en el México Colonial*. México D.F.: Fondo de Cultura Económica, 1974.

Israel, Jonathan I. *Dutch Primacy in World Trade, 1585–1740*. Oxford: Oxford University Press, 1989.

Israel, Jonathan I. *Razas, Clases Sociales y Vida Política en el México Colonial, 1610–1670*. México, D.F.: Fondo de Cultura Económica, 1980.

Israel, Jonathan I. *The Dutch Republic and the Hispanic World, 1606–1661*. New York: Oxford University Press, 1982.

Israel, Jonathan I. *The Dutch Republic: Its Rise, Greatness, and Fall, 1477–1806*. Oxford: Clarendon Press, 1995.

Jian, Hang, and Qiuhui, Guo. *Chinese Arts and Crafts* (translated by Zhou Youruo and Song Peiming). Beijing: China Intercontinental Press, 2006.

Kagan, Richard L. *Pleitos y Pleiteantes en Castilla, 1500–1700*. Salamanca: Junta de Castilla y León, 1991.

Kanki, Kaizo. "Artes Industriales Namban." *Archivo Español de Arte* 196 (1976): 455–67.

Kawamura, Yayoi. "Coleccionismo y Colecciones de la Laca Extremo Oriental en España desde la Época del Arte Namban hasta el Siglo XX." *Artigrama* 18 (2003): 211–30.

Klein, Herbert S. *The American Finances of the Spanish Empire. Royal Income and Expenditures in Colonial Mexico, Peru, and Bolivia, 1680–1809*. Albuquerque, NM: University of New Mexico Press, 1998.

Krahe, Cinta. *Chinese Porcelain in Habsburg Spain*. Madrid: Madrid, CEEH, 2016.

Kuwayama, George. *Chinese Ceramics in Colonial Mexico*. Honolulu, HI: University of Hawaii Press, 1997.

Lavallé, Bernard. *Recherchers sur l'Apparition de la Conscience Créole dans la Vice-Royauté du Pérou. L'Antagonisme Hispano-Créole dans les Orders Religieuses (XVIe–XVIIe Siècles)*. Lille: Université de Lille, 1982.

Lemire, Beverly. *Fashion's Favourite: The Cotton Trade and the Consumer in Britain, 1660–1800*. Oxford: Oxford University Press, 1991.

Levy, Evonne, and Mills, Kenneth, ed. *Lexikon of the Hispanic Baroque. Transatlantic Exchange and Transformation*. Austin, TX: University of Texas Press, 2013.

Lim, Ivy Maria. "From Haijin to Kaihai: The Jiajing Court's Search for a Modus Operandi along the South-eastern Coast (1522–1567)." *Journal of the British Association for Chinese Studies* 2 (2013): 1–26.

Lister, Florence C., and Lister, Robert H.. "The Potters' Quarter of Colonial Puebla, Mexico." *Historical Archeology* 18, no. 1 (1984): 87–102.

Lockhart, James, and Schwart, Stuart B. *Early Latin America. A History of Colonial Spanish America and Brazil*. Cambridge: Cambridge University Press, 1983.

Lorenzo Sanz, Eufemio. *Comercio de España con América en la Época de Felipe II. Tomo I: Los Mercaderes y el Tráfico Indiano*. Valladolid: Diputación Provincial de Valladolid, 1986.

Luque Talaván, Miguel, and Machado López, Marta M., ed. *Un Océano de Intercambios: Hispanoasia (1521–1898). Homenaje al Profesor Leoncio Cabrero Fernández*. Madrid: Ministerio de Asuntos Exteriores, 2008.

Lynch, John. *Spain under the Habsburgs*. Oxford: Oxford University Press, 1981.

Martínez López-Cano, María P. *La Génesis del Crédito Colonial en la Ciudad de México, Siglo XVI*. México, D.F.: UNAM, 2001.

Martínez López-Cano, María P., and del Valle Pavón, Guillermina, ed. *El Crédito en Nueva España*. México, D.F.: Instituto de Investigaciones Históricas, 1998.

Martínez Shaw, Carlos, and Oliva Melgar, José M., eds. *El Sistema Atlántico Español Siglos XVII–XIV*. Madrid: Marcial Pons, 2005.

Mason, Peter. "From Presentation to Representation: *Americana* in Europe." *Journal of the History of Collections* 6, no. 1 (1994): 1–20.

Mazzotti, José A., and Zevallos Aguilar, U. Juan, ed. *Asedios a la Heterogeneidad Cultural. Homenaje a Antonio Cornejo Polar*. Philadelphia, PA: Asociación Internacional de Peruanistas, 1996.

McCants, Anne E. "Exotic Goods, Popular Consumption, and the Standard of Living: Thinking about Globalization in the Early Modern World." *Journal of World History* 18, no. 4 (2007): 433–62.

Mesquida, Juan O. "La Población de Manila y las Capellanías de Misas de los Españoles: Libro de Registros, 1642–1672." *Revista de Indias* 70, no. 249 (2010): 469–500.

Mesquida, Juan O. "The Early Years of the Misericordia of Manila (1594–1625)," *Review of Culture* 14 (2005): 59–81.

Mills, C. Wright. *The Power Elite*. Oxford: Oxford University Press, 2000 (originally published in 1956).

Molà, Luca. *The Silk Industry of Renaissance Venice*. Baltimore, MD: Johns Hopkins University Press, 2000.

Morán, José M., and Checa, Fernando, *El Coleccionismo en España. De la Cámara de las Maravillas a la Galería de Pinturas*. Madrid: Cátedra, 2005.

Morgan, Philip D., and Green, Jack P., ed. *Atlantic History: A Critical Appraisal.* Oxford: Oxford University Press, 2009.

Morineau, Michel. *Incroyables Gazettes et Fabuleux Métaux. Les Retours des Trésors Américains d'Aprés les Gazettes Hollandaises (XVIe–XVIIe Siècles)*. London: Cambridge University Press, 1985.

Müir, Edward. *Fiesta y Rito en la Europa Moderna*. Madrid: Editorial Complutense, 2001.

Muñoz Navarro, Daniel, ed. *Comprar, Vender y Consumir. Nuevas Aportaciones a la Historia del Consumo en la España Moderna*. Valencia: Servei de Publicacions de la Universitat de València, 2011.

Navarro, Germán. *El Despegue de la Industria Sedera en la Valencia del Siglo XVI*. Valencia: Generalitat Valencia, 1992.

North, Douglass C. *Structure and Change in Economic History*. New York: Norton, 1981.

North, Douglass C. *Institutions, Institutional Change and Economic Performance*. Cambridge: Cambridge University Press, 1990.

North, Douglass C., and Thomas, Robert P. *The Rise of the Western World: A New Economic History*. Cambridge: Cambridge University Press, 1973.

North, Douglass C., and Weingast, Barry R. "Constitutions and Commitment: The Evolution of Institutions Governing Public Choice in Seventeenth-Century England." *Journal of Economic History* 4 (1989): 803–32.

North, Michael, ed. *Artistic and Cultural Exchanges between Europe and Asia*. Farnham: Ashgate, 2010.

Núñez Roldán, Francisco. *La Vida Cotidiana en la Sevilla del Siglo de Oro*. Madrid: Sílex, 2004.

Obregón, Gonzalo. "El Aspecto Artístico del Comercio con Filipinas." *Revista Artes de México* 143 (1971): 74–97.

O'Brien, Patrick. "Contentions of the Purse between England and its European Rivals from Henry V to George IV: A Conversation with Michael Mann." *Journal of Historical Sociology* 19, no. 4 (2006): 341–63.

Ogilvie, Sheilagh. *Institutions and European Trade. Merchant Guilds, 1000–1800*. Cambridge: Cambridge University Press, 2011.

Oliva Melgar, José M. *El Monopolio de Indias en el Siglo XVII y la Economía Andaluza. La Oportunidad que Nunca Existió*. Huelva: Universidad de Huelva, 2004.

Olivencia Ruiz, Manuel. *Arbitraje: Una Justicia Alternativa (Una Vision Histórica desde la Mueva Ley)*. Córdoba: Universidad de Córdoba, 2006.

Ollé, Manel. *La Empresa de China. De la Armada Invencible al Galeón de Manila*. Barcelona: Acantilado, 2002.

O'Rourke, Kevin, and Williamson, Jeffrey G.. "After Columbus: Explaining Europe's Overseas Trade Boom, 1500–1800." *Journal of Economic History* 62, no. 2 (2002): 428–39.

O'Rourke, Kevin, and Williamson, Jeffrey G. *Globalization and History: The Evolution of a Nineteenth Century Atlantic Economy*. Cambridge, MA: MIT Press, 1999.

Osterhammel, Jürgen, and Petersson, Niels P. *Globalization: A Short Story*. Princeton, NJ: Princeton University Press, 2003.

Parker, Geoffrey. *The Army of Flanders and the Spanish Road, 1567–1659*. Cambridge: Cambridge University Press, 2004.

Pearson, Stacey. "The Movement of Chinese Ceramics: Appropriation in Global History." *Journal of World History* 23, no. 1 (2012): 9–39.

Pérez, Béatrice, and Clément, Jean-Pierre, ed. *Des Merchands entre Deux Mondes. Pratiques et Représentations en Espagne et en Amerique (XVe–XVIIIe Siècles)*. Paris: PUPS, 2007.

Pérez Carrillo, Sonia. "Imitación de la Laca Oriental en Muebles Novohispanos del Siglo XVIII." *Cuadernos de Arte Colonial* 3 (1987): 51–78.

Pérez García, Manuel, and de Sousa, Lucio ed. *Global History and New Polycentric Approaches. Europe, Asia and the Americas in a World Network System*. Singapore: Palgrave, 2018.

Phelan, John L. *The Hispanization of the Philippines: Spanish Aims and Filipino Responses, 1565–1700*. Madison, WI: University of Wisconsin Press, 2010.

Pierce, Donna. "Popular and Prevalent: Asian Trade Goods in Northern New Spain, 1590–1850." *Colonial Latin American Review* 25, no. 1 (2016): 77–97.

Pierson, Stacey. "The Movement of Chinese Ceramics: Appropriation in Global History." *Journal of World History* 23, no. 1 (2012): 9–39.

Pietschmann, Horst, ed., *Atlantic History. History of the Atlantic System, 1580–1830*. Göttingen: Vandenhoeck & Ruprecht, 2002.

Pike, Ruth. *Aristócratas y Comerciantes. La Sociedad Sevillana en el Siglo XVI*. Barcelona: Ariel, 1978.

Pomeranz, Kenneth. *The Great Divergence: China, Europe and the Making of the Modern World Economy*. Princeton, NJ: Princeton University Press, 2002.

Ptack, Roderich, ed. *China, the Portuguese, and the Nanyang: oceans and routes, regions and trade (c. 100'- 1600)*. Aldershot and Burlington, VT: Ashgate/Variorum, 2004.

Rahn Philips, Carla. *Six Galleons for the King of Spain. Imperial Defense in the Early Seventeenth Century*.

Redondo Cantera, María J., ed. *El Modelo Italiano en las Artes Plásticas de la Península Ibérica durante el Renacimiento*. Valladolid: Universidad de Valladolid, 2004.

Reid, Anthony. *Southeast Asia in the Age of Commerce, 1450–1680. Volume One: The Lands below the Winds*. New Haven, CT: Yale University Press, 1988.

Richards, John F., ed. *Precious Metals in the Late Medieval and Early Modern World*. Durham, NC: Duke University Press, 1983.

Riello, Giorgio, and Roy, Tirthankar, eds. *How India Clothed the World. The World of South Asian Textiles, 1500–1850*. Leiden: Brill, 2009.

Riello, Giorgio. "Asian Knowledge and the Development of Calico Printing in Europe in the Seventeenth and Eighteenth Centuries." *Journal of Global History* 5 (2010): 1–28.

Riello, Giorgio. *Cotton. The Fabric That Made the Modern World*. Cambridge: Cambridge University Press, 2013.

Roessingh, Marius P. H. "Dutch Relations with the Philippines: A Survey of Sources in the General State Archives, The Hague, Netherlands." *Asian Studies* 5, no. 2 (1967): 377–407.

Romano, Ruggiero. *Coyunturas Opuestas. La Crisis del Siglo XVII en Europa e Hispanoamérica*. México, D.F.: Fondo de Cultura Económica, 1993.

Romano, Ruggiero. *Moneda, Pseudomonedas y Circulación Monetaria en las Economías de México*. México, D.F: Fondo de Cultura Económica, 1998.

Rowe, William T. *China's Last Empire. The Great Qing*. Harvard University Press, 2010.

Rubial García, Antonio, ed. *La Ciudad de México en el Siglo XVIII (1690–1780). Tres Crónicas*. México, D.F.: Consejo Nacional para la Cultura y las Artes, 1990.

Rubial García, Antonio, ed. *Historia de la Vida Cotidiana en México. II: La Ciudad Barroca*. México, D.F.: Colegio de México, 2005.

Sales Colín, Ostwald. *El Movimiento Portuario de Acapulco. El Protagonismo de Nueva España en la Relación con Filipinas, 1587–1648*. México, D. F.: Plaza y Valdés, 2000.

Sánchez-Albornoz, Nicolás. *La Población de América Latina. Desde los Tiempos Pre-Colombinos al Año 2000*. Madrid: Alianza, 1973.

San Ginés Aguilar, Pedro, ed. *Cruce de Miradas, Relaciones e Intercambios*. Granada: Universidad de Granada, 2010.

Sanz Ayán, Carmen. *Estado, Monarquía y Finanzas. Estudios de Historia Financiera en Tiempos de los Austrias*. Madrid: Centro de Estudios Políticos y Constitucionales, 2004.

Schäfer, Dagmar, ed. *Cultures of Knowledge. Technology in Chinese History*. Leiden: Brill, 2012.

Schurtz, William L. *El Galeón de Manila*. Madrid: Ediciones de Cultura Hispánica, 1992.

Seabra, Isabel Leonor. *A misericórdia de Macau (séculos XVI a XIX): irmandade, poder e caridade na idade do comércio*. Macao and Lisbon: University of Macau and University of Porto, 2011.

Seijas, Tatiana. *Asian Slaves in Colonial Mexico. From Chinos to Indians*. Cambridge: Cambridge University Press, 2015.

Slack, Edward S. "The *Chinos* in New Spain: A Corrective Lens for a Distorted Image." *Journal of World History* 20, no. 1 (2009), 35–67.

Sluiter, Engel. *The Gold and Silver of Spanish America, ca. 1572–1648*. Berkeley, CA: University of California Press, 1998.

Smith, Robert S. "Sales Taxes in New Spain, 1575–1770." *Hispanic American Historical Review* 28, no. 1 (1948): 2–37.

Smith, Robert S. "Antecedentes del Consulado de México." *Revista de Historia de América* 15 (1942): 299–313.

Smith, Robert S., and Ramírez Flores, José. *Los Consulados de Comerciantes de Nueva España.*

Smith, Woodruff D. *Consumption and the Making of Respectability, 1600–1800.* London: Routledge, 2002.

Soberanes Fernández, José L., ed. *Memoria del III Congreso de Historia del Derecho Mexicano.* México, D.F.: UNAM, 1983.

Soria Mesa, Enrique. *La Nobleza en la España Moderna. Cambio y Continuidad.* Madrid: Marcial Pons, 2007.

Souto Mantecón, Matilde. "Los Consulados de Comercio en Castilla e Indias: Su Establecimiento y Renovación (1494–1795)." *Anuario Mexicano de Historia del Derecho* 2 (1990): 227–50.

Souza, George B. *The Survival of Empire. Portuguese Trade and Society in China and the South China Sea, 1630–1754.* Cambridge: Cambridge University Press, 2004.

Styles, John. "Product Innovation in Early Modern London." *Past and Present* 168 (2000), 124–69

Subrahmanyam, Sanjay. *The Portuguese Empire in Asia, 1500–1700. A political and Economic History.* London and New York: Longman, 1993.

Subrahmanyam, Sanjay. "Holding the World in Balance: The Connected Histories of the Iberian Overseas Empires, 1500–1640." *American Historical Review* 112 (2007): 1359–85.

Sugaya, Nariko. "Spanish Colonial Manila in Transition: Trade and Society at the Turn of the Nineteenth Century," 愛媛大学法文学部論集. 人文学科編 36 (2014): 19–32.

Swope, Kenneth M. *The Military Collapse of China's Ming Dynasty, 1618–44.* London: Routledge, 2014.

TePaske, John, and Klein, Herbert S. "The Seventeenth-Century Crisis in New Spain: Myth or Reality?." *Past and Present* 90 (1981): 116–35.

TePaske, John, Klein, Herbert S., et al. *Royal Treasuries of the Spanish Empire* (3 vols.). Durham, NC: Duke University Press, 1982.

TePaske, John J. (edited by Kendall W. Brown). *A New World of Gold and Silver.* Leiden: Brill, 2010.

Tolentino Martínez, Jessica M., and Rosales Ortega, Rocío. "La Producción de Talavera de Puebla y San Pablo del Monte, Tlaxcala: Un Sistema Productivo Local en Transformación." *Revista Pueblos y Fronteras* 6, no. 11 (2011): 198–235.

Torres Sánchez, Rafael, ed. *Capitalismo Mercantil en la España del Siglo XVIII.* Pamplona: EUNSA, 2000.

Torquemada, Juan de (edited by Miguel León-Portilla). *Monarquía Indiana.* México, D.F., 1973–1985.

Tracy, James D., ed. *The Polical Economy of Merchant Empires. State Power and World Trade, 1350–1750*. Cambridge: Cambridge University Press, 1991.

Tracy, James D., ed. *Rise of Merchant Empires. Long-distance Trade in the Early Modern World, 1350–1750*. Cambridge: Cambridge University Press, 1993.

Tracy, James D. *The Founding of the Dutch Republic: War, Finance, and Politics in Holland, 1572–1588*. Oxford: Oxford University Press, 2008.

Tremml-Werner, Birgit M. "The Global and the Local: Problematic Dynamics of the Triangular Trade in Early Modern Manila." *Journal of World History* 23, no. 3 (2012): 555–86.

Tremml-Werner, Birgit M. *Spain, China, and Japan in Manila, 1571–1644. Local Comparisons and Global Connections*. Amsterdam: Amsterdam University Press, 2015.

Trentmann, Frank, and Nützandel, Alexander, ed. *Food and Globalization. Consumption, Markets and Politics in the Modern World*. Oxford: Berg, 2008.

Trevor-Roper, Hugh R. "The General Crisis of the Seventeenth Century." *Past and Present* 16 (1959): 31–64.

Trivellato, Francesca. *The Familiarity of Strangers. The Sephardic Diaspora, Livorno, and Cross-Cultural Trade in the Early Modern Period*. New Haven, CT: Yale University Press, 2009.

Valladares, Rafael. *Castilla y Portugal en Asia (1580–1680). Declive Imperial y Adaptación*. Leuven: Leuven University Press, 2001.

Vickery, Amanda. *Behind the Closed Doors. At Home in Georgian England*. New Haven: Yale University Press, 2009.

Vila Vilar, Enriqueta. *Los Corzo y los Mañara. Tipos y Arquetipos del Mercader con Indias*. Sevilla: Escuela de Estudios Hispano-Americanos, 1991.

VVAA. *Actas II Coloquio Historia de Andalucía. Andalucía Moderna*. Córdoba: Monte de Piedad y Caja de Ahorros, 1983.

VVAA. *Actas del III Congreso Internacional del Barroco Americano. Territorio, Arte, Espacio y Sociedad*, 2001 (via http://www.upo.es/depa/webdhuma/areas/arte/actas/3cibi/documentos/008f.pdf).

VVAA. *Alonso Sánchez Coello y el Retrato en la Corte de Felipe II*, VVAA. Madrid: Museo del Prado, 1990.

VVAA. *El Galeón de Manila. Catálogo*. Madrid: Ministerio de Educación, 2000.

VVAA. *El Mueble Mexicano. Historia, Evolución e Influencias*. México, D. F.: Fomento Cultural Banamex, 1985.

VVAA. *East Asian Lacquer. The Florence and Herbert Irving Collection*. New York: Metropolitan Museum of Art, 1991.

VVAA. *El Quijote en sus Trajes*. Madrid: Ministerio de Cultura, 2005.

VVAA, *La Documentación Notarial y la Historia.*, vol. 2. Santiago de Compostela: Universidad de Santiago de Compostela, 1984.

VVAA. *La Grandeza del México Virreinal: Tesoros del Museo Franz Mayer*. México, D.F.: Museo Franz Mayer, 2002.

VVAA, *Presencia Italiana en Andalucía. Actas del III Coloquio Hispano-Italiano*. Sevilla: CSIC, 1989.

VVAA. *Talaveras de Puebla. Cerámica Colonial Mexicana, Siglos XVII a XXI*, VVAA. Barcelona: Museu de Ceràmica de Barcelona, 2007.

Von Glahn, Richard. "Myth and Reality of China's Seventeenth-Century Monetary Crisis." *Journal of Economic History* 56, no. 2 (1996): 429–54. .

Von Glahn, Richard. *Fountain of Fortune. Money and Monetary Policy in China, 100–1700*. Berkeley, CA: University of California Press, 1996.

Vries, Peer. *Via Peking back to Manchester: Britain, the Industrial Revolution, and China*. Leiden: Leiden University, 2003.

Weatherill, Lorna. *Consumer Behaviour and Material Culture, 1660–1760*. London: Routledge, 1988.

Wimer, Javier, ed. *El Galeón del Pacífico. Acapulco-Manila. 1565–1815*. México, D.F.: Instituto Guerrerense de Cultura, 1992.

Wong, Roy B. *China Transformed. Historical Change and the Limits of the European Experience*. Ithaca, NY: Cornell University Press, 1997.

Yanes Rizo, Emma. "La Loza Estannífera de Puebla. De la Comunidad Original de Loceros a la Formación del Gremio (1550–1653)." PhD thesis, México, D. F.: UNAM, 2013.

Yuan-kang, Wang. "Managing Regional Hegemony in Historical Asia: The Case of Early Ming China." *The Chinese Journal of International Politics* 5 (2012): 129–153.

Yun Casalilla, Bartolomé, and Thomspon, Ian A. A., eds. *The Castilian Crisis of the Seventeenth Century. New Perspectives on the Economic and Social History of Seventeenth-Century Spain*. Cambridge: Cambridge University Press, 1994.

Yun Casalilla, Bartolomé. "The American Empire and the Spanish Economy: An Institutional and Regional Perspective." *Revista de Historia Económica – Journal of Iberian and Latin American Economic History* 16, no. 1 (1998): 123–56.

Yun Casalilla, Bartolomé, and Torras Elias, Jaume ed. *Consumo, Condiciones de Vida y Comercialización*. Valladolid: Junta de Castilla y León, 1999.

Yun Casalilla, Bartolomé. *Marte contra Minerva. El Precio del Imperio Español*. Barcelona: Crítica, 2004.

Yun Casalilla, Bartolomé. " 'Localism', Global History and Transnational History. A Reflection from the Historian of Early Modern Europe." *Historik Tidskrift* 127, no. 4 (2007): 659–678.

Yun Casalilla, Bartolomé, and Ramos Palencia, Fernando, eds. *Economía Política desde Estambul a Potosí. Ciudades Estado, Imperios y Mercados en el Mediterráneo y en el Atlántico Ibérico, c. 1200–1800*. Valencia: Publicacions de la Universitat de Valèncía, 2012.

Yuste López, Carmen. *El Comercio de la Nueva España con Filipinas, 1590–1785*. México, D.F.: Instituto Nacional de Antropología e Historia, 1984.

Yuste López, Carmen, ed. *Comercio Marítimo Colonial. Nuevas Interpretaciones y Últimas Fuentes*. México, D. F.: Instituto Nacional de Antropología e Historia, 1997.

Yuste López, Carmen. *Emporios Transpacíficos. Comerciantes Mexicanos en Manila, 1710–1815*. México, D.F.: UNAM, 2007.

Zemon Davis , Natalie. *The Gift in Sixteenth-Century France*. Madison: University of Wisconsin Press, 2000.

[3]   Webpages

http://www.insidemydesk.com/hdd.html
http://www.iisg.nl/hpw/data.php#southamerica
http://gpih.ucdavis.edu/files/Spain_1351-1800.xls

Index